A Short History of Islam
From Pre-Islamic Times to the Colonial Period

S.E. Al-Djazairi

The Institute of Islamic History

A Short History of Islam (S.E. Al-Djazairi)

Published by
The Institute of Islamic History, Manchester 2006
www.theislamichistory.com
email:info@theislamichistory.com

Distributed by
The World of Islam
211 Wilmslow Road
Manchester M14 5AG
0161 256 3232
www.islam1.co.uk
email: islam@islam1.co.uk

ISBN
0-9553313-0-7
978-0-9553313-0-5

Printed and bound by Antony Rowe Ltd.
www.antonyrowe.co.uk

Maps: Z. al-Hamad
Art works and design: Z. al-Hamad

Acknowledgements

I am very grateful to a number of people. The second, third, and part of the fourth, chapters have been written under the critical direction of Mohammad Hatahet, owner and manager of the World of Islam (Manchester). Without his contribution, these chapters would not have been completed to the required standards. My thanks also go to C.M. Zaimeche and Najah Hatahet who both read through the manuscript and made many corrections. My warmest gratitude goes to Zeyd al-Hamad who has done an exceptional work on the maps and other art works. L Ball and F. Zafar are to be thanked for various other contributions. Finally, I am grateful to The World of Islam Bookshop, Manchester, for sponsoring this work.

CONTENTS

List of Maps[1]

1: Arabia and Early Events of Islamic History
2: Campaigns against Byzantium and Persia (633-8)
3: The Campaigns of Qutaybah and Ibn Qasim
4: Expansion of Islam
5: Lands of Eastern Islam (10th-11th Centuries)
6: North Africa, Iraq and Syria (9th -11th Centuries)
7: The First Crusades (1096-1146)
8: Crusaders/Ayyubids/Mamluks and Mongols to 1260
9: The End of the Crusader East
10: Western Islam (12th-mid 13th Century)
11: The Expansion of Islam in Africa
12: Expansion of Islam in South East Asia
13: The Expansion of Islam in India
14: The Decline of the Ottomans

---

[1] The maps are by Z. Al-Hamad.
The maps have been inspired by works referred to in this work, and have been drawn to
reflect the contents of this book.

Foreword
(By Mohammed Hatahet)

`Read in the name of your Lord
Who created, created man from a clot.
Read for your Lord is the Most Gracious.
It is He Who teaches by means of the pen.
Teaches man what he does not know.'
Qur'an 96: 1-8.

Some 14 centuries ago, these verses were revealed to Mohammed (PBUH). They started up his mission as a messenger of Allah to mankind. The revelation of the Qur'an was a turning point in the history of humanity. The mission of the messenger as a mercy to the worlds accompanied by the Qur'an as a guide to that which is most right had a crucial impact on humanity. A Divine command was sent to humans to read and write. It carried people from an age of ignorance into one of learning.

No civilisation prior to Islam could boast schools or universal learning. From the time of Adam up to the time of Mohammed, the world was generally illiterate. Mohammed himself was an illiterate in a nation where illiteracy was generalised. At the time of Mohammed's mission, no more than ten people could read and write in Makkah. By the time of his death, twenty three years later, more than a hundred thousand could read the Qur'an. There were also 3000 public schools, mainly located in mosques. In less than two centuries, the whole Muslim world was filled with libraries, academies, universities, observatories, and places of learning of diverse sorts. The Christian West, then, was going through its Dark Ages.

This revolutionary impact on learning began with Islam. It is in the year 610 that the history of Islam began. This book is about that history. Although retaining an academic form, it is still accessible to the general reader. It is brief but it offers a comprehensive view of the history of Islam and Muslims. Above all, it uncovers historical facts that, for one reason or another, have been hidden in other works, yet, these facts are crucial for correct understanding of Islamic history.

A Word of Warning

It is imperative to note that this work relies to a large extent on non Muslim sources dealing with Islam, faith and history. In many places their approach will be at odds with the Islamic approach to similar concepts. There are indeed complex matters of the faith, aspects of the language and terminology which Western sources fail to grasp when dealing with Islam. Moreover, although many Western sources cited here (such as Gibbon) praise Islam in places, in others they lash violently at the faith and the Prophet (PBUH).

Western authors who praise aspects of Islam and Muslim history also use in their text and even in the titles of their works anti Islamic expressions. The 19th century historian, R.B. Smith, for instance, is very favourable in most places to Islam, but the title of his work refers to Mohammedanism (i.e that Prophet Mohammed (PBUH) himself created the faith), and Smith constantly insists that, however good Islam is, it is always inferior to Christianity.[2] Another 19th century historian who is also very favourable to Islam, and who is guilty of similar weaknesses is Davenport. In his book, *An Apology for Mohammed,*[3] he constantly uses the expression Mohammedanism and Mohammedans when referring to Islam and Muslims respectively.

Most Western authors also praise many aspects of Islam and its history, but also tell us that Islam has been borrowed from Christianity and Judaism.[4]

Many Western authors praise Islam, its civilisation and the Arabs then attack other Muslim groups such as the Turks, Berbers, etc. Le Bon and Lane Poole, who are widely used in this work, belong to this category.[5]

Generally, Western writers who are favourable to aspects of Muslim history and civilisation unremittingly attack what they call Orthodox Islam, that is Sunni Islam, and pour their invective on it.[6] One such historian cited early in this work is Syed Ameer Ali,[7] hence seemingly a Muslim. This is not the case. This was a pen name most probably for E.G. Browne, famed for his work on Muslim medicine. Indeed their writing style is similar, and they

---

[2] R.B. Smith: *Mohammed and Mohammedanism*; London; Smith Elder; 1876 ed.
[3] J. Davenport: *An Apology for Mohammed and the Koran;* J. Davy; London; 1869; p. 2.
[4] Such as H. Kung et al: *Christianity and the World Religions*; Doubleday; London; 1986. Or W.M. Watt: *Muslim Christian Encounters*; Routledge; London; 1991.
[5] G. Le Bon: *La Civilisation des Arabes;* Syracuse; 1884.
S. Lane-Poole: *The Moors in Spain;* Fisher Unwin; London; 1888.
[6] Such as G.E. Von Grunebaum: *Medieval Islam,* The University of Chicago Press, 1954. Or G.Wiet et al: *History of Mankind;* Vol 3: The Great Medieval Civilisations; tr. from the French; George Allen &Unwin Ltd; UNESCO; 1975.
[7] Syed Ameer Ali: *The Spirit of Islam;* Methuen; London; 1967 ed; p. lxviii.

both worked at Cambridge. They share the same devotion to Muslim civilisation and the same hostility to Sunni Islam. The reason for Browne changing his name could be due to the fact that he was a closet Muslim. Or, possibly, the cover/pseudonym could give him the opportunity to lash out at Islam from within, or from a `Muslim' point of view.

Other Western writers such as Hillenbrand, in her book on the crusades, praise aspects of Islamic history, but undermine it in other places.[8] Hillenbrand also says that she writes from an Islamic perspective to give justice to Islamic history, but in fact does not.

A historian of non Western origin who wrote one of the best works on Islamic history is Hitti.[9] Philip Hitti is a great admirer of Islamic civilization, and proud of his Arab origins, yet he considers the Qur'an a forgery and Islam a force of backwardness.[10]

Thus, readers should be constantly aware when using these sources.

---

[8] C. Hillenbrand: *The Crusades, Islamic Perspectives,* Edinburgh University Press; 1999.

[9] P.K.Hitti: *History of the Arabs*, MacMillan, London, 1937 ed.

[10] P.K. Hitti: *Islam and the West: An Historical, Cultural Survey*; Princeton, 1962.

INTRODUCTION

There is no book on Islamic history, from the early times to the present or recent period, written by a Muslim in a language other than Arabic. There are good works on specific Islamic historical subjects, or distinct periods, written by Muslims in English, French, Spanish, etc. But, Islamic history, stretching from the early times to our era, written and taught by Muslims in any other language than Arabic, from an Islamic perspective, has not yet been written or taught. The Islamic history that is written and taught today in most countries, including Muslim countries, is also, and overwhelmingly, by non Muslims. Even when Muslims have written and taught aspects of Islamic history, especially in non Arabic speaking countries, they have tended to use non-Muslim sources without taking account of the distortions and distorting techniques, used by the majority of such non-Muslim historians to alter the reality of Islamic history negatively. As an instance, any person visiting a number of Muslim schools in the UK today and becoming aware of history that is being taught to Muslims, would tear their hair in disbelief at a history so thoroughly distorted, so poorly presented, so biased against the Muslims, one is baffled at such Muslim criminal incompetence. The blind adherence to history written by non-Muslims is the worst mistake committed by any historian calling himself/herself Muslim.

As the first chapter of this work amply shows, non-Muslim historians, as a general rule, have completely distorted, and fundamentally ruined Islamic history. They have, for instance, suppressed from knowledge some of the best episodes of such history. They have also suppressed some crucial facts in history. For instance, to this day, nobody knows what happened to the millions of Muslims who lived at one point in Spain, and the countless hundreds of thousands who once lived in Sicily. Non-Muslim historians have also over-inflated divisions amongst Muslims, most particularly dwelling on the early rifts which marked Islamic history. They have given great place to dissolute rulers who were the least keen on Islam, whether such rulers were Abbasids, or Fatimids, or Safavids. On the other hand,

1

non-Muslim historians have completely played down some of the greatest moments of Islamic history when they have not completely removed them. For instance, they have given little attention to the Aghlabid role in North Africa. In general, non Muslim historians also describe Muslim military victories as nothing other than small gains in skirmishes. In their opinion, Muslim victories, whether against the crusaders, or colonial powers, or other foes, were always won against weak, diminished, armies. The Muslim victory against the Mongols at Ain Jalut, in 1260, which saved Muslims from mass extermination, for instance, was, according to them, won by a large Muslim army against Mongol shepherds. The recent Algerian War of Independence (1954-1962) is seen as nothing more than a series of terrorist activities, and Algerian independence is said to be a gift France gave to Algeria. Muslim heroes are generally depicted as cunning, dissolute, murderous, and even those who once benefited of non-Muslim sympathies, such as Salah Eddin Al-Ayyubi (d.1193), have their life and deeds tarnished. Correspondingly, non-Muslim historians, with few exceptions, have turned Genghis Khan, Hulagu, Timur the Lame, colonial powers, etc, who massacred millions of Muslims, into benefactors of Islam, that somehow by such massacres they brought rejuvenation and progress to the Islamic land. Finally, in the great scheme of rewriting history in modern books, we find that it was the Muslims who mass enslaved Africans; that the Muslims were the worst slave traders in history; that the colonisation of Africa by Western powers was in order to end this Islamic scourge. We also read that the pirates who murdered and enslaved millions were the Muslims, whilst in truth, it was the Muslims who were victims of such pirate attacks. We also read today that the Muslims were perpetrators of genocides, when in truth they were victims of them. And even when it comes to events as recent as the Bosnian genocide (1992-5), and mass rape of Muslim women, we read and hear today that the Muslims were at best equally responsible of barbaric deeds and mass rape as the other parties.[11]

Thus, unless Muslims begin to re-write their history, based on facts and backed by evidence, Islamic history, left in the hands of others, is going to remain completely reshaped, the good made into bad and the bad made into excellent, and people of all ages fed these distortions.

---

[11] The latest instance of this comes from Channel Four News on 13 December 05 at 7pm. The News reader in the introduction on a report on the effects of mass rape in Bosnia held that all parties, including the Muslims, were responsible for rape, when in truth, 99% of the victims of mass rape, just as of mass slaughter, were the Muslims. Thus, if events as recent as these can be distorted in their essence, those centuries old bear no relationship whatsoever with reality.

This book raises the need for re-writing Islamic history, not by dismissing Western sources altogether, but by making a careful use of them. Which is not the case today: nearly all Muslim historians either use Western sources uncritically and thus end up reproducing Western distortions of Islamic history under a Muslim garb; or they ignore Western sources altogether, and end up losing good reference sources, and also losing the Western style of writing, a style better appreciated by Western educated Muslims and non-Muslims.

Both these approaches are avoided in this work. This work relies on both Muslim and non Muslim sources, old and recent. It uses non-Muslim sources critically, though, and does not dwell on the darker episodes of Islamic history whilst ignoring the positive as non-Islamic works tend to do.

This work seeks to be nearest to the truth as possible and to rectify the distortions of Muslim history as much as it can. Whilst it seeks to remain as honest as possible, it avoids dwelling on the worst atrocities and genocides. It is not the aim of this author to make an exaggerated representation of killings amongst Muslims so as to give and perpetuate a barbaric picture of them as non-Muslim historians generally do. Nor is it the aim of this author to dwell on genocides of Muslims by Westerners so as to re-open wounds or perpetuate hatred. One touches on such instances of atrocities, but only succinctly to make an argument, and then move on.

This work deals with Islamic history from the Pre-Islamic era till the colonial period. It tries to do so as succinctly as it can. It does not say everything and cannot say everything. This work begins a task, which others are under the obligation to improve and complete.

The first chapter discusses the forms and manners history, in general, and Islamic history, in particular, is distorted.

The second looks at Pre-Islamic Arabia and its surroundings, and the rise of Islam.

The third chapter gives an overview of Islam.

The fourth chronicles the history of Islam under the first four caliphs, and the early expansion of Islam.

The fifth makes an outline of the outstanding events, which occurred between the 9th and 11th centuries throughout the lands of Islam.

The sixth is a summary of the crusade period (1095-1291).

The seventh chapter looks at the history of Muslim Sicily and Spain, and their loss by the Muslims.

The eighth charts the rise and progress of Ottoman Turkey.

The ninth makes an outline of Islam in Africa, China, India, and South East Asia.

The tenth and final chapter looks at the colonial period, and the impact of colonisation on Islamic lands.

ONE

HISTORY AND ITS DISTORTIONS
(And the Need for Rewriting Islamic History)

This chapter looks at historical distortions and the techniques used to rewrite history. It focuses on Islamic history, which is the most distorted of all, especially on Western hands.

1. History as a Distorted Science:

Scores of independent sources have noted the distortions by Western historians. Writing in the mid 1930s, Sarton preached against the `double standard of morality which poisons our intellectual atmosphere.'[12] He insisted that accuracy has the same meaning in history as in science, and that the scientist who has two standards of truth, one for his scientific work, the other for his historical work, ought not be allowed to discredit academia but only himself. No matter what his `scientific' reputation may be, as opposed to his `historical' one, he should be revealed in his true colours, as an incompetent scholar, or a dishonest one, or both, `as one who debases our knowledge and defiles his own temple.'[13]

Likewise, Hartner observes how:
`Our time witnesses a most unfortunate tendency to write pretentious `syntheses' on the basis of either of a wholly insufficient factual knowledge

---

[12] G. Sarton: *The Study of the History of Mathematics*: Harvard University Press, 1936; p.27.
[13] Ibid.

or of preconceived theories-religious, philosophic, sociological maintained only by twisting and suppressing facts at the author's pleasure.'[14]

Geyl, too, says:

`I have done battle with historical myths in my time. I have seen (or thought I saw) historians being led astray by blind streaks in their minds due to their devotion or their partisanship.'[15]

And Daumas notes:

`One must take into account that printed sources have often suffered at their author's hands a distortion, whether unintentional or enforced, when measured against strict historical truth.'[16]

Such is the scale of historical distortions that a number of works have been devoted to this subject alone. Fischer, for instance, looks at the manners, forms, and reasons for historical distortions. [17] Geyl, too, in a work on the use and abuse of history, observes:

`Looking around, the first thing I discover is that the world's thinking is full of history mutilated or falsified, of historical myths, which are not, on account of their remoteness from past reality, any the less potent in the politics, national or international, of the present.'[18]

History aimed at the masses, schools and colleges is largely distorted, and can hardly be challenged by research (which is not the aim, nor the qualification, of either the masses or school and college children). Fischer observes that many historical fallacies are perpetrated by historians who appear to have mistaken their mission for `the titillation of illiterate thrill-seekers.'[19] Many works of poor historical value, Fischer adds, are also urged upon innocent children by well meaning librarians and school teachers.[20] Glubb also ponders on the suppression of whole chunks of history, even centuries, from Western history, questioning:

---

[14] W. Hartner: Essay review of O. Neugebauer: A History of Ancient Mathematical Astronomy, Verlag, 1975; 3 vols; in *Journal for the History of Astronomy*; 9; pp 201-12; at p. 201.

[15] P. Geyl: *Use and Abuse of History*, Yale University Press, 1955; p.78.

[16] M. Daumas: The History of technology: Its limits; its methods; tr into English and notes by A. Rupert Hall; in *History of Technology*, 1976; pp 85-112; p.91.

[17] D.H. Fischer: *Historians' Fallacies*, London: Routledge & Kegan Paul, 1971. Introduction: xxi.

[18] P Geyl: *Use and Abuse*; op cit; p.75.

[19] D.H. Fischer: *Historians' Fallacies*; op cit; p. 71.

[20] Ibid; pp. 71-2.

`If knowledge of the history of the period from the 7th to the 12th centuries is vital to the comprehension of the development of Europe, why, it may be asked, had it never been taught?'[21]

Today's writing of history, just as the media's impact and culture, due to the power of Western civilisation, is mainly the preserve and monopoly of the Western Whites, who write and re-shape history according to their own perceptions of it. `Modern civilisation's myriad pretensions to objectivity' says Menocal `have unfortunately tended to obscure the facts that much of our writing of history is as much a myth making activity as that of most primitive societies... We are prone to forget that history is written by the victors and serves to ratify and glorify their ascendancy, and we forget how many tracks are covered in that process.'[22]
This follows a pattern adopted by mainstream modern Western historians who remove the darkest pages of Western history, for instance.[23] Instead, a brighter, more alluring image of the Christian West is rebuilt, a history, which contradicts fundamentally historical truth.[24] And whilst Western history is rehabilitated, other histories are darkened. And no history is darkened and distorted as much as Islamic history.

2. The Generalised Distortion of Islamic History:

In a few words, the bulk of non-Muslim writing on Islam has primarily consisted on one hand in suppressing the positive and favourable about Islamic history, and on the other, in re-attributing to Islam all past misdeeds. Thus, anything that is favourable and that can be identified with Islamic history, such as the rise of modern science, or gardening, or architectural innovations, tolerance, etc, has been suppressed from Islamic

---

[21] J. Glubb: *A Short History of the Arab peoples*, Hodder and Stoughton, London, 1969; p.289.
[22] M.R. Menocal: *The Arabic Role in Medieval Literary History*; University of Pennsylvania Press; Philadelphia; 1987; at p. 1.
[23] Compare, for instance, any of the works by modern historians cleansed of such dark pages with an older Western source, which caught events as they were taking place; i.e: W. Howitt: *Colonisation and Christianity*: Longman; London; 1838.
[24] D E. Stannard: "Genocide in The Americas" in *The Nation*, October 19, 1992; pp. 430-4; W. Howitt: *Colonisation and Christianity*; op cit; R. Garaudy: *Comment l'Homme devient Humain*. Editions J.A, 1978.

history, and granted to the West. Then, on the other hand, everything, from the burning of dissidents, to enslavement of Africans, to piracy, etc, has been increasingly attributed to Islam and Muslims.

Hostility to Islam, rather than historical truth, is the prime reason behind the negative writing relating to Islamic history to this day.[25] The hostile, distorted depiction of Islam has its sources in the Middle Ages as highlighted by Daniel,[26] Sardar and Davies,[27] Southern,[28] and others. `The disgrace of the Christians, Daniel holds, `was to attack Islam for so many reasons…. In this area we can only say that Europeans have on the whole maintained towards the Arabs a constant reserve which seems to run consistently through the whole medieval period up to the present day.'[29] Smith insists that nearly all those who had approached Islam did so only to vilify and misrepresent it, writing from preconceived positions.[30] A dark picture was painted of Islam to contrast with the light self image of Christianity, and every crime imaginable was popularly associated with Islam, Smith adds.[31]

Prophet Mohammed (PBUH) has been a particular target of centuries of Western Christian calumny. Smith insists that with rare exceptions, all Western Christian depiction saw him as nothing other than a rank impostor.[32] Calumnies and non existent victories were concocted at pleasure against the Prophet, the `destroyer of idols,' whom they transformed into `an idol of God,' adds Smith.[33] Davenport, too, notes how an unfavourable image was made of the Prophet, that he was subject to epileptic fits `to impute that morbid affection to the apostle as a stain upon his moral character…'[34] Equally Forster observes that they were predisposed to think ill of Mohammed, writing `crude and undigested theories' to bear on their subjects and `bend the facts to accommodate them.'[35]

---

[25] A. Thomson: *Barbary and Enlightenment*: Brill; Leiden; 1987; pp. 37-8.

[26] N. Daniel: *The Arabs and Medieval Europe*; Longman Librairie du Liban; 1975.

[27] Z. Sardar; M-W. Davies: *Distorted Imagination*; Grey Seal Books; London, 1990.

[28] In R.W. Southern: *Western Views of Islam in the Middle Ages*, Harvard University Press, 1978.

[29] N. Daniel: The Arabs; op cit; p.319.

[30] R.B. Smith: *Mohammed*; op cit; p. ix.

[31] C. Bennett: *Victorian Images of Islam*; Grey Seal; London; 1992; p. 77.

[32] R.B. Smith: *Mohammed*; op cit; p. 81.

[33] Ibid; p. 75 fwd.

[34] J. Davenport: *An Apology;* op cit; p. 14.

[35] C. Forster: *Mohamedanism Unveiled*; London; James Duncan and John Cochran; 1829; I; p. 4.

Tolan expands on the motivations for the distorted images painted of Islam and the Prophet:
'Both as a rival religion and as a rival civilization, Islam was tremendously successful. It was hence appealing, intriguing, and frightening. The attraction of Muslim learning, Muslim culture, and Muslim sophistication was extremely strong... But the more Christians were attracted to Islam, the stronger others felt the need to condemn it-for it was this attraction, more than the might of Muslim armies, that was most threatening to Christendom.'[36]
The principles of Islam are 'neither so pernicious nor so absurd as many have imagined,' notes Jackson, and yet 'they have been vilified from error or for the purpose of exalting Christian doctrine.'[37]
Watt adds that Western Christendom found it necessary to paint such dark images of Islam and the Prophet to compensate for the feeling of inferiority as Europe was tributary to Islam in terms of science and learning.[38] Nonsense was, thus, accepted, and sound sense was distorted, concludes Daniel.[39]

The leading figures and the dynasties that stood for Islam are an object of the same vilification. Ashtor, en par with the vast majority of non-Muslim writers, depicts very much unfavourably the first four caliphs of Islam and the companions of the Prophet in asserting, for instance:
'Governors and even caliphs engaged in various speculations, withholding the pay due to the military or hoarding great quantities of wheat, so that the prices should rise and hindering others from selling their grain. In fact, several of the high ranking companions of the Moslem prophet and the Arab governors were great merchants. It seems, however, that the estates they acquired in various ways yielded them even greater sums and were the main source of their great riches.'[40]
The same author, just like nearly every non Muslim writer, savages the Seljuks and Mamluks, attributing to them all the woes of Islam, from corruption to barbaric deeds, to debauchery....[41] This hostility to such peoples has its true reasons, though. It was the Seljuks who defended the land of Islam, and saved it from total extermination when the crusades

---

[36] J.V. Tolan ed: *Medieval Christian Perceptions of Islam*; Routledge; London; 1996; preface; pp. xix-xx.
[37] J. Grey Jackson: *An Account of the Empire of Morocco*; 3rd ed; London; 1814; p 208.
[38] M.W. Watt: l'Influence de l'Islam *Revue des Etudes Islamiques*, Vol 41; p. 154.
[39] N. Daniel: *Islam and the West*; Oneworld; Oxford; 1993; p.302.
[40] E. Ashtor: *A Social and Economic History of the Near East in the Middle Ages;* Collins; London; 1976; p. 24.
[41] Ibid; chapter VI; pp. 209 ff.

(1095-) arrived and wiped out millions of Muslims.[42] Had it not been for the Seljuks, who fought in that crucial period when the Muslims were weak and disunited (1095-1145), it is certain the fate of Muslims would have been the same as that of the tens of millions of natives elsewhere, who failed to fight back and were exterminated to the last.[43] As for the Mamluks, it is they who not only fought back and stopped the Mongols at Ain Jalut in 1260, after the Mongols had already slaughtered millions of Muslims, but it is also they who threw out the crusaders from Palestine in 1291.[44]

The same hostility has been shown to the Berbers and Turks; Muslim history being cleansed of favourable images of the Turks, most particularly. Le Bon, for instance, whilst praising Islam and the Arabs, blames Islamic decline on the Turks and Berbers.[45] And the reason, again, as the chapter on the Ottomans (chapter 8) will show, is that it was the Ottomans who fought on behalf of Islam for centuries, from the 14th to the 20th century.

A great deal of writing and broadcast today attributes slave trading to the Muslims. Channel Four, in its programme Empire, broadcast in 2003, praises the achievements of the British Empire and gives the primary role for the abolition of the trade to devout Christian figures, and puts the blame for some of the worst aspects of the trade on the Muslims.[46] We are also told by another source that the Western military invasion of Africa in the 19th century was in fact aimed to ending this `Muslim scourge.'[47] We are thus told that in the mid 1850s, David Livingstone, the Scottish missionary,

---

[42] See accounts of the crusaders' slaughter of Muslim populations in every single town and city they conquered, slaying millions in the process. See, for instance:
-J.W. Draper: *A History of the Intellectual Development of Europe*; Vol I; Revised edition; George Bell and Sons, London, 1875.
-S. Runciman: *A History of the Crusades,* 3 vols, Cambridge University Press, 1962.
-Ibn al-Athir: *Al-Kamil fi'l Tarikh*; 12 Vols; ed C.J. Tornberg; Leiden and Uppsala; 1851-76.
[43] W. Howitt: *Colonisation and Christianity*: op cit; pp. 173 fwd in particular.
[44] See, for instance:
- Baron G. d'Ohsson: *Histoire des Mongols*: La Haye et Amsterdam; 1834.
- U. and M.C. Lyons: *Ayyubids, Mamluks and Crusaders, Selection from the Tarikh al-Duwal wal Muluk of Ibn al-Furat*; 2 vols, W. Heffer and Sons Ltd, Cambridge, 1971.
[45] G. Le Bon: *La Civilisation des Arabes*; Cyracuse; 1884.
[46] Broadcast on S4C on 18 February 03.
[47] H.A.L. Fisher: *A History of Europe (from the Beginning of the 18th Century to 1937)*; Eyre and Spottiswoode; London; 1952 ed. P. 1033; Also television programme Empire, broadcast on the British television channel, Channel Four, seen by this author on the Welsh equivalent of the same channel: S4C on 18 February 03.

'brought home to the imagination of the British public the horrors of the Arab slave trade, which had its centre in Zanzibar;'[48] and which England went to Africa to put an end to.[49] Even today, we are shown Christian missionaries at the forefront of the fight against 'Muslim slave trading' in Africa.[50] And if we happen to see Black slaves in white households in films today (i.e in Gone With The Wind), they are the happiest of all creatures, or as Loewen notes, they are not slaves, but mere "servants" with happy lives.[51]

This contradicts history fundamentally. Firstly, although domestic slavery has always existed in Africa, as in the Islamic land, it is, in the words of Garaudy, the Christian West that traded people en masse like commodities.[52] And it is a lie to see in slave trading some sort of continuity to what happened before in Africa.[53] Never had Africa made of slavery a means of production, whereby hundreds of thousands of Black men laboured to death to enrich masters in the fields or in the mines. There were in African societies domestic slaves, more or less integrated to the family, and field slaves (delinquents or war prisoners made to work), but never the way they were to made to toil, very often to death, by Western slave traders in the colonies.[54] Slave trading implemented by Western nations, Garaudy explains, is radically different: it is about deportation, and the scale of it is phenomenal, and without any common measure with traditional slavery.[55] In 1540, only 400 Africans were deported, a figure, which rose to reach nearly 300,000 slaves every year in the 18th century.[56] The slave trade dominated relations between Europe, Africa and America between 1680 and 1830, notes Vidrovitch.[57] Slave trading even became a Western state monopoly as early as 1528 by a decree of the champion of the Catholic faith: Charles Quint, imposing the chase of slaves.[58] The slave trade developed into an industry organised by the state; in France, the minister Colbert and the King Louis the XIVth in Versailles sorted in good conscience the questions concerning slaves in the Antilles in creating and encouraging commercial companies through

---

[48] H.A.L. Fisher: *A History of Europe;* p. 1033.
[49] Ibid.
[50] Such as Everyman on BBC1 on 29 January 2001.
[51] James W. Loewen at: http://www.uvm.edu/~jloewen/intro.html
[52] R. Garaudy: *Comment l'Homme;* op cit; pp.276-7.
[53] Ibid; p.274.
[54] Ibid.
[55] Ibid; p.275.
[56] Ibid.
[57] Catherine. C. Vidrovitch: Villes Africaines anciennes: une civilisation mercantile pre-negriere dans l'Ouest Africain, XVI et XVII em siecles; *ANNALES*: Vol 46; pp 1389-1435; at p.1390.
[58] R. Garaudy: *Comment l'Homme;* op cit; pp.276-7.

which the traffic was operating.[59] Likewise, the trade involved the highest echelons of the British establishment. The outcome was the thriving cities of France and England, and their booming economies at the height of the slave trade in the 18th century.[60] Three centuries of slave trading and one century of colonialism, however, destroyed the African continent.[61] The hardship experienced by Africans during ocean travel, or on the plantations, remains unique in its horrors. John Gabriel Stedman, who went to Surinam in 1771 to help suppress one of many slave revolts there, in his book,[62] quotes a white colonist who describes the torture-execution of a slave:

"Not long ago," this colonist told Stedman, "I saw a black man hanged alive by the ribs, between which with a knife was first made an incision, and then clinched an Iron hook with a chain. In this manner, he kept living three days, hanging with head and feet downwards and catching with his tongue the drops of water, it being the rainy season, that were flowing down his bloated breast, while the vultures were picking in the putrid wound."[63]

Due to losses during capture, transportation etc, 100 million Africans perished as a result of the slave trade.[64]

Piracy, according to the generalised Western view, was also a North African deed that targeted Christian shipping, inflicting terrible cruelties on innocent Christians, and justifying Western military invasion of North Africa. Thus J. Grey Jackson, an early 19th century apologist for Western military invasion of North Africa, writes:

'The first principle of this barbarous and sanguinary government (Algerian-Turkish rule), according to the African adage, is to 'maintain the arm of power, by making streams of blood flow without intermission around the throne.' He claims that this government 'reflects disgrace on Christendom' and that the bombardment (of Algiers) like that of Lord

---

[59] R. Pernoud: Pour en finir; op cit; p.85.

[60] M. Craton: Sinews of Empire: A Short history of British Slavery; Garden City; NY; Doubleday; 1974.
D. B. Davis: The Problem of Slavery in Western Culture; Ithaca; New York; Cornell University Press; 1966.

[61] R. Garaudy: Comment; op cit; p. 274.

[62] John Gabriel Stedman: Narrative of a Five Years Expedition Against the Revolted Negroes of Surinam; London; 1813.

[63] In T. Morganthau: Slavery: How It Built the New World; in Newsweek; Special Issue, Fall/Winter 1991; pp. 66-9.

[64] R. Garaudy: Comment; op cit; p.275.

Exmouth in 1816 is insufficient punishment for `the repeated insults offered by these ruffians to civilised Europe.''[65] France used the excuse of piracy to colonise Algeria in 1830 (and in the process caused the death of ten million Algerians.)[66] Today, `illustrious scholars,' specialising on the Islamic world,[67] and broadcasting corporations,[68] also adhere to the notion of Muslim piracy and its barbaric deeds. Some of these sources also justify the French military `intervention to end it (piracy).'[69] And yet, again, piracy was a Western deed before it became Muslim, and it inflicted the worst woes on Muslims.[70] Piracy against Islam, Bresc says:

`Highlights one of the important pages of maritime history, and the systematic looting of which the Muslims were victim. Until the Maghrebi and Turkish fleets began to register victories at sea, widespread looting of Muslim wealth, of men, and goods, considerably weakened the coastal economies of the Maghrib.'[71]

Indeed, it was Western piracy which enriched the West[72] and destroyed the once thriving and dominant Muslim trade and economic system.[73]

The genocide of Muslims during the crusades (1095-1291), equally, is rewritten from a false, anti Islamic perspective. Re-writers today do away with the worst crimes that had been inflicted on the Muslims. Thus, modern writers such as Wiet et al say that:

`The essential causes of the Crusade are probably to be found in the temperament and splendid vitality of Western Europe at that time..... Jerusalem taken on 15 July 1099, the day of Christ passion.'[74]

---

[65] J.Grey Jackson: *An Account of Timbuctu and Hausa;* London; 1820; pp 457-63, in A.Thomson: *Barbary and Enlightenment*: Brill; Leiden; 1987; p. 131.

[66] M. Lacheraf, in L.Blin: *l'Algerie du Sahara au Sahel*, l'Harmattan, Paris, 1990; note 3, p 112.

[67] I.e C. Brockelmann: *History of the Islamic Peoples*; Routledge and Kegan Paul; London; 1950 reprint; p. 292; p. 397.

[68] BBC 2: Time Watch; seen on 10 January 2003.

[69] C. Brockelmann: *History of the Islamic Peoples*; op cit; speaks of France being provoked by the repeated Algerian insults, provocations to which France had no other choice than to respond; see pp. 292; p. 397 etc.

[70] H. Bresc: la Course Mediterraneene au Miroir Sicilien (XII-Xvem Siecle); In *Politique et Societe en Sicile; XII-Xv em siecle*; Variorum; Aldershot; 1990; pp. 91-110.

[71] Ibid; p. 102.

[72] G. Fisher: *The Barbary Legend;* Oxford; 1957.
I.M. Lapidus: *Muslim Cities in the Later Middle Ages*: Harvard University Press; Cambridge Mass; 1967.
F. Braudel: *Grammaire des Civilisations*; Flammarion, 1987.

[73] See R.B. Serjeant: *The Portuguese off the South Arabian Coasts*, Oxford; 1963.

[74] G. Wiet, V. Elisseeff; P. Wolff; and J. Naudu: *History of Mankind;* op cit; p.273.

The same authors say that `despite the heroic effort of the kings of Jerusalem the counter offensive which Saladin launched from Egypt culminated in the fall of the city (1187). The subjugation of Frankish Syria by the Moslems, which had been postponed by the intervention of the Mongols, now went ahead.'[75]

This is contradicted by contemporary accounts, whether by Muslims or Christians. Indeed, as to be extensively highlighted in chapter six, such accounts tell us of mass slaughter of Muslims, and cannibalism, torture, rape, treachery and greed on the part of the crusaders of unmatched proportions.

Other than distorting Islamic history, a major aim of Western academia dealing with Islam has been to use its expertise of the subject, and its awareness of the divisions amongst Muslims, most particularly, to exploit them in the war on Islam. Western attention to Islam is, as Arenal points out, to put focus on, and use every sign of local identity.[76] Hence, to this day and for centuries, the West, through its academia, media, and politicians, has worked diligently to stir local conflicts amongst Berbers, Kurds, Arabs, Shias, Sunnis, Turks, etc, so as to serve Western ends. During the colonial era, for instance, the French implemented many policies to stir conflict between Arabs and Berbers in Algeria and Morocco.[77] The English successfully conquered India by splitting Muslims between themselves, and by splitting them from their other subjects: Jats, Sikhs, etc.[78] Today, the same can be seen everywhere, divisions and differences amongst Muslims being used to stir conflict between them so as to ease Western domination over them.

It is also widely obvious that instead of setting aside Western stereotypes of Islam, Western scholarship is eager to reinforce them.[79] We find, again and again, Arenal observes, the same obsessions with decadent Islam.[80] In the words of Sardar and Davies:
`Armed with the tools of the new disciplines, Orientalist attacks on Islam became more intense, more confident, more pervasive, they ascribed

---

[75] Ibid; pp.273-4.

[76] M. Garcia-Arenal: Historiens de l'Espagne, historiens du Maghreb au 19em siecle. Comparaison des stereotypes *ANNALES: Economies, Societes, Civilisations:* Vol 54 (1999); pp. 687-703; p.702.

[77] J.J. Cook: The Maghrib through French Eyes; 1880-1929; in *Through Foreign Eyes;* edited by A.A. Heggoy; University Press of America; 1982; pp. 57-92; p. 91.

[78] E. Driault: *La Question d'Orient*; Librairie Felix Alcan; Paris; 1921; p. 63.

[79] M. Garcia-Arenal: Historiens de l'Espagne, op cit; p.702.

[80] Ibid.

ridiculously large and important roles to minorities: Christians, Jews, Ismailis, assassins, Hellenists, certain features of Sufi thought (Hallajism is a `religion of the cross'), anyone or anything which to their mind represented the antithesis of Islam and could undermine its basis.'[81]

3. An Instance of Distortion: The Fate of the Muslims of Spain:

The history of the Muslims in Spain is a good instance to highlight how Islamic history is distorted by the suppression of their accomplishments, and also the suppression of the terrible fate they suffered.

One manner the Islamic impact on the history of Spain has been removed was by the destruction of the Islamic legacy as here highlighted by Scott: `The sumptuous edifices which abounded in every city have disappeared or have been mutilated almost beyond recognition. Barbaric violence has annihilated the palaces which lined the Guadalquevir, and whose richness and beauty were the admiration of the world. Ecclesiastical malignity has demolished to their very foundations or sedulously effaced the characteristics of the innumerable temples raised for the propagation of a hostile religion, and the extent of this systematic enmity may be inferred from the suggestive fact that of the seven hundred mosques required for the worship of the Moslem capital, but one has survived. Diligent antiquarian research has failed to establish even the sites of all but three or four of the remainder, of whose existence and splendour both history and tradition afford abundant and indisputable evidence. The ignorance and prejudice of successive generations have, in addition to the above named destructive agencies, contributed their share, and no unimportant one, to the obliteration of these memorials of Arab taste and ingenuity.'[82]
Philip II, the 16th century Spanish monarch, went as far as ordering that every stone in Toledo which bore Arabic inscription to be destroyed.[83]

---

[81] Z. Sardar-M.W. Davies: *Distorted Imagination*; op cit; p. 43.
[82] S.P. Scott: *History of the Moorish Empire*; in 3 vols; The John Lippincott Company; Philadelphia; 1904; vol 2; pp.557-8.
[83] Ibid; p.576.

The Spanish Muslim phase is also largely absent in modern Spanish history. The subject of Muslim influence on Spain, Monroe observes, is inadequately handled in major universities today.[84] Menocal, one of the more recent Arabists, also notes that the Muslim question has suffered distortions, and been impoverished in ways that others have not been.[85] This exclusion of the Andalusian and Sicilian Muslim literary world from the general medieval European frame of reference, as Menocal concludes, hampers decisively Muslim Spanish history.[86] Puertolas notes that `a truly surprising simplism is revealed as the norm in which so many Spaniards have been `educated' in recent years, the subject being reduced to `the grossest Hollywood terms of good guys and bad guys-Christians and Muslims respectively.'[87]

This same history which suppresses the Muslim heritage in Spain, also suppresses the woes Muslims suffered in that country. This is a more common practice amongst modern works. One goes through old sources, such as Lea's History of the Inquisition, especially the section devoted to the Muslims, and one comes across terrible deeds inflicted on Muslims.[88] Another older source, Scott, also depicts the mistreatment of Muslims.[89] Old contemporary sources, written by Spaniards themselves, soldiers, even, also speak of the terrible fate of the Muslims. A Spanish soldier, Perez de Hita, who fought the civil wars of Grenada (1570s),[90] for instance, says how Muslim women, terrified at the advance of the Spanish forces, aware no prisoners would be taken:

`Unable to withstand the attack, they went out on a cliff overlooking the sea, and embracing each other, and shouting their pain and sorrow, plummeted to their deaths. Others sought to put the idea of Christian mercy to the test and constructed crude crosses not out of pieces of wood. Kneeling before the soldiers they would cry: `I Christian sir, I Christian'.

---

[84] J.T. Monroe: The Hispanic-Arabic World: in *Americo Castro and the Meaning of Spanish Civilisatio;* J. Rubia Barcia ed; University of California Press, Berkeley, 1976, op cit; pp. 69-90; p. 87.

[85] Maria Rosa Menocal: *The Arabic Role in Medieval Literary History,* University of Pennsylvania Press, Philadelphia, 1987; p.92.

[86] Ibid; p.92.

[87] Julio Rodriguez Puertolas: A Comprehensive View of Medieval Spain: in *Americo Castro,* op cit; pp 113-34; p.121.

[88] H. C. Lea: *A History of the Inquisition of Spain,* 4 vols; The Mac Millan Company, New York, 1907.

[89] S.P. Scott: *History;* op cit.

[90] Perez de Hita: Guerras civiles; Blanchard-Demouge ed; 2 vols. In Rhona Zaid: The Guerras civiles de Granada: the idealisation of assimilation; (vol.ii, 79) (Vol II, 79) in J.V. Tolan ed: *Medieval Christian Perceptions of Islam;* Routledge; London; 1996; pp. 313-30.

But no one in that squadron offered any Christian charity, and the Moorish women were forced to jump from the cliffs.'[91] Perez de Hita describes the cruelties of the soldiers, and hardly conceals admiration for the Muslim reluctance to abandon their faith and heritage.[92]

Modern works, on the other hand, especially the very recent ones, with one or two exceptions, write a completely different history. A modern historian, taken at random, Conrad, in his new version of the history of the Spanish wars against the Muslims, does not refer to a single massacre of Muslims.[93] For instance, he speaks of the taking of Barbastro by the Christians from the Muslims in 1063, but does not say a word of the slaughter of the Muslim population and the mass rape of Muslim women in front of members of their families or in mosques, which happened on that occasion.[94] He does not fail, though, to say, that when the Muslims retook the town the following year they slaughtered the Christian garrison.[95] Another historian, Cardaillac, en par with most modern Western scholars, and the Catholic Church,[96] cleanses history of such crimes.[97]

Burning a human alive is the worst crime committed by any entity at all times of history. Modern Western history suppresses from knowledge this terrible deed inflicted on Muslims.[98] This contradicts historical reality, which shows that the Inquisition was established to undertake the job of uprooting Islam by the use of torture and burning at the stake.[99] In 1531, the Valencia tribunal, for instance, had fifty eight trials for heresy, with some 45 burnings in person, most of whom Muslims.[100] An average of at least one Muslim was burnt alive every week, and this happened for twelve years, 1528-1540, in the city.[101] At the Seville auto de fe of September 24, 1559, two Muslim apostates were burnt; one had carried Muslims to `Barbary' and the other had taken his wife and children there.[102] A letter to Philip II, from

---

[91] Ibid; pp. 326-7.
[92] Ibid.
[93] P. Conrad: *Histoire de la Reconquista*; Que Sais je? Presses Universitaire de France; Paris; 1998.
[94] Ibid; p. 49.
[95] Ibid.
[96] In June 2004 the Church came out with a new, cleansed history of Spain.
[97] *Les Morisques et l'Inquisition*: Edited by L. Cardaillac; Publisud; Paris; 1990.
[98] Hardly any modern work refers to this.
[99] H.C. Lea: *A History of the Inquisition;* op cit; See volume three.
[100] Arch.Hist. Nacional, Inquisition de Valencia, Legajos 98, 300.; H.C. Lea: A History of the Inquisition in Spain; op cit; p.358
[101] A. Thomson; M.A. Rahim: *Islam in Andalus*; Taha; London; 1996; p.187.
[102] H.C Lea: *The Moriscos of Spain*; op cit; p.189.

the inquisitors of Saragossa, June 6, 1585, said that in that day five culprits were burnt.[103] Over the period 1549-1622, the Inquisition of Saragossa had burnt 1,817 men; and 758 women.[104] Hernando de Palma, a Muslim, accused of teaching and conducting Islamic ceremonies, denied and overcame severe torture, then confessed. He was burnt in Toledo in 1606.[105] Not just happy to burn Muslims alive, the Dominican Inquisitor, Bleda, writing in 1604, commented that: when they are about to be burnt alive, the Muslims always read their Islamic lines (shahada), and threw a curse on the 'Holy Church,' and he concluded that, 'they should have their mouths gagged so as to stop them from insulting our true faith'[106]

There is no need to dwell on the numbers of Muslims who have been exterminated, the problem being instead with historians who love cogitating and playing with statistics to bring the figures of victims down. Generally one of them uses his 'scholarship' to cut the numbers of such victims by a certain ratio. He is then followed by another, who refers to the one before him, and using diverse techniques cuts down the numbers of his predecessor. Another follows, refers to his predecessor, and further cuts down the latter's figures, and so on and so forth. By the time we get to our day, there are hardly any victims of Western crimes.

Cardaillac, with Dedieu, rely on Lapeyre to cut down the numbers of Muslims who were eliminated from Spain. In the Kingdom of Valencia, for instance, the number of Muslims at the beginning of the 16th century is put at just about 70,000.[107] We are not told what happened to the millions who once lived in the country, and if told, their disappearance is blamed on demographic crises, and emigration.[108] In a passage, Lapeyre refers to Regla 'who had the great merit to destroy the legend of the 50,000 Moors of Catalonia, whom the historians piously transmitted without any critical effort. Even he (Regla) has overestimated these figures. By admitting 10,000 he still remains above the true figure.'[109]

In his work, Lapeyre, who remains the source of reference for the countless many who cut down the numbers of Muslims exterminated in

---

[103] Ibid; p.118.

[104] Les Morisques et leur temps; *Table ronde Internationale*: 4-7 July 1981; Montpellier; CNRS; Paris; 1983; p. 527

[105] H.C. Lea: *A History of the Inquisition in Spain*; op cit; pp.199-200.

[106] In R. De Zayas: *Les Morisques et le racisme d'Etat*; ed Les Voies du Sud; Paris; 1992; pp.471-2.

[107] H. Lapeyre: *Geographie de l'Espagne Morisque*; SEVPEN, 1959; pp. 29-30 in L. Cardaillac; J.P. Dedieu: Introduction a l'Histoire des Morisques; in *Les Morisques et l'Inquisition*: op cit; pp 11-28; at p.15.

[108] Ibid; p.13.

[109] Regla; la expulsion, p 263; in H. Lapeyre: *Geographie*; p.98.

Spain, reduces their numbers to a mere few thousands.[110] If Lapeyre is correct, where have the millions of Muslims who lived in Spain gone? If one takes the population of Muslim Cordova as an illustration, archaeologists excavating parts of the city suggest that the population was as much as a million on account of the very great area covered by the Muslim city, which Levi Provencal says was about 8 times the size of the modern city.[111] A figure of a million inhabitants of the city would accord well with the figures given by the various authors, most of them very conservative and very reliable, cited by al-Maqqari: 200,000 houses for the common people and 60,300 for the more important elements; or even 300,000 houses.[112] This completely contradicts the ridiculous figures given by Lapeyre, and leaves open the question: where have the millions of Muslims of Spain, indeed, gone?

Modern Western historians, in general, also blame Islam and Muslims themselves for their extermination in Spain. Lapeyre, again, admits that the Muslim population was en masse ethnically cleansed, but as he puts it, it was 'a brutal solution, perhaps, but it simplified things.'[113] 'The power of resistance of numerous minorities is not to be demonstrated, especially when this is a faith as tenacious as Islam', he adds.[114]

For Perez, another historian:
'The minorities living under the status of protected minorities first under Muslims, then under Christian, had a pejorative meaning; ... Once the reconquista completed, no reason was there to maintain such a situation. Spain had now become a nation like others in Christian Europe...The Moors, descendants of the Mudedjares, had refused to assimilate; they had to be expelled in the early 17th century.'[115]

According to Cardaillac and Dedieu:
'The Moors were building alliances with the enemies of Spain in North Africa and with the Turks, and other European enemies to invade the country. Denunciations of such Moors multiplied, and they were not without foundations.'[116]

---

[110] H. Lapeyre: *Geographie de l'Espagne Morisque*; op cit.
[111] E. Levi Provencal: *Histoire de l'Espagne Musulmane;* in 3 Volumes; Paris, Maisonneuve, 1953 Vol III; pp. 362-3.
[112] Al-Maqqari: *Nafh Al-Tib*. Translated by P.De Gayangos: *The History of the Mohammedan Dynasties in Spain*; 2 vols; The Oriental Translation Fund; London, 1840-3; pp. 214-5.
[113] H. Lapeyre: *Geographie;* op cit; p. 119.
[114] Ibid; p. 120.
[115] J. Perez: Chretiens; Juifs et Musulmans en Espagne; Le mythe de la tolerance religieuse (VIII-XV e siecle); in *Histoire*, No 137; October 1990.
[116] L. Cardaillac; J.P. Dedieu: Introduction; op cit; p.24

And:

'Why expulsion? Why now? Political considerations won, and the decision was justified by the rising threat and all the fears just described.'[117]

These Western justifications for the elimination of the Muslims fail to make the parallel with the Christians living under the Muslims in crusader times, or under the Turks, in later centuries. During the crusades, the local Christians, Maronites and Armenians in particular, sided with the Crusaders and the Mongols, and massacred Muslims in considerable numbers.[118] Yet once the Muslims (led by the Mamluks) took the upper hand, they could have wiped out every Maronite and Armenian on account of their alliance with the crusaders and the Mongols, and on account of their direct participation in the mass slaughter of Muslims. None of this happened. Both Maronites and Armenians have survived to our day amidst Muslim communities.

Finally, some modern Western historians justify the extermination of Muslims on the ground that Islam and Muslims constitute a disease. Hence, Conrad sides with Menendez Pidal, who in his *Historia de Espana*, concludes that:

'After many centuries of forced neighbourhood with the Christians, this exotic race never integrated into Spain, neither to its faith nor to its collective ideals, nor to its character, the Moors never assimilated and lived like a cancerous growth in the Spanish flesh.'[119]

---

[117] Ibid; p.25.

[118] See, for instance, J.J. Saunders: *Aspects of the Crusades*, University of Canterbury, 1962.

S. Runciman: *A History of the Crusades*, op cit.

K.S. Salibi: The Maronites of Lebanon under Frankish and Mamluk rule; 1099-1516; *Arabica* IV; 1957.

[119] R. M. Pidal: *Historia de Esapana dirigida por Ramon Menendez Pidal'* Vol 2; Madrid; 2nd edition; 1966; p. 41.

4. Ways and Methods to Distort Islamic History:

One of the first and most obvious practices to maintain the distorted depictions of Islamic history is to bar, as much as possible, from entry into academia and historical studies any person deemed unsuitable, i.e anyone not ready to reproduce the fallacies of Islamic studies.

Also effective is the technique of hounding out `bad academics' (i.e historians who seek to alter the institutionalised fallacious learning), or by putting pressure on them not to write on certain subjects, or in a manner too favourable to Islam and Muslims. Returning to the history of Spain and its Islamic dimension, for instance, Castro says:
`Until not many years ago my opinions on this matter (the role of Islam in Spanish history) were the same as everyone else's. When in 1938 I wrote an essay on certain problems of the fifteenth and sixteenth centuries, I noticed how difficult it was to introduce the Islamic element into the historical picture, or to leave it out, and I ended up by improperly avoiding the question.'[120]
Confirming this, Monroe points out how for centuries, any mention of the Muslims and their role in the formation of Spanish culture, has drawn furiously hostile response from Spanish scholarship.[121] Just as Menocal fairly recently experienced, noting in her long preface:
`No specific of any of the theories called `Arabist' can be successful so long as the most general views we have of the medieval period are as hostile to the notions of such influence and interaction as they currently are.'[122]

The same attacks are unleashed on anyone challenging the hostile depiction of Islam in other fields. A couple of illustrations suffice here. When in 1958, Singer, assisted by Hall and Holmyard completed the edition of the large `History of Technology,'[123] which gave a greater place to the Orient in modern technological upsurge, the response was extremely hostile from established academia. Lynn White Junior and his hordes of followers, responded with great hostility to Singer's epilogue: `East and West in Retrospect.' White used the quarterly review Speculum[124] and, above all,

---

[120] ESH, pp.47-48: SSH, p.82. See also AVH (1949), (1970) in Guillermo Araya Goubet: The Evolution of Castro's theory; op cit; pp. 41-66; p.43.
[121] J.T. Monroe: The Hispanic-Arabic World; op cit; p. .69.
[122] M.R. Menocal: *The Role;* op cit; p. xiii.
[123] C.J. Singer et al: *History of Technology*; 5 vols; Oxford at the Clarendon; see vol 2 (1956); particularly pp. 753-77.
[124] Vol 33, 1958, pp. 130-5.

Technology and Culture,[125] a quarterly set up soon after Singer's book, and with him (White) taking one of the leading positions in that journal, to fiercely lash out at Singer's above quoted chapter because of its strong support for Islamic and Chinese science.

White's attack on Singer was by no means new or isolated. Hence, Rashdall[126] violently mauled Ribera[127] for the latter's view that Islamic higher learning influenced Western higher learning and the birth of universities in the West. Sanchez Albornoz literally led a war of attrition[128] against Castro because of the latter's support for the Islamic foundations of Spanish culture.[129] Renaud, the Frenchman, who was part of the French colonial enterprise in Morocco, savaged Castiglione's history of medicine for its too pro-Islamic tones.[130] Fisher who condemned the Barbary legend that Muslim corsairs were beasts infesting the seas,[131] drew upon himself extreme hostility.[132] Equally, when Forster wrote some favourable accounts of Islam,[133] he met with considerable criticism. *The Methodist Magazine* ascribed to his pro Islamic views `a satanic origin, or at least a satanic `helping hand whose `agency, dark, active, malignant and intense, would be employed to give it success and extension;' and this was even when Forster saw the Prophet (PBUH) as the `Antichrist' and made an analogy of Islam with popery.[134] Massignon, too, suffered from the same hostility when he said that he was struck by the spiritual value of Muslim religious experience and disturbed by the historical injustices inflicted against Islam, both as a religion and a group of peoples, oppressed and despised. He and his

---

[125] Vol 1, 1958, at pp. 340-1.

[126] H. Rashdall: *The Universities of Europe in the Middle Ages*, ed F.M Powicke and A.G. Emden, 3 Vols, Oxford University Press, 1936.

[127] J. Ribera: *Dissertaciones y opusculos*, 2 vols, Madrid, 1928.

[128] S. C. Albornoz: *L'Espagne Musulmane*, French translation of earlier Spanish version, Paris, 1985.

[129] A.Castro: *Espana en su historia. Cristianos, moros y judios*. Buenos Aires: Losada, 1948, 709 pp; see *The Spaniards, an Introduction to their History;* tr. by W. F. King and S. Margaretten; University of California Press; Berkeley; 1971.
A.Castro: *La realidad historica de Espana.* 2ed. Edited by Paulino Garagorri with additions and corrections from Castro's papers. Madrid: Alianza-Alfaguara, 1974.

[130] H.P. J. Renaud reviewing A. Castiglioni: Histoire de Medicine, 1 vol, Paris, Payot, 1931; in *Hesperis*; Vol 12: 1931; pp 248-50.

[131] G. Fisher: *The Barbary Legend*; Oxford; 1957.

[132] A. Thomson: *Barbary*; op cit; p. 125.

[133] C. Forster: *Mohametanism Unveiled*; London; James Duncan and John Cochran; 1829.

[134] The Methodist Magazine, p, 75 in C. Bennett: *Victorian Images of Islam*; Grey Seal; London; 1992; p.39.

followers were charged 'of Islamising heresy' by outraged supporters of Church integrity.[135]

Cleansing away 'bad' academics also means cleansing their names from bibliographies, references, and eventually from all knowledge. An example amongst the hundreds that can be cited here is one of the latest examined by this author: Philip Conrad's History of the Reconquista.[136] In his bibliography (pp 125-6), Conrad gives a good place to historians hostile to Islam: Perez, Lapeyre, Menendez Pidal, Albornoz...., and suppresses from his bibliography sources such as Castro, Levi Provencal, Lea, Lane Poole, Dozy etc, that not only recognise the Islamic impact on Spanish history, but also show the crimes of the Catholic Church towards the Muslims in Spain.

There is also a technique consisting in disappearing centuries from history. These suppressed centuries (7th –14th), during the middle ages, correspond to the very period of Islamic ascendancy, and remain essential for understanding the very foundation of Western science and civilisation.[137] Centuries are disappeared which, as Glubb notes, make 'the subsequent story of the rise of Europe largely incomprehensible.'[138]

If centuries are easy to erase, it is even easier to erase unwanted facts, i.e facts with which modern historians disagree. Every author goes further than his predecessor in the suppression of facts to such a point that any subject of history, eventually, ends up being thoroughly cleansed of all unwanted facts and their sources. To legitimise such a cleansed history, modern historians refer to each other; quote each other (and praise each other). Many such techniques of selective suppressions of facts to present a wholly distorted version of history of civilisation, for instance, have been studied by Emeagwali.[139] She notes how techniques vary from changes of names, to removal of data, to open misuse of facts.[140] Another instance of suppression of facts relates to the history of the crusades. A whole crusade,

---

[135] See introduction to the work of R.Dagorn, *le Geste d'ismael d'apres l'onomastique et la tradition Arabe*; Geneva; 1980. M. Rodinson: *Europe;* op cit; p. 78.

[136] P. Conrad: *Histoire de la Reconquista*; op cit.

[137] As noted by P. Benoit and F. Micheau: The Arab intermediary: in *A History of Scientific Thought*; ed M. Serres; Blackwell, 1995; pp 191-221; at p. 191.

[138] J. Glubb: A Short History; op cit; p.135.

[139] At http://members.aol.com/Sekglo/racism.htm
This is a May 2001 modified version of an earlier paper published by G.T. Emeagwali in Science and Public Policy; *Jounal of the International Science Policy Foundation*, Surrey; UK; Vol 16; No 3; 1989;

[140] Ibid.

the real second crusade, that took place in 1100-1, has been removed from knowledge altogether, as if it never happened. Only in very few works on the subject, such as by Oldenbourg, do we read that in 1100-1, no less than four Christian armies, altogether between 250,000 and half a million men, invaded the Orient, aiming at destroying the Islamic caliphate once for all, and wiping out the very existence of Islam.[141] These armies were decimated by the Turkish forces of Kilij Arslan and Ghazi, without registering one single gain. This inglorious adventure, Oldenbourg notes, is passed under total silence by historians.[142] Indeed, in nearly every single book by Westerners on the history of the crusades, the second crusade did not take place in 1100-1, but in 1144; the great Muslim victories of 1101 completely passed in silence.

Other techniques used to falsify history consist in the suppression of subjects form courses, and the suppression of unwanted book titles from references handed to students. Books are made as difficult for access as possible, some of the best books placed in special collections with strict access. One is not referring to the Vatican Library, here, but to many university libraries. Of course, manuscripts are even harder to get at. And finally there is the technique of restricting access to works that are not included in the university library, and that can be sought from elsewhere. Here reasons such as high costs, restricted loans, etc, being invoked to justify the non accessibility.

Another dominant technique in distorting Islamic history is to refrain from correcting fallacies about it as long as they depict Islam unfavourably. A good instance of this relates to the burning of the library of Alexandria, which Bar Hebraeus (13th century) attributed to the Muslims, and which was subsequently adopted by nearly all Western sources to support the view that Islam is hostile to learning. Voltaire, the 18th century French philosopher, for instance, cunningly, forgave the Muslims for 'burning the Library of Alexandria' 'haven't they by that also destroyed monumental errors of men,' as he put it.[143] Even if that account of the Muslim burning of such library dates five centuries after the supposed incident took place (7th century), and no mention was ever made of it by contemporary sources, the Muslims were still blamed for it. Research has also proved that the said library was burnt by Christian

---

[141] Z.Oldenbourg: *The Crusades*; Weinfeld and Nicolson: English tr. London; 1966; pp. 174-5.
[142] Ibid; pp. 183.
[143] Voltaire: Essai sur les Moeurs; Chapter VI; in P.Martino: *l'Orient dans la Literature Francaise au 17em et 18em siecles*; Librarie Hachette; Paris; 1906. p. 319.

zealots centuries before the Muslim entered Egypt.[144] To this day, though, the Muslims are blamed for the deed.

Other than written rhetoric, it is an old Western art to exploit the power of images for the purpose of exaggerating the 'barbaric' side of Muslims. During the crusades, for instance, whilst the Franks were slaughtering their way into the Muslim land,[145] their draughtsmen were able to create a completely different image of both deed and foe. This is seen in the illustrations of the chronicles of William of Tyre (1130?-90).[146] The Muslims are distinguished from the Franks by their exaggerated physical features, to the limits of caricature. The reader would easily recognise the evil nature of the Muslim characters, like today with villains in comics.[147]

The use of images is even more effective today. Hence, an English daily, in its edition of 25 January 03, on page two, showed the Prince of Wales talking to a Muslim woman completely shrouded in black. On that particular occasion, the Prince of Wales came across tens of Muslim women all wearing a diversity of cloaks, and yet the paper, en par with the rest of the media, chose that image to depict Muslim women. The same daily a week later, on 1 February, returned to the issue of a woman tried for adultery in Nigeria, and used the very powerful image of her holding a small baby to turn her trial into an Islamic crime against motherhood.

Cinema is another effective form of weaponry to promote the superiority of the Westerner and the animal primitiveness of the Muslim. In the film El-Cid, Charlton Heston is El-Cid. He is the courageous, loyal, humane, Christian figure, fighting the black faced, vile, cruel, fanatic Muslim. In truth, mass slaughter in Spain was of the Muslim population who lived in the country.[148] As for El-Cid, he was 'treacherous and cruel, a violater of altars, and a breaker of his own faith.'[149] As Dozy insists, the romantic history of the Cid is a tissue of inventions.[150]

---

[144] E. Gibbon: *The Decline and Fall of the Roman Empire*; vol 5; op cit; pp 474-5.

[145] See S. Runciman: *The Crusades*; op cit.

[146] M. Balard: Les Musulmans d'apres les illustrations de Guillaume de Tyr, in *De Toulouse a Tripoli;* Colloque held between 6 and 8 December, 1995, University of Toulouse; 1997; pp 143-51; illustrations pp. 152-66.

[147] Ibid; pp. 143-4.

[148] See H.C. Lea: *A History of the Inquisition in Spain*, in four volumes, The MacMillan Company, New York, 1907, volume three.

J. Read: *The Moors in Spain and Portugal*; Faber and Faber, London, 1974.

[149] S. Lane-Poole: *The Moors in Spain*; Fisher Unwin; London; 1888; p.192.

[150] R. Dozy: Spanish Islam, in S.Lane Poole: *The Moors in Spain;* p. 192.

The Need for Re-Writing Islamic History:

So much more could have been said about historical fallacies and the particular distortions of Islamic history. Enough has been said, though to reach certain important conclusions.

This author is firmly convinced that amongst the crucial factors, which divide the West and Islam into two hostile camps, is the misunderstanding of each other. The fundamental reason behind such misunderstanding is precisely the distorted depictions of Islam and Muslims, and the constant pouring, if not to say bombardment, of minds with such distorted depictions. These distorted depictions have origins in a history written from the vantage of hostility. Such hostility feeds itself from events in history, and also from the manner historical events have been fed into the non Islamic minds. Any writing and any approach to Islamic history has, indeed, perpetuated the same distorted images of Islam and Muslims. The conclusion, hence, is, if the present East-West conflict is to be tackled, a new look at the writing and teaching of Islamic history is crucial. The history of Islam, especially in relation to the West, needs to be cleansed as much as possible from the false and derogatory. There is a great need to set aside the usual approach, which consists in writing and teaching Islamic history from the one and only perspective of seeking to darken the Muslim subject as much as possible, falsify the history of such subject, and hence register an ideological victory. This victory has not, is not, and will not be achieved. The aim is to live side by side and cohabit on equal terms regardless of differences. The public, both Muslim and non Muslim, needs to look at history from a more realistic perspective, where truth is the central consideration. No progress is made on lies, slur or demeaning the other. Progress will be made only on firmer, truer, grounds, hence a new history.

This new history, as this writer begins to write, and that will, hopefully, be followed up and improved by others, seeks to be as nearest the truth as possible. This history incorporates dark instances of the shared past. It does not dwell on them, though. The need is to do justice to historical events, not to use them to sour the present. This history engages the combined efforts and writings of both Muslims and non Muslims, past and present. It aims at being a history that both Muslims and non Muslims can read and comprehend, a history that seeks to bring closer the two publics. Certainly it is not perfect for either, but it is the history that both publics, hopefully, can begin to build upon for a future, and better history.

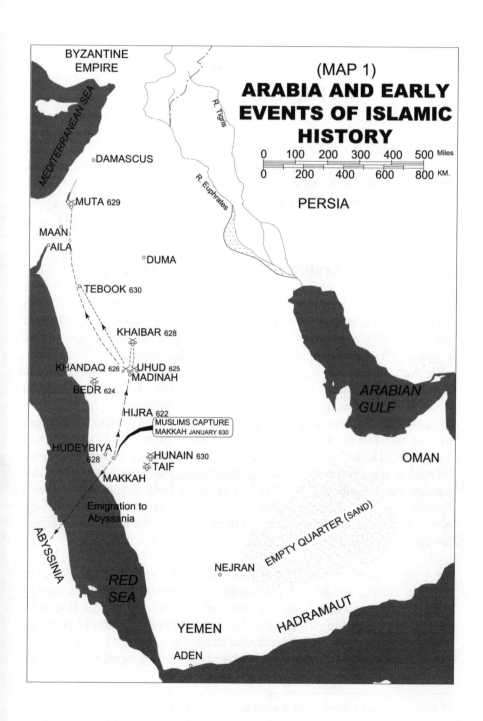

TWO

THE RISE OF ISLAM

This chapter looks at the social, historical and religious background of the rise of Islam. It focuses on pre-Islamic Arabia and its surrounding regions, most particularly the social and religious conditions prior to the rise of Islam. The text, then, looks at the progress of Islam in the Arab peninsula.

1. Pre-Islamic Arabia and its Surrounding Regions:

Nothing captures best the changes Islam made upon pre-Islamic Arab society than the following instance, when the Abyssinian king asked about the new religion a group of Muslims who had sought refuge in his kingdom, Dja'far, cousin of the Prophet (PBUH) answered:
`We were plunged in the dark meanders of ignorance; we adored idols. Ruled by our passions, we only recognised the law of the strongest, until God has chosen a man from our race, illustrious by his birth, for very long respected for his virtues. This Prophet had taught us to profess the oneness of God, to reject the superstitions of our fathers, to despise Gods of stones and wood. He ordered us to flee vice, to be honest in our discourse, faithful to our promises and word, affectuous and generous towards our parents and neighbours. He has forbidden us from despoiling women's honour, and from robbing orphans. He recommended us prayers, giving alms, and fasting. We have believed in his mission; we have respected the laws and the morale that he brought us on behalf of God.'[151]

Pre-Islamic Arabia did not lack positive traits. The Arab was never short of courage, honour, pride and generosity. His fairness at war is a quality anterior to Islam, which Islam reinforced and institutionalised. Le Bon notes how before the advent of Islam, the Arab nomads lived in a state of perpetual war but their hostilities were conducted according to a strict code of honour. No tribe aspired to exterminate or enslave another. Compared with the cruel

---

[151] G. Le Bon: *La Civilisation des Arabes,* Syracuse; 1884; p.68.

28

methods used by the `civilised' nations of the nineteenth century, Arab tribal wars were scarcely more than a game, says Le Bon.[152] The object of the Arab warrior, Glubb adds, was not so much to win the war as to gain glory. This attitude produced a certain `sporting' spirit between the combatants. No glory could be won by treachery or stealth, even if it resulted in a victory. Sometimes the date and place of a battle were fixed by agreement long before the event to ensure that neither side stole an unfair advantage.[153]

These qualities apart, pre-Islamic society was swamped by dreadful conditions of diverse sorts. One of the worst practices of pre-Islamic Arabia was idolatry. Here is Gibbon's depiction of such a state:
`Each tribe either found or introduced in the Caaba (Kaaba) their domestic worship: the temple was adorned, or defiled, with three hundred and sixty idols of men, eagles, lions, and antelopes; and most conspicuous was the statue of *Hebal (Hubal)*, of red agate, holding in his hand seven arrows, without heads or feathers, the instruments and symbols of profane divination.... The devotion of the ruder ages was content with a pillar or a tablet; and the rocks of the desert were hewn into gods or altars, in imitation of the black stone of Mecca, which is deeply tainted with the reproach of an idolatrous origin. From Japan to Peru, the use of sacrifice has universally prevailed; and the votary has expressed his gratitude, or fear, by destroying or consuming, in honour of the gods, the dearest and most precious of their gifts.... The cruel practice was long preserved among the Arabs; in the third century, a boy was annually sacrificed by the tribe of the Dumatians; and a royal captive was piously slaughtered by the prince of the Saracens, the ally and soldier of the emperor Justinian. A parent who drags his son to the altar exhibits the most painful and sublime effort of fanaticism: the deed, or the intention, was sanctified by the example of saints and heroes; and the father of Mahomet (Mohammed (PBUH) himself was devoted by a rash vow, and hardly ransomed for the equivalent of a hundred camels.'[154]

The majority of the tribes were addicted to fetishism of a very low type. Makkah was, at this time, the centre of a far reaching idolatry, ramifications of which extended throughout the tribes of the peninsula. In the Kaaba were included three hundred and sixty idols, including *Hubal*.[155] The Kinana tribe, closely allied to the Quraish (the leading family of Makkah) politically and by blood, besides the star Aldobaran, served the goddess *Uzza*,

---

[152] Ibid; p.338.
[153] J. Glubb: *A Short History;* op cit; p.25.
[154] E. Gibbon: *The Decline and Fall;* op cit; vol 5; pp.329-30.
[155] R. B. Smith: *Mohammed and Mohammedanism;* op cit; p. 102.

represented by a tree at a place called *Nakhla*, a day and half's journey from Makkah.[156] Animals and plants, the gazelle, the horse, the camel, the palm tree, inorganic matter like pieces of rock, stones, etc, formed the principal objects of adoration.[157] The Hawazin, who roamed towards the south east of Makkah, had for their favourite idol the goddess Lat, located at Tayef. Manat was represented by a rock on the caravan road between Makkah and Syria.[158] *Yaghuth* was worshiped under the form of a lion; *Sawa* of a woman; *Ya'uk* of a horse; *Nasr* of an eagle.[159]

Among some tribes in the case of a death, a camel was sacrificed on the tomb, or allowed to die from starvation, in the belief that it would serve as a conveyance for the deceased in a future existence. Some believed that when the soul separated itself from the body, it took the shape of a bird called *Hama* or *Sada*. If the deceased was the victim of a violent death, the bird hovered over the grave, crying *askuni*, (Give me a drink) until the murder was avenged.[160] Belief in jinns, ghouls and oracles rendered by their idols, whom they consulted by means of pointed arrows, called Azlam or Kiddah, was universal. Each tribe had its particular idols and particular temples. The priests and hierophants attached to these temples received rich offerings from the devotees. Often there arose sanguinary conflicts between the followers or the worshipers of rival temples.[161]

The scattered branches of the Christian Church in Asia and Africa were at variance with each other, and had adopted the wildest heresies and superstitions. They were engaged in perpetual controversies and torn to pieces by the disputes of the Arians, the Sabeians, Nestorians, and Eutychians, whilst the general barbarism and ignorance which were found amongst the clergy caused great scandal to the Christian religion, and introduced universal profligacy of manners among the people.[162] In Arabia, the deserts swarmed with ignorant and infatuated Cenobites, or recluses, wasting their lives in vain but fiery speculations, and then rushing, often armed, in mobs into the cities, preaching their fantasies in the churches, and enforcing agreement to them by the sword.[163]

---

[156] Syed Ameer Ali: *The Spirit of Islam;* op cit; pp. lxvi.
[157] Ibid; pp. lxvi-ii.
[158] Ibid; pp. lxvi.
[159] R. B. Smith: *Mohammed and Mohammedanism*; op cit; p. 102.
[160] Syed Ameer Ali: *The Spirit of Islam; op cit*; p. lxvii.
[161] Ibid.
[162] J. Davenport: *An Apology*; op cit; p. 3.
[163] Ibid.

"let's eat and drink for tomorrow we die"

Just as it was idolatrous pre-Islamic Arab society was devoid of social mores. The Arabs believed neither in a future state nor in the creation of the world, but attributed the formation of the universe to nature, and its future destruction to time. Debauchery and robbery prevailed everywhere, and since death was regarded as the end, so strictly called, of existence, so was there neither recompense for virtue nor punishment for vice.[164] As among the Hindus, polygamy was practised to an unlimited extent. A widow was considered an integral part of her deceased husband's patrimony, and passed into the use of the son; and the atrocious and inhuman practice of burying female infants was universal.[165]

The pagan Arab indulged to the utmost the vice of drunkenness, and prided himself upon his capacity to absorb great quantities of liquor. There were some Himyarite princes who obtained an unenviable immortality by drinking themselves to death.[166] Gambling was so popular in the desert that the Bedouin often staked his liberty, his most priceless possession, on the toss of a pebble.[167] He gloried in the name of brigand, and regarded the capture of a caravan as the principal object of life, and it was not unusual for him, after plundering the dead, to mutilate them with a brutal malignity, and he tested guilt or innocence by ordeals of fire and water.[168]

The Arabs, Smith sums up, were careless, sceptical, materialistic: `they believed that death was extinction: a few believed in a future life and a future judgment; `let's eat and drink, for tomorrow we die' is the Epicurean tone of the majority of the poems that have come down to us. What a contrast they were in this respect to Mohammed, and what a Herculean difficulty did this temperament of theirs place in the way.'[169]

Just as they were addicted to drinking and gambling, the Arabs were passionately addicted to dancing and singing. Dancing and singing, as in other eastern countries, were practiced by a class of women occupying a servile position, who were called *Kiyan,* or in the singular, *Kayna,* and whose immorality was proverbial. Yet they were held in the highest estimation and the greatest chiefs paid public court to them.[170] The moral depravity of the

---

[164] Ibid; p. 2.
[165] W. Durant: *The Age of Faith,* op cit; pp. 167 ff; Syed Ameer Ali: *The Spirit of Islam;* p. lxiv.
[166] S.P. Scott: *History of the Moorish Empire;* op cit; p. 23.
[167] Ibid.
[168] Ibid.
[169] R. B. Smith: *Mohammed;* op cit; p. 104.
[170] W. Durant: *The Age of Faith,* op cit; pp. 167 ff; Syed Ameer Ali: *The Spirit of Islam;* op cit; p. lxiv.

people is evidenced by the fact that these women used to give receptions which were attended by all the men of light and leading in the city.[171]

Makkah, the place where the Prophet (PBUH) was born and grew, and today the hub of Islam, prior to Islam, was the centre of the commercial activity which has distinguished the Arabs at all times from the other nations of the East. From Makkah radiated the caravans which carried to the Byzantine dominions and to Persia the rich products of Yemen and the far famed India, and brought from Syria the silks and stuffs of the Persian cities. But they brought with them more than articles of trade; in the train of these caravans came all the luxurious habits and vices which had corroded the very heart of the neighbouring empires.[172] Greek and Persian slave girls, imported from Syria and Iraq, beguiled the idle hours of the rich with their dancing and singing, or ministered to their vices. The poet, whose poems formed the pride of the nation, sang only to the joys of the present life, and encouraged the immorality of the people. And no one reminded themselves of the morrow.[173]

Pre-Islamic Arab society was also excessively violent, a condition outlined by Gibbon:

`Each Arab, with impunity and renown, might point his javelin against the life of his countrymen. The union of the nation consisted only in a vague resemblance of language and manners; and in each community, the jurisdiction of the magistrate was mute and impotent. Of the time of ignorance which preceded Mohammed, seventeen hundred battles are recorded by tradition: hostility was embittered with the rancour of civil faction; and the recital, in prose or verse, of an obsolete feud, was sufficient to rekindle the same passions among the descendants of the hostile tribes. In private life every man, at least every family, was the judge and avenger of his own cause. The nice sensibility of honour, which weighs the insult rather than the injury, sheds its deadly venom on the quarrels of the Arabs: the honour of their women, and of their beards, is most easily wounded; an indecent action, a contemptuous word, can be expiated only by the blood of the offender; and such is their patient inveteracy, that they wait whole months and years the opportunity of revenge. A fine or compensation for murder is familiar to the Barbarians of every age: but in Arabia the kinsmen of the dead are at liberty to accept the atonement, or to exercise with their own hands the law of retaliation. The refined malice of the Arabs refuses even the head of the murderer, substitutes an innocent for the guilty person, and transfers the penalty to

---

[171] Ibid.
[172] Ibid.
[173] Ibid.

the best and most considerable of the race by whom they have been injured. If he falls by their hands, they are exposed, in their turn, to the danger of reprisals, the interest and principal of the bloody debt are accumulated: the individuals of either family lead a life of malice and suspicion, and fifty years may sometimes elapse before the account of vengeance be finally settled.'[174]

Women before Islam were seen as intermediary creatures, between man and the animal world, their only purpose being that of procreation, and slaving for their masters. The Arabs practiced both polyandry and polygamy to an extent rarely countenanced by other barbarians. Polygamy was universal and quite unrestricted; equally so was divorce, at least as far as the man was concerned. One woman, whose career would seem to be unique in the history of matrimonial achievement, was celebrated for having been the wife of forty husbands.[175] Omm Charijeh distinguished herself, even amongst the Arabs, by having forty husbands. In a society where communal marriage prevailed, the passion of jealousy was necessarily unknown.[176] A husband could dismiss his wife on the merest whim, and then, if he so pleased, might recall her again under the influence of a similar whim. [177]

One of the worst practices of pre-Islamic Arabia was its treatment of new born girls. A new born girl was deemed a calamity, and the custom of burying girls alive was the normality. Under the pretext of preventing future dishonour, he (the Arab) often buried his female children alive. Smith, thus, tells us:
'The most barbarous practice of these 'times of ignorance,' was the burying alive of female children as soon as they were born; or worse, still, as sometimes happened, after they had attained the age of six years. The father was generally himself the murderer. 'Perfume and adorn', he would say to the mother, 'your daughter, that I may convey her to her mothers.' This done, he led her to a pit dug for the purpose, bade her look down into it, and then as he stood behind her, pushed her headlong in, and then filling up the pit himself levelled it with the rest of the ground.'[178]
From such unspeakable atrocities as this did Islam deliver the people.[179]
Le Bon narrates this story (told initially by Caussin de Perceval):

---

[174] E. Gibbon: *The Decline and Fall*; op cit; vol 5; pp. 323-4.
[175] S.P. Scott: *History of the Moorish Empire*; op cit; p. 23.
[176] Ibid.
[177] R. B. Smith: *Mohammed*; op cit; p. 97.
[178] Ibid; pp 95-6.
[179] S.P. Scott: *History of the Moorish Empire*; op cit; p. 23.

'Cays, a chief of the Benu-Tenim tribe one day met with the Prophet (PBUH) who had one of his daughters seated on his lap.
'What is that yew you have there?'
'My child,' said the Prophet.
'By God!' said Cays, 'I don't have little girls like that; I buried them all alive!'
'Fool! Shouted the Prophet; God must have emptied your heart of every human emotion. You've never experienced the gentlest feelings given to a man to experience.'[180]
And so, Islam suppressed this practice and similar others such as the annual offering of virgins to the Nile, under Islam, the girls were replaced by a symbolic wooden replica.[181]

---

[180] G. Le Bon: *La Civilisation;* op cit; p. 316.
[181] Al-Muqaddasi: *The Best Divisions for Knowledge of the Regions*, a translation of his *Ahsan at-taqasim fi Ma'rifat al-Aqalim* by B.A. Collins, Centre for Muslim Contribution to Civilization, Garnet Publishing Limited, Reading, 1994; at p.190.

A Story of Idolatry from Pre-Islamic Arabia

The religious ideas or superstitions of the Arabs varied as much as did the objects of their worship. A father not un-frequently sacrificed his own child to appease an angry God. Divination by arrows was a favourite method of finding out the will of God. In the Kaaba was an idol with seven arrows. The number most commonly employed, though, was three arrows. One of them was marked with the words: My Lord hath commanded thee; a second My Lord hath forbidden thee; the third being left blank. The Arab was always ready to consult these arrows, but not always so ready to abide by their decision. A certain prince was anxious to avenge the murder of his father. He consulted an idol of much repute by drawing from three arrows in his presence. On one of them was written the word `command;' on the second: `prohibition;' and the third: `delay.' He drew out `prohibition'; dissatisfied, he shuffled the arrows a second time, and the second time drew out the same. Twice again, he shuffled them, and each time with the same result. In his anger he broke the arrows into pieces and threw them at the idol's head, exclaiming:
`Wretch! If it were thy father who had been killed, thou wouldst not have forbidden his being avenged.'[182]

---

[182] Caussin de Perceval; II; p. 310; in R.B. Smith: *Mohammed*; op cit; p. 103.

2. Beginning of Islam:

Davenport says:
`Mohammed (PBUH), a simple Arab, united the distracted, scanty, naked and hungry tribes of his country into one compact and obedient body, and presented them with new attributes and a new character among the people of the earth. In less than thirty years, they defeated the Emperor of Constantinople, overthrew the kings of Persia, subdued Syria, Mesopotamia, Egypt; and extended conquests from the Atlantic to the Caspian Sea, and to the Oxus; from which limits, during twelve centuries, its political sway has never, with the exception of Spain (and Sicily) only, receded; while the faith has continued to extend, and is, at this hour, extending in Northern Asia, in Central Africa, and on the Caspian.'[183]
Durant, too, says:
`When Prophet Mohammed began preaching Islam, Arabia was a desert flotsam of idolatrous tribes; when he died it was a nation.'[184]

It was four years after the death of Justinian, the Byzantine emperor, in 570, that was born at Makkah, in Arabia, the man who, of all men, Draper says, has exercised the greatest influence upon the human race-Mohammed.[185]
Prior to Mohammed (PBUH), the Arabs were adorers of a multitude of Gods; stones and objects of great diversity, including lumps of sugar or items of equal value or just anodyne objects to the modern observer. He, Mohammed, preached a monotheism which quickly `scattered to the winds the empty disputes of the Arians and Catholics, and irrevocably wrenched from Christianity more than half, and that by far the best half of her possessions, since it included the Holy Land, the birthplace of our faith, and Africa, which had imparted to it its Latin form.'[186]
However, there was much to happen, first, before that wrenching took place.

Mohammed was born a few months after his father died,[187] inheriting nothing other than two camels, a few sheep and a slave named Barakat.

---

[183] J. Davenport: *An Apology;* op cit; pp. 54-5.
[184] W. Durant: *The Age of Faith*; op cit; p.174.
[185] J.W. Draper: *A History of the Intellectual Development of Europe*; 2 vols, George Bell and Son, London, 1875; vol 1; p.329
[186] Ibid.
[187] This outline on the life of the Prophet is mainly derived from the introduction to *The Qur'an, a New translation* by M.A.S. Abdel Haleem; Oxford University Press; 2004-5; pp. x-xi; and J. Davenport: *An Apology*; op cit; pp 5-15.

When Mohammed was six years old his mother, Amina, died. After her death, the care of the orphan devolved to his paternal grandfather Abd-Al Mutalib. Two years later he also died, and Abu Taleb, Mohammed's uncle, took charge of the boy treating him as one of his own children. Mohammed continued in his uncle's employment. Mohammed enjoyed great respect for his judgment and trustworthiness, as was reflected by his nickname al-Amin, the trusted one.[188] He was recommended to a rich widow, Khadidjah, for whom he traded. Impressed by his honesty and good character, she proposed marriage to him. He was 25 and she was 40. They were married for over twenty five years until her death.

It was in the fortieth year of his life, that while passing the month of Ramadhan on Mt Hira, he lay wrapped in his mantle during the silent watches of the night, that he heard a voice calling him by name. Uncovering his head, there suddenly broke in upon him a flood of light of such intolerable splendour and intensity that he swooned away. Mohammed raised his eyes and saw the angel in the likeness of a man, standing in the Sky above the horizon.
`Read!' said the angel.
`I know not how to read,' said Mohammed.
`Read in the name of your Lord, the Creator of all things,
Who made man from a clot!
Read, and thy Lord is the Most Bounteous,
Who taught man the use of the pen,
And Who taught man that which he knew not.'
Mohammed stood quite still, turning away his face from the brightness of the vision, but whithersoever he might turn his face, there always stood the angel confronting him. `Mohammed! You are the Apostle of God the Most High, and I, I am the angel Gabriel.'[189]
The Voice said again O Mohammed you are Allah's Messenger, and I am Gabriel.' Mohammed remained thus a long while till at length the angel vanished.
When, later, he returned to his wife Khadidjah, he told her his experience.[190]

Khadidjah, who of all people was the closest him, became his first convert. The next were Zeid, his Arab slave, to whom he granted freedom, and his

---

[188] J. L. Esposito: *Islam, the Straight Path;* Oxford University Press; 1998. P. 6.
[189] J. Davenport: *An Apology;* op cit; p. 15.
[190] Introduction to *The Meaning of the Glorious Qur'an;* by M. M. Pickthall; Taha; London; p. x.
M.M. Pickthall was English born, and converted to Islam, before in 1930 making a translation of the Qur'an into English.

own cousin, Ali, the son of Abu Taleb. A merchant from Makkah, called Abu Bekr, a quiet, pleasant man, became his fourth disciple, and the first man from outside his household to do so.[191]

The first years of Mohammed's preaching were difficult, marked by resistance and rejection by Quraish. While there was a trickle of converts, opposition to Mohammed (PBUH) was formidable.[192] For the powerful and prosperous oligarchy of Makkah, the monotheistic message of this would be reformer, with its condemnation of the socioeconomic inequities of life, constituted a direct challenge not only to traditional polytheistic religion but also to the power and prestige of the establishment, threatening their economic, social, and political interests.[193] The Prophet denounced false contracts, usury, and the neglect and exploitation of orphans and widows. He defended the rights of the poor and the oppressed, asserting that the rich had an obligation to the poor and dispossessed. This sense of social commitment and responsibility was institutionalized in the form of religious tithes or taxes on wealth.[194]

After four years, the Prophet's disciples only numbered about seventy. The Quraish particularly resented the Prophet's insistence on the destruction and removal of idols. Quraish, Glubb notes, were proud of their idol temple. Men from all over Arabia came to it as pilgrims and bought many commodities, which they imported. If as the Prophet insisted, the idols were destroyed, both the prestige and the commerce of Makkah would suffer.[195] Quraish, Durant says, were even more disturbed by Mohammed's welcome to slaves than by the new religion.[196]

'The people of Makkah were hardened in their unbelief by superstition and envy,' says Gibbon: 'The elders of the city, the uncles of the Prophet, affected to despise the presumption of an orphan, the reformer of his country. The Koreishites (Quraish) had long been jealous of the pre-eminence of the family of Hashem... Mohammed was guilty of deserting and denying the national deities... They (Quraish) repeatedly addressed Abu Taleb in the style of reproach and menace. "Thy nephew reviles our religion; he accuses our wise forefathers of ignorance and folly; silence him quickly, lest he kindles tumult and discord in the city. If he

---

[191] J. Glubb: *A Short History;* op cit; p. 30
[192] J. L. Esposito: *Islam, op cit;* P. 7.
[193] Ibid.
[194] Ibid.
[195] J. Glubb: *A Short History*; op cit; p.32.
[196] W. Durant: *The Age of Faith*; op cit; p.165.

perseveres, we shall draw our swords against him and his adherents, and thou wilt be responsible for the blood of thy fellow-citizens."[197]

The Prophet (PBUH) took great risks in conveying the message. The early years in Makkah brought terrible reaction. The people of Makkah jeered at him and his friends. They threw their refuse in his face and boycotted his whole tribe regardless of whether they were Muslims or not. Mohammed took his call to Ta'if, but was pelted with stones and chased away.[198] The weight and moderation of Abu Taleb eluded the violence of religious faction, and the Prophet withdrew himself to various places of strength in the town and country. As he was still supported by his family, the rest of the tribe of Quraish engaged themselves to renounce all intercourse with Mohammed's family, neither to buy nor sell, neither to marry not to give in marriage, but to pursue them with implacable enmity, till they should deliver the person of Mohammed to the justice of the gods.[199] The decree was suspended in the Kaaba before the eyes of the nation; Quraish besieged the Prophet and his most faithful followers, intercepted their water, and inflamed their mutual animosity by the retaliation of injuries and insults.[200]

Gradually, however, many early enemies of Islam became its most ardent defenders. Omar Ibn al-Khattab, future caliph (634-644), was one of the most uncompromising of such enemies. He drew his sword in rage over the Prophet's "blasphemies" against the gods of the Quraish.[201] The version by the early Islamic historian, Ibn Hisham (d. 218H/833), of Omar's conversion, reads:
'Omar Ibn al-Khattab, who afterwards became Caliph, was among the bitterest opponents of Islam in early days. He set out one day, sword in hand, with the intention of killing the Prophet- "this Sabaean who has split the unity of Quraysh, calls their ideals foolish and their religion shameful, and blasphemes their gods"-when a friend who met him dissuaded him, reminding him that if he slew the Prophet he would have to reckon with the vengeance of a powerful clan:
"Thinkest thou that the Banu 'Abd Munâf would let thee walk on the earth if thou hadst slain Muhammad?" for tribal pride survived religious

---

[197] E. Gibbon: *The Decline and Fall*; op cit; vol 5; p. 354.
[198] I.R. and L.L. Al-Faruqi: *The Cultural Atlas of Islam*; Macmillan Publishing Company; London; 1986; p.119.
[199] E. Gibbon: *The Decline and Fall*; op cit; vol 5; p. 355.
[200] Ibid.
[201] I.R. and L.L. Al-Faruqi: *The Cultural Atlas*; op cit; p.119.

difference. "Is it not better for thee to return to the folk of thine own house and keep them straight?"

Omar asked: "which of the folk of my house?'

"Thy brother-in-law and cousin, Sa'id ibn Zeyd, and thy sister, Fatimah daughter of Al-Khattab, for, by Allah, they have become Muslims and followers of Muhammad in his religion, so look thou to them."

Then Omar returned, enraged against his sister and brother-in-law, and there was with them in the house Khabâb ibn Arit, having with him a leaf on which was written Ta Ha (Surah/Chapter of the Qur'an) which he was reading aloud to them. When they heard the noise of Omar's coming, Khabâb hid in a closet that they had in the house and Fatimah took the leaf and hid it under her thigh. But Omar had heard the sound of Khabâb's reading as he drew near the house, and when he entered he said:

"What was that mumbling which I heard?"

They said: "Thou hearest nothing."

Omar said: "Yea, by Allah! And I have already been informed that you have become followers of Mohammed in his religion." Then he attacked his brother-in-law Sa'id ibn Zeyd, but Fatimah sprang to keep him off her husband and he struck and wounded her.

And when he had done that, his sister and his brother-in-law said to him: "Yes, we are Muslims and we believe in Allah and His messenger, so do what you will!"

But when Omar saw the blood upon his sister he was sorry for what he had done, and he said to his sister: "Give me that leaf from which I heard you reading just now, that I may see what this is that Muhammad has brought." And Omar was a scribe.

When he said that, his sister said: "We fear to trust thee with it."

He said: "Fear not!" and swore by his gods that he would return it to her when he had read it.

And when he said that, she hoped for his conversion to Al-Islam, but said: "O my brother, thou art unclean on account of thine idolatry and none may touch it save the purified."

Then Omar went out and washed himself, and she gave him the leaf on which Ta Ha was written and he read it. And when he had read it he said: "How excellent are these words!" and praised it highly.

When he heard that, Khabâb came out to him and said: "O Omar, I hope that Allah has brought you in answer to the prayer of the Prophet, for only yesterday I heard him saying: O Allah! Strengthen Al-Islam with Abu'l-Hukm ibn Hishâm or Omar ibn Al-Khattab; and Allah is Allah, O Omar!"

At that, Omar said: "O Khabâb, direct me to Mohammed that I may go to him and make surrender."[202]
The conversion of Omar took place in the fifth year of the Prophet's mission (ninth before the Hijrah) soon after the departure of the emigrants to Abyssinia. At that time this Surah, Ta Ha, was already written down and in circulation.

As Islam earned new members, Quraish grew into greater animosity to the faith and to the Prophet (PBUH). Quraish sought to bribe Mohammed to relinquish his mission. They offered to accept Islam on condition that he modified it so as to make room for their gods as intercessors with Allah, offering to make him their king if he would give up attacking idolatry.[203] His answer was unequivocal: "if they should place the sun on my right hand, and the moon on my left, they should not divert me from my course."[204]

Fear of blood feud deterred Quraish from using violence upon Mohammed or his freemen followers, but they inflicted terrible pains on converted slaves. Abu Bekr, one of the Prophet's earliest followers had by years of commerce saved 40,000 pieces of silver; now he used 35,000 to buy the freedom of as many converted slaves as he could.[205] It was also conveyed that recantation under duress was forgivable.[206]

When the Prophet (PBUH) saw that he could not protect his companions from exposure to persecution and that he was spared of it because of his rank with Allah and his uncle Abu Taleb, he said to them:
`You may go to Abyssinia, for the king there is fair and will not cause injustice to anyone and it is a friendly country (so you may stay there) until Allah will relieve you from your affliction.'[207]
Thereupon his companions went to Abyssinia. This was the first migration of Islam. Amongst those who emigrated were the future caliph Uthman Ibn Affan with his wife, Ruqayyah, the daughter of the Prophet. Eighty three was

---

[202] Ibn Hisham: *Sirat Rasul Allah*; part one; pp. 119-20 in The meaning of the Glorious Qur'an (Pickthall); op cit; pp. 226-7.
[203] Introduction to *The Meaning of the Glorious Qur'an* (Pickthall); pp. xii-xiii.
[204] E. Gibbon: *The Decline and Fall*; op cit; vol 5; p. 353.
[205] W. Durant: *The Age of Faith;* op cit; p. 165.
[206] Ibid.
[207] In Ibn Hisham: *Sirat Ibn Hisham: Biography of the Prophet* as abridged by Abdus Salam M. Harun; Al-Falah Foundation; Cairo; 2000; p.56.

the total number of those who went to Abyssinia apart from the little children.[208]

In the year 619, the Prophet lost in a very short space of time two of his dearest relatives: his uncle Abu Taleb, and his wife Khadidjah. With the death of Abu Taleb, the Prophet lost a support and stay in his personal life, and a fortification and protection against the Quraish.

The death of Abu Taleb was about three years before the Emigration to Madinah, and during this period, Quraish began to increase their maltreatment and insult him in a way they would have never had the courage to do when his uncle was alive.[209] Suffering severe persecution, the Prophet (PBUH) went to Taif to seek support from the Thaqif. Ibn Hisham narrates:

`Arriving at Taif, the Prophet headed to certain personalities of the Thaqif who were then their notables and chiefs, namely three brothers: Abd Yalil, Mas'ud and Habib. The Prophet sat with them, called them to Islam and asked their support against his adversaries at home. `I will tear the cloths of the Ka'abah if Allah has sent you as a Messenger! Said one of them. `Did not Allah find anyone other than you to send? Said the second. `I swear by Allah ,that I will never have any contact with you. If really you are the Messenger of Allah, then you are too dangerous to reply to your words; and if you are belying Allah, then I feel it is imperative not to speak to you,' said the third.

So the Prophet got up and said to them:

`Seeing that you have acted as you have keep the matter secret,' for he did not like that his people would know it, so that they would further hurt him. On the contrary they (the three brothers) stirred up their louts and slaves to scorn him and ridicule him as he was pursued by a mob. He sought refuge and rested against the shade of a wall of a vineyard of an orchard possessed by Utbah ibn Rabi'ah and his brother Shaybah who were in it at that time watching him.

When the Prophet reached safety, he said:

`O Allah! to You I complain of my weakness of my helplessness, and my insignificance before men. O Most merciful of the merciful, You are the Lord of the helpless and You are my Lord! Into whose hands would You entrust me? Into the hands of a remote person who would scowl at me, or to an enemy who You have given control over my affairs? If You are not angry with me, I do not care; but Your clemency is more wide for me. I

---

[208] Ibid.
[209] Ibid; p. 77.

42

seek refuge with the Light of Your Countenance, whereby all darkness is illuminated, and of Which all affairs are ordered in this world as well as in the Hereafter, from (any possibility) that You should send down Your anger or that I should incur Your wrath. It is for me to return to you until You are well satisfied! There is no means nor might save with You!'
Seeing him in this difficult situation, Utbah and Shaybah were moved on the grounds of kinship and compassion, and sent him a young Christian slave with a tray of grapes.'[210]

The Prophet went on preaching the message, and whenever a chance came at the season of pilgrimage, he contacted Arab tribes to invite them to believe in Allah and that he was a Prophet who had been sent by Him. He met a number of Madinah residents at the season of pilgrimage to whom he expounded Islam and recited the Qur'an.[211] They listened to his preaching and became Muslims saying:
'There is no tribe that is so divided by hatred and rancour as our people are, and may Allah bring them together through you. So, let us go and invite them to this religion of yours; and if Allah unites them in it, no man will be mightier than you.'[212]
They left the Prophet and went back to Madinah believing in Islam. They were six from the Khazraj tribe, and reaching Madinah they told their people about the Prophet calling on them to embrace Islam until it became widely spread amongst them.[213] Subsequent arrivals from Madinah during the following pilgrimage season gave their first pledge to the Prophet, that they will not associate anything in worship with Allah, that they will not steal, nor commit illegal sexual acts, nor that they will kill their children, or utter slander intentionally.[214]
More pledges were made, and in the last pledge to the Prophet, one Udabah ibnus Samid said:
'We gave a pledge to the Prophet (PBUH) that we would listen and obey in times of plenty as well as in scarcity, under likable and dislikable circumstances, and that we would not prefer ourselves to the other Muslims, and that we would not disagree with those who are in authority, and that we would speak the truth wherever we are, and that we would never fear the blame of the blamers.'[215]

---

[210] Ibid; pp.79-80.
[211] Ibid; p.84.
[212] Ibid.
[213] Ibid.
[214] Ibid; p.85.
[215] Ibid; p.89.

Following these pledges, the Prophet ordered his companions to emigrate to Madinah, whilst he remained in Makkah.

In Makkah itself, taking advantage of the death of Abu Taleb, Abu Jahl, who succeeded to the principality of the community, a zealous idolater, convened an assembly of Quraish and their allies, to decide the fate of the Apostle.[216] His death was resolved; and they agreed that a sword from each tribe should be buried in his heart, to divide the guilt of his blood.[217] An angel revealed their conspiracy to the Prophet; and flight to Madinah was the only resource.[218] The assassins came to the Prophet's house, and watched at the door. They were to strike him as he came out, whether at night or in the early morning, but a blindness fell upon the would be murderers, and the Prophet passed them by without they could see him, on his way to the house of Abu Bekr.[219] The assassins meanwhile were deceived by the figure of Ali, who reposed on the bed, and was covered with the green vestment of the Apostle.[220]

Three days Mohamed and his companion, Abu Bekr, were concealed in the cave of Thor, at the distance of a league from Makkah; and in the close of each evening, they received from the son and daughter of Abu Bekr a secret supply of intelligence and food. The assassins, still continuing the pursuit, explored every haunt in the neighbourhood of the city; they arrived at the entrance of the cave, but the providential deceit of a spider's web and a pigeon's nest at its entrance (both miraculously placed there,) made them conclude the cave to be empty, and they renewed their search in a different direction.[221] "We are only two," said Abu Bekr. "There is a third," replied the Prophet; "it is God Himself."[222]

---

[216] E. Gibbon: *The Decline and Fall*; op cit; vol 5; p. 355.
[217] Ibid.
[218] Introduction to *The Meaning of the Glorious Qur'an* (Pickthall); op cit; p. xiv.
[219] Ibid; p. xv.
[220] E. Gibbon: *The Decline and Fall*; op cit; p. 355.
[221] J. Davenport: *An Apology;* op cit; p. 30.
[222] E. Gibbon: *The Decline and Fall*; op cit; vol 5; p. 356.

3. The Prophet (PBUH) in Madinah:

Mohammed was welcomed in Yathreb, and in his honour, its citizens changed its name to that of *Madinat al-nabi* (the city of the Prophet, Madinah). This year, 622, of the flight of the Prophet from Makkah to Madinah, was the beginning of the so-called Hijra (emigration), and the beginning of the Muslim Hijri calendar.

Upon arrival in Madinah, Mohammed (PBUH) built the first mosque in Islam, and spent most of his time there, teaching and remoulding the character of the new Muslims from unruly tribesmen into a brotherhood of believers.[223] Guided by the Qur'an, he acted as teacher, judge, arbitrator, adviser, consoler, and father figure to the new community.[224] One of the reasons the people of Madinah had invited the Prophet to migrate there was the hope that he would be a good arbitrator between their warring tribes, as indeed proved to be the case.[225] Mohammed also made a pact of mutual solidarity between the immigrants (known as the *Muhajirrun*) and the Muslims of Madinah (known as the *Ansars*) (helpers), an alliance based not on tribal but on religious solidarity, a departure from previous social norms.[226] Mohammed also made a wider pact between all the tribes that they would support one another in defending the city under attack, and each tribe would be equal under this arrangement, including the Jews, and all free to practice their religion.[227]

It was during the time of the Prophet's time in Madinah that took place a series of armed encounters between the armies of Islam and those of Quraish. The first of these was at Bedr (623). Abu Sufyan led the Quraish caravan from Syria. Sensing that the Muslims were following him, he sent Damdam al Ghifäri to mobilize the Quraish.[228] These were fearful of a stab in the back by their neighbour tribe, the Kinanah. When the chief of Kinanah reassured them, they marched to face Mohammed and his party of 314 companions.[229] The Muslims, who had set out in search of a caravan guarded by thirty or forty riders, now confronted a force of over

---

[223] *The Qur'an, a New Translation* (M.A.S. Abdel Haleem); op cit; p. xii.
[224] Ibid.
[225] Ibid.
[226] Ibid.
[227] Ibid.
[228] I. Rand LL. Al-Faruqi: *The Cultural Atlas*; op cit; p. 205.
[229] Ibid.

1,000.[230] At any rate, the caravan had already escaped. The Prophet gave the Muslims the choice of withdrawing or pressing ahead for a confrontation with the Makkans; the decision to press on was unanimous and enthusiastic.[231] The Muslims encamped at Bedr, where they awaited the arrival of the enemy.

The preparation for the battle, under the Prophet's supervision, is told by Ibn al-Khatir, as derived from Ibn Ishaq. Ibn Ishaq says:

`Habban B. Wasi'b. Habban related to me, from sheikhs of his tribe, that when the Messenger of God (SAAS) lined up his forces at the battle of Bedr, he held an arrow which he used to indicate how they should adjust their position. He passed by Sawwid b. Ghaziyya, an ally of the Banu Adi b. al-Najjar, and a little ahead of the line. He poked him in the belly with the arrow, saying: 'straighten up, Sawwad!'

"He replied: 'O Messenger of God, I swear by Him Who sent you with the truth and justice that you hurt me! So let me retaliate!'

"The Messenger of God (SAAS) promptly uncovered his stomach and said: 'Retaliate then!' Sawwad hugged him and then kissed his stomach.

The Messenger of God asked: 'why did you do that, Sawwad?'

He replied: `O Messenger of God, you can see what is about to happen; I wanted my last contact with you to be my skin touching yours.'

The Messenger of God (SAAS) then spoke a prayer for him.'[232]

The Muslim army was formed of more than three hundred men; they mounted by turns a train of seventy camels (the camels of Yathreb were formidable in war); but such was the poverty of the Prophet's first disciples, that only two could appear on horseback in the field.[233]

In the fertile and famous vale of Bedr, three stations from Madinah, Mohammed was informed by his scouts of the caravan that approached on one side; of the Quraish, the much larger army advanced on the other. A slight entrenchment was formed to cover the Muslim troops and a stream of fresh water that glided through the valley.

Ibn Hisham narrates the main battle, of which extracts here:

`The two parties moved closed to each other. The Prophet had commanded his companions not to attack until he gave the order, and if they were encircled by the enemy, they were to resist them with showers of arrows. He himself remained in the hut with Abu Bekr. The battle of Bedr took place on Friday morning of the seventh of Ramadhan.

---

[230] Ibid.

[231] Ibid.

[232] Imam Abu'l Fida Ismail Ibn Khatir: *The Life of the Prophet Mohammed; A Translation of al-Sira al-Nabawiyya;* tr by T. Le Gassick; Centre for Muslim Contribution to Civilisation; Garnet Publishing; 1998; vol 2; p. 272.

[233] E. Gibbon: *The Decline and Fall;* op cit; vol 5; pp. 361-2.

The Prophet was appealing to Allah for victory which He had promised him. Then the Prophet spoke to the people, encouraging them:
`By Allah in Whose hand is the soul of Mohammed, no man will be killed this day while fighting against the enemy constantly and expecting Allah's reward, forwarding not withdrawing but Allah will admit him in Paradise.'
The Prophet then took a handful of gravel and said in the direction of Quraish: `may confusion seize these faces.' Then he cast the pebbles at them and ordered his companions to counter attack.[234]
Both armies heard the thunder of his voice: their fancy beheld the angelic warriors: the Quraish trembled and fled: seventy of the bravest were slain; and seventy captives adorned the first victory of the faithful.[235]

This success was followed by the disastrous encounter at Uhud (just outside Madinah). In 624, following Bedr, Quraish was ready to march again, having put in the field an army of 3,000 men, including 200 horsemen, and about 1,000 men in heavy armour, advancing to the vicinity of Madinah.[236]
In Madinah, after the Prophet (PBUH) completed the Friday prayer, he preached to the congregation and enjoined them to fight hard and well. Having finished his address and prayer, he called for his armour and dressed in it. He then made the announcement to the people that they were to go forth to battle. Aware of all this, some men of good sense observed: `The Messenger of God ordered us to remain in Madinah and he knows best about God and what He wants; revelation comes to him from heaven.'
They addressed him: `O messenger of God, remain here, as you told us to do.'
He replied: `It is not fitting for a Prophet who has put on armour for war and given the order to proceed to battle the enemy to return without fighting. I did call upon you to do that, but you insisted on going out to battle. You must fear God and remain firm in the violence when you meet the enemy. Look for what it is God has ordered you, and do it.'[237]
On the way to the battle, the Prophet was passing with his army by a spot when a blind man heard the voice of the Prophet, and began tossing dirt into their direction, saying: `by God, if I knew I'd strike no one but you, Mohammed, I'd hit you in the face with this!'
The Muslims charged to him to kill him, but the Prophet said: `don't kill him! This sightless fellow is blind both in his heart and in his eyes!'[238]

---

[234] Ibn Hisham: *Sirat Ibn Hisham*; op cit; p.133.
[235] Gibbon: *The Decline and Fall*; op cit; pp. 361-2.
[236] I. Rand LL. Al-Faruqi: *The Cultural Atlas;* op cit; p. 205.
[237] Imam Abu'l Fida Ismail Ibn Khatir: *The Life of the Prophet Mohammed;* op cit; vol 3; p. 16.
[238] Ibid; p. 18.

When the Prophet and his army came down the defile from Mount Uhud, at the head of the valley, he positioned his camels and his men, and said: 'Let no one begin fighting before I give the order to attack.'[239]

The Prophet then sent back a group of young men from the battle, not permitting them to be present at the fighting because of their youthfulness.[240]

As Quraish advanced to the field of battle, the resentment of the public and private loss at Bedr stimulated Abu Sufyan (the leader of Quraish) to collect this army; and his wife Hind, with fifteen matrons of Makkah, incessantly sounded their timbrels to animate the troops, and to magnify the greatness of Hubal, the most popular deity of the Kaaba.[241] Quraish troops numbered more than 3,000 men, while the standard of Islam was upheld by seven hundred believers: the disproportion of numbers was not more alarming than in the field of Bedr.[242]

The Prophet organised the Muslims in a compact formation with a front of 1,000 yards (a strategy, which is excellently presented today by a former Pakistani Army General, A.I Akram.)[243] The Prophet placed his right wing at the foot of the spur and his left wing at the foot of a low hill, about 40 feet high and 500 feet long, called Ainain. The Muslim's right was safe, but their left could be turned from beyond Ainain.[244] So, to meet this danger, the Prophet placed 50 archers on Ainain from which they could command the approaches along which the Quraish could manoeuvre into the Muslim rear. These archers were given the express order not to leave their positions.[245] The Prophet appointed Abd Allah B. Jubayr as head of the archers, and said:

'Fend off the cavalry from us with your arrows, so that they don't come at us from the rear. Whether the battle goes for or against us, hold your position so that we can't be attacked from your direction.'[246]

Quraish advanced in the form of a crescent; and the right wing of cavalry was led by Khalid Ibn Al-Walid, the fiercest and most successful of the Arab warriors, but the Muslims were skilfully posted on the declivity of the hill, and the weight of the Muslim charge impelled and broke the

---

[239] Ibid; pp. 18-9.
[240] Ibid; p. 19.
[241] E. Gibbon: *The Decline and Fall*; op cit; vol 5; p. 363.
[242] Ibid.
[243] Lt General A.I. Akram: *Khalid Ibn Al-Waleed;* Maktabah; Publishers and distributors; Birmingham; England; 2004; p. 23.
[244] Ibid.
[245] Ibid.
[246] Imam Abu'l Fida Ismail Ibn Khatir: *The Life of the Prophet Mohammed*; op cit; vol 3; pp. 18-9.

centre of the idolaters.[247] Quraish began to waver, and the Muslims pressed harder in their assault, causing several standard bearers of Quraish to fall killed or wounded.[248] Under strong Muslim assault, panic set in the Quraish ranks, and they fled in disorder, pursued by the Muslims. As Quraish fled, and the Muslims entered their camp, the two mobile wings of Quraish stood firm, both Khalid and Ikrimah, their leaders, keeping their men under complete control, not permitting a single rider to retreat.[249] Khalid watched the confused situation, as he was, capable of a high degree of patience, waiting for an opportunity to strike.[250] It soon came. As the Muslim archers, tempted by the spoil, against the Prophet's strict orders, left their positions, Khalid mounted a swift attack on the few archers who still remained, falling on them from behind.[251] Muslim ranks fell into disarray, and the Prophet would have been killed were it not for a handful of fiercely loyal companions who shielded him with a ring of steel. Nonetheless he received at least one blow which knocked out one of his molars.[252] Word spread that the Messenger of God had been killed, and the shout resounded that: `Mohammed has been killed! Go back home before they (Quraish) get you and kill you!'

Then, a Muslim, Annas B. Al-Nadr stood up and shouted:
`People, even if Mohammed has been killed, Mohammed's God has not. Fight on for what Mohammed strived for. O God, I apologise to You and seek Your forgiveness for what these people have said.' He then gripped his sword and fought valiantly until he was killed.[253]

The Prophet had been indeed wounded in the face with a javelin; two of his teeth were shattered with a stone; yet, in the midst of tumult and dismay, he reproached the infidels with the murder of a Prophet, and blessed the friendly hand that wiped his blood, and conveyed him to a place of safety.[254] That hand was that of Talha, who had shielded him, and was himself struck by an arrow that paralysed his hand. A man from Quraish advanced shouting he wanted to kill the Prophet, and thrusting forward with his sword, but the Prophet pierced him through the chain mail over his chest.[255] The man's injury although slight caused him to die the following day.[256]

---

[247] E. Gibbon: *The Decline and Fall;* op cit; p. 363.
[248] Lt General A.I. Akram: *Khalid Ibn Al-Waleed;* op cit; p. 28.
[249] Ibid.
[250] Ibid.
[251] I. Rand LL. Al-Faruqi: *The Cultural Atlas;* op cit; p. 205.
[252] Ibid.
[253] Imam Abu'l Fida Ismail Ibn Khatir: *The Life of the Prophet Mohammed;* op cit; p. 31.
[254] E. Gibbon: *The Decline and Fall;* op cit; vol 5; p. 363.
[255] Imam Abu'l Fida Ismail Ibn Khatir: *The Life of the Prophet Mohammed;* op cit; p. 31.
[256] Ibid.

At the end of battle, seventy Muslims died; they fell, said the Apostle, in pairs, each brother embracing his lifeless companion. Their bodies were mangled by the inhuman females of Makkah; and the wife of Abu Sufyan tasted the entrails of Hamza, the uncle of Mohammed.[257] Quraish might applaud their superstition, and satiate their fury; but the Muslims soon rallied in the field.[258]

In 626 Abu Sufyan and Quraish resumed the offensive, this time with 10,000 men.[259] Unable to meet such a force in battle, Mohammed (PBUH) defended Madinah by digging a trench before the city, he himself leading the work of digging it.[260] The trench was completed when the enemy clans, 10,000 strong, arrived. The Prophet's army, 3,000 went to face them, the trench separating the two armies. For nearly a month, the Muslim army was exposed to showers of arrows in constant expectation of attack from an army much superior in numbers. To make matters worse, news came that the Banu Kuraiza had defected to the side of Quraish.[261] The women and children had been put in their homes, which were unguarded, and some of the Muslims asked to leave the battle front to go back to protect their families. The case of the Muslims seemed humanly hopeless.[262] The trench was, however, an unexpected obstacle in front of Quraish. Khalid Ibn al-Walid, and his co-leader Iqrimah, attempted to cross it. Iqrimah, with a squadron managed to reach over to the Muslim side at a favourable spot.[263] With Iqrimah's group was the gigantic figure of Amr Bin Abdu Wud. The group stood in front of the Muslims, and the giant figure yelled at the Muslims for individual combat with him, provoking them with his blasphemous taunts. Ali, the future caliph, advanced to meet him in duel.[264] At some point Ali overpowered his enemy, a dagger in his hand close to Amr's throat, but Amr gathered the spittle in his throat and spat into the face of Ali.[265] Instead of finishing him, Ali rose calmly from Amr's chest, wiped his face, and stood a few paces away gazing solemnly at his adversary:

'Know O Amr, I only kill in the way of Allah and not for my private motives. Since you spat in my face, my killing of you may be from a desire

---

[257] E. Gibbon: *The Decline and Fall;* op cit; vol 5; p. 363.
[258] Ibid.
[259] W. Durant: *The Age of Faith*; op cit; p. 165.
[260] Introduction to Sura 33 in *The Meaning of the Glorious Qur'an;* (Pickthall); op cit; p. 299.
[261] Ibid.
[262] Ibid.
[263] Lt General A.I. Akram: *Khalid Ibn Al-Waleed;* op cit; p. 59.
[264] Ibid; p. 60 ff.
[265] Ibid; p. 63.

for personal vengeance. So, I spare your life. Rise and return to your people.'[266]
The giant figure of Amr rose, but instead of returning to his people decided to fight for victory. The duel resumed, as fierce as before, Amr attacking Ali with a terrible blow, but missing, inflicting only a slight wound on him. Carried by his attack, he could not fend Ali's reflex, who, with his sword, inflicted a mortal blow on Amr.[267] As Amr fell to the ground, the cry of *Allah U Akbar!* was thundered by 2000 Muslim throats.[268] Invigorated by this success the Muslims attacked the rest of Quraish intruders, killing some, forcing the rest to retreat, before the Muslims reinforced the guard around this spot of the ditch, thwarting an attempt by Khalid to repeat Ikrimah's successful crossing.[269]
Things reached a stalemate until one Tuesday night Madinah was struck by a storm. Cold winds lashed at the allied camp and howled across the valley, and the temperature dropped sharply.[270] The allied camp was exposed, and the storm seemed to hit their camp with a vengeance, putting out the fires, knocking down cooking pots, carrying away tents.[271] The Quraish and their allies sat huddled under their blankets and cloaks as the storm raged around them, waiting for an end of it that would not come.[272] Disheartened, the Quraish and their allies packed up what was left of their belongings and fled to Makkah.[273] Sura 33 of the Qur'an says on the event:
'O You who believe, remember God's goodness to you when mighty armies massed against you. We sent a violent wind and invisible forces against them. God sees all that you do. They massed against you from above and below, and your eyes rolled (with fear), your hearts rose into your throats, and you thought (ill) thoughts of God. There the believers were sorely tested and deeply shaken: the hypocrites and the sick at heart said: 'God and His Messenger promised us nothing but delusions.'.....
Say, if God wishes to harm you, who can protect you? If God wishes to show you mercy, who can prevent Him?'[274]

Altogether, in the years spent in Madinah, the Prophet planned sixty five campaigns, of which 27 he personally led.[275] At the height of these successes,

---

[266] Ibid.
[267] Ibid.
[268] Ibid.
[269] Ibid; p. 64.
[270] Ibid; p. 65.
[271] Ibid.
[272] Ibid.
[273] I. Rand LL. Al-Faruqi: *The Cultural Atlas*; op cit; p. 207.
[274] Sura 33; verses. 9-17.
[275] In W. Durant: *The Age of Faith*; op cit; p. 165.

the Prophet passed with Quraish the treaty of Al-Hudeybiyah, which was to secure a ten years' truce. For ten years there were to be no hostilities between the parties. The Prophet was to return to Madinah without visiting the Kaabah, but in the following year he might perform the pilgrimage with his comrades, Quraish promising to evacuate Makkah for three days to allow him doing so. Deserters from Quraish to the Muslims during the period of the truce were to he returned; not so deserters from the Muslims to Quraish. Any tribe or clan who wished to share in the treaty as allies of the Prophet might do so, and any tribe or clan who wished to share in the treaty as allies of Quraish might do so.[276]

There was dismay among the Muslims at these terms. They asked one another: "Where is the victory that we were promised?"

It was during the return journey from Al-Hudeybiyah that the surah entitled "Victory" was revealed. This truce proved, in fact, to be the greatest victory that the Muslims had till then achieved. War had been a barrier between them and the idolaters, but now both parties met and talked together, and the new religion spread more rapidly. In the two years which elapsed between the signing of the truce and the fall of Makkah the number of converts was greater than the total number of all previous converts. The Prophet travelled to Al-Hudeybiyah with 1400 men. Two years later, when Quraish broke the truce, he marched against them with an army of 10,000.[277]

In the 8th year of the Hijra, that is two years into the treaty of Al-Hudeybiyah, Quraish broke the truce. They attacked a tribe, which was in alliance with the Prophet and massacred many amongst them even in the sanctuary of Makkah.[278] The Prophet (PBUH) summoned all men capable of bearing arms, and marched to Makkah. Quraish were overawed, and their cavalry were routed even without bloodshed.[279] In the year 630, the Prophet entered his native city. The inhabitants expected vengeance for their past deeds.[280] After the entry of the Prophet in Makkah, Scott says, 'with a magnanimity unequalled in the annals of war, a general amnesty was proclaimed and but four persons, whose offences were considered unpardonable, suffered the penalty of death.'[281]

---

[276] Introduction to *The Meaning of the glorious Qur'an* (Pickthall); op cit; pp. xxii-xxiii.
[277] Ibid.
[278] Ibid; p. xxiv.
[279] Ibid.
[280] Ibid.
[281] S.P. Scott: *History of the Moorish Empire;* op cit; Vol 1; p.90.

It was the same forbearance the Prophet showed to Zaynab Bt. Al-Harith, the wife of Sallam B. Mishkam. She served him a roast sheep, which she had poisoned. The Prophet chewed a bit, but he did not swallow it. His companion, Bishr B. al-Bara B. Marur, did. The Prophet spat his bit, saying: `this bone informs me that it has been poisoned.' He summoned the woman, who confessed the deed. He asked: `what led you to do this?' She replied: `How you have afflicted my people is not hidden from you. So I said, if he is a Prophet, he will be informed, but if he is a king, I shall be rid of him.'
The Prophet forgave her. His companion, Bishr, died of the food he had eaten.[282]

---

[282] *The History of al-Tabari (Tarikh al-rusul wa'l muluk;)* tr. by M. Fishbein; State University of New York Press; 1997; vol 3; pp. 123-4.

An Account of the Prayers that the Prophet Spoke After the Battle of Uhud

(In that battle the Muslims were defeated, and the Prophet was nearly killed)

`O God, to You is due all praise. O God, there is no grasping what You have dispersed, nor dispersing what You grasp. There is no guiding aright those whom You have led astray, nor any leading astray of those You have guided. There is no giving of what You have prevented, nor any prevention of what You have given. There is no drawing close what You have distanced, nor any distancing what You have drawn close. O God, spread forth You blessings, Your mercy, Your generosity and Your favours upon us.
`O God, I ask You enduring blessings that never change nor cease. O God, I ask You for blessings at a time of deprivation, and security at a time of fear.
`O God, I seek refuge with You against the evil of what You have given us, as well as from the evil which You have saved us.
`O God, have us view faith with favour, and endear it to us well. Have us view disbelief, immorality and disobedience with antipathy. Place us among those who are well guided.
`O God, take us to Yourself as Muslims and give us life as Muslims. Place us among the virtuous, not the shamed or the demented.
`O God, do battle with those disbelievers who give the lie to Your messengers, and who oppose them. Torment and punish them. O God, do battle against those disbelievers who were given the scripture, O God of the Truth.'[283]

---

[283] Imam Abu'l Fida Ismail Ibn Khatir: *The Life of the Prophet Mohammed;* op cit; pp. 53-4.

Khalid Ibn Al-Walid's Conversion to Islam

It was during the truce of al-Hudeybiyah that Khalid Ibn al-Walid converted to Islam. Lt General Akram offers us an outline of this episode, of which the following extracts:

`After the Prophet's pilgrimage, serious doubt entered Khalid's mind regarding his religious beliefs. He had never been deeply religious and was not unduly drawn towards the gods of the Kaabah. He had always kept an open mind. Now he began to ponder deeply on religious matters, but did not share his thoughts with anyone. And then it flashed across his mind that Islam was the true faith. This happened about two months after the Prophet's pilgrimage.

Having made up his mind about Islam, Khalid met Ikrimah and some others and said:

`It is evident to the intelligent mind that Mohammed is neither a poet nor a sorcerer, as the Quraish allege. His message is truly divine. It is incumbent on all sensible men to follow him.'

Ikrimah was stunned by the words of Khalid: `Are you abandoning our faith? He asked incredulously.

`I have come to believe in the true Allah.'

`It is strange that of all the Quraish you should say so.'

`Why?'

`Because the Muslims have killed so many of your dear ones in battle. I for one shall certainly not accept Mohammed, nor shall I ever speak to you again unless you give up this absurd idea. Do you not see that the Quraish seek the blood of Mohammed'?

`This is a matter of ignorance,' replied Khalid.

When Abu Sufyan heard from Ikrimah of Khalid's change of heart, he sent for both the stalwarts: `Is it true what I heard? He asked Khalid.

`And what did you hear?'

`That you wish to join Mohammed.'

`Yes. And why not? After all Mohammed is one of us. He is a kinsman.'

Abu Sufyan flew into a rage and threatened Khalid with dire consequences, but was restrained by Ikrimah:

`Steady, O Abu Sufyan!' said Ikrimah. `Your anger may well lead me also to join Mohammed. Khalid is free to follow whatever religion he chooses.'

Ikrimah, the nephew and bosom friend, had stood up for Khalid in spite of their religious differences.

That night Khalid took his armour, his weapons and his horse, and set out for Madinah. On the way he met two others travelling in the same direction: 'Amr Ibn Al-'As (one of the future greatest generals of Islam, and the conqueror of Egypt) and Uthman Ibn Talha (son of the Quraish standard bearer at Uhud) and there was mutual astonishment when they found that each was travelling to Madinah with the same purpose, for each had regarded the other two as bitter enemies of Islam. The three seekers arrived in Madinah on May 31, 629 (H) and went to the house of the Prophet. Khalid entered first and made his submission. He was followed by 'Amr and then Uthman. All three were warmly welcomed by the Prophet; their past hostility was forgiven...

Khalid, now 43 and in the prime of life, was glad to be in Madinah. He met old friends and found that he was welcomed by all. The old feuds were forgotten.'[284]

[284] Lt General: A.I. Akram: *Khalid Ibn Waleed*; op cit; pp. 70-1.

4. Early Progress of Islam:

After the Prophet's entry to Makkah, his first deed was to destroy the idols. Al-Tabari (d.923) narrates some instances of idol destruction:
`In this year, five nights before the end of Ramadan, Khalid b. al-Walid destroyed al-'Uzza in the lowland of Nakhlah. Al-'Uzza was an idol of the Banu Shayban, a subdivision of Sulaym, allies of the Banu Hashim. The Banu Asad b. 'Abd al-'Uzza used to say it was their idol. Khalid set out for it, and then he said: "I have destroyed it." (The Messenger of God) said: "Did you see anything?" "No," said Khalid. "Then," he said: "go back and destroy it." So Khalid returned to the idol, destroyed its temple, and broke the idol. The keeper began saying: "Rage, O 'Uzza, with one of thy fits of rage!" whereupon a naked, wailing Ethiopian woman came out before him. Khalid killed her and took the jewels that were on her. Then he went to the Messenger of God and gave him a report of what had happened. "That was al-'Uzza," he said, "and al-'Uzza will never be worshiped [again]."[285]
According to al-Waqidi: `in this year [the idol] Suwa' was destroyed.' He was at Ruhat and belonged to the tribe of Hudhayl. He was a stone. The person who destroyed it was 'Amr b. al-'As. When he reached the idol, the keeper asked him, "What do you want?" 'Amr replied: "To destroy Suwa." The keeper said: "you cannot destroy him." 'Amr b. al-'As said to him: "You are still in falsehood." 'Amr destroyed him but found nothing in his treasury. Then 'Amr said to the keeper: "What do you think?" He replied: "I have become a Muslim, by God."[286]

The Havazen and Quraish tribes commanded by Abalak, being deeply incensed at seeing their sacred idols demolished, took up arms, and appeared in battle array in the Valley of Honain, about three miles from Makkah. Twelve thousand men, including two thousand men from Makkah, recently converted, promised themselves an easy victory over these tribes. But being unexpectedly assailed by a storm of arrows, the Muslim army, terrified by so sudden an attack, was about to make a disgraceful retreat. Mohammed (PBUH) rushed into the thickest of the fight, and by his valour arrested the flight of his army, and ultimately defeated his foe.[287] After a long and vigorous pursuit, the Havazen tendered their submission, and their leader set the example to his people of

---

[285] *The History of al-Tabari;* op cit; pp. 187-8.
[286] Ibid; p. 188.
[287] J. Davenport: *An Apology;* op cit; pp. 44-5.

57

embracing the new faith. Six thousand prisoners, twenty four thousand horses, four thousand mouhars, and the like number of ounces of silver, fell into Muslim hands. The division of this rich spoil was about to be made when deputies arrived, who, with tears and lamentations, besought Mohammed not to ruin so many families; upon which, the Prophet assembling his soldiers addressed them with these few and simple words: 'Muslims, your brothers have come to you led by repentance! They have besought me to give freedom to their fathers, mothers and children, and restore to them their property and effects. I could not resist their prayer. Your approval will afford me heartfelt satisfaction; but should any one think himself injured thereby, let him speak, and I will promise to indemnify him at the next battle, when Allah shall vouchsafe unto us richer spoils.'

Not a murmur was heard when Mohammed finished his appeal; everything taken was restored, all the captives were freed, and the spirit of religion and justice replaced that of violence and rapine.[288]

Following the establishment of Islam, an upsurge of impostors took place. Musailima had written to Mohammed offering to share the land: 'From Musailima the Apostle of God to Mohammed the Apostle,' he wrote, 'Let us divide the earth between us, half to you and half to me.'

The reply, however, was discouraging: 'From Mohammed the Apostle of God to Musailima the Liar. The earth is the Lord's. He causes such of his servants to inherit it as he pleases.'[289]

Musailima was soon eliminated.

Another false prophet was Tulaiha at the head of the tribe of Beni Asad. A Muslim column of four thousand strong was sent against him under the command of Khalid Ibn al-Walid (now a Muslim general), and the Beni Asad were defeated.[290]

Islam brought about many changes and reforms, which will be considered in the following chapter. Briefly, here, these include believing in Allah, alone, performing daily prayers, and other religious obligations, improving the condition of women by restricting polygamy, placing restraints upon divorce, securing to widows immunity from destitution, and preventing female infanticide.[291] Under Islamic rule, in return for a moderate tribute, the Christians of Arabia were taken under the Muslims' protection, and so were the Jews, both Christians and Jews being people of the book, and so

---

[288] Ibid.
[289] J. Glubb: *A Short History*; op cit; p.43.
[290] Ibid.
[291] S.P. Scott: *History of the Moorish Empire*; op cit; Vol 1; p.103.

benefited of freedom of worship, to practice trades, keep property and wealth, and so on.

The Prophet had endeavoured to extend the call to Islam to the people and princes of adjacent countries from his time at Madinah. The emperor of Byzantium, the ruler of Egypt, and the Negus of Abyssinia, who had turned Muslim, responded with kind words. The emperor of Persia and the chieftains of the buffer states in Northern Arabia rejected the call with contempt and defiance. The Prophet had sent a letter to Badham, Viceroy of Yemen, to be forwarded to Khosroes, King of Persia. Khosroes tore the letter into pieces, ordering Badham either to restore the Prophet to his right mind, or to send him his head. [292] As soon as this insult was made known to the Prophet, he exclaimed: 'thus shall Allah asunder the kingdom of Khosroes, and reject his supplications.' Khosroes was soon after murdered by his son Sirses.[293]

The ruler of Dhat al Tall, a vassal of Byzantium, killed the Prophet's companions who were sent to present Islam to him and his people.[294] The governor of Busra, another agent of Byzantium, killed the Muslim delegate upon hearing him deliver his message. Some Muslim historians have reported that Emperor Heraclius himself gave the order to the provincial governors to mobilize and engage in hostilities.[295] Three thousand Muslim men were equipped for the retribution. The Prophet exhorted them to display their courage in the cause of the Most High. At the same time, however, he enjoined them to collect their booty not from the tears of the provincials, but from the public treasuries of the conquered state: 'In avenging my injuries, said he, 'molest not the harmless religious persons of domestic seclusion; spare the weakness of the softer sex, the infant at the breast, and those who, in the course of nature, are hastening from this scene of mortality. Abstain from demolishing the dwellings of the unresisting inhabitants, and destroy not the means of subsistence; respect their fruit trees, no injure the palm, so useful to Syria for its shade and so delightful for its verdure.'[296]

At the battle, which took place at Mu'tah, in today's Jordan, the Greeks were vastly superior in number (including Arab auxiliaries) an army of

---

[292] J. Davenport: *An Apology;* op cit; pp. 40-1.
[293] Ibid.
[294] I.R. and L.L. Al-Faruqi: *The Cultural Atlas of Islam;* op cit; p. 138.
[295] M H. Haykal: *The Life of Mohammed;* tr. I.R. Faruqi; Indianapolis: American Trust Publications; 1976; pp. 338-89.
[296] J. Davenport: *An Apology;* op cit; pp 41-2.

100,000. This battle is outlined by Lt General Akram in good detail.[297] For the sake of space and convenience, however, Davenport's short outline is chosen.[298] At first, Davenport says, the Muslims were repulsed in the first attack, and lost successively three generals: Zeid; Jaafar, and Abd Allah Ibn Rawah. Zeid fell like a soldier in the foremost ranks. The death of Jaafar was heroic and memorable. His right hand having been severed from the arm, he shifted the standard to his left, and upon losing this his remaining hand, he embraced the sacred banner with his bleeding stumps until transfixed with fifty honourable wounds. Abd Allah filling the vacant place, cried aloud: `forward; and victory or paradise is our own.' A Greek lance determined the alternative, but the falling standard was seized by Khalid; nine swords were broken in his hand, and his valour withstood and repulsed the almost overwhelming forces of the Christians. Victory at length declared itself for the Muslims, and Khalid, whose skill and intrepidity had so greatly contributed to insure it, had, as a reward, the honourable title of the `Sword of God,' conferred upon him by the Prophet.[299]

The Muslim spirit of bravery in this battle was typified by 'Abd Allah ibn Rawahah, a companion of the Prophet. Before engaging the enemy, he told his men: "Brothers! That which some people fear might happen to us is precisely the reason why we came here; namely, martyrdom. We Muslims fight neither with numbers nor equipment. Our only power is in our faith, which God has graciously granted to us. Rise to battle and march forward! One of the two greatest blessings shall be ours: either victory or martyrdom. In either case we are the winners."[300]
A similar spirit moved the Muslims confronting the Persian Empire. The Persian supreme commander, in an attire so resplendent and covered with gold that he could hardly move, sent after the Muslim commander who was clad in the usual desert attire. 'What brings you here to fight us?" the Persian asked. The Muslim commander answered: "that humans may stop worshipping humans and offer worship to the Creator of humans. To fulfil this end, our men are as eager to die as your men are eager to live."[301]
This spirit, as this work will show, was to mark all Muslim armies that fought under the banner of Islam in the following centuries; a spirit that preserved the Muslim nation against the woes and onslaughts of those who sought to destroy it.

---

[297] Lt. General A.I. Akram: *Khalid Ibn Waleed*; op cit; pp. 74ff.
[298] J. Davenport: *An Apology;* op cit; pp. 41-2.
[299] Ibid; p. 42.
[300] I.R. and L.L. Al-Faruqi: *The Cultural Atlas*; op cit; p. 138.
[301] Ibid.

The Prophet's Last Message

The Prophet's constitution, though originally fortified by abstinence and a simple diet, had for years given evidence of decline, a consequence of the poison administered to him years before by Zaynab bent al-Harith. After a short illness, he died in the arms of his wife Ayesha, on the eighth of June, 632.[302]

Just before he died, the Prophet gave his farewell message at Mount Arafat, of which the main extracts are:
`O people, lend me an attentive ear, for I don't know whether, after this year, I shall ever be amongst you again. Therefore listen to what I am saying to you very carefully and take these words to those who could not be here.
O people, just as you regard this month, this day, this city as sacred, so regard the life and property of every Muslim as a sacred trust.
Return the goods entrusted to you to their rightful owners.
Hurt no one so that no one may hurt you.
Remember you will indeed meet your Lord, and that He will indeed reckon your deeds.
Allah has forbidden you to take usury (interest), therefore all interest obligation shall henceforth be waived. Your capital, however, is yours to keep. You will neither inflict nor suffer any inequity.
Beware of Satan, for your safety of your religion. He has lost all hope that he will ever be able to lead you astray in big things, so beware of following him in small things.
O people, it is true that you have certain rights with regard to your women, but they also have right over you. Remember that you have taken them as your wives only under Allah's trust and with his permission. If they abide by your right then to them belongs the right to be fed and clothed in kindness. Do treat your women well and be kind to them for they are your partners and committed helpers. And it is your right that they do not make friends with any one of whom you do not approve, as well as never be unchaste.
O people, listen to me in earnest, worship Allah, perform your five daily prayers (Salat), fast during the month of Ramadan, and give your wealth in Zakat. Perform Hajj if you can afford to.

---

[302] S.P. Scott: *History of the Moorish Empire*; op cit; Vol 1; p.91.

All mankind is from Adam and Eve, an Arab has no superiority over a non Arab, nor a non Arab has any superiority over an Arab; also a White (person) has no superiority over a Black, nor a Black has any superiority over a White except by piety and good deed.

Learn that every Muslim is a brother to every Muslim, and that the Muslims constitute one brotherhood.

Remember, one day you will appear before Allah and answer for your deeds.

So beware, do not astray from the path of righteousness after I am gone.

O people, no Prophet or Apostle will come after me and no new faith will be born.

Reason well, therefore, O people, and understand my words which I convey to you. I leave behind me two things, the Qur'an and my example, the Sunnah, and if you follow these you will never go astray.

All those who listen to me shall pass on my words to all others and those to others again; and may the last ones understand my words better than those who listen to me directly. Be my witness O Allah, that I have conveyed Your message to Your people.'

Important Events in the Prophet's Life[303]

-570:	Birth of Mohammed (PBUH) (August 20).
-576:	Death of Mohammed's Mother.
-595:	Mohammed Marries Khadidjah.
-610:	Call to Prophethood: Beginning of the Revelation of the Qur'an.
-613:	Public Preaching of Islam Begins.
-615:	First Muslim Migration to Abyssinia.
-617:	Second Migration to Abyssinia.
-619:	Death of Khadidjah; Death of Abu Talib.
-621:	First Meeting of Aqabah.
	Al-Isra' wal Mi'raj (Night Journey and Ascent to Heaven)
-622:	Second Meeting of al-Aqabah.
	Attempted Assassination of the Prophet by the Makkans.
July 16:	The Hijrah (The Prophet's migration to Yathrib).
-1 H/622:	The Prophet builds Mosque and residence in Madinah.
	The Prophet founds the First Islamic State.
-2 H/624:	Battle of Bedr.
-3 H/626:	Battle of Uhud.
-5 H/627:	Battle of the Ditch.
-6 H/628:	Al-Hudeybiyah Peace Treaty.
-7 H	Campaign of Khaybar.
	The Prophet sends delegates to present Islam to neighbouring Monarchs.
-7 H/629:	Khalid Ibn al-Walid and 'Amr Ibn al-'As accept Islam.
-8 H/630:	Campaign of Makkah.
	The Makkans Accept Islam.
	Destruction of idols and Cleansing of Ka'bah.
	Campaign of Hawazim and Hunayn.
-10 H/632:	Farewell Pilgrimage of the Prophet.
-11 H	Death of the Prophet (PBUH).

---

[303] Partly derived from I and L. Al-Faruqi: *The Cultural Atlas*; op cit; pp. 124-5.

THREE

ISLAM

It is impossible to write a history of Islamic peoples and their shared events with others if the central element, that is the faith of Islam, is not comprehensively (though not too excessively) looked at. A minimum understanding of Islam is necessary. This chapter offers a brief outline of Islam, its main tenets, its differences with other faiths, and finally, the generalised misconceptions about Islam.

1. On the Basics of Islam:

In Islam, first and foremost, every order from God carries the same compulsions. It is not for man to grade His rulings as more or less important. Whether the individual finds them likeable or dislikeable, the precepts of the Qur'an are unchangeable and non selective.[304] No individual, or group of individuals, or hierarchy, or ruler, however great their powers, can decide on matters of the faith; to alter, or to adapt the faith to circumstances or needs.

Islam consists in believing in God, alone, performing prayers, fasting, distributing alms, and pilgrimage to Makkah. It also stresses the inviolability of human life, banning the consumption of alcohol and pork, usury, gambling and adultery.

---

[304] The Qur'an ought to be read in Arabic, most preferably, its meaning being better understood in its original language. There are, however, translations in other languages, such as:
- *The Meaning of the Glorious Qur'an;* by M. M. Pickthall; Taha; London;
- *The Holy Qur'an: Text, Translation and Commentary;* by A.Yusuf Ali; 1934.
- *The Qur'an: A New Translation* by M.A.S. Abdel-Haleem; Oxford World Classics; Oxford University Press; 2004-5.

The moral prescriptions of the Qur'an, as outlined by Le Bon, are charity, good deeds, hospitality, moderation of desires, abiding by one's word, the love of the next person, respect for parents, and protection for widows and orphans. [305]

The injunction regarding washing and cleanliness is an accessory to prayer. Sale in his `Preliminary dissertation,'[306] says:
`That his followers might be more punctual in this duty, Mohammed is said to have declared that the practice of religion is founded on cleanliness, which is the one half of the faith, and the key to prayer, without which it will not be heard by God. That these expressions may be better understood Al-Ghazali reckons four degrees of purification; of which the first is the cleansing of the body from all pollution and filth; the second the cleansing of the members of the body from all wickedness and unjust actions; the third, the cleansing of the heart from all blameable inclinations and odious vices; the fourth, the purging of man's secret thoughts from all affections, which may divert their attendance from God; adding that the body is but the outward shell with respect to the heart, which is as the kernel. And for this reason he complains of those who are superstitiously solicitous in exterior purifications, avoiding those persons as unclean who are not as scrupulously nice as themselves, and at the same time have their minds lying waste and overrun with pride, ignorance and hypocrisy. Whence it plainly appears with how little foundation the Muslims have been charged by some writers with teaching, or imagining that these formal washings alone cleanse them from their sins.'[307]

In Islam, belief is between the faithful and his or her God. No intermediary is to forgive or apportion the blame, or commend or recommend a new line or path. The Prophet was so alive to the danger attending priesthoods in political states, and of their tendency to corrupt all governments, that he disapproved of the allowance of any such institution, and desired that every Muslim should possess a copy of the Qur'an, and be his own priest.[308]   All the faithful needs from another faithful, better learned in the matters of the faith, and enjoying the respect of the community are clarifications, and clarifications alone, and that is the task of the Imams, in general.

---

[305] G. Le Bon: *La Civilisation des Arabes,* Syracuse; 1884; p.337.
[306] G. Sale in E.M. Wherry: *Commentary on the Quran;* London; Traubner and Co Ltd; 1896; vol I; p. 139.
[307] In J. Davenport: *An Apology;* op cit; p. 71.
[308] Ibid; p. 72.

Islam, Davenport explains, is likewise free from suspicion and ambiguity; and the Qur'an is a glorious testimony to the oneness of God. Rejecting the worship of idols and men, of stars and planets, on the rational principle that whatever is born must die; that whatever rises must set; and whatever is corruptible must perish and decay. Muslims adore an infinite and eternal Being without form or place, without issue or similitude, present to our most secret thoughts, existing by the necessity of His own nature, and deriving from Himself all intellectual perfection.[309]

The understanding of the Qur'an knows of no hermeneutical problems such as affect the Bible. The only hermeneutic the Qur'an knows is lexicographic; the only possible question concerns the meaning a given word had at the time of revelation, which the word is then assumed to have had throughout the fourteen centuries.[310]

Islam, in both Qur'an and tradition (Hadith), has both spiritual and social dimensions, as well as economic and political ones. Thus, Caliph Omar (caliph: 634-644) said:

`Prayer carries us halfway to God, fasting brings us to the door of His palace, almsgiving lets us in.'[311]

The traditions abound in stories of generous Muslims; Hassan, for example, was said to have three times in his life divided his substance with the poor, and twice given away all that he had.[312]

The acceptance of Islam, moreover, conferred equal rights with the conquering body and emancipated the vanquished states from the conditions which every conqueror, since the world existed up to the period of Mohammed (PBUH), had invariably imposed. Islam put an end to infanticide then prevalent in the surrounding countries. It put an end to slavery, the adscription to the soil. It administered even handed justice, not only to those who professed its religion, but also to those who were conquered by its arms. It reduced taxation, the sole tribute to the state consisting of one eight. It freed commerce from charges and impediments; it freed professors of other faiths from all fixed contributions whatsoever to the dominant creed.[313]

---

[309] Ibid; p. 73.

[310] I.R. and L.L. Al-Faruqi: *The Cultural Atlas*; op cit; p. 107.

[311] G. Sale: *Commentary on the Quran;* op cit; vol I; p.43.

[312] W Durant: *The Age of Faith*; op cit; p.214.

[313] J. Davenport: *An Apology;* op cit; p. 81.

a. The Qur'an:

The Qur'an is a text of 114 *suwar (sing. sürah)* or chapters, 6,200 ayats or verses, 77,934 words, and 323,671 letters. It was revealed in Makkah and Madinah and their environs-hence the characterization of its *suwar* as Makki or Madani-several verses at a time.[314] It has been revealed to Mohammed over a period of twenty-three years. It is approximately four-fifths the size of the New Testament, and its chapters are arranged according to length, not chronology. The longer chapters, representing the later Madinah revelations, precede the shorter, earlier Makkah revelations to Mohammed.[315] Except for the first few revelations, which took the Prophet completely by surprise, each of the revelations had a situational context to which it spoke. Most of these, if not all, are known to scholars as *asbab al nuzal* (the situational causes of revelation).[316] From the first to last, each revelation was first impressed upon the Prophet's memory, who then conveyed the revelations verbatim to his companions, who memorized and recited them in turn, and finally recorded them in a text. At the end of his life, Mohammed had about 30,000 contemporaries who had heard and memorized the Qur'an in whole or in part. Several of them could read and write and had committed the Qur'an to writing in part or in toto. Certainly, writing materials were crude: leather, bones, stone or wood, cloth, and papyrus.[317] The text has been preserved absolutely intact. Not one jot or title has changed. Diacritical marks have been added and the calligraphy has been improved to facilitate its correct reading and recitation. Its parts stand today in exactly the same order in which the Prophet was instructed by the Angel to arrange them.[318]

Since revelation of the Qur'an was a cumulative process over some twenty-three years, the Prophet arranged and rearranged the revelations year by year.[319] This took place during the month of fasting-Ramadan-when the Angel Gabriel would instruct the Prophet where to intercalate and include the new passages, and the Prophet would then recite liturgically and publicly all that had been revealed up till then in the new order given to him by the Angel. For fourteen centuries, following this practice of the Prophet, Muslims by the hundreds of thousands have

---

[314] I.R. and L.L. Al-Faruqi: *The Cultural Atlas*; op cit; p. 100.
[315] J. L. Esposito: *Islam, the Straight Path;* Oxford University Press; 1998; p. 17.
[316] I.R. and L.L. Al-Faruqi: *The Cultural Atlas*; op cit; p. 100.
[317] Ibid.
[318] Ibid; p. 99.
[319] Ibid; p. 100.

liturgically and publicly recited the Qur'an from memory.[320] Under Islamic law, recitation of the Qur'an in *salat*-the ritual of worship-may not be interrupted except by loss of ritual purity or death; but it can and should be interrupted in case of error in the recitation. In that case any other worshipper may raise his voice with the correct recitation of the misread, omitted, or mispronounced passage.[321]

The Qur'an was also committed to writing. Being illiterate, the Prophet engaged a scribe to write down the revelation. Many others wrote it down as well. In the year Mohammed died, all the revelations written by the Prophet's scribe were collected and stored in the house of Hafsa, the Prophet's wife and daughter of Omar, the second caliph.[322] Twelve years later, under the third Caliph, Uthman (644-56), as many non-Peninsular Arabs and non-Arabic-speaking peoples converted to Islam and recited the Qur'an with some mistakes, the Prophet's scribe was ordered to head a commission of the Prophet's literate companions, of those who were most able in memory, to prepare a written text of the Qur'an.[323] This was completed within the year, and Uthman ordered that several copies to be made and distributed.[324] Except for the diacritical marks and some improvements of orthography and calligraphy, the Qur'an extant in every Muslim home around the world today, or kept and recited from memory by the millions, is identical to the material that was recited and conveyed by the Prophet to his companions fourteen centuries ago.[325]

Abdel Haleem provides useful explanatory notes in the introduction to his translation of the Qur'an, and one of the best sections of this introduction relates to the stylistic features of the Qur'an. The Qur'an, Abdel Haleem explains, has its own style. It is necessary to mention some of the important features of this style. The reader should not expect the Qur'an to be arranged chronologically or by subject matter. The Qur'an may present, in the same sura (chapter,) material about the unity and grace of God, regulations and laws, stories of earlier prophets and nations and the lessons that can be drawn from these, and descriptions of rewards and punishments on the Day of Judgement. This stylistic feature serves to reinforce the message, to persuade and to dissuade. This technique may appear to bring repetition of the same themes or stories in different suras

---

[320] Ibid.
[321] Ibid.
[322] Ibid.
[323] *The Qur'an: A New Translation* by M.A.S. Abdel-Haleem; op cit; p. xvi.
[324] Ibid.
[325] I.R. and L.L. Al-Faruqi: *The Cultural Atlas*; op cit; p. 100.

but, as the Qur'an is above all a book of guidance, each chapter adds to the fuller picture and to the effectiveness of the guidance. For instance, in the midst of discussion about divorce and settlements, it suspends the introduction of regulations and instructs the believers to keep up prayer and stand in obedience to God (2: 237-8), later to resume discussion of the divorce regulations. While urging people to give in charity, it shifts to the Throne verse (2: 255) to describe the glory of God and refer to the time when no one can intercede for anyone else. Having reminded people of God's power, it resumes its injunctions to give in charity. In a religion that seeks to affect people's belief and behaviour in all aspects of life it is not enough to say something once or twice. Moreover, if the material on God, on earlier prophets, or on the Day of Judgment were each dealt with only once, the effect would be so all pervasive. This technique compresses many aspects of the Qur'anic message into any one chapter (sura), each forming a self contained lesson. This is particularly useful as it is rare for anyone to read the whole Qur'an at once: it is mainly used in short sections during worship and preaching as well as by individuals or on television and radio in daily readings and broadcast.

A central feature of Qur'anic style is the contrast between this world and the next (each occurring exactly 115 times), between believers and disbelievers, and between Paradise and hell. This has been studied in great detail, and scholars have found remarkable patterns of contrasts: angels and devils, life and death, secrecy and openness, and so on, occurring exactly the same number of times.[326] This sense of balance in the text is continued in passages where the Prophet is instructed to say, 'Now the truth has come from your Lord: let those who wish to believe in it do so, and let those who wish to reject it do so' (18: 29) and "There is no compulsion in religion: true guidance has become distinct from error' (2: 256) (one of the names the Qur'an gives for itself al-Furqan-the book that distinguishes right from wrong (25: 1).[327]

One stylistic feature that makes the Qur'an particularly effective is that God speaks directly to people (e.g. 56: 57-73) and to the Prophet, often using 'We', the first person plural of majesty, to represent Himself. It involves the readers/listeners by questioning, directing, and urging them, alternating this with information (e.g. 56: 47-74).[328]

The Qur'an always offers justifications for its message, supporting it with logical argument, for example in explaining the Oneness of God (e.g.: 21:

---

[326] A.Nawfal: *Al-Ijaz al-Adabi lil Qur'an al-Karim;* Cairo; 1976.
[327] *The Qur'an: A New Translation* (Abdel-Haleem); op cit; pp. xix-xx.
[328] Ibid; p. xx.

21-2; 23: 91; 36: 78-83). The Qur'an supports its statements with reference to the past (the history of earlier nations and prophets), to the present (to nature as a manifestation of God's wisdom, power, and care), and to the future (life in the hereafter and Judgment), besides reminding people constantly of God and his attributes.

Another aspect of the Qur'an, Abdel Haleem adds, is that it does not name individuals, with rare exceptions such as prophets and angels, but uses generalisation. One method of achieving this is the use of general words like 'those who or 'whoever', giving the message universal application. Thus, in permitting Muslims to defend themselves, it gives permission generally to those who have been driven unjustly from their homes (22: 40 ff.). This will apply at any time or place. When it urges the Prophet to deliver the message, even when dealing with his own personal situation and feelings, instead of saying 'You should deliver the message and fear none but God', it speaks of 'those who deliver God's messages and fear only Him and no other: God's reckoning is enough' (33: 39). Reformers, preachers, and anyone standing for the truth can apply this readily to themselves, because such statements are put in a proverbial style. Verses of the Qur'an are therefore readily quoted and inscribed on plaques which can be hung on the walls of offices, houses, courtrooms, and so on as an inspiration or a reminder.[329]

b. The Message of the Qur'an:

Islam, through the Qur'an, teaches that God's signs have occurred in several forms: in nature, history, and Scripture. God's existence can be known through creation; nature contains pointers or "signs" of God, its creator and sustainer (3: 26-27). The history of the rise and fall of nations, victory and defeat, provides clear signs and lessons of God's sovereignty and intervention in history (30: 2-9). In addition, God in His mercy determined to reveal His will for humankind through a series of messengers: "Indeed, We sent forth among every nation a Messenger, saying: 'serve your God, and shun false gods' "(16: 36) (see also 13: 7, 15: 10, 35: 24). The verses of revelation are also called signs of God. Thus, throughout history, human beings could not only know that there is a God but also know what God desires and commands for His creatures.[330]

---

[329] Ibid; pp. xix-xxi.
[330] J. L. Esposito: *Islam, the Straight Path;* op cit; p. 17.

As Abdel Haleem explains, the Qur'anic material revealed to the Prophet in Makkah is distinguished by scholars from the material that came after the Migration (Hijra) to Madinah. In the Makkah period, the Qur'an was concerned mainly with the central belief in Islam-the unity of God as evidenced by His 'signs' (ayat), to the prophethood of Mohammed, and the Resurrection and final Judgement and these themes are repeatedly stated in order to emphasise and to reinforce Qur'anic teachings.[331] The Qur'an refers to believing in more than one God as shirk (partnership): the sharing of several gods in the creation and government of the universe.[332] The Makkans also initially denied the truth of Mohammed's message, and the Qur'an refers to earlier prophets many of them also mentioned in the Bible, for instance Noah, Abraham, Jacob, Joseph, Moses and Jesus, in order both to reassure the Prophet and his followers that they will be saved, and to give a warning to their opponents that they will be punished.[333] The Qur'an emphasises that all these prophets preached the same message and that the Qur'an was sent to confirm the earlier messages. It says that Muslims should believe in all of them without making any distinction between them (2: 285).[334]

In the Makkan suras, the Qur'an gives arguments from embryology and from nature in general (36: 76-83; 56: 47-96; 22: 5-10) to explain how the Resurrection can and will take place; the Qur'an always seeks to convince by referring to history, to what happened to earlier generations, by explanations from nature, and through logic.[335]

In the Madinah suras, by which time the Muslims were no longer the persecuted minority but an established community with the Prophet as its leader, the Qur'an introduces laws to govern the Muslim community with regard to marriage, commerce and finance, international relations, war and peace. Examples of these can be found in Suras 2, 3, 4, 6, 8, and 9.[336] This era also witnessed the emergence of a new group, the hypocrites, who pretended to profess Islam but were actually working against the Islamic state, and these 'hypocrites' are a frequent theme in the Madinah suras. We also see here discussion of the 'People of the Book' with particular reference to the Jews and Christians, both those contemporary with the Prophet and those in the past.[337]

---

[331] *The Qur'an: A New Translation* (Abdel-Haleem); op cit; p. xvii.
[332] Ibid.
[333] Ibid.
[334] Ibid.
[335] Ibid; p. xvii-xviii.
[336] Ibid.
[337] Ibid.

The Qur'an is acknowledged as the fundamental code, not only of theology, but of civil and criminal jurisprudence, and the laws which regulate the actions and the property of humans are governed by the immutable sanctions of the will of God. In other words, the Qur'an is a religious, social, civil, commercial, military, judicial, criminal, penal code; it regulates everything, from the ceremonies of religion to those of daily life; from the salvation of the soul to the health of the body; from the rights of all to those of each individual; from the interests of the individual to those of society; from morality to crime; from punishment here to that in the life to come.[338] The Qur'an includes rules concerning modesty, marriage, divorce, inheritance, feuding, intoxicants, gambling, diet, theft, murder, fornication, and adultery. Out of the 6200 verses of the Qur'an, 100 deal with ritual practices, 70 discuss personal laws, 70 civil laws, 30 penal laws, and 20 judiciary matters and testimony.[339]

The Qur'an condemns debauchery and excesses of every kind (chapters 4; 17); usury (chapter 2); avarice and pride (4; 17; 18); slander and calumny (104); covetousness (4; 33); Hypocrisy (4; 63); the thirsting after worldly goods (100; 102); it ordains, on the contrary, alms giving (2; 3; 30; 59; 57; 90); filial piety (4; 17; 29; 46); gratitude towards God (5); fidelity to engagements (5; 16); sincerity (6; 17; 23; 83); justice (5; 6), especially to orphans (13; 90), and without respect of persons (80); chastity and decency even in words (24; 25); the ransoming of captives (13; 90); benevolence (28); forgiveness of injuries (3; 16; 24; 43); the returning of good for evil (23); and the walking in the path of virtue, not with the view of obtaining the approbation of the world, but for being acceptable unto God (22).[340]

The socioeconomic reforms of the Qur'an are among its most striking features. Exploitation of the poor, weak, widows, women, orphans (4: 2; 4: 12) and slaves is vividly condemned: 'those who live off orphans' property without having any right to do so will only suck up fire into their bellies, and they will be exposed to burning flame (4: 10).

False contracts, bribery, abuse of women, hoarding of wealth to the exclusion of its subordination to higher ends, and usury are denounced. The Qur'an demands that Muslims pursue a path of social justice.[341]

Although slavery was not abolished, slave owners were encouraged to emancipate their slaves, to permit them to earn their freedom, and to give

---

[338] J. Davenport: *An Apology;* op cit; pp. 71-2.
[339] A. Khallaf: *A Concise History of Islamic legislation;* (Arabic) Kuwait; 1968; pp. 28-9.
[340] J. Davenport: *An Apology;* op cit; pp. 77-8.
[341] J. L. Esposito: *Islam, the Straight Path;* op cit; p. 29.

them some of God's wealth which he has given you' (24:33).[342] Forcing female slaves into prostitution was condemned.

Women and the family were the subjects of more wide ranging reforms affecting marriage, divorce, and inheritance. Marriage was a contract, with women entitled to their dowry (4: 4). Polygamy was restricted (4: 3), and men were commanded to treat their wives fairly and equally (4: 129). Women were given inheritance rights in a patriarchal society that had previously restricted inheritance to male relatives.[343]

The Muslim's mission is to be servant of God and to spread God's rule is both an individual and a community obligation. The Qur'an emphasizes the social dimension of service to God, for it is on earth and in society that God's will is to govern and prevail. Similarly, as God had sent His prophets and revelation to the Jews and then to the Christians, He declares in the Qur'an that the Muslims now constitute the new community of believers who are to be an example to other nations:

'Thus We made you an *umma* (nation) justly balanced, that ye might be witness over the nations" (2: 143).[344]

Guided by the word of God and the Prophet, the Muslim community has a mission to create a moral social order:

"You are the best community evolved for mankind, enjoining what is right and forbidding what is wrong" (3: 110).

This command has influenced Muslim practice throughout the centuries, providing a rationale for political and moral activism. Government regulations, Islamic laws, and the activities of religious police who watch public behaviour have all been justified as expressions of this moral mission to command the good and prohibit evil. Again, the Prophet (PBUH) and the first Muslim community are seen as exemplifying this ideal, implementing the socially just society envisioned by the Qur'an.[345]

---

[342] Ibid; p. 79.
[343] Ibid.
[344] J. L. Esposito: *Islam, the Straight Path;* op cit; pp. 28-9.
[345] Ibid; p. 29.

c. The Beauty of the Qur'an:

Muslims, regardless of their national language, memorize and recite the Qur'an in Arabic whether they fully understand it or not.[346] In contrast to Judaism and Christianity, whose Scriptures were not only translated into Greek and Latin at an early date but also disseminated in vernacular languages, in Islam Arabic has remained the language of the Qur'an and of religious learning.[347]

Since the Qur'an is God's book, the text is perfect, eternal, and unchangeable; which is the miracle of inimitability of the Qur'an, that the ideas, language, and style of the Qur'an cannot be reproduced. The Qur'an proclaims that even the combined efforts of human beings and jinns could not produce a comparable text (17: 88).

Without a doubt, the Qur'an is beautiful, indeed, the most beautiful literary composition the Arabic language has ever known. Its beauty, however, is not the consequence of faith but its very cause.[348] The aesthetic judgment-that the Qur'an is beautiful, is a critical judgment, reached through literary analysis. Hence, its beauty is not only held by Muslims but also by non-Muslims conversant with the literary aesthetics of the Arabic language. Instead of beauty depending upon the divine origin and flowing out of faith in that origin, the divine origin of the Qur'an is the reasoned consequence of its literary beauty.[349]

Reluctant to forsake their gods, to abandon their traditions and alter their customs, the Makkans denied the authority of the new teaching, alleging that rather than God, the source and author of the Qur'an was Mohammed or some teacher from whom the Prophet borrowed these words.[350] The so-called word of God or revelation was not divine but human, all too human, and hence devoid of commanding authority. What proof did Mohammed have that it was divine? Could he produce a miracle such as Moses and Jesus had performed?[351] The Qur'an answered them that in his own accord he was unable, that he commanded no superhuman power, and that in the process of revelation, he was a passive patient receiving what was given

---

[346] Ibid; p. 19.
[347] Ibid.
[348] I.R. and L.L. Al-Faruqi: *The Cultural Atlas*; op cit; pp. 102-3.
[349] Ibid.
[350] Ibid; pp. 103-4.
[351] Qur'an 17: 90-93.

by the divine source.[352] The proof that the Qur'an was the word of God devolved upon the Qur'an itself. It constituted its own proof by its inimitability, its superior beauty, and its moving appeal which no human composition can match.[353]

The Qur'an invited the opponents to produce a similar book,[354] ten *suwar* (chapters) like any in the Qur'an.[355] But none would rise to the challenge, despite the fact that the Arabs regarded themselves the masters of poetry and literary eloquence, and the Makkans, the very head of that pinnacle. The Qur'an reduced the challenge, asking them to produce one *surah* like any of the Qur'an whose short *suwar* had fewer than thirty words, and inviting them to bring their own gods to help.[356]

Poets and men of letters from all over Arabia were called to the rescue and were promised the greatest prizes for their compositions. One of them, al Walid ibn al Mughirah, listened to the Qur'an recited by the Prophet and felt admiration for it. Abu Jahl, the Makkan leader, approached him to bolster his resistance and promised him the wealth of Makkah. Al-Walid listened again to the Qur'an and spoke out without hesitation: "I am the first connoisseur of poetry and letters in Arabia, and I speak with unquestionable authority. This Qur'an is not the work of humans, nor of *jinn*. It has a very special beauty, a very special ring. It is replete with light and beauty, surpassing everything known."[357]

Other poets and contenders presented their compositions as well, only to be declared failing by one another and their own sponsors. By its words, the Qur'an wielded an awesome power, fascinating, shattering, composing, and moving. Whatever their predicament or social position, those who heard it and apprehended its meanings fell prostrate before the divine presence it signified.[358]

In addition to its place as a religious text, the Qur'an was central to the development of Arabic linguistics and provided the basis for the development of Arabic grammar, vocabulary, and syntax.[359] The Qur'an objectified all the norms of the Arabic language.[360] It was from the Qur'an

---

[352] Qur'an: 41: 6.

[353] I.R. and L.L. Al-Faruqi: *The Cultural Atlas*; op cit; pp. 103-4.

[354] Qur'an: 18: 110; 52:34.

[355] Qur'an: 11: 13.

[356] Qur'an: 17:88.

[357] Mohammed Ibn Ishaq (151/769) and Mohammed Ibn Hisham (218/834): *Sirat al-Nabiy Salat Allahu Alayhi wa Sallam;* ed by M.M. Abd Al-Hamid; Cairo; 1963; vol 1; pp. 174-5.

[358] I.R. and L.L. Al-Faruqi: *The Cultural Atlas*; op cit; pp. 102-4.

[359] J. L. Esposito: *Islam, the Straight Path;* op cit; p. 19.

[360] I.R. and L.L. Al-Faruqi: *The Cultural Atlas*; op cit; pp. 105-6.

that the Arabist derived his grammar, the linguist his morphology, the poet his figures of speech. It was the standard and norm of all that pertains to Arabic.[361] Thus attached to the Qur'an as its sublime instance, the Arabic language passed beyond the flux of time and became as eternal and unchangeable as the Qur'an itself, its ideal exemplification. Indeed, the Muslim mind never permitted any separation of the Qur'an from its Arabic language.[362]

---

[361] Ibid.
[362] Ibid.

The Miracle of the Qur'an

Muslim tradition is replete with stories of those who converted to Islam on hearing its inimitable message and of those pagan poets who failed the Qura'nic challenge (10:37-38) to create verses comparable with those contained in the Qur'an.[363] According to tradition, Lebid Abu Rabia, a native of Yemen, and one of the seven whose verses constituted the Mu'alakat (a series of prizes suspended in the Kaaba), was still an idolater when Mohammed announced Islam. For some time no poet could be found to compete with him, but at length the chapter of the Qur'an entitled Bakara (sura 2) was affixed to a gate in the same temple, and Lebid was so overcome by the first few verses as to declare that they could only have been produced by the inspiration of God Himself, and he forthwith embraced Islam.[364]

The passage from the Qur'an which affected this conversion was the following:

`There is nothing doubtful in this book: it is a direction to the pious who believe in the unseen;

Who observe the appointed times of prayer, who distribute alms out of what We have bestowed upon them;

Who believe in the revelation that has been sent down unto thee (Mohamed), as well as in that delivered unto the Prophets before thee, and who are certain of the Hereafter;

Such, verily, are under the guidance of their Lord, and they shall prosper.

As for the disbelievers, whether thou warn them or thou warn them not it is all one for them; they believe not.

Allah hadth sealed their hearing and their hearts, and on their eyes there is covering. Theirs will be an awful doom.

And of mankind are some who say: we believe in Allah and the Last Day, when they believe not.

They think to beguile Allah and those who believe, and they beguile none but themselves; but they perceive not.

In their hearts is a disease, and Allah increaseth their disease. A painful doom is theirs because they lie.

And when it is said to them: make no mischief on earth, they say we are peacemakers only (2: 2-14).[365]

---

[363] J. L. Esposito: *Islam, the Straight Path;* op cit; p. 19.
[364] J. Davenport: *An Apology;* op cit; p. 68.
[365] Ibid.

2. On Differences of Islam With Other Faiths:

Christians and Jews, as a rule, have not accepted the Qur'an as divine revelation.[366] Islam on the other hand, accepts both faiths as Godly. Islam has never interfered with the dogmas of any faith, never persecuted, never established an inquisition, never aimed at proselytism. It offered its religion, but never enforced it: `let there be no compulsion in religion.'[367]

Islam, as clearly stated in the Qur'an, is not new, but is the religion of Abraham, which has subsequently been distorted by the Israelites.[368] Esposito explains that:
`Mohammed was not the founder of Islam; he did not start a new religion. Like his prophetic predecessors, he came as a religious reformer. Mohammed maintained that he did not bring a new message from a new God but called people back to the one, true God and to a way of life that most of his contemporaries had forgotten or deviated from. Worship of Allah was not the evolutionary emergence of monotheism from polytheism but a return to a forgotten past, to the faith of the first monotheist, Abraham. The Prophet brought a revolution in Arabian life, a reformation that sought to purify and redefine its way of life. False, superstitious practices such as polytheism and idolatry were suppressed. Such beliefs were viewed as the worst forms of ingratitude or unbelief, for they contradicted and denied the unity or oneness *(tawhid)* of God. Polytheism, or association *(shirk)* of anything with Allah, was denounced as the worst of sins, idolatry. For Mohammed, the majority of Arabs lived in ignorance *(jahiliyya)* of Allah and His will as revealed to the Prophets Adam, Abraham, Moses, and Jesus.'[369]

Islam adjures the Jews to obey their Law, Christians to obey the Gospel (5: 72); but principally to accept also the Qur'an as God's latest pronouncement as the earlier revelations had been corrupted and abused; now the new one would unite them, cleanse them, and offer all mankind an integrating, invigorating faith.[370] In Islam, Jesus (PBUH) has been sent to bring religion back from Jewish heresies to the true path. Jesus was a Prophet, but after a

---

[366] G.E. Von Grunebaum: *Medieval Islam,* The University of Chicago Press, 1954; p.13.
[367] J. Davenport: *An Apology;* op cit; p. 81.
[368] J. Glubb: *A Short History*; op cit; p.32.
[369] J. L. Esposito: *Islam, the Straight Path;* op cit; P. 12.
[370] W. Durant: *The Age of Faith*; op cit; p.186.

time, his followers also adulterated his teaching.[371] Ibn Khaldun enlightens
further on this matter:
`The largest following of Jesus were his companions, the Apostles... The
Apostles divided into different groups. Most of them went to the country of
the Romans and made propaganda for the Christian religion. Peter was the
greatest of them. He settled in Rome, the seat of the Roman emperors. They
then wrote down the Gospel that had been revealed to Jesus, in four
recensions according to their different traditions. Mathew wrote his Gospel in
Jerusalem in Hebrew. It was translated into Latin by John, the son of
Zebedee, son of the (Apostles). (The Apostle) Luke wrote his Gospel in Latin
for a Roman dignitary. (The Apostle) John, the son of Zebedee, wrote his
Gospel in Rome. Peter wrote his Gospel in Latin and ascribed it to his pupil
Mark. These four recensions of the Gospel differ from each other. Not all of
it is pure revelation, but (the Gospels) have an admixture of the words of
Jesus and of the Apostles. Most of (their contents) consists of sermons and
stories. There are very few laws in them.'[372]

The three monotheist religions (Judaism, Christianity and Islam) believe in
one supreme God; Christianity added, however, that the one God appears in
three distinct persons. Davenport reminds how it is clearly stated in the
Qur'an:
`O people of the Book- that is to say `O Jews and Christians, let not your
worship transgress just bounds; say naught that is contrary to truth, when
you speak of God; Jesus, the Messiah, the son of Mary, is nothing more
than a Prophet of God. Believe then in God and His prophets, and make no
mention of the Trinity. Set just bounds to your discourses. God is only one
God; all praise be unto Him! God hadth no son'.[373]

Christians describe human beings as God's children, and God is not just the
Lord, but the father, too.[374]Islam considers this a disguised polytheism, and
proclaims with passionate emphasis the oneness of God.[375] `There is no god
but Allah, and Mohammed is his Prophet.' Such strict monotheism allows no
place for Christian trinity. The oneness of God is the cornerstone of Islam
(literally, `submission to God's will'). For the Muslims God has no son; he

---

[371] J. Glubb: *A Short History*; op cit; p.32.
[372] Ibn Khaldun: *The Muqaddimah*, tr. F. Rosenthal, Bollingen series, XLIII; New York,
Princeton University Press, 1958, Vol I, pp 472-481.
[373] J. Davenport: *An Apology;* op cit; p. 75.
[374] Joseph van Ess: Islamic Perspectives: In H. Kung et al: *Christianity and the World
Religions*; Doubleday; London; 1986; p.72,
[375] W. Durant: *The Age of Faith*, op cit; p.176.

does not 'beget'.[376] God is not simply the One, but the Only One, to Whom all things are returned, and Who takes care of all things. He is the Lord, and He is the Merciful One.[377] Jesus in Islam is only a Prophet. Mohammed, in fact, warned against any attempt on the part of the Muslims to deify him.[378] When the newly converted chief of an Arab tribe said to the Prophet, 'Thou art our king,' the Prophet answered quickly: 'The King is God, not I.'[379] When the Prophet died, Abu Bekr addressed the crowd that had gathered outside the dwelling in which he died:

'Whoever worshipped Mohammed, let him know that Mohammed is dead; but whoever worshiped God, let him know that God lives and dies not!'[380]

In Islam the Prophet has no divine powers either; and the ability to work miracles is especially repudiated by him as unnecessary for religious conviction.[381]

Equally, in Islam, there is no idea of mediator. Mohammed is the bringer of salvation only in the sense of information. Otherwise every bridge between heaven and earth is deliberately torn down: There are no sacraments, no cult images, no church music.[382] Islam is hostile to the organised church and monasticism.[383] There was not a single town entered by the Muslims that did not have some idol for its protector. Remembering the strict recommendations of the Prophet against this deadly sin, prohibited at once by the commandment of God and repudiated by the reason of man, Draper says, the Muslims' first deed was to destroy all the images.[384]

As Esposito notes, in Islam:

'God ordains; humankind is to implement His will. Human responsibility and mission are of cosmic proportion, and people will be judged on the cosmic consequences of their acts. As God's trustees on earth, the measure of human actions, and indeed life, is the extent to which the Muslim contributes to the realization of God's will on earth. This responsibility lies squarely on each individual's shoulders, since no one can bear another's responsibility or suffer for another:

---

[376] J. Van Ess: Islamic Perspectives: op cit; p.72,
[377] Ibid; p.71.
[378] D. J. Geanakoplos: *Medieval Western Civilisation, and the Byzantine and Islamic Worlds*, D.C. Heath and Company, Toronto, 1979. p.147.
[379] Santillana, loc cit., p.286. in G.E. Von Grunebaum: *Medieval Islam;* op cit; p.154.
[380] P. Lunde: *Islam*; Dorling Kindersley; London; 2002.
[381] S.P. Scott: *History of the Moorish Empire*; op cit; Vol 1; p.106.
[382] Joseph van Ess: Islamic perspectives; op cit; p.71.
[383] George M. Lamsa: Selections from the Quran; op cit; p.3.
[384] J.W. Draper: *A History of the Intellectual Development of Europe*; op cit; p.417.

'Nor can a bearer of burdens bear another's burden, and if one heavily laden crieth (for help) to (bear) his load, not the least portion of it can be carried (by the other). . . . And whosoever purifies himself does so for the benefit of his own soul. (35: 18) . . . And whatever good you do, you shall not be denied the just reward of it... As for the unbelievers, their riches shall not avail them, neither their children against God; those are the inhabitants of the fire, dwelling therein forever. (3: 115-16).[385]

Regarding personal responsibility, as Esposito explains, the story of the Fall in the Qur'an differs from that in the Bible in its teaching. It is Adam, not Eve, who is tempted by the devil. Unlike the Judeo-Christian tradition, woman in the Qur'an is not portrayed as the cause of the Fall. Moreover, the sin of Adam and Eve is just that-their own personal sin, an act of disobedience for which they, and they alone, are responsible. Unlike Christianity, there is no notion of an inherited "original" sin, committed by the ancestors of the human race, for which all humanity suffers. Sin is not a state of being; it is the result of an act of disobedience, failure to do or not to do what God commands or prohibits. In Islam, indeed, the consequences of sin, like human responsibility, belong solely to those who commit sin. And human beings are not sinful by nature; as they are created, or finite creatures, they are naturally limited, weak, and subject to temptation.

The Biblical and Qur'anic stories about the consequences of the Fall reveal the basis for the divergence between Christianity and Islam. The Bible views the Fall as the cause of man's flawed nature and existence; the Qur'an finds here the story of sin, God's mercy and repentance. In the Bible, the Fall brings a life of shame, disgrace, and hardship: to the woman God said: "I will greatly multiply your pain in childbearing; in pain you shall bring forth children, yet your desire shall be your husband, and he shall rule over you."

And to Adam He said: "Because you have listened to the voice of your wife, and have eaten of the tree of which I commanded you, you shall not eat of it, cursed the ground because of you, in toil you shall eat of it all the days of your life; thorns and thistles it shall bring forth to you" (Genesis: 3: 16-18).

In sharp contrast, the Qur'an teaches that after Adam disobeys God but repents, God extends to Adam His mercy and guidance: "But his Lord chose him. He turned to him and gave him guidance" (20: 122). Adam turned away from Satan and sin and turned back to God; Adam repented, and God forgave. This is sin and repentance in Islam. The Muslim is one

---

[385] J. L. Esposito: *Islam, the Straight Path;* op cit; pp. 26-7.

who submits to God by following His will, sin is disobedience or refusal to submit. It is the arrogance and ingratitude of creatures who forget or turn away from their Creator and Sustainer. Repentance is remembering or returning to God's path, the straight path of Islam. There is little or no emphasis on feelings of shame and disgrace or guilt. What God commands, and what His awesome character engenders, is fear of God *(taqwa)*. *Taqwa* means self-protection or fear of God. This attitude or disposition follows from belief in an all-powerful, omnipresent God (an ever-present God who is as near as one's jugular vein), who has commanded submission or obedience to His will and before whom the Muslim is morally responsible and accountable. It is the response of the believer who knows what he or she must do and who lives life ever mindful of the eternal consequences that await on the Last Day.

The duties and obligations of Muslim life, as well as its rewards and punishments, fall equally on men and women:

'The believers, men and women, are guardians of one another; they enjoin good and forbid evil, perform the prayer, give alms, and obey God and His Prophet (9: 71)... Whoever does a righteous deed, whether man or woman, and has faith, we will give a good life; and we shall reward them according to the best of their actions (16: 97).'[386]

3. On Some Distortions of Islam:

Many distorted depictions of Islam have been made through the centuries in Christendom, and it would be impossible to address all at this stage. Amongst the earliest was by John of Damascus, who wrote that: 'arose among the Arabs a man named Mamed, who became acquainted with the Old and New Testaments, and later, after discoursing with an Arian monk, 'established his own sect', which he imagined to be a new religion.[387] For a Byzantine chronicler,[388] it was instead a Nestorian monk called Bahira who converted 'Mamed' to heresy and convinced him he was a great prophet. Another version is by Gauthier de Compiègne in Chartres (12th century), which speaks of Mohammed as a poor child raised by a baron

---

[386] Ibid; pp. 27-8.

[387] John of Damascus: *De haeresibus*, *Patrologia Graeca*, vol. 94, 761-71; in Von Grunebaum: *Medieval;* op cit; p. 43.

[388] *Confutatio Agarenozum*, *Patrologia Graeca*, vol. 104, 1383-1448.

who made his fortune in Persia, India and Ethiopia, and whose trust Mohammed wins.[389] Another version presents Mohammed as a former cardinal who, out of pique at having been passed over in a papal election, went off to Arabia and started a rival religion.[390] Another that a monk who became a cardinal named Nicolas, who to take revenge on his attackers, makes of the Prophet the instrument of his revenge. Then Nicolas becomes the Prophet himself. Hence Prophet Mohammed was initially in Rome, celebrated and adulated, but because angry for not having been elected pope, founds a new rival religion.[391] The Romances of Baphomet, so common in the 14th and 15th centuries, attributed every crime to the Prophet, just as the Athanasians did to Arius. `He is a Cardinal, who having failed to obtain the object of every Cardinal's ambition, invents a new religion to revenge himself on his brethrens.'[392] In the end, the Prophet becomes the agent of `Perverse Jews,' and also heretic Christians: Nestorians, Jacobites, Arians, etc, depending on who makes the attack on Islam.[393]

These distortions are `most divorced from reality, and most remote from any contact with Islam,' Daniel notes.[394] They were very often a concoction of untrue accounts which were deliberate, probably malicious, misrepresentations; and some totally absurd, based on pure fantasy, Daniel adds.[395] Hence, when Guibert of Nogent (d. ca 1124-30) spoke about the Prophet in his Gesta Dei per Francos,[396] he may have garbled his name and pushed him a few centuries forward in time, says Southern, but he was not to be denied the chance to reproduce the usual hostile image; an image hardly based on truth, but the fruit of popular opinion and legend.[397] Distorted image, which persisted through the centuries, and so much so even Christian viceroys who lived long in Muslim countries, knew nothing of the Prophet, his message or his life.[398] Thus the ignorance of Islam as a religion persisted and the misconceptions about Muslim belief remained profound,

---

[389] Gauthier de Compiègne. *Otia Machometi. In* E. Edelstand du Méril, *Poesies populaires latines du moyen âge* (Paris, 1977).

[390] B. Lewis: *Cultures in Conflict*; Oxford University Press; 1995; p. 30.

[391] E. Doutte: Mahomet Cardinal, in *Memoires de la societe d'agriculture... sciences et arts de la Marne*; Second serie; Vol 1; 2nd part; Chalons; 1899; pp 233-43.

[392] R. B. Smith: *Mohammed*; op cit; p. 78.

[393] M. T. D'Alverny: Pierre le venerable et la Legende de Mahomet: *A Cluny, Congres Scientifique...* 9-11 July 1949; CNRS; 1950; pp 161-170; at p. 163.

[394] N. Daniel: *The Arabs and Medieval Europe*, Longman, Librairies du Liban, 1975; p.232.

[395] Ibid.

[396] *Gesta Dei per Francos*, bk.1, caput 3 in patrologia latina, ed. J.P. Migne; Paris, 1853; Vol 156; col.689.

[397] R.W. Southern: *Western Views of Islam in the Middle Ages*, Harvard University Press, 1978; p.31.

[398] S.P. Scott: *History of the Moorish Empire;* op cit; Vol 1; p.91.

Sweetman concludes.[399]

Further distorted depictions attribute extremism to Islam. In truth, Islam frowns on ascetism, and condemns monascitism (7: 27). Muslims are to enjoy the pleasures of life with good conscience, but in moderation.[400] Marriage is the natural state of man.[401] The Prophet (PBUH) repeatedly affirmed that he was a preacher, whose mission was the regeneration and the happiness of mankind.[402] In fact, Islam is the perfect vehicle of happiness. Spokesmen as far apart as al-Afghani (d.1897) and Heykal (1888-) have stressed Islam's unique capacity to produce happiness.[403]

As for liberty, Islamic jurists have reached a twofold conclusion:

1) Liberty finds its limit in its very nature, because liberty unlimited would mean self destruction-and that limit or boundary is the legal norm, or law.

2) No limit is arbitrary, because it is determined by its utility or the greatest good of the individual or for society. Utility, which is the foundation of law, traces also its boundary and extent.'[404]

It is also widely claimed that Islam is the enemy of learning and science. Thus, Diderot, the 18th century philosopher, claims that the Prophet was the worst enemy of reason; that he could not read or write, and so this encouraged Muslims to be hostile to, and have contempt for knowledge, which, thus, secured the survival of Islam.[405] And with the exception of the Qur'an, `all books were burned, either because they were superfluous if they contained only what was in it or they were pernicious if they contained anything that was omitted from it.'[406]

Yet, as Davenport rightly points out, that in reply to the almost stereotyped assertion that Islam is in the present day an enemy to science and letters, `it has been observed, that so far from this being the truth, Islam has outstripped the enlightenment of our age by making instruction a fundamental law. Every child must be put to school in its fifth year. It is the duty of the state to instruct the citizen, that he may understand the laws

---

[399] J.W. Sweetman: *Islam and Christian Theology*; Lutterworth Press; London; 1955; Vol I; Part II; p. 63.

[400] W. Durant: *The Age of Faith*; op cit; p.214.

[401] J.W. Draper: *A History of the Intellectual Development of Europe*; op cit; p.331

[402] S.P. Scott: *History of the Moorish Empire;* op cit; Vol 1; p.96.

[403] G.E. Von Grunebaum: *Medieval Islam;* op cit; p.233.

[404] D. de Santillana, in *The Legacy of Islam*, ed. Sir T. W. Arnold and A. Guillaume; Oxford, 1931; p. 292.

[405] D. Diderot: *Oeuvres Completes*; Vol VIII, Paris; 1975; p. 230.

[406] Ibid.

he has to obey, and of the family to teach the child the means by which he may acquire his livelihood.'[407]

Vast accomplishments by Islam in sciences and civilisation also coincided with the peak of Islamic power: 7th-13th centuries, and it was Islam, which dragged the Christian West out of barbarism.[408]

It is generally held that Islam was spread by the sword, and violence and terror are always associated with Islam and Muslims today. There are many instances of these assertions around us today. Yet in truth, there is nothing in Islam that promotes violence and terror. Islam derives from the concept of Salam (peace) and stresses the inviolability of human life. Killing the innocent cancels every other act of piety. Violence is condoned in Islam only in self defence. Davenport devotes an excellent chapter to this matter.[409] He cites in support the patent that the Prophet granted to the monks of Mount Sinai, and to the Christians, in general, which went:

`Article IX: And those who live quietly and solitary upon the mountains, they shall exact neither poll tax nor tithes from their incomes, neither shall any Muslim partake of what they have, for the labour only to maintain themselves.

Article XI: Neither in time or far shall they take them out of their habitation, nor compel them to go to wars, not even shall they require of them any poll tax.'

Article XIII: Do not molest those who have veneration for the Books that are sent from God, but rather, in a kind manner, give of your good things to them, and converse with them, and hinder every one from molesting them.'

And in three out of the eighteen articles, the Prophet warns those who might break this covenant, in article XVI stating:

`Whosoever acts contrary to this my grant, or gives credit to anything contrary to it, becomes truly an apostate from God and his Apostle, because this protection I have granted to them according to this promise.'

Then in article XVII: And by this I ordain that none of my nation shall presume to do or act contrary to this promise until the end of the world.'[410]

Moreover, as Scott insists, force alone could have never enabled the Muslims, as they are presented, `a tumultuous horde of barbarians, unaccustomed to concerted action and impatient of the restraints of military discipline, to overwhelm three great empires in less than a century.'[411] The

---

[407] J. Davenport: *An Apology*; op cit; p. 95.
[408] See: S.E. Al-Djazairi: *The Hidden Debt to Islamic Civilisation*; Bayt Al-Hikma; Manchester; 2005.
[409] J. Davenport: *An Apology;* op cit; pp. 140-50.
[410] Ibid.
[411] S.P. Scott: *History of the Moorish Empire*; op cit; Vol 1; p.95.

policy of Islam was to inculcate its principles by argument rather than to provoke opposition by invective.[412] The arrival of Islam has been often seen by those whose territories were subject to it as a liberation, never a threat to their faith, and by Christians who believed in the message of Islam.[413] Chapter 9 of this work, in particular, will show how Islam expanded in diverse continents without recourse to any military force or presence.

Acts of violence by Muslims have remained minimal throughout history. There is no instance of genocide of any race, or suppression of an entity committed by Islam. This does not mean that all Muslims always act in a perfect, ideal manner. Far from it. However, as Jameelah sums up:
'Despite all the imperfections, which are inevitable in this imperfect world, traditional Muslim society throughout the centuries of its ascendancy was free from the curses of nationalism, imperialism, class conflicts, racial discrimination, inquisition, heresy hunts, routine torture of war and political prisoners, bloody sectarian strife, large scale illicit and perverted sex, sex crimes, illegitimate children and alcohol addiction, which cast their shadows over Christendom.'[414]

Another myth is 'Islamic intolerance,' contradicted by both the Qur'anic message and historical reality. The Qur'an forbids arguing with the People of the Book (i.e Christians and Jews) except in the best way, and urges the Muslims to say:
'We believe in what was revealed to us and in what was revealed to you; our God and your God are one (and the same) (29: 46). God addresses Muslims, Jews and Christians with the following: 'We have assigned a law and a path to each of you. If God has so willed, He would have made you one community, but He wanted to test you through that which He has given to you, so race to do good: you will all return to God and He will make clear to you the matters you differed about' (5: 48).[415] The Qur'an allows Muslims to eat the food of the People of the Book and marry their women (5:5).[416]
Throughout history, under Islam, Jews and Christians could practise their faith, keep their laws and elect their own judges.[417] Nearly a thousand years later, Glubb notes, people in Europe were still being tortured and burned alive for their faith. And in general, the Ottomans continued the policy of religious toleration which they had inherited from the Arabs.[418]In the

---

[412] Ibid.
[413] C. Cahen: l'Acceuil des Chretiens a l'Islam, in *Revue d'Histoire des Religions*, 1963.
[414] M. Jameelah: *Islam and Orientalism*; M.Y. Khan and Sons; Lahore; 1981; p. 49.
[415] *The Qur'an: A New Translation* (M.A.S. Abdel-Haleem); op cit; p. xvi.
[416] Ibid; p. xxv.
[417] J. Glubb: *A Short History*; op cit; p. 251.
[418] Ibid.

centuries of Muslim presence in Southern Europe, no existing religion was interfered with. No counts were appointed to govern or oppress the conquered. 'No unworthy prelates were assigned to rich sees as the result of intrigue or corruption,' Scott points out.[419] The Christian populations were secure in the protection of their own laws and the enjoyment of their ancient religious privileges; their restrictions confined to a show of outward respect for the institutions of their masters and the regular payment of tribute; and all acts of violence and oppression were punished.[420] Islam, Scott notes, was 'an idea of the Deity so simple, and yet so comprehensive, that no mind, however bigoted, could conscientiously reject it; which moulded into an harmonious system the jarring interests of antagonistic races, and, by its maxims of toleration.'[421]

Benevolence is commended by the Prophet as the first of all virtues; a benevolence which reaches to all creatures.
'To all the brute creation,' writes Miss Pardoe (City of the Sultan) the Turks are not only merciful, but ministering friends; and to so great an extent do they carry this kindness towards the inferior animals that they will not kill an unweaned lamb, in order to spare unnecessary suffering to the mother; and an English sportsman, who had been unsuccessful in the chase, having on one occasion, in firing off his piece previously to disembarking from his caique, brought down a gull that was sailing above his head, was reproached by his rowers with as much horror and emphasis as though he had been guilty of homicide.'[422]

Under Islam, individuals, regardless of status or race, or ethnicity, enjoyed rights little equalled elsewhere, and even today. The Prophet was visited by an Abyssinian who addressed him with this question: 'You Arabs excel us in every respect; you are more shapely, and of more gainly colour; also the Prophet has risen amongst you. Now, if I believe in your mission shall I be awarded a seat in Paradise alongside of the believing Arabs?' 'Yes,' the Prophet assured him. 'And the black skin of the Abyssinian will spread splendour at a distance of a thousand years.'[423]
The offspring of a black mother and white father was admitted to full equality; and Blacks were not excluded from high office in the whole of the Islamic realm. From 946 to 968, Egypt was governed by Kafur, a Black

---

[419] S.P. Scott: *History*; op cit; vol II;: p. 194
[420] Ibid; vol 1; p.270.
[421] Ibid; p.96.
[422] Extracts from A.Ubbicini: *La Turquie Actuelle*; 1855. p.78.
[423] Slightly abridged from I. Goldhizer, *Muhammedan* Studies: ed and tr. by S.M. Stern; London; Allen and Uniwin; 1971, I.74.

person born in Slavery.[424] Mamluk slave aristocracies, Turkish and Circassian, for many generations ruled de facto in Baghdad, and de jure in Egypt.[425] Islam also permits marriage with slave girls, and accepts that the offspring of such unions is to be considered legitimate, and so rose many amongst such off-springs into the greatest houses of Islamic aristocracy. Only three Abbasid caliphs were born of free mothers, and all these belong to the 8th century (i.e the first century of Abbasid power).[426] Under Mehdi, both heads of departments in Baghdad and governors of provinces tended increasingly to be freed slaves of the Abbasid family.[427]

Despite all such facts, the deliberate misrepresentations of Islam go on even today. This is noted by Vitkus, who says:
`Unfortunately, the demonisation of Islam and misunderstanding of Islamic society and religion that this essay recounts are still prevalent in the dominant ideology of the West. Today, many of the stereotypes described above continue to shape the image of Islam produced by the mass media in North America, Europe, and other parts of the world.[428] If we examine, in particular, the American representation of Islam in mass media journalism during the last 10-15 years, we will find ample evidence for an unbroken tradition depicting Islamic people as violent, cruel, wrathful, lustful, and so on. With the end of the Cold War, America needed a new ideological bogey man to serve as an alleged external threat; and perhaps this explains the recent resurgence of anti Islamic imagery, a revival that draws upon a venerable tradition of anti Islamic demonisation that began in the medieval period and acquired some of its present features in the 16th and 17th centuries.'[429]

Having taken a generalised look at Islam, and issues related to its perception and depiction, return must be made now to the history of the Islamic lands following the death of the Prophet, and the inception of the first four caliphs.

---

[424] G.E. Von Grunebaum: *Medieval Islam*; op cit; p.210.
[425] Ibid; p.177.
[426] Ibid; p.202
[427] J. Glubb: *A Short History;* op cit; p.99.
[428] See J. Esposito: *The Islamic Threat: Myth and Reality;* Oxford; 1992.
[429] D.J. Vitkus: Early Modern Orientalism: Representations of Islam in 16th and 17th century Europe; In *Western Views of Islam in Medieval and Early Modern Europe;* Edited by D.R. Blanks and M. Frassetto; St Martin's Press; New York; 1999; pp. 207-30; p. 226.

FOUR

THE FIRST FOUR RIGHTLY GUIDED CALIPHS AND THE EARLY PROGRESS OF ISLAM

The first four caliphs of Islam, Abu Bekr, Omar, Uthman, and Ali, are the greatest figures of Islam after the Prophet (PBUH). They followed the Prophet, and after his death, all four pursued the Prophet's mission. Despite the difficulties, which generally Western historians over emphasise so as to darken Islamic history, the achievements of these first great figures of Islam remain unique in Islamic history. This chapter looks at their character and accomplishments.

This chapter also looks at the advance of Islam in the first two centuries of the Hijra. It looks at the military aspects, first, how vast lands were brought under the Islamic sway. It then looks at how people became Muslims not because of the sword, as generally non-Muslim historians hold, but, instead, became Muslims by pure conviction, that is finding in Islam a faith that fulfilled both their spiritual and material needs.

1. The First Four Caliphs:

Gibbon, says:

'The courage of Abu Bekr, Omar, and Othman, had indeed been tried in the persecution and wars of the Prophet; and the personal assurance of paradise must have taught them to despise the pleasures and dangers of the present world. But they ascended the throne in a venerable or mature age; and esteemed the domestic cares of religion and justice the most important

90

duties of a sovereign. Excepting the presence of Omar at the siege of Jerusalem, their longest expeditions were the frequent pilgrimage from Medina to Mecca; and they calmly received the tidings of victory as they prayed or preached... The austere and frugal measure of their lives was the effect of virtue or habit, and the pride of their simplicity insulted the vain magnificence of the kings of the earth.'[430]

Gibbon has great praise for Ali, too:

`The zeal and virtue of Ali were never outstripped by any recent proselyte. He united the qualifications of a poet, a soldier, and a saint: his wisdom still breathes in a collection of moral and religious sayings; and every antagonist, in the combats of the tongue or of the sword, was subdued by his eloquence and valour. From the first hour of his mission to the last rites of his funeral, the apostle was never forsaken by a generous friend, whom he delighted to name his brother.'[431]

To these first caliphs, nothing came before Islam and their mission on earth, and all might, power and wealth on this earth counted for very little. Abu Bekr (Caliph 632-634) lived in patriarchal simplicity, and in the first six months of his short rule, he travelled back and forth daily from al-Sunh (where he lived in a modest household with his wife, Habiba), to his capital Madinah, and received no stipend since the state had at that time hardly any income.[432] Abu Bekr enjoined his daughter Ayesha to take a strict account of his private patrimony, that it might be evident whether he were enriched or impoverished by the service of the state. He thought himself entitled to a stipend of three pieces of gold, with the sufficient maintenance of a single camel and a black slave; but on the Friday of each week he distributed the residue of his own and the public money, first to the most worthy, and then to the most indigent, of the Muslims.[433] The remains of his wealth, a coarse garment, and five pieces of gold, were delivered to his successor, who lamented with a modest sigh his own inability to equal such an admirable model.[434]

The humanity of the caliphs was also boundless, whether at peace or at war. Caliph Abu Bekr despatched a circular letter to the Arab tribes. It said:

"In the name of the most merciful God, to the rest of the true believers. Health and happiness, and the mercy and blessing of God, be upon you. I praise the most high God, and I pray for his Prophet Mohammed. This is

---

[430] E. Gibbon : *The Decline and Fall;* op cit; vol 5; p. 399 .
[431] Ibid; p. 381
[432] Ibn al-Athir: *Usd al-Ghabah fi Ma'arifat al-Sahabah* (Cairo; 1286 (H); vol iii; p. 219.
[433] E. Gibbon: *The Decline and Fall;* op cit; p. 400.
[434] Ibid.

to acquaint you that I intend to send the true believers into Syria to take it out of the hands of the infidels. And I would have you know, that the fighting for religion is an act of obedience to God."

"Remember," said the successor of the Prophet, "that you are always in the presence of God, on the verge of death, in the assurance of judgment, and the hope of paradise. Avoid injustice and oppression; consult with your brethren, and study to preserve the love and confidence of your troops. When you fight the battles of the Lord, acquit yourselves like men, without turning your backs; but let not your victory be stained with the blood of women or children. Destroy no palm-trees, nor burn any fields of corn. Cut down no fruit-trees, nor do any mischief to cattle, only such as you kill to eat. When you make any covenant or article, stand to it, and be as good as your word. As you go on, you will find some religious persons who live retired in monasteries, and propose to themselves to serve God that way: let them alone, and neither kill them nor destroy their monasteries…..'[435]

Shortly after the victory of Ajnadayn, Caliph Abu Bekr died at the age of sixty-three, and was buried beside the Prophet Mohammed. Jarir Mu'awiya said: `God's Messenger was taken when he was sixty three years old; Omar was to be killed when he was sixty three years old, and Abu Bekr died when he was sixty three years old.'[436]

Before he died, Abu Bekr instructed:

`Give back what we have of the Muslims' money, for I will not acquire anything of this property. My land, which is in such and such a place is given to the Muslims as compensation for what I have acquired from their property. He transferred that to Omar along with milch camels, a slave who was a blade whetter, and velvet worth five dirhams.' Omar said: `He has caused troubles for all after him.'[437]

Abu Bekr's last words were:

`My Lord, take me as a Muslim and join me with the righteous.'[438]

Abu Bekr was succeeded by Omar ibn al-Khattab, another father-in-law of the Prophet (through the marriage of Hafsa), as the second Caliph (634-44) with the additional title of *Amir al-Mu'minin*, meaning 'Commander of the Faithful.' Before he died, Abu Bekr summoned separately some of the leading figures, one of whom was Uthman B. Affan (who was to

---

[435] Ibid; pp 415-7.
[436] *The History of Al-Tabari*; op cit; vol XI; tr by K.Y. Blankinship; p. 132.
[437] Ibid; p. 153.
[438] Ibid; p. 138.

become the third caliph). Abu Bekr said: `O Abu Abdallah, inform me about Omar.'
Uthman responded: `You are better informed about him.'
Abu Bekr said: `Let me decide O Abu Abdallah.'
Uthman said: `O God, my knowledge about him is that what he does in private is better than what he shows openly, and that there is no-one like him amongst us.'
Abu Bekr said: `May God have mercy on you, O Abu Abdallah. Do not mention anything that I have mentioned to you.'
Uthman said: `I will do as you said.'[439]
After he appointed Omar as his successor, Abu Bekr received the visit of Talhah B. Ubaydallah, who said: `Have you made Omar your successor over the people, even though you have seen the way the people are treated by him, even when you are with him? How then will he be if he is alone with them, after you have met your Lord and He asks you about those you were responsible for?
Abu Bekr, who was lying down, said: `Sit me up,' and they sat him up. He then answered Talhah: `Is it with God that you frighten me? When I meet God my Lord, and He questions me, I will say: `I have left the best of Your people as successor in charge of Your people.'[440]

Omar belonged to the politically unimportant Makkan clan of Adi ibn Kab, but was a man of strong determination, a keen sense of duty and a remarkable gift for administration. Omar's accession to the Caliphate turned out to be of immense value to Islam. Throughout his reign of ten years (634-644) of expanding empire, he remained a man of sincere religious convictions, deep personal humility and extreme austerity, and made up for his lack of experience in dealing with the practical problems of government by shrewd judgement of men and motives, and political acumen.[441] He laid the foundations of what was later to become the classical Islamic state, the glorious decade of his rule seeing the first phase of its vast expansion, before the Umayyad (661-750) expanded it still further.[442] In his ten years of rule, the Muslims conquered an empire, and although he humbled the Byzantine and Persian Emperors, he remained always pious, simple and compassionate.[443] Prisoners-of-war brought to Madinah expected to see palaces and imperial pageantry such as they had

---

[439] Ibid; p. 146.
[440] Ibid; p. 153.
[441] H.U. Rahman: *A Chronology of Islamic History: 570-1000 CE*; Mansell Publishing Limited; London; 1989; p. 21.
[442] Ibid.
[443] J. Glubb: *A Short History;* op cit; p. 63.

witnessed in Constantinople or in Ctesiphon. Instead, in the glaring, dusty square of a little mud-brick town, they would find a circle of Arabs sitting on the ground. One of them, a tall lean man, barefoot and wearing a coarse woollen cloak, would prove to be the world's most powerful emperor.[444] He owned, we are told, one shirt, and one mantle only, both conspicuous for their patchwork.[445] He slept on a bed of palm leaves and had no concern other than the maintenance of the purity of the faith, the upholding of justice and the ascendancy and security of Islam.[446] The messenger bearing good news of Muslim victories took with him to Caliph Omar two large chests filled with precious stones from the treasures of the Great King. As there was no treasury or strong-room in Madinah, the chests were deposited for the night in a room in Omar's house. But the old man was worried at the presence of such wealth. The hoarding of treasure, he felt, showed a lack of faith in God's power to provide. In the morning, he summoned the messenger and told him to take the chests away, sell the contents and distribute the proceeds among the soldiers.[447]

The conquest of foreign lands was a new experience for the Muslims and raised the important question for the second Caliph of deciding for the first time on what principles the conquered territories were to be governed. He had to pronounce on many fundamental issues encountered for the first time, and his innovative decisions set precedents for his successors.[448] Caliph Omar was acknowledged as the chief creator of the Muslim system of administration, having laid down the working principle that Arabs should not acquire landed property in conquered territories.[449] Under his system, the conquering general of a new territory became its governor, but most of the subordinate officers were allowed to retain their posts. The Muslims established themselves in large towns, and provided the military garrisons, but civil administration was left largely in the hands of the local chiefs.[450]

The conquered territories were divided into compact provinces so that their resources could be developed separately under their respective governors, who were appointed by the Caliph. But he retained the old

---

[444] Ibid.

[445] Ibn Sa'd: *Kitab al-tabaqat al-Kabir (The Great book of Classes);* ed Sachau; Leiden, Brill, 9 vols, 1904-28; vol iii; p. 1; pp. 237-9.

[446] P.K. Hitti: *History of the Arabs*; op cit; p. 176.

[447] J. Glubb: *A Short History*; op cit; p. 60.

[448] H.U. Rahman: *A Chronology;* op cit; pp. 21-2.

[449] S.M. Ikram: *Muslim Civilisation in India;* ed by by A.T. Embree; Columbia University Press; New York; 1964; p. 11.

[450] Ibid.

political divisions, currency and machinery of civil administration; the Muslim law now prevailed everywhere, but only for Muslims. The non-Muslims were dealt with according to their own laws and by their own religious leaders who were also responsible for collecting and paying the communities taxes to the government.[451] The 9th century Muslim historian Al-Baladhuri (d. 892) tells us that Caliph Omar appointed a judge for Damascus and the Jordan, and another for Hims and Qinnasrin, which makes him the first to establish the institution of judgeship.[452]

Caliph Omar established a highly developed fiscal system in which the public treasury raised its revenue through various forms of taxation including personal and land, and administered a register of those entitled to a state pension. It included the relatives of Prophet Mohammed, those who had served the cause of Islam and the soldiers with their wives and children.[453] In this way, he established for the first time the principle that it was the state's duty to provide to these groups of people. Also, the soldiers were now assigned a fixed stipend from the public treasury so that they could devote all their time to military training, which had not been possible when their remuneration was only a share of the booty acquired in a battle.[454]

The sense of justice never deserted Caliph Omar, who addressed his governor at Basra in these terms:

'People have an aversion from their rulers, and I trust to Allah that you and I are not overtaken by it, stealthily and unexpectedly, or by hatreds conceived against us. See to the execution of the laws even if it be for only one hour of the day, and if two matters present themselves to you, the one godly and the other worldly, then choose as your portion the way of God. For the present world will perish and the other world remain. Strike terror into wrong doers and make heaps of mutilated limbs out of them. Visit the sick among Muslims, attend their funerals, open your gate to them and give heed in person to their affairs, for you are but a man amongst them except that God has allowed you the heaviest burden.'[455]

Omar was succeeded by nearly sixty year-old Uthman ibn Affan (Caliph 644-56), the Prophet's son in law (through the marriage of Ruqayya). Uthman, who was a wealthy merchant, became a Muslim quite early in the

---

[451] H.U. Rahman: *A Chronology;* op cit; p. 22.
[452] Al-Baladhuri: *Kitab Futuh al-Buldan;* Ed de Goeje, Brill, 1866; tr English of P.K. Hitti; and German tr of O. Rescher, 2 vols; p. 217 (Hitti).
[453] H.U. Rahman: *A Chronology;* op cit; p. 22.
[454] Ibid.
[455] Ibn Qutaiba: *Uyun al-ahbar*, ed. C. Brockelmann; Berlin and Strasburg, 1900-1908, p. 28.

Prophet's mission. His conversion to Islam, as the first Muslim of high social standing, caused a sensation in Makkah and raised the morale of the early converts.[456]

The early part of his twelve-year reign saw the continuation of the conquests started in the time of Omar. Vast areas of lands became Muslim under Uthman's caliphate, including the complete conquest of Iran, Azerbaidjan and parts of Armenia.[457] Uthman was very pious, and a well meaning old man. In the years 650-2, he established a commission to prepare a text of the Qur'an from a copy made during the reign of the first Caliph, Abu Bekr, and safely stored with him.[458] Uthman ordered that a number of copies should be made out of this, to be distributed to different parts of the Muslim world as the official copy of the Qur'an, a copy which remained recognised throughout the Islamic world for the last fourteen centuries as the authentic document of the Qur'an as revealed to Prophet Mohammed.[459]

In the year 656, sedition arose amongst Muslims. Although the Muslim caliph was the ruler of a vast land, he still lived a very simple life with no personal protection and was easily accessible to his subjects. Even after the murder of Omar by a non Muslim slave, it had not been seen necessary to appoint bodyguards for the caliph's protection.[460] On 17 June of that year, the old Caliph was murdered in his house whilst he read the Qur'an, which was spread on his lap.[461]

Ali succeeded to the Caliphate in 656. He was the Prophet's cousin and son in Law (through his marriage to Fatima, the daughter of the Prophet). Ali had become Muslim at the age of ten. In his youth, he had taken part in many famous battles such as Bedr, Uhud, and Khaybar, and had displayed rare courage in the service of Islam.

The sedition amongst Muslims went on under Ali, and he was himself assassinated in 661.

Despite these murders, under the first four caliphs, and also in the succeeding century, up to 750, Islam made considerable territorial advance.

---

[456] H.U. Rahman: *A Chronology;* op cit; p. 30.
[457] P.K. Hitti: *History of the Arabs*; op cit; p. 176.
[458] The Qur'an: *A New Translation* (M.A.S. Abdel- Haleem); op cit; p. xvi.
[459] Ibid.
[460] H.U. Rahman: *A Chronology;* op cit; p. 33.
[461] Ibn Sa'd: *Kitab al-tabaqat al-Kabir*; op cit; vol iii; p. 1; p. 52.

Gibbon's impression of Caliph Omar

`The abstinence and humility of Omar were not inferior to the virtues of Abu Beker: his food consisted of barley bread or dates; his drink was water; he preached in a gown that was torn or tattered in twelve places; and the Persian satrap, who paid his homage to the conqueror, found him asleep among the beggars on the steps of the mosque of Medina. The increase of the revenue enabled Omar to establish a just and perpetual reward for the past and present services of the faithful. Careless of his own emolument, he assigned to Abbas, the uncle of the Prophet, the first and most ample allowance of twenty-five thousand drachms or pieces of silver. Five thousand were allotted to each of the aged warriors, the relics of the field of Bedr; and the last and meanest of the companions of Mohammed was distinguished by the annual reward of three thousand pieces. One thousand was the stipend of the veterans who had fought in the first battles against the Greeks and Persians; and the decreasing pay, as low as fifty pieces of silver, was adapted to the respective merit and seniority of the soldiers of Omar. Under his reign, and that of his predecessor, the conquerors of the East were the trusty servants of God and the people; the mass of the public treasure was consecrated to the expenses of peace and war; a prudent mixture of justice and bounty maintained the discipline of the Muslims, and they united, by a rare felicity, the despatch and execution of despotism with the equal and frugal maxims of a republican government.'[462]

---

[462] E. Gibbon: *The Decline and Fall*; op cit; vol 5; p. 400.

2. Islamic Advance after the Prophet:

Prior to the Arab advance, in the 7th century, the two powers bordering on the Arab land were the Byzantine and Persian empires, wherein a state church was engaged in active persecution and thereby alienating a large section of the subject populations.[463] However, at the time, so weak were the Arabs, Glubb notes, neither the Persian nor the Byzantine empires had constructed any defences to protect their territories from the Arabs. To avoid against raids by these desert tribes, however, both empires maintained subject dynasties of Arab princes.[464] In eastern Syria and Damascus, the princely family of Beni Ghassan held sway, its head enjoying the title of a Roman patrician. On the lower Euphrates, the Arab Lakhmids were subject princes of the Great King. The two Arab dynasties occupied themselves fighting each other. This system of Arab satellite princedoms guarding the desert flanks of both empires, however, broke down by a curious coincidence just a few years before the Muslims began to move.[465]

From the time the move began under the second Caliph Omar (634-644), then proceeded under the Umayyad, until it was halted under the Abbasids, in 750, about a century elapsed during which the Muslims wrested from the two empires Persia itself, Syria, Palestine, Egypt, and North Africa. The Muslims reached the Iberian Peninsula in 711, which they took in 714. Further successes to the east meant that by the advent of the Abbasids in 750, the Islamic land stretched from today's Spain to China. Christianity was forever expelled from Palestine, from Asia Minor, from Egypt, whence issued the great doctrine of Trinitarian orthodoxy; from Cartage, who imposed her belief on Europe.[466] Only Constantinople resisted, even if in 670, a Muslim fleet sailed through the Dardanelles and laid siege to Constantinople itself. In 672, another fleet captured Rhodes and later on twice raided Sicily. In 677, however, the Muslims abandoned their fruitless attacks on the walls of Constantinople.[467]

These Islamic advances in different parts are looked at, but only in a brief outline. Islamic conquests on their own merit deserve a large book.

---

[463] De Lacy O'Leary: *Arabic Thought and its Place in History*, Kegan Paul, London, 1922; p.64

[464] J. Glubb: *A Short History*; op cit; p.23.

[465] Ibid; pp.23-4.

[466] J.W. Draper: *A History*; op cit; p.332

[467] J. Glubb: *A Short History*; op cit; p.72.

a. Campaigns Against Persia: [468]

Khalid Ibn al-Walid's departure to Syria with half or the better Muslim armed forces had left that area unprotected. Al-Muthanna had come to Madinah to ask for help, and Caliph Abu Bekr, on his deathbed (634), had ordered recruitment of a new army to be sent to the eastern front against Persia. His successor, Caliph Omar, fulfilled the order by calling for fresh recruits.[469]

The new Persian emperor Yazdigird appointed Rustum to the command of the front against the Muslims. Rustum began by sending delegates to the cities that had made covenants of peace with the Muslims, urging them to renege on their agreements.

Soon, the two armies faced each other near Hirah. There they fought the Battle of the Bridge, which resulted in the loss of several thousand Muslim lives. The rest of the army withdrew under the command of al-Muthanna. Reinforcements soon arrived from Madinah. A month later, the two armies stood again face to face at al Buwayh (between Kufa and Najaf) on the western side of the Euphrates. The Persians were now in the same position as the Arabs had been in the previous battle. The bridge was seized by al-Muthanna. Denied access and a passage for retreat, the Persian army was destroyed. The Muslims reoccupied al-Anbar and 'Ayn al Tamr, advanced to and took Hirah, and penetrated deeply into the plain between the two rivers. Soon they stood before the gates of al-Madain.

Al-Muthanna died a month after his victory from the wounds he suffered at Buwayh.

Caliph Omar appointed a close companion of the Prophet to assume command of the eastern front. This was Sa'd ibn Abi Waqqas, a veteran of the Battle of Bedr, a man about forty years old. He was sent forth with an army of 5,000 men, with the promise that more would come later. The Muslims, agile and quick of foot because they wore no armour, were perfectly at home in the deserts adjoining the Euphrates. The Persians, on the other hand, were laden with armour. They brought to battle thirty-three elephants to lead the attack. Yazdigird, the Persian king, had ordered Rustum, his general, to waste no time and to attack the Muslim army. Rustum gave the order, and his army crossed to Qadisiyyah, forty-five miles from the Euphrates, in the desert. The battle took place there in the spring of 15H/637. The Muslims won, and pursued their enemies to and

---

[468] Outlined from: I. Rand LL. Al-Faruqi: *The Cultural Atlas*; op cit; p. 215.
[469] Ibid.

beyond Madain (the twin cities of Seleukia and Ctesiphon, on either bank of the Tigris). Although the caliph had instructed Sa'd to stop there and not to advance deeper into Persia, the Muslims moved forward. An engagement at Jalala', in the north, followed by another at Mosul added more defeats on the Persians. The last major battle took place at Nihawand (ancient Ebatana), and the remnant of the Persian army was completely destroyed. Khuzistan, Elam, Pars, and Persepolis fell in 28-29H/649-650. Khurasan, Makran, and Baluchistan (all in modern Central-Southern Asia) were also subdued; Yazdigird was assassinated by one of his own generals at Merw in 651.[470]

Nothing is more indicative of the spirit that moved the Muslims in these battles than the conversation, as reported by the historian al Baladhuri (d.892),[471] between Rustum, the commanding general of the Persians, and al Mughirah ibn Shu'bah, the Muslim delegate. Without ceremony, al Mughirah entered the carpeted hall riding on his horse and seeking to sit at the side of Rustum. When he was prevented from doing so, he remained standing by his horse. Rustum suggested that, since the Arab tribesmen were moved to this war by their poverty and lack of food, the Persians would gladly give them wealth and food in plenty, provided they promised to return home. Al Mughirah answered: "We are here neither for food nor wealth, but to reorient your men from adoration of men to adoration of the one God. Our men are as eager to lay down their lives for this cause as your men are eager to preserve theirs. I call you to Islam. If you accept, you are one of us. If you do not, I offer you the peace of Islam and ask you to pay the jizyah. If you do not accept this, then war.'[472]

---

[470] Ibid.

[471] Al-Baladhuri: *Kitab Futuh al-Buldan;* op cit.

[472] In Ibn al-Athir: *Kitab al-Kamil*; Cairo 1885-1900; vol 2; p. 179.

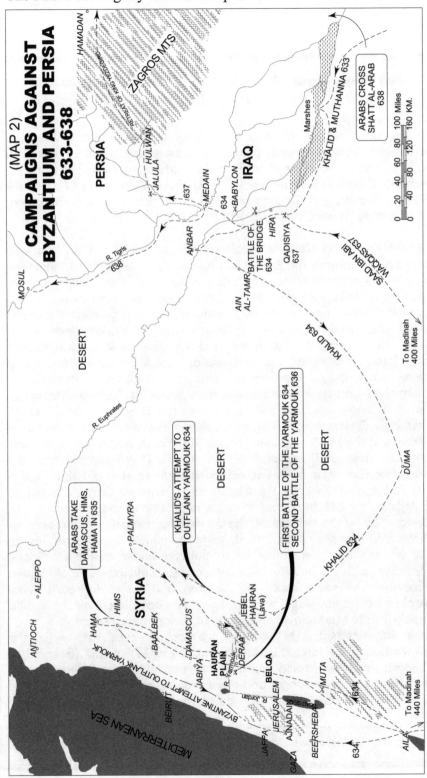

(MAP 2)

CAMPAIGNS AGAINST
BYZANTIUM AND PERSIA
633-638

The Campaigns of Khalid Ibn al-Walid in Syria and Palestine

Khalid Ibn al-Walid was initially a great enemy of Islam. When he embraced Islam, he became one of, if not the greatest, Muslim general in history. This is the story of some of his campaigns compiled from Al-Faruqi's *Cultural Atlas of Islam*,[473] E. Gibbon's *Decline and Fall of the Roman Empire,* and Akram's first class study of the military campaigns of *Khalid Bin Waleed* (Walid):

`It took Khalid Ibn Walid only eighteen days to cross the desert from east to west and surprise the Byzantines by emerging behind their lines. The march took place in March 634, and is regarded as the greatest military feat in the history of the region. Going southwest from Hirah, Khalid arrived at Dawmat and gained it for Islam. He then proceeded through Wadi Sirhan to Quraqir, where he crossed one of the driest deserts in the world, outflanking the Byzantines and the other Muslim columns. Five days later, his army arrived at Suwa or Sab' Abar, where they found some water below the surface near an acacia tree. Replenishing themselves and their animals, the men drove to Tadmur (Palmyra), seized it, and moved southwest to meet the Byzantines from behind their lines. On the way, he fought the Byzantines at Qarvatayn and Marj Rāhit, and the Muslims gained victory. The march continued southward, and the cities of Busra and al Fihi (Greek Pella) surrendered. The retreating Byzantine army was attacked again at Man al Suffar; and in the Autumn of 23H/635 the Muslim army entered Damascus, before Ba'albak, Hims, Hamah, and other towns of Syria were subdued.
Undaunted by this defeat, the Byzantine ruler, Heraclius raised another army, and thought of another strategy to counter the Muslims. Just as the Muslims were invincible when fighting under desert conditions, Heraclius, with his heavily armoured army, could move safely within Palestine. The route south was shorter, and he could reach Wadi 'Arabah before any Muslims could. There, he hoped to cut off the Muslim supply lines to Madinah, and the road of their possible retreat.
Heraclius marched south via Caesarea on the coast, aiming at the elimination of the force the Muslims had left at Bi'r al Sab' (Beersheba) in south Palestine. Khalid heard of this march, and hastened to meet him. Khalid took the longer and more arduous road. He joined with the other Muslim forces under 'Amr ibn al 'As. Without delay, he marched

---

[473] I. Rand LL. Al-Faruqi: *The Cultural Atlas*; op cit; p. 214.

northward to meet Heraclius halfway between Caesarea and Bi'r al Sab'. The two armies fought at Ajnadayn, between the Mediterranean coast and Bayt Jibrin. The Muslims registered a great victory.

After all these encounters, only the Byzantine force at Dir'ah remained. Khalid returned to that front forthwith, rallied all the Muslim forces, and confronted the enemy. With their defeat at Ajnadayn and their loss of the territories to the north, the Byzantine position at Dir'ah became untenable. Heraclius ordered a retreat to a small plain on the banks of the Yarmuk River which was surrounded with high cliffs, a position he regarded as defensible. [474]

Akram gives an excellent depiction of the Battle of Al-Yarmuk, a battle fought over a number of days. Akram's depiction, like all his narrations of Khalid's campaigns, derived from original Islamic sources, and personal visits to these battle-fields, is enriched with tactical sketches and maps. Nothing can do justice to such description, except Akram's own text, which is, too long, though, to be reproduced here. From Akram, however, is borrowed an account of the meeting that took place between the Byzantine general, George, and Khalid Ibn al-Walid just before the battle:

`Then a Roman general by the name of George emerged from the Roman centre and rode towards the Muslims. Halting a short distance from the Muslim centre, he raised his voice and asked for Khalid. From the Muslim side Khalid rode out, delighted at the thought that the battle would begin with himself fighting a duel. He would set the pace for the rest of the battle.

As Khalid drew nearer, the Roman general made no move to draw his sword, but continued to look intently at Khalid. The Muslim advanced until the necks of the horses crossed, and still George did not draw his sword. Then he spoke, in Arabic:

`O Khalid, tell me the truth and do not deceive me, for the free do not lie and the noble do not deceive. Is it true that Allah sent a sword from heaven to your Prophet?... and that he gave it to you?.... and that never have you drawn it but your enemies have been defeated?'

`No,' replied Khalid.

`Then why are you known as the sword of Allah?'

Here Khalid told George the story of how he received the title of Sword of Allah from the Holy Prophet. George pondered this a while, then with

---

[474] Ibid.

a pensive look in his eyes, asked: `Tell me, to what do you call me?'
`to bear witness,' Khalid replied `that there is no god but Allah and that Mohammed is his slave and Messenger, and to believe in what he has brought from Allah.'
`If I do not agree?'
`Then the jizya (Poll Tax) and you shall be under our protection.'
`If I do not agree?'
`Then the sword!'
George considered the words of Khalid for a few moments, then asked: `What is the position of one who enters your faith today?'
`In our faith there is only one position: All are equal!'
`Then I accept your faith.'[475]
To the astonishment of the two armies, which knew nothing of what had passed between the two generals, Khalid turned his horse and Muslim and Roman rode slowly to the Muslim army. On arrival at the Muslim centre George repeated after Khalid: `there is no god but Allah; Mohammed is the Apostle of Allah.'
(A few hours later, the newly converted George would fight heroically for the faith which he had just embraced and would die in battle. On the auspicious note of this conversation began the battle of Yarmuk.'[476]

Gibbon narrates the battle of al-Yarmuk:
`It was incumbent on the Muslims to exert the full powers of their valour and enthusiasm against the forces of the emperor, who was taught, by repeated losses, that the rovers of the desert had undertaken, and would speedily achieve, a regular and permanent conquest. From the provinces of Europe and Asia, fourscore thousand soldiers were transported by sea and land to Antioch and Caesarea: the light troops of the army consisted of sixty thousand Christian Arabs of the tribe of Ghassan. Under the banner of Jabalah, the last of their princes, they marched in the van; and it was a maxim of the Greeks, that for the purpose of cutting diamond, a diamond was the most effectual.
A report of these mighty preparations was conveyed to the `Saracens' (Muslims) in their camp of Emesa, and the chiefs, though resolved to fight, assembled a council: the faith of Abu Obeidah would have expected on the same spot the glory of martyrdom; the wisdom of Khalid advised an honourable retreat to Palestine and Arabia, where they might await the reinforcements of their friends, and the attack of the unbelievers. A speedy messenger soon returned from Madinah, with the blessings of Omar and Ali, and a reinforcement of eight thousand Muslims. In their way they

---

[475] From al-Tabari: *Tarikh al-Umum wal Muluk*; Cairo; 1939; vol 2; p. 595.
[476] A. I. Akram: *Khalid Bin Waleed*; op cit; pp. 387-8.

overturned a detachment of Greeks, and when they joined at Yarmuk the camp of their brethren, they found the pleasing intelligence, that Khalid had already defeated and scattered the Christian Arabs of the tribe of Ghassan.

Khalid assumed his station in the front, his colleague, Abu Obeidah, was posted in the rear, that the disorder of the fugitive might be checked by his venerable aspect. The last line was occupied by the sister of Derar, with the Arabian women who had enlisted in this holy war, who were accustomed to wield the bow and the lance. The exhortation of the generals was brief and forcible: "Paradise is before you, the devil and hell-fire in your rear." Yet such was the weight of the Roman cavalry, that the right wing of the Muslims was broken and separated from the main body. Thrice did they retreat in disorder, and thrice were they driven back to the charge. In the intervals of action, Abu Obeidah visited the tents of his brethren, prolonged their repose by repeating at once the prayers of two different hours, bound up their wounds with his own hands, and administered the comfortable reflection that the infidels partook of their sufferings without partaking of their reward. Four thousand and thirty of the Muslims were buried in the field of battle; and the skill of the Armenian archers enabled seven hundred to boast that they had lost an eye in that meritorious service. The veterans of the Syrian war acknowledged that it was the hardest and most doubtful of the days which they had seen. But it was likewise the most decisive: many thousands fell by the swords of the Muslims; many, by mistaking the ford, were drowned in the waters of the Yarmuk. Christian writers confess and bewail the bloody punishment of their sins.'[477]

A few days after news of the Muslim victory had reached him, Abu Bekr died. He had been caliph for a little more than two years. Omar Ibn al Khattab succeeded him as Caliph. The new ruler appointed Abu 'Ubaydah ibn al Jarrah governor of Syria, and proceeded in person to inspect the new territories, the garrisons, and their generals, and to define their status rights, and obligations. He arrived at al Jabiyah, one of the camps of the Muslim army north of the Yarmuk battlefield. Jerusalem, which was until then under siege, offered to open its gates. Ready to make peace with the Muslims, the bishop of Jerusalem requested Omar to take charge of the city in person. Omar acquiesced to his request, journeyed to Jerusalem, and took over its keys in the year 25H/637. It was on this occasion that he executed the covenant known as the Covenant of Omar, which offers Christians freedom of practice of faith and other rights under Muslim rule.[478]

---

[477] E. Gibbon: *The Decline and Fall*; op cit; vol 5; pp. 432-4.
[478] I. Rand LL. Al-Faruqi: *The Cultural Atlas*; op cit; p. 214-5.

b. Egypt:[479]

According to an old tradition, when Omar came to accept the surrender of Jerusalem, the Muslim general, 'Amr ibn al 'As, asked the caliph's permission to advance into Egypt. The Caliph seems to have hesitated and the matter remained open. In the autumn of 639, however, 'Amr ibn al 'As, who had been at Caesarea, marched southwards down the coast of Palestine with only three thousand and six hundred men.[480]

He had reached Rafah, on the border between Palestine and Sinai, when he received a letter sent post-haste by the Caliph from Madinah. Before opening the despatch, 'Amr, crossing the Palestine-Egypt border, marched on to Al-Arish, where he read the Caliph's letter:

"If, when you receive this letter, you are still in Palestine," Omar had written, "you should abandon the operation. If, however, you have already crossed into Egypt, you may proceed."[481]

'Amr knew what was in the letter, and did not open it until he got into Egypt, and then innocently enquired from those standing near, whether he was in Palestine or Egypt. When they replied that they were in Egypt, he ordered the continuation of the march. This event occurred on 12th December, 639.[482]

The first fortified place which the Muslims struck was al-Farama (Pelusium), the key to eastern Egypt, in the middle of January 640; followed by Bilbeys, north east of Cairo, before reaching the strong castle of Babylon, at the southern tip of the Delta. There, a considerable Byzantine force had been concentrated; the Governor of Egypt, the Patriarch Cyrus, was also in the fortress.[483] On 6th June, 640, reinforcements from Madinah arrived at Heliopolis (five miles north east of the modern city of Cairo), some six miles north-east of Babylon, from which it was separated by a sandy plain.[484] The Muslim army still numbered about a third of the total Byzantine army, yet in July 640, a huge battle took place midway between the two camps. The Byzantine army was utterly routed, and its commander was obliged to take refuge behind

---

[479] See The History and Conquest of Egypt, North Africa and Spain, known as the *Futuh Misr of Ibn Abd al-Hakam;* Edited from the manuscripts in London, Paris, and Leyden by C. C. Torrey; New Haven; Yale University Press; London; Milford.

[480] J. Glubb: *A Short History;* op cit; p. 57.

[481] Ibn Abd al-Hakam: *Futuh Misr;* op cit; pp. 56-7.

[482] P.K. Hitti: *History of the Arabs*; op cit; p. 160.
J. Glubb: *A Short History;* op cit; p. 57.

[483] Ibn Abd al-Hakam: *Futuh Misr*; op cit; pp. 53; 58; A.J. Butler: *The Arab Conquest of Egypt;* Oxford; 1902; pp. 245-7.

[484] J. Glubb: *A Short History*; op cit; p. 57.

the walls of the fortress.[485] Cyrus, the archbishop of Alexandria and representative of the emperor who came to defend Babylon, returned to Alexandria after the fall of Babylon with the following description of the Muslims:

`We have witnessed a people to each and every one of whom death is preferable to life, and humility to prominence, and to none of whom this world has the least attraction. They sit not except on the ground, and eat naught but on their knees. Their leader (emir) is like unto one of them: the low cannot be distinguished from the high, nor the master from the slave. And when the time of prayer comes none of them absents himself, all wash their extremities and humbly observe their prayer.'[486]

Asking for a delegation to meet him at al-Rawdah to negotiate peace, Cyrus was shocked to receive it headed by a black person, Ubadah Ibn al-Samit.[487] To save Alexandria from defeat, the Patriarch Cyrus-a strange character who became easily despondent in difficult circumstances and as cruel when he felt secure-quickly entered into peace negotiations.[488] Cyrus agreed to pay tribute to Ibn al 'As, to keep the peace, and to maintain a Muslim garrison in the city.[489] After a few brief negotiations, he signed an agreement for surrender, stipulating that the Christians would pay tribute to the conquerors, but be free to practice their own religion. A clause was added making the agreement subject to ratification by the Emperor Heraclius.[490] In Constantinople, however, the emperor categorically refused to ratify the surrender.

War resumed. After a siege of six months, the city of Babylon was captured by the Muslims, on April 6, 641, the cry of *Allahu Akbar* echoing victoriously in the halls of the fortress.[491]

After reducing the eastern borders of the Delta, 'Amr Ibn al-'As found himself in front of the capital of Egypt, Alexandria. The city was guarded by seemingly impregnable walls and fortresses, a strong garrison of 50,000, and the Byzantine navy; the Muslim besiegers, on the other hand, were much inferior in number and equipment, and had not a single ship, no siege machines, and no immediate sources of supply for their troops.[492] The Muslims were first repulsed, but they remained resilient in their

---

[485] P. K. Hitti: *History*; op cit; p. 160; J. Glubb: *A Short History*; op cit; p. 57.
[486] The report is from Ibn Abd al-Hakam: *Futuh Misr*; op cit; p. 65.
[487] P. K. Hitti: *History;* op cit; p. 163.
[488] H.U. Rahman: *A Chronology;* op cit; p. 29.
[489] I. Rand LL. Al-Faruqi: *The Cultural Atlas*; op cit; p. 216.
[490] J. Glubb: *A Short History;* op cit; p. 57.
[491] Al-Baladhuri: *Kitab Futuh al-Buldan;* op cit; p. 213.
[492] P. K. Hitti: *History*; op cit; p. 164.

enterprise. Patriarch Cyrus, who had made earlier agreements with the Muslims and was dismissed because of that, was restored by the new Byzantine Emperor, Constans. On 8th November 641 Cyrus signed an agreement surrendering the whole of Egypt to the Muslims. The terms of the new treaty were severe for the Byzantines, who were forced to leave this rich province, but the local Christians and the Jews received from the Muslims the same favourable treatment which had previously been accorded to the 'People of the Book' in Syria, Palestine and Iraq.[493] The inhabitants would be allowed the free practice of their religion. The Byzantine army that has been allowed a year's grace to evacuate the country did so, and in September 642, the evacuation was complete.[494] However, toward the end of 645, the Alexandrians appealed to the Emperor Constans, who dispatched some 300 ships under Manuel, an Armenian, to reclaim the city.[495] The Muslim garrison of 1000 men was slaughtered, and Alexandria was once more in Byzantine hands, and a base for attack on Muslim Egypt.[496] 'Amr Ibn al-'As returned, and met the Byzantines at Nikiu, inflicting on them a terrible defeat, and early in 646, the second capture of Alexandria took place.[497]

The Muslim taking of Egypt was the occasion of the 13th century Christian historian, Bar Hebraeus (Abu Al-Faraj Ibn al-Ibri), to make a false charge, repeated blindly by a number of Muslim and Western historians after him. Bar Hebraeus claimed that Caliph Omar had ordered the destruction of Alexandria's famous Ptolemaic library.[498] In fact, that library was first burned in 48 B.C.E. by Julius Caesar and then destroyed completely in 389 C.E. by Christian zealots.[499] Rather than destroying, the Muslims reorganised and improved the country. 'Amr reopened the ancient canal linking the Nile to the Red Sea, and completed many engineering works.[500] The garrison of Babylon had already surrendered two months after the death of Heraclius, and six months later 'Amr started building a permanent military camp, named al-Fustat, near this fortress; a military colony, which later grew into a thriving metropolis and continued to be the Muslim capital of Egypt until 973.[501]

---

[493] H.U. Rahman: *A Chronology;* op cit; p. 29.

[494] J. Glubb: *A Short History*; op cit; p. 59.

[495] Al-Baladhuri: *Kitab Futuh al-Buldan;* op cit; p. 221.

[496] P. K. Hitti: *History*; op cit; p. 166.

[497] Ibid.

[498] Abu al-Faraj Ibn al-Ibri: *Tarikh Mukhtasar al-Duwal;* ed. A. Salibani; Beirut; 1890; pp. 175-6.

[499] E. Gibbon: *The Decline and Fall*; op cit; vol 5; pp 474-5.

[500] P. K. Hitti: *History*; op cit; p. 165.

[501] H.U. Rahman: *A Chronology;* op cit; p. 29.

In 28 H/649, under the caliphate of Uthman, the Muslims built a fleet, and from Alexandria and other ports of the eastern Mediterranean shore, they launched an attack upon Cyprus and wrenched it from Byzantium. In 34H/655 the maritime battle of Dhu al Sawari (that of the masts), in which 500 Greek ships were destroyed, put an end to Greek hegemony in the eastern Mediterranean.[502] The fall of Alexandria opened the way for the Muslims to march westward toward Libya. Barqah (Pentapolis) was conquered by 'Amr ibn al 'As with little or no resistance. The people of Tripoli offered tribute the same year; and 'Amr's successor, 'Abdullah ibn Sad ibn Abu Sarh, moved westward into Ifriqyah (Africa) and forced Carthage to pay tribute as well.[503]

c. North Africa:

The term North Africa is a general one, and it is the equivalent to the term al-Maghrib used by Arab historians and geographers to describe the entire area extending from the western boundaries of Egypt to the Atlantic Ocean.[504] The modern historian, Taha, offers an excellent introductory chapter on the political geography of the region and also Spain, prior to the Muslim arrival.[505]

When 'Amr was once more made governor of Egypt by the first Umayyad ruler, Mua'wiya, he sent his nephew, Uqba ibn Nafi', to conquer North Africa.[506] Uqba reached modern Tunisia, fifteen hundred miles from his base in Egypt. Here, realizing that the country could not be controlled without a local capital, in 670 he established a military base at Al-Qayrawan (modern Tunisia), as the early Muslims had done at Kufa and Basra.[507] When Uqba Ibn Nafi', heading the Muslim army in the Maghrib reached the valley of al-Qayrawan, he spent the night there with his

---

[502] Ibn Abd al-Hakam: *Futuh;* op cit; pp. 189-1.
[503] Al-Baladhuri: *Kitab Futuh al-Buldan;* op cit; pp. 237-8 (Arabic text); I. Rand LL. Al-Faruqi: *The Cultural Atlas;* op cit; p. 216.
[504] A.D. Taha: *The Muslim Conquest and Settlement of North Africa and Spain;* Routledge; London; 1989; p. 19.
[505] Ibid; pp. 19 ff.
[506] On the Muslim entry into North Africa, See Ibn al-Idhari: *Al-Bayan al-Maghrib fi Akhbar al-Maghrib;* ed R. Dozy; Leyden; 1848.
[507] J. Glubb: *A Short History;* op cit; pp. 72-3.

companions. The following morning, he stopped at the entrance of the barren valley, and tradition has it that he hailed loudly:

'Dwellers of the valley, leave, for we are stopping here!' He gave the order three times. Soon, serpents, scorpions, and many other creatures began to crawl away. The Muslim warriors stood bewildered, gazing at the exodus taking place from the morning until they were made uncomfortable by the intense heat. Then, seeing that all creatures had deserted the place, they installed themselves in the valley. Forty years after this day, it was said, the people of Ifriqya could not find a serpent or a scorpion even when they were offered a thousand dinar for one.'[508]

This new military base like Basra, Kufa, and Fustat, was later to develop into a famous city with the Great Mosque. It was in 670, that Uqba Ibn Nafi' laid the first stone for the mosque, then the palace of government, and then houses for his soldiers as well as a wall 2750 yards long.[509] Al-Qayrawan became the capital of Muslim North Africa and the base for further expansion into North Africa later, during the Umayyad period.

The struggle in North Africa was three-cornered. The Byzantines, with their provincial capital in Carthage, held a number of coastal fortresses extending as far west as Tangier. The interior of the country was held by the Berbers. Now the Arabs had arrived on the scene.[510] Uqba was a man of remarkable courage, enterprise and simple loyalty. He failed to exploit the political possibilities of the situation by playing off the Berbers against the Byzantines, instead, with early Muslim enthusiasm, he attacked both simultaneously.[511] In 682, he carried out an extraordinary military foray. From the newly established base at Al-Qayrawan, he marched twelve hundred miles to the west until he reached the River Sus in modern Morocco. Here tradition depicts him as riding his horse into the Atlantic Ocean and declaiming, sword in hand: "God is most great! If my course were not stopped by this sea, I would still ride on to the unknown kingdoms of the west, preaching the unity of God, and putting to the sword the rebellious nations who worship any other god but Him."[512]

Riding carelessly back to the east, elated by this splendid march, he was ambushed at Tahudha in the Aures mountains (Algeria) by the Berbers (in 683); he and his men fighting on until all were killed.[513] As soon as his

---

[508] Ibn abd al-Hakem in J. Fontaine and P. Gresser: *Le Guide de la Tunisie*; Editions La Manufacture; Besancon; 1992; p. 306.
[509] G. Iver: Kairawan; *Encyclopaedia of Islam*; first series vol 4; pp. 646-9; p. 647.
[510] J. Glubb: *A Short History*; op cit; p. 73.
[511] Ibid.
[512] Ibid.
[513] A.D. Taha: *The Muslim Conquest;* op cit; p. 66.

death was known, the Berbers rose in revolt, and the Muslim forces, which had remained in Al-Qayrawan, reduced in numbers, retreated from al-Qayrawan.[514]

In 695, the Arabs, under the command of Hassan ibn Numan, and in alliance with Berber tribesmen, one of them Hilal b. Tharwan al-Luwaiti, general of the Muslim armies, returned to North Africa.[515] Al-Qayrawan fell without any opposition. Hassan then attacked Carthage, the main Byzantine stronghold on the coast and captured it. With the fall of the capital, the remnant of the Roman army abandoned their fortresses and left the country. This was the final expulsion of the Byzantines from their African Stronghold.[516] In 698, in order to repel the Byzantine danger and sudden attack on the coast, Hassan founded the new town of Tunis, near Carthage, which was to become the base for the Muslim fleet in North Africa.[517]

With the Romans driven out, the Muslims were then confronted with the Berber tribe of the Jarawa Jews, who lived in the eastern Aures, led by a queen, to whom the Arabs had given the name al-Kahina.[518] At first, the Kahina had considerable success, defeating the Arabs on the River Nini, but acting on the belief that the Arabs were only after booty, she wrought havoc to the Tunisian countryside so that the Arabs would have no incentive to return.[519] A decisive battle was fought near Gabes (Modern Tunisia), where she was defeated, then pursued by Arab warriors, she was eventually killed in the Aures Mountains in the spot called Bir al-Kahina (Al-Kahina's Well).[520]

Hassan Ibn Numan offered the Berbers favourable peace terms, and encouraged the spread of Islam amongst them; the Berbers, soon, in large numbers, converting to the new faith, joined its army.[521] It was one such Berber, Tariq Ibn Ziyad, who was to push the Muslim presence into Spain.

---

[514] Ibid.
[515] Ibid; p. 69.
[516] Ibid.
[517] Ibid; p. 71.
[518] Ibn al-Idhari: *Al-Bayan al-Maghrib* ; op cit; vol 1; pp. 20-4;
J.M. Abun Nasr: *A History of the Maghrib;* Cambridge University Press; 1971; p. 70.
[519] J.M. Abun Nasr: *A History of the Maghrib;* p. 70.
[520] Ibid.
[521] A.D. Taha: *The Muslim Conquest;* op cit; p. 71.

d. Spain:

The Muslims crossed into Spain in the year 711. In 531, a hundred and seventy years earlier, the Goths had conquered Spain, where they had become an idle aristocracy, living in luxury and pleasure.[522] Scott writes that they held banquets, defiled by drunken orgies, and not infrequently the scenes of violence and even homicide, were celebrated.[523] Without literature, save a fragmentary translation of the Bible, 'the most pitiless of conquerors, destruction was with them a passion, and war an amusement.'[524] The Muslim armies, which defeated them, were led by Tariq who crossed the sea into the peninsula in 711.[525]

In 92H/711, Tariq ibn Ziyad landed near the rock at the southern end of the Iberian Peninsula. The rock has since that time been known as "Jabal Tariq" (the mountain of Tariq)-or in its later corrupted form, Gibraltar. The Muslim forces moved, each horseman provided with a copper pot, a leather bag for provisions, and a bottle for water; the infantry carrying nothing but their arms.[526] The camp equipage was loaded on trains of pack-mules; military and political considerations requiring and enforcing the observance of the strictest discipline.[527] The Muslim and Christian armies met on the banks of the Guadalete. Roderick Goth's army comprised about 120,000 men; Tariq's numbering somewhere between 12 and 17,000 men.[528] Before the battle, Tariq is said to have addressed the Muslims with the following words:

'Where can you fly? The enemy is in your front, the sea at your back. By Allah! There is no salvation for you but in your courage and perseverance. Consider your situation: here you are on this island like so many orphans cast upon the world; you will soon be met by a powerful enemy surrounding you on all sides like the infuriated billows of a tempestuous sea, and sending against you his countless warriors, drowned in steel, and

---

[522] J. Glubb: *A Short History*; op cit; p. 80.
[523] S.P. Scott: *History*; op cit; Vol 1; p.166.
[524] Ibid.
[525] For good early Islamic sources on the Muslim entry in Spain, see Anonymous: *Akhbar Majmu'a,* ed. Lafuente y Alcantara, Madrid, 1867;
Ibn al-Qutiyya: *Tarikh Iftitah al-Andalus,* ed. Madrid, 1868, trans. J. Ribera, Madrid, 1926.
Al-Dabbi: *Bughyayt al-Multamis fi Tarikh Rijal al-Andalus;* ed Francisco Codera and J. Ribera; Madrid; 1884-5; p. 303.
[526] S.P. Scott: *History*; op cit; Vol 1; p.249.
[527] Ibid.
[528] A. Thomson and M. A. Rahim: *Islam in Andalus*; Ta Ha Publishers Ltd; London; 1996; p.14.

provided with every store and description of arms. What can you oppose to them? You have no other weapons than your swords, no provisions but those you may snatch from the hands of your enemies, you must therefore attack them immediately, or otherwise your wants will increase, the winds of victory may no longer blow in your favour, and perhaps the fear that lurks in the hearts of your enemies may be changed into indomitable courage. Banish all fear from your hearts; trust that victory shall be ours, and that the unbelieving king will not be able to withstand the shock of our arms.'[529]

The Muslims won a crushing victory. This battle, Scott insists, justly ranked with the great and decisive victories in history, considering the relative number of the combatants, the duration of the action, and the importance of its results.[530]

Following this victory, Tariq marched on, conquering one place after the other either after a brief siege or through direct assault.[531] Tariq marched to Toledo, the capital, following the old Roman road, called Anibal, and found the city abandoned. There he left some troops to defend the city with the local Jewish assistance, and he continued his campaign pursuing the enemy.[532] Tariq dispatched troops to Malaga, Elvira, Murcia and Cordoba, the latter city taken on behalf of the Muslims by the Byzantine convert to Islam, Mughith al-Rumi.[533]

The following year, Musa ibn Nusayr, the commanding Muslim general, arrived on the scene with 10,000 fresh troops. His objectives were the fortified towns which Tariq had avoided on his march. Madina, Sidonia and Carmona, Seville, and Merida all fell to the Muslims before the end of the year. Muslim troops continued their advance into Aragon, Leon, the Asturias, and Galicia. The conquest of Saragosa sealed the fate of Spain, which the Muslims renamed al Andalus.[534]

The Muslim conquerors behaved with their usual leniency. The churches were divided between Muslims and Christians. Crown lands, or those of landowners who had fled the country, were confiscated and Christians and Jews paid a poll-tax.[535] The conquest was indeed not an unmitigated

---

[529] Al-Maqqari: *Nafh Al-Tib;* tr by P.De Gayangos: *The History of the Mohammedan Dynasties in Spain*; 2 vols; The Oriental Translation Fund; London, 1840-3; vol 1; p. 273.
[530] S.P. Scott: *History*; op cit; Vol 1; p.232.
[531] Al-Maqqari: *Nafh Al-Tib;* op cit; vol 1; Appendix, xiviii.
[532] A.D. Taha: *The Muslim Conquest;* op cit; p. 93.
[533] Ibid; pp. 91-2.
[534] I. Rand LL. Al-Faruqi: *The Cultural Atlas*; op cit; p. 217.
[535] J. Glubb: *A Short History*; op cit; pp. 80-1.

disaster for the people. The Muslims were more tolerant than the Goths. Serfs and slaves, by professing Islam, could obtain their freedom. The Jews, who had been persecuted by the Goths, were under the Muslims free to practice their religion.[536]

The pacification of Spain was quickly completed, except for a remnant of Christians in the mountains of Galicia (North of Spain). The failure to completely subdue Galicia was to cost the Muslims dear, for the future Christian attacks on Muslim Spain were to begin from that same territory. The conquest of Galicia was in fact interrupted by the vicissitudes of politics. In September 714, both Musa Ibn Nusayr and Tariq ibn Ziyad, while still campaigning hard in the mountainous region of Galicia in Spain, received orders from caliph al-Walid in distant Damascus to report to him about the conquest. They reluctantly turned their backs on Narbonne and Europe.[537] Musa, leaving his second son, Abdul Aziz, in charge of the newly acquired territory, made a long overland journey via Africa, Egypt and Palestine, with Tariq, a long convoy of Berber chiefs, Gothic princes laden with crown jewellery, prisoners-of-war and slaves carrying enormous booty, including the famous table, gifts of gold, silver and pearls, and many other Spanish treasures.[538] When Musa, at the head of this triumphal procession, reached Syria in February 715, Caliph al-Walid was lying on his death bed. Soon al-Walid's harsh and vengeful brother Suleyman (r 715-7) took over the Caliphate and proved himself to be but a poor shadow of his father and brother. Instead of applauding the great achievements, he accorded humiliating treatment to the heroes whom he regarded as too powerful and potentially dangerous.[539] Musa's and Tariq's aim was, indeed, to march through southern France, and then march across southern Europe, and link up with the Muslims in the East, hence conquering the whole of Western Christendom.[540] The two generals were dismissed in disgrace, and they spent the rest of their days in destitution and obscurity; Musa, an old and broken man, ending his days in poverty in a small oasis near Madinah.[541] Musa about whom al-Hijazi says:

`He always surrounded his person with holy men and virtuous friends, whom Allah the Almighty selected to be the instruments of His glory and power, as well as the means of establishing the fame of Musa, a fame that

---

[536] Ibid.

[537] A. Thomson and M.A. Rahim: *Islam in Andalus*; op cit; p. 25.

[538] A.D. Taha: *The Muslim Conquest;* op cit; p. 100.

[539] See Al-Maqqari: *Nafh Al-Tib;* op cit; vol 1; p.293.

[540] A. Thomson and M.A. Rahim: *Islam in Andalus*; op cit; p. 24.

[541] J. Glubb: *A Short History;* op cit; p. 81.

shall last throughout day and night, and which the course of ages shall not impair; although it was tarnished in his days by becoming the victim of that cruel enemy against whom a noble minded man had no power, I mean envy and hatred, those two vices so common in people of narrow minds.'[542]

The Muslims did not stop in Spain but continued their march into France until they reached Poitiers/Tours, where the battle with Charles Martel stopped their northward thrust in 113H (October, 732.)[543] This battle, as Hitti correctly points out, was embellished by Western authors, turning it into one of the greatest victories in history, whilst in truth, the Muslim army, already slimmed in numbers and weakened by internal divisions, lifted its camps, and left south, to return stronger later on.[544] Indeed, Avignon fell into Muslim hands two years later in 734; Lyons, Narbonne, and most of the area of the Provence down to the Mediterranean, two years thereafter.[545] In 792 two armies were raised by order of the Umayyad Caliph of Spain, Hisham 1 (788-796) to carry the flag of Islam deeper into the northwest and northeast corners of the Iberian Peninsula; the latter column met with greater success than the former.[546]

e. The Lands to the East (7th and 8th Centuries):

During the rule of Caliph Uthman, in the years 650-2, Abd Allah Ibn Amir, governor of Basra, launched a series of successful attacks into the eastern provinces of Persia. He marched through Khurasan, overrunning Herat, Merw, and Balkh. A column from his army crossed the Hindu Kush, and captured Kabul while still another concentrated on the southern region capturing Makran. Thus the eastern boundaries of the Muslim empire were pushed as far as the River Oxus (Modern Amu Darya), reached the Indian border, which paved the way for future eastward conquests.[547]

---

[542]Al-Maqqari: *Nafh Al-Tib;* op cit; vol 1; p. 298.
[543] Al-Dabbi: *Bughyayt al-Multamis fi Tarikh Rijal al-Andalus*; op cit; p. 333.
[544] P.K. Hitti: *History;* op cit; pp. 500-1.
[545] Ibid; p. 501.
[546] I. Rand LL. Al-Faruqi: *The Cultural Atlas*; op cit; p. 217.
[547] H.U. Rahman: *A Chronology;* op cit; pp. 33-4.

Zayyad Ibn Sumya was the son of a vagrant slave girl of Makkah. Due to his great abilities he was appointed by Caliph Ali as governor of southern Persia, and after the murder of Caliph Ali, he was appointed governor of Kufa and Basra. It was he who crossed the Oxus in 671 and took Bukhara.[548]

Subsequent developments were to take place under the leadership of al Hajjaj ibn Yusuf al Thaqafi (d.95H/714), who laid down the pen, and distinguished himself in pacifying the Hijaz. He was appointed governor of the eastern provinces in 74/694 in order to pacify them.[549] He did it with an arm of steel, and mobilized the region to undertake further expansion of Islam in Asia.[550] From his newly built capital city called Wasit (medial), which he built in 702, halfway between Kufa and Basra,[551] he controlled the whole of the eastern land until his death in June, 714.[552]

During his military campaigns, Al Hajjaj picked three outstanding generals and sent them in different directions with three well-equipped armies.

'Abdul Rahman ibn al Ash'ath went to Kabul and subdued its king, Zunbil, who had refused to pay the customary tribute, in 80/700.[553]

Al-Hajjaj had Qutayba ibn Muslim appointed governor of Khurasan in 704 with his base at Merw, and following his appointment, Qutayba, an outstanding soldier, made considerable progress in the unknown territory of Central Asia.[554] Qutayba launched a series of successful campaigns and established a permanent Muslim foothold in 'the land beyond the river (Oxus)' (modern Amu Darya); and conquered, or re-conquered, places such as Balkh in 85H/705; Bukhara, Samarqand, and Khwarizm (modern Khiva) in the short period of two years (91-93H/710-712); Farghanah was conquered a year later, and Kashgar (in Chinese Turkestan) in 96/715.[555] In Samarqand, Qutayba fell upon a number of idols, whose devotees expected instant destruction to overtake him who dared outrage them. Undeterred, the Muslim general set the images on fire with his own hands, an act which resulted in a number of conversions to Islam.[556] From

---

[548] J. Glubb: *A Short History*; op cit; pp. 71-2.

[549] P.K. Hitti: *History of the Arabs*; op cit; p. 207.

[550] On Al-Hajjaj, see Ibn al-Athir: *Kitab al-kamil*; ed K.J. Tornberg; 12 vols; Leiden; 1851-72. vol iv.

[551] Yaqut al-Hamawi: *Mu'Ajam al-Buldan*; Wustenfeld Edition; in six volumes; Leipzig; 1866. vol iv; pp. 881-2.

[552] P. K. Hitti: *History;* op cit; p. 208.

[553] Ibid; pp. 208-9.

[554] Al-Baladhuri: *Kitab Futuh al-Buldan;* op cit; p.423.

[555] I. Rand LL. Al-Faruqi: *The Cultural Atlas;* op cit; p. 216.

[556] Al-Baladhuri: *Kitab Futuh al-Buldan;* op cit; p.421.

Kashgar a delegation was sent to the Emperor of China to demand his submission, a suggestion apparently received with philosophic good humour by 'The Son of Heaven.'[557] It was then that the Muslims learned from the Chinese the secret of the manufacture of paper, which they introduced into the Islamic land and subsequently passed on to Europe.[558] While Qutayba ibn Muslim was advancing into Central Asia, Muhammad ibn Qasim, a son in law of Hajjaj, with six thousand horsemen was advancing in what is today Pakistan.[559] He advanced through southern Persia, subdued Makran, pushed on through what is now termed Baluchistan, and in 711-12, reduced Sind, the lower valley and delta of the Indus.[560] He marched against Daybul (modern Karachi) which fell after a siege, where Muslims used heavy artillery pieces operated by 500 men.[561] After Daybul, in the hot summer of 712, the Arab armies crossed the river and faced the armies of Dahar, the ruler of Sind; the two armies engaging in a fierce battle won by the Muslims. Dahar lost his life in the battlefield, the Hindu army was crushed, and fled, and Ibn Qasim captured Brahmanabad.[562] From Lower Sind, the Muslim general marched on Upper Sind, towards Punjab. Multan, the leading city was well fortified, but was taken in 713, thus making Ibn Qasim the master of the whole of Sind and part of Punjab.[563]

This was the climax of Umayyad expansion in the east. The achievement of spreading Islam in the area remained permanent. An increasing number of conversions to Islam followed, particularly under Caliph Omar II Ibn Abd Al-Aziz (r. 717-20), when a fairer system of taxation for non-Arab Muslims was introduced, and a large number of these new converts joined the Arab army in Khurasan. Bukhara and Samarqand were destined to become great centres of Islamic intellectual and cultural life, and over the centuries to come, Islam spread even into China from this firm base.[564]

This conquest of the easternmost extremity of the Muslim realm was not, however, followed up on any large scale by Muslims for another three centuries, that is until the rule of Sultan Mahmud of Ghazna (r. 998-1030) (see chapter five). The Abbasids (who came to power in 750) halted the

---

[557] J. Glubb: *A Short History;* op cit; p. 81.
[558] Ibid.
[559] S.M. Ikram: *Muslim Civilisation in India;* op cit; p. 7.
[560] P.K. Hitti: *History;* op cit; p. 210.
[561] S.M. Ikram: *Muslim Civilisation in India;* op cit; p. 7.
[562] Ibid.
[563] Ibid; p. 8.
[564] H.U. Rahman: *A Chronology;* op cit; p. 67.

expansion of Islam. The vagaries of internal Islamic politics also got in the way. Moreover some caliphs were very weak and inimical to Islam. One of them, the Umayyad ruler, Suleyman (ruled 715-717), was amongst the worst. Debauched and conspicuous in his manners and behaviour, he dismissed the great Muslim generals: Musa Ibn Nusayr and Tariq Ibn Zyad, the conquerors of Spain, and he had Muslim generals slain on his orders, including Mohammed Ibn Qasim, the conqueror of Sind, and Qutayba, the conqueror of Central Asia. He forced Ibn Qasim to resign, accused him of many offences, and then had him executed after having inflicted on him terrible torture.[565]

---

[565] S.M. Ikram: *Muslim Civilisation in India;* op cit; p. 8.

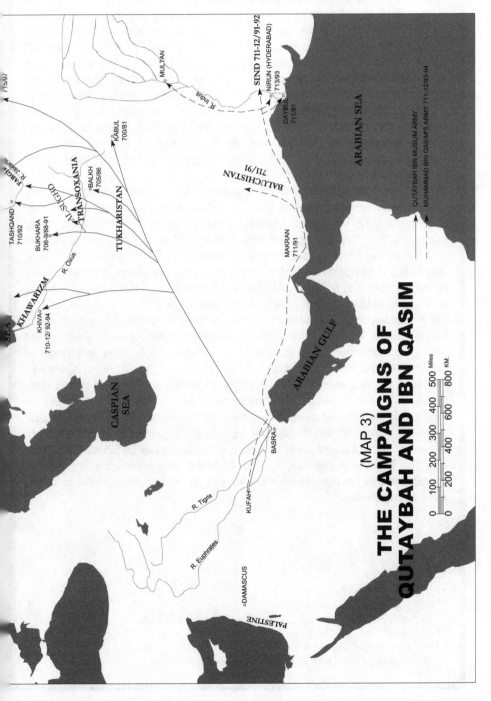

(MAP 3)
THE CAMPAIGNS OF
QUTAYBAH AND IBN QASIM

The Umayyads

In 661, following the assassination of Caliph Ali, Mu'awiya was proclaimed caliph. This is the beginning of the Umayyad dynasty which was to last until 750. Mu'ayiwa moved the capital from Madinah to Damascus. This meant the abandonment of the simplicity of the early caliphate for the palatial life, a significant change in the history of Islam. The first Umayyad ruler also established hereditary rule, imposing his son Yazid as his heir, which was yet another major deviation from early Islamic precepts of election of the ruler. Dissentions followed this move, and in the ensuing conflict, Husseyn, the grandson of the Prophet, and his small group of followers were massacred at Kerbala, not far from Kufa. Further upheaval occurred, which resulted in serious harm caused to the holy sites of Madinah and Makkah.

Some Umayyad rulers, whether in the east or in the west, were debauched, blood thirsty tyrants. One of them was Sulayman (ruled 715-17), already mentioned, who had great Muslim generals executed. After the death of Hisham, in 743, the Umayyad declined rapidly. The new caliph was Waleed II, a son of the frivolous but harmless Yazeed II. Waleed was a libertine, a drunkard, a blasphemer and a cynic. He was killed after a reign of only fifteen months. On 17th April, 744, his head, impaled on the point of a lance, was paraded through the streets of Damascus.[566]

Other Umayyad rulers were, however, authors of great accomplishments. In 685, Caliph Abd Al-Malik came to power. He ruled for twenty years, and set up an administrative structure, and made Arabic the language of administration. He changed the public registers (diwan) from Greek to Arabic in Damascus, and from Pahlawi to Arabic in Iraq and the Eastern provinces.[567] The transition must have been slow, beginning under Abd al-Malik and continuing during the reign of his successor, Al-Walid (caliph 705-715).[568] Abd Al-Malik also set up a postal system,[569] using relays of horses for the conveyance of travellers and dispatches between Damascus and the provincial capitals.[570] Abd Al-Malik also issued the first Islamic coinage. In 695, he had struck the first gold dinars and silver dirhems, which were purely Arabic.[571]

---

[566] J. Glubb: *A Short History*; op cit; p. 88.
[567] P.K. Hitti: *History;* op cit; p. 217.
[568] Al-Baladhuri: *Kitab Futuh al-Buldan;* op cit; pp. 191; 193; 300-1.
[569] Al-'Umari: *Al-Ta'arif bi al-Mustalah al-Sharif*; Cairo; 1312 H; p. 185.
[570] P.K. Hitti: *History;* op cit; p. 218.
[571] Al-Baladhuri: *Kitab Futuh al-Buldan;* op cit; p. 240.

Abd Al-Malik's viceroy in Iraq, al-Hajjaj, minted silver in al-Kufa in the following year.[572] Al-Hajjaj also dug a number of new canals and restored the large one between the Tigris and the Euphrates. He drained and tilled submerged or uncultivated lands.[573] He also took the initiative in introducing diacritical marks into Arabic orthography to distinguish similarly written letters, and inserting vowel signs above and below the consonants.[574] In this orthographic reform he was prompted by the desire to prevent errors in the recitation of the sacred text.[575]

Omar II, Ibn Abd Al-Aziz (ruled 717-20), was also an illustrious Umayyad ruler. Despite his short rule, Omar distinguished himself in many ways. His ideal was to follow in the foot-steps of his illustrious maternal grandfather, Omar (Ibn Al-Khattab), his simplicity, devotion, and frugality reminding of his illustrious predecessor, indeed.[576] He wore clothes that had many patches, and mingled with his subjects freely, that when one came to petition him he found it difficult to recognise him.[577] Omar also banned the practice of cursing Caliph Ali from the pulpit at the Friday prayer, which had been introduced by the first Umayyad ruler. Omar also introduced fiscal reforms which relieved non-Arab Muslims from tribute that had been introduced in previous Umayyad rule.[578]

The Umayyad were also responsible for some great architectural accomplishments. In 691, Abd al-Malik erected in Jerusalem the magnificent Dome of the Rock.[579] Al-Walid enlarged and beautified the Great Mosque of Makkah and rebuilt that of al-Madinah, besides erecting a number of schools and places of worship and endowed institutions for the lepers, the lame and the blind.[580] He was perhaps the first ruler in medieval times to build hospitals for persons with chronic diseases, and the many lazar houses which later grew up in the West followed the Muslim precedent.[581]

During Umayyad rule, the Muslim armies made many of the conquests described above, including those of North Africa and Spain, whilst in the East, they reached the frontiers of China.

---

[572] Yaqut al-Hamawi: *Mu'ajam al-Buldan;* ed. F. Wustenfeld. 6 vols. Leipzig, 1866-70. vol iv; p. 886.
[573] P.K. Hitti: *History;* op cit; p. 219.
[574] Ibn Khallikan: W*afayat al-Ayan wa-Anba Abna al-Zaman,* Cairo, 1299 (H); vol 1; pp. 220-1. (De Salne version at pp. 359-60).
[575] P.K. Hitti: *History;* op cit; p. 220.
[576] Ibn al-Jawzi: *Sirat Omar Ibn abd –Al-Aziz;* Cairo; 1331 (H); pp. 173-4; 145 ff.
[577] Ibid.
[578] Ibn al-Athir: *Kitab al-kamil*; op cit;; vol v; p. 37.
[579] P.K. Hitti: *History;* op cit; p. 221.
[580] Al-Baladhuri: *Kitab Futuh al-Buldan;* op cit; p. 47; Al-Tabari: vol 2; p. 1271.
[581] P.K. Hitti: *History*; op cit; p. 221.

3. The Non Military Progress of Islam:

Islam progressed not just owing to military success, but also due to other factors.

Islamic success, then as today, owed very much to the rapid conversions of the conquered people, which in turn owed much to their discovery of Islam. The message of Islam (looked at in the previous chapter) with its emphasis on good morality and social justice; its banning of vices such as gambling, alcohol consumption, adultery, and the burial of female infants; its stressing humility, respect for parents, tolerance of other faiths, the freeing of slaves and serfs; its easy understanding, and much else, proved of great appeal to countless many.

Early Muslim rulers under whom most such conquests were made also contributed greatly to enhance the appeal of Islam. One such ruler was Omar (Caliph 634-644) under whom Syria, Egypt, Palestine, Persia, and Iraq came into the Muslim realm. Omar, Durant says, was tall, broad-shouldered, and passionate; bald headed, and with dyed beard. Time and responsibility had matured him into a rare mixture of hot temper and cool judgement. Having beaten a Bedouin unjustly, he begged the Bedouin-in vain-to inflict an equal number of strokes upon him.[582] Tradition reports that he scourged his son to death for repeated drunkenness.[583] Muslim historians report that he owned but one shirt and one mantle, patched and re-patched; that he lived on barley bread and dates, and drank nothing but water; that he slept on a bed of palm leaves, hardly better than a hair shirt; and that his sole concern was the propagation of the faith by letters and by arms.[584] Omar went barefoot and possessed only one shirt, while the immense treasures of Byzantium and Persia were spread at his feet after both had been vanquished.[585] When the messenger bearing the good news took with him to the Caliph two large chests filled with precious stones from the treasures of the Great King (of Persia), Caliph Omar summoned the messenger and told him to take the chests away, sell the contents and distribute the proceeds among the soldiers.[586] The statutory fifth sent to Madinah, had hitherto been immediately distributed by the Caliph to the poor of the town.[587] When Omar

---

[582] Sir W. Muir: *The Caliphate*; Smith and Elder and Co; London; 1883. p.198.
[583] P.K. Hitti: *History*; op cit; p. 176.
[584] W. Durant: *The Age of Faith*; op cit; p.189.
[585] J. Glubb: *A Short History;* op cit; p.84.
[586] Ibid; p.60.
[587] Ibid; p.56.

conquered Egypt he rejected the advice of Zubayr to divide the land amongst his followers. `Leave it,' said Omar, `in the people's hands to nurse and to fructify.'[588] Despite his humbling of both Byzantine and Persian emperors, he remained always pious, simple and compassionate.[589] Prisoners of war brought to Madinah expected to see palaces and imperial pageantry such as they witnessed elsewhere, instead, they saw a tall, lean man, barefoot and wearing a coarse woollen cloak, although he was the world's most powerful `emperor.'[590] The Caliph himself had no money and ate the same simple diet as his fellow citizens.[591]

Historians, however hostile to Islam, never refrain from comparing Omar's peaceful entry into Jerusalem (in 637) with that of the crusaders centuries later in July 1099 (when tens of thousands of Muslims were slain in cold blood). Here is Gibbon's version of the Muslim capture of the city: `The siege of Jerusalem lasted four months; not a day was lost without some action of sally or assault; the military engines incessantly played from the ramparts; and the inclemency of the winter was still more painful and destructive to the Arabs. The Christians yielded at length to the perseverance of the besiegers. The patriarch Sophronius appeared on the walls, and by the voice of an interpreter demanded a conference. He proposed, in the name of the people, a fair capitulation, with this extraordinary clause, that the articles of security should be ratified by the authority and presence of Omar himself. The conqueror of Persia and Syria (Caliph Omar) was mounted on a red camel, which carried, besides his person, a bag of corn, a bag of dates, a wooden dish, and a leather bottle of water. Wherever he halted, the company, without distinction, was invited to partake of his homely fare, and the repast was consecrated by the prayer and exhortation of the commander of the faithful. When he came within sight of Jerusalem, the caliph cried with a loud voice, "God is victorious. O Lord, give us an easy conquest!" and, pitching his tent of coarse hair, calmly seated himself on the ground. After signing the capitulation, he entered the city without fear or precaution; and courteously discoursed with the patriarch concerning its religious antiquities. Sophronius bowed before his new master. At the hour of prayer they stood together in the Church of the Resurrection; but the caliph refused to perform his devotions, and contented himself with praying on the steps of the Church of Constantine. To the patriarch he disclosed his prudent and honourable motive. "Had I yielded," said Omar, "to your

---

[588] Sir W. Muir: *The Caliphate*; op cit; p. 170.
[589] J. Glubb: *A Short History;* op cit; p.63.
[590] Ibid.
[591] Ibid; p.56.

request, the Muslims of a future age would have infringed the treaty under colour of imitating my example."[592]

Deeds such as these contradict the view that Muslim progress was due to the sword alone, Draper notes.[593] The sword may change an acknowledged national creed, but it cannot affect the consciousness of men. Profound though its argument is, something far more profound was demanded before Islam 'pervaded the domestic life of Asia and Africa, before Arabic became the language of so many different nations,' adds Draper.[594] Islam abstained from forceful conversion, even in North Africa, often cited as a case of such forced conversions. Forster, as had Sale, pointed out that in North Africa, Islam flourished apart from reliance on 'political domination' and that its 'votaries' were 'unshackled by the restraints' of a Muslim government.[595] The Muslims, Durant notes, could have devastated or confiscated everything, like the Mongols or the Magyars or the raiding Norse; instead they merely taxed.[596] Under Muslim rule, the condition of the serfs was greatly improved, whilst tribute was regulated by law, and ceased to depend upon capricious demands.[597] Conquered lands, while forming a part of the public domain, could not be acquired by those who had conquered them, and continued to be occupied and tilled by their former proprietors.[598] Lands were measured, records were systematically kept, roads and canals were multiplied or maintained, rivers were banked to prevent floods; Iraq, formerly half desert, was again a garden of Eden; Palestine, recently so rich in sand and stones, was fertile, wealthy and populous.[599] Doubtless there were imperfections in the Islamic rule, Durant notes, but:
'The caliphs gave reasonable protection to life and labour, kept career open to talent, promoted for three to six centuries the prosperity of areas never so prosperous again, and stimulated and supported such a flourishing of education, literature, science, philosophy, and art as made western Asia, for five centuries, the most civilised region in the world.'[600]

During the early Islamic period, Le Bon holds, the morality of the Arabs was everywhere higher than that of all other people, most particularly the

---

[592] E. Gibbon: *Decline and Fal*; op cit; vol 5; pp. 435-6.
[593] J.W. Draper: *A History*; op cit; p.332.
[594] Ibid.
[595] C. Forster: *Mohamedanism unveiled*; London; James Duncan and John Cochran; 1829. I; p. 15.
[596] Will Durant: *The Age of Faith*; op cit; p.227.
[597] S.P. Scott: *History of the Moorish Empire*; op cit; Vol 1; p.259.
[598] Ibid; p.130.
[599] G. Le Strange: *Palestine under the Moslems*; London; 1890; p. 24.
[600] W. Durant: *The Age of Faith*; op cit; p.227.

Christians.[601] Their sense of justice, moderation, care, tolerance towards vanquished people, the respect of their agreements, their chivalrous character, contrasted sharply with the conduct of other people, most particularly that of the Europeans, during the Crusades, Le Bon adds.[602] At war, non-combatants were unmolested, and pillage was forbidden under pain of death, and no property was destroyed except when resistance or violence was offered the troops.[603] One particular trait was that the engagements entered into with their allies were performed by the Muslims with scrupulous fidelity.[604] On The Muslims who went to fight for the emperor in China and then were granted the right to stay there, `they are animated in general of a great spirit of rightness and honesty,' says Le Bon. `Those who hold public functions are liked and respected by the populations, and those who deal in trade have an excellent reputation. They are charitable due to religious principles, and seem only to form one and large family all of whose members protect and support each other.'[605]

The success of Islam was also due to its equalitarian nature; all believers of equal standing;[606] before the law, in particular, and in the absence of antagonistic class distinctions in Muslim society.[607] Esposito notes that whilst recognizing differences in status, wealth, and tribal origin, the Qur'an teaches the ultimate supratribal (trans-national) unity and equality of all believers before God.[608] Common faith, not tribal or family ties, binds the community together. The Qur'an envisions a society based on the unity and equality of believers, a society in which moral and social justice will counterbalance oppression of the weak and economic exploitation.[609] Belief and action are to be joined; Muslims are not only to know and believe, but also to act and implement.[610] Worship and devotion to God embrace both private and public life, affecting not only prayer, fasting, and pilgrimage, but social behaviour as well.[611] No priestly class

---

[601] G. Le Bon: *La Civilisation des Arabes*, op cit; p.338.
[602] Ibid.
[603] S.P. Scott: *History of the Moorish Empire*; op cit; Vol 1; p.249.
[604] Ibid; p.259.
[605] G. Le Bon: *La Civilisation des Arabes*, op cit; p.48.
[606] F. Artz: *The Mind of the Middle Ages*; 3rd ed revised; The University of Chicago Press, 1980. p.137.
[607] J.W. Thompson: *Economic and Social history of the Middle Ages 300-1300*; New York, 1928, p.193.
[608] J. L. Esposito: *Islam, the Straight Path;* op cit; p. 29.
[609] Ibid.
[610] Ibid.
[611] Ibid.

relegates the layman to the background, either.[612] In Islam every man is his own priest,[613] and Muslim society was free from 'the evils of an ambitious and avaricious clergy like the bishops and abbots, qualities, which stamp early Islam with a new and refreshing vigour,' says Thompson.[614] No one was too insignificant to have his name inscribed upon the official registers at Madinah; and even slaves, women, and newly born infants were, as well as the most renowned warriors, regularly paid their state allowance.[615] Islam's legislation about women, marriage, and the family, the care of orphans, the poor, the slaves and the insane was equally high.[616]

It is from pure monotheism that derives the immense simplicity of Islam, and it is in this simplicity that must be sought the secret of its strength, Le Bon says.[617] Easy to understand, it offers its adepts no mystery and none of these contradictions which are so common in other beliefs, and which very often hurt good sense. One God, absolutely unique to adore; all humans equal in front of Him; a small number of regulations to observe, paradise as reward if these precepts are observed, hellfire as retribution, if they are not observed. Nothing could be as clear and far from misunderstanding.[618] The Muslim, whatever his social rank, knows exactly what he has to believe, and can without any difficulty expose the rules of his religion in a few words. For a Christian to risk to talk of trinity and trans-substantiation, or some analogous mystery, he has to be doubled of a theologian acquainted with all subtleties of dialectic.[619] 'Islam,' Davenport pursues, 'is a religion, moreover, stripped of all controversy, and which, proposing no mystery to offer violence to reason, restricts the imagination of men to being satisfied with a plain, invariable worship. It is a religion from which all worship of saints and martyrs, relics and images, all mystery and metaphysical subtlety, all monastic seclusion and enthusiastic penance is banished.'[620] All this, added to a feeling of charity and justice, with which Islam is imprinted, has certainly very much contributed to its diffusion in the world, Le Bon adds.[621]

Smith holds that Islam:

---

[612] G.E. Von Grunebaum: *Islam*, Greenwood Press, Publishers, 1961.p.76.
[613] J.W. Thompson: *Economic and Social history*, op cit; p.193.
[614] Ibid.
[615] S.P. Scott: History of the Moorish Empire; op cit; Vol 1; p.130.
[616] F. Artz: *The Mind of the Middle Ages*; op cit; p.137.
[617] G. Le Bon: *La Civilisation des Arabes*, op cit; p.89.
[618] Ibid.
[619] Ibid.
[620] J. Davenport: *An Apology;* op cit; p. 80.
[621] G. Le Bon: *La Civilisation des Arabes*, op cit; p.89.

'Is that religion which alone gives stability to the tottering fabric, and is the one principle of life amidst all the jarring elements of destruction. It is the religion which merges all colours, ranks, and races in the consciousness of a common brotherhood. It is the religion which elevates the mind by drawing it from the transitory to the eternal, and which gives to the half-starved or ill used peasant that courage in calamity, that calm amidst confusion, and that ineffable dignity in distress, which is found nowhere else but in Islam.'[622]

The conclusion belongs to Durant who says:
'Gradually the non-Muslim populations adopted the Arabic language and dress, the laws and faith of the Qur'an. Where Hellenism, after a thousand years of mastery, had failed to take root, and Roman arms had left the native gods unconquered, and Byzantine orthodoxy had raised rebellious heresies, Islam had secured, almost without proselytism, not only belief and worship, but a tenacious fidelity that quite forgot the superseded gods. From China, Indonesia, and India through Persia, Syria, Arabia, and Egypt to Morocco and Spain, the Islamic faith touched the hearts and fancies of a hundred peoples, governed their morals and molded their lives, gave them consoling hopes and a strengthening pride.'[623]

---

[622] R.B. Smith: *Mohammed;* op cit; pp. 308-9.
[623] W. Durant: *The Age of Faith;* op cit; p. 219.

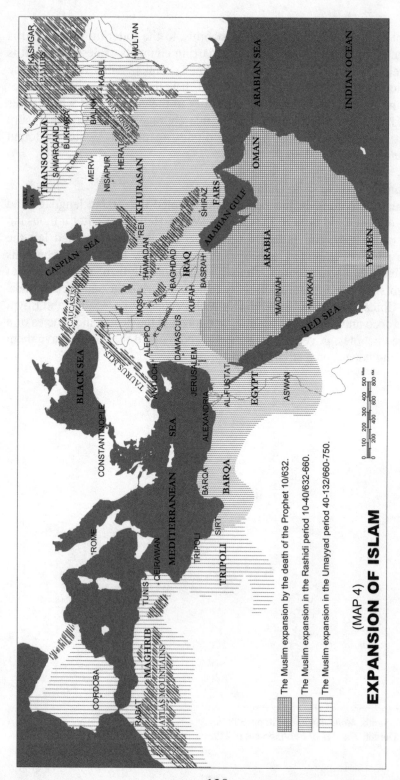

The Muslim expansion by the death of the Prophet 10/632.

The Muslim expansion in the Rashidi period 10-40/632-660.

The Muslim expansion in the Umayyad period 40-132/660-750.

(MAP 4)

EXPANSION OF ISLAM

FIVE

THE ISLAMIC LAND (9th-11th CENTURIES)

The vast expansion of Islam under the first four caliphs and the Umayyads (who ruled between 661 and 750) came to an end under the Abbasids (750-1258). Although some Muslim dynasties such as the Aghlabids of Tunisia, and the Ghaznavids of northern India, recorded some advances, there were no substantial territories brought under Islam. Instead, during the period under consideration here, between the 9th and 11th centuries, we witness the rise of widespread conflict amongst Muslims. As a result of this infighting, some regions were devastated, bearing the scars to this very day. This infighting also invited external invasions of the Muslim land.

1. Iraq and Arabia:

The period up to 750 was a period of great advances as the previous chapter showed. However such advances stopped when the Abbasids took power in 750. The advent of the Abbasids followed the destruction of the preceding Umayyad Dynasty. The Umayyad had begun their rule following the first rightly guided caliphs. Umayyad rule was marked by a great territorial advance and an enlargement of the Muslim land. The Umayyad, however, deviated from the Islamic ethos of electing the ruler, and began rule by hereditary succession. Hereditary succession, history shows, rarely guarantees the best ruler.

The Abbasids had obtained power in 750 by what today we should call subversive propaganda. Under their rule, it was claimed that 'inequities of the wicked Umayyad' would cease, and the reign of peace, mercy, justice and happiness would spread over the earth. These dreams had been quickly dispelled by the Blood Shedder (As-Saffah ruled 750-754) and his successor. The Abbasids came to power by massacring the whole Umayyad family, men, women, children, in one of the worst episodes of Islamic history. The

Abbasids also halted the Islamic advance. If the Abbasids were no worse than the Umayyad, they were certainly no better.[624]

Under the Abbasids, Islamic culture witnessed some bright moments, as the outline below shows. However, in counterpart, also arose many non-Islamic behaviours and manners. The luxuries and culture of waste became generalised. In Baghdad, everything was plastered with gold. Not only was it used to adorn the women but also the pillars and the roof beams of the houses. The buckles of the men's belts were gold, which likewise covered the hilts and scabbards of their swords and daggers, and the saddles and the bridles of their horses.[625]

Women, many of them concubines collected from distant countries, were adorned by the lavish use of jewels and pearls. Everywhere abounded the silks and embroidered fabrics, the priceless carpets and cushions, the sparkling fountains, the soft music and the exotic perfumes of the private apartments.[626]

It is this sort of life style, which was taken from the Abbasids to Spain by a man called Ziriab, who took there all these corrupt, effeminate mannerisms, and generalised them to much of Muslim society. This description by Scott is very illuminating on such corrupting impact:

`The character of the Mussulmans of Spain was defiled by all the vices which follow in the train of prodigal luxury and boundless wealth. Among these drunkenness was one of the most common. Personnages of the highest rank were not ashamed to appear in public while intoxicated... National degeneracy early indicated the approaching and inevitable dissolution of the empire. The posterity of the conquerors, who in three years had marched from Gibraltar to the centre of France, became in the course of a few generations cowardly, effeminate, corrupt.'[627]

A capable Abbasid ruler, Mutassim (833-842), was succeeded by his son Wathiq on 5th January 842. A complete contrast to his fiery and dominating father, Wathiq was fond of eating and drinking. He never travelled, visited the provinces or engaged in military campaigns. He played the lute and composed more than a hundred musical works. He took little interest in government, which he left entirely to his vizier. He died in 847 after a reign of six years.[628]

---

[624] J. Glubb: *A Short History*; op cit; p. 95.
[625] Ibid; p. 105.
[626] Ibid.
[627] S.P. Scott: *History*; op cit; Vol II, at pp 648 and 650.
[628] J. Glubb: *A Short History*; op cit; p. 116.

From 869 to 883, southern Iraq was in the hands of the so-called Zanj rebels, most of whom were revolted slaves who worked in the marshes east of Basra. The Muslim historian, Al-Tabari, discusses the Zanj rebellion in great detail, a rebellion, which was particularly disastrous, as it put an end to the profitable Oriental trade which, coming up the Gulf to Basra, provided great wealth to the Abbasids.[629]

In 892, the weak Caliph Mutamid died and was succeeded by his energetic and capable nephew Mutadhid, who set himself to restore the power of the Caliphate. Hope seemed to revive under Mutadhid until, in 900, the Carmathian rebellion broke out in Arabia. In the neighbourhood of Kufa, Gibbon says, a preacher, of the name of Carmath, who relaxed the duties of ablution, fasting, and pilgrimage, allowed the indiscriminate use of wine and forbidden food, and nourished the fervour of his disciples by the daily repetition of fifty prayers.[630] Operating from their base, in the Kufa region, the Carmathians proclaimed the suspension of the *shari'a* (the sacred law of Islam), and mustered around them the peasants of southern Iraq and the tribes of the nearby desert.[631] Carmath's twelve apostles dispersed themselves among the Bedouins, and the success of their preaching seemed to threaten Arabia with a new revolution.[632] The Carmathians conducted repeated raids on Iraq, Syria, and in 904 invaded the Yemen and plundered Zabid, and between 911 and 915, a short lived Carmathian regime was established in Sana'a.[633] The Carmathian movement, Hitti insists, developed into a most malicious growth in the body politics of Islam, and to shed the blood of their opponents, even if Muslims, the Carmathians considered legitimate.[634] Between the 10th and 11th centuries, the Carmathians kept Syria and Iraq drenched in blood.[635] Al-Tabari, who was a contemporary to the event, devotes considerable amounts of writing to the progress of, and upheavals caused by the Carmathians.[636] The Carmathians preyed on pilgrims to Makkah's caravans, and massacred thousands amongst the faithful. An account by Al-Tabari describes, how in the year 906, they attacked caravans: 'The criminals (i.e the Carmathians) had come to Wasiqah, and before leaving they had made the watering places there unusable, filling the

---

[629] *The History of Al-Tabari*; op cit; vol XXXVII.
[630] E. Gibbon: *The Decline and Fall*; op cit; vol 6; 1925 ed; p. 49.
[631] K. Salibi: *A History of Arabia*; Caravan; New York; 1980; p. 103.
[632] In E. Gibbon: *The Decline and Fall*; op cit; vol 6. p. 49.
[633] K. Salibi: *A History of Arabia*; op cit; p. 103.
[634] P.K. Hitti: *History*; op cit; p. 445.
[635] *The History of Al-Tabari*; op cit; vol XXXVIII; (tr F. Rosenthal) esp. pp. 81 ff.
[636] Ibid.

ponds and wells with the corpses of camels and horses whose bellies were split open….. The criminals found the rear of the caravan unaware and fell upon them from that direction. They thrust their lances into the sides and bellies of the camels which fell upon the fighters in the caravans and crushed them. They, thus, overpowered them and put them to the sword, killing them to the last man, except those they made slaves. They then dispatched horsemen several miles beyond Al-Aqbah where they encountered those who had escaped the slaughter. They granted them guarantees of safe conduct then returned and killed all of them. They took captives the women they liked and seized all the money and goods… the bodies of the slain formed a large hill. Some of the wounded had fallen amongst the dead… The Carmathian women always went around among those killed with their children who offered them water. Those who talked to them (indicating they were still alive) were finished off.
Reportedly about twenty thousand pilgrims were in the caravan. All of them were killed, except a small number… The money and splendid goods seized by the Carmathians in this caravan were reportedly worth two million dinars.'[637]

Another year, the Carmathians allowed the pilgrims to proceed without interruption; then, Abu Taher, the Carmathian leader, stormed Makkah, and trampled on the most venerable relics of Islam.[638] Thirty thousand pilgrims were put to the sword; the sacred precincts were polluted by the burial of three thousand dead bodies; the well of Zemzem overflowed with blood; the golden spout was forced from its place; the veil of the Kaaba was divided, and the Black Stone was borne away in triumph to their capital.[639]

The Carmathian state fell subsequently, but its doctrine was passed on to the Fatimids of Egypt, Hitti notes, and from one of them was to erupt the Ismaili or Assassin movement,[640] which would play a crucial role in the subsequent period and the crusades.

The Carmathian episode was no lone dark episode of the period. The early years of the 10th century were marked by an unending succession of riots, rebellions and military seizures of one sort or another. One Caliph was assassinated; the next was blinded by his own troops, who plundered

---

[637] Ibid; pp. 175-6.
[638] E. Gibbon: *The Decline and Fall*; op cit; p. 50.
[639] See: Ibn al-Athir: *Kamil;* op cit; vol viii; p. 63;
E. Gibbon: *The Decline and Fall*; op cit; pp. 50-1.
[640] P.K. Hitti: *History;* op cit; p. 446.

his palace.[641] Then, in 913, western Persia was invaded by the Daylamites, a warlike horde originating in the mountains at the southern end of the Caspian Sea.[642] They were extremely hostile to the Abbasid Caliph. Under their tribal chiefs, the Buwaihids, they occupied the whole of west Persia, establishing their capital in Shiraz.[643] In 945, Ahmed ibn Buwaih, whose father had claimed descent from the ancient Sasanid kings so as to bolster up dynastic prestige,[644] marched out of Shiraz and occupied Baghdad unopposed. The Caliph Mustakil was obliged to recognize his authority and to bestow on him the honorific title of *Muizz al Dawlah* (he who makes the state mighty.)[645] This was not enough, and on the fortieth day, Muizz al-Dawlah insisted that his name be mentioned in the Friday khutba (sermon), and his name stamped on the coinage.[646] On 29 January, 946, at the audience of the ambassadors of Khurasan, and in the presence of a trembling multitude, the caliph was dragged from his throne to a dungeon by the Daylamites, through the streets of his own capital beneath the blows and jeers of the Daylamite soldiers.[647] His palace was pillaged, his eyes were put out, and throughout their century of supremacy (945-1055), the Buwaihids made and unmade caliphs at will.[648]

The Buwaihids were to stay in power until 1055, when their rule was terminated by the Seljuk Turks.

---

[641] *The History of Al-Tabari*; op cit; vol xxxviii; op cit; pp. 190-1.

[642] P.K. Hitti: *History;* op cit; p. 470.

[643] E. Gibbon: *The Decline and Fall;* op cit; p. 54.

[644] Ibn Khallikan: *Wafayat al-Ayan wa-Anba Abna al-Zaman*, Biographical Dictionary, tr., M. De Slane Duprat, Paris and Allen & Co., London, 1843. vol 1; p. 98.

[645] J. Glub: *A Short History;* op cit; p. 120.

[646] Ibn al-Athir: *Kitab al-kamil*; vol viii; op cit; p. 337.

[647] E. Gibbon: *The Decline and Fall*; op cit; p. 56; J. Glub: *A Short History*; op cit; p. 120.

[648] P.K. Hitti: *History*; op cit; p. 471.

The Brilliance of the Abbasid Caliphate

Muslim civilisation and culture is not the result of Abbasid rule as the unfortunate reading of history conveys. Muslim culture and civilisation arose straight after the birth of Islam, its early accomplishments: hospitals, architecture, irrigation, schools, universal learning, medicine, astronomy and many sciences, all being anterior to the arrival of the Abbasids. All Muslim sciences also derive directly from Islam. Furthermore, the brilliance of Umayyad civilisation in Andalusia and the Aghlabid in Tunisia compare favourably with that of the Abbasid. And following the sack of Baghdad in 1258 by the Mongols, Islamic civilisation thrived in Egypt, North Africa, Syria, under the Ottomans and in Muslim India.

Having said this, it must be, however, recognised that the Abbasids contributed largely to the brilliance of Islamic culture and civilisation. *The Bayt al-Hikma* or House of Wisdom was established in Baghdad in the 9th century. It was primarily a research and translation institute; the first academy of science of its genre. It had a library, scientific equipment, a translation bureau, and an observatory. Teaching in Bayt al-Hikma included rhetoric, logic, metaphysics and theology, algebra, geometry, trigonometry, physics, biology, medicine, and surgery.[649]

Under Caliph Al-Mamun (ruled 813-833), Islamic astronomy made its greatest early strides. Al-Mamun had an observatory completed in 829, a major landmark in the history of astronomy, from which, in the year 830, was determined the position of the solar apogee at $82°39'$.[650] Astronomers at al-Mamun's court also found the inclination of the ecliptic to be $23°33'$.[651] Al-Mamun also supervised two geodetic surveys in Iraq for the purpose of determining the length of a degree of the meridian, reaching a result of a degree being equal to 562/3 miles.[652] The earth circumference was found to be 40,253.4 kms (the accurate figure being 40,068.0 km through the equator, and 40,000.6 km through the poles.)[653] One of the astronomers at the court was Habash al-Hasib (d.864) who made observations of solar and lunar eclipses and of planetary positions at Baghdad, Samarra and Damascus. He compiled astronomical tables and gave the first instance of

---

[649] F.B. Artz: *The Mind of the Middle Ages*; op cit; p. 151.

[650] W. Hartner: The Role of Observations in ancient and medieval astronomy; in *The Journal of History of Astronomy*; Vol 8; 1977; pp 1-11; at p. 8.

[651] J.L.E. Dreyer: *A History of Astronomy From Thales to Kepler*; Dover Publications Inc, New York, 1953, p.246.

[652] Ibid.

[653] M. A. Kettani: Science and Technology in Islam: The underlying value system, in *The Touch of Midas; Science, values, and environment in Islam and the West*; Z. Sardar ed: Manchester University Press, 1984, pp 66-90; p. 75.

a determination of time by an altitude, besides introducing the notion of shadow (umbra versa) corresponding to our tangent. He also compiled a table of tangents, probably the earliest of its kind.[654]
In medical sciences and practice, in Baghdad alone, in the 10thcentury, there were nearly a thousand physicians; and the population, the ordinary and the less so, found in the hospitals places and means for healing.[655] One of the main medical scholars exerting in Baghdad was the Persian scholar, Al-Razi, who came from Ray, near today's Tehran. Al-Razi wrote more than 100 books covering a variety of diseases and medical subjects.[656] Al-Razi's *Al-Hawi* was translated on the order of Charles of Anjou in the 13th century by Faraj Ibn Salim (Faragut), and was propagated in numerous manuscripts in the following centuries.[657] Latin versions of Al-Razi were published at Milan in 1481, at Venice in 1483, 1490, 1493; Bergamo 1497; 1498; 1500; 1506; 1509; and 1510, and at Lyons in 1510.[658]

Ibn Fadlan, in the 10th century, accompanied a mission from the Caliph al-Muktadir (Caliph 902-8) to the Volga Bulgars. His particular role on that journey was to read out the letter from the Caliph to the king, to present him with gifts and to supervise the teaching of Islamic laws to the Bulgars. The Embassy left Baghdad in June 921.[659] The journey and the description of the various tribes encountered by the embassy are vividly described by Ibn Fadlan in his *Risala.*[660] He describes his experiences and the people and places he visited, the Khazzars, and the manners and customs of the Rus.[661] This is not just the earliest account in Arabic of the Volga region, it also gives the topography of the surrounding region, approximately up to 60 degree North latitude, it is also an important source of anthropology on various populations of the region.[662]

---

[654] G. Sarton: *Introduction to the History of Science*; 3 vols; The Carnegie Institute of Washington; 1927-48.
vol I, op cit; p.545.
[655] N.L. Leclerc: *Histoire de la medecine Arabe*; 2 vols; Paris; 1876.
[656] G.M Wickens: The Middle East as a world centre of science and medicine; in *Introduction to Islamic Civilisation*, ed by R.M. Savory; Cambridge University Press, Cambridge, 1976; pp 111-8; at p 116.
[657] N. Daniel: *The Arabs;* op cit; p.305.
[658] D. Campbell: *Arabian Medicine and its Influence on the Middle Ages;* Philo Press; Amsterdam; 1926; pp. 70-1.
[659] M. Canard: Ibn Fadlan, in *Encyclopaedia of Islam*; New edition, vol 3; Brill; Leiden, 1971; p. 759.
[660] S. Al-Dhhan: *Risalat Ibn Fadlan*; Dar Sadir; Beirut; 1993.
[661] For a long account of Ibn Fadlan's travel to the Volga Bulgars, see M. Canard: Les Relations de voyage d'Ibn Fadlan chez les Bulgares de la Volga; In *Annales de l'Institut d'Etudes Orientales*; Vol 16; 1958; pp 41-146; S.M. Ahmad: *A History of Arab-Islamic Geography*; Amman; Albany; 1995; M. Dunlop: *Arab Civilisation, to AD 1500*, Longman, Librarie du Liban, 1971, pp 169-70.
[662] S.M. Ahmad: *A History of Arab-Islamic Geography*, op cit; p. 112.

The Abbasid caliphate also excelled at architecture and urban design. The outline by Lassner on the foundation of Samarra (today's Iraq) in the 9th century is an excellent illustration of this.[663] Samarra, the second great capital of the Abbasid caliphate, was situated along the Tigris some sixty miles (ninety-seven kilometres) north of Baghdad. The city was subject to meticulous planning; several thoroughfares running almost the entire length and breadth of the city. The main thoroughfare was the "Great Road" (*shari' al-a'zam*), called al-Sarjah, extended the entire length of the city. With later extensions it ran some 20 miles (32 kilometres) and was reported to have been 300 feet (91 meters) wide at one point. The part of the road, which still exists, although somewhat narrower (240 feet or 73 meters), testifies, indeed, to dimensions that were staggering. The great government buildings, the Friday mosque and the city markets were all situated along al-Sarjah; and it was throughout the entire history of the city the main line from which most of the city's traffic radiated toward the Tigris and inland. The Great thoroughfare was extended from the outer limits of Samarra, and feeder channels that brought drinking water flanked both sides of the road.[664]

---

[663] J. Lassner: Samarra; *Dictionary of the Middle Ages*; J.R. Strayer Editor in Chief; Charles Scribner's Sons; New York; 1982 ff; vol 10; pp. 642-3.
[664] Ibid; pp. 643.

2. India and Central Asia:

It was a Turk, Mahmud of Ghazna (d. 1030), who resumed the Muslim advance in the East, principally in India. He had taken part in all of his father's campaigns against the Hindu, and he became ruler of the kingdom of Ghazna (comprising of Afghanistan and Northern Persia) at the age of about twenty-seven.[665] Initially, Mahmud's father, Subuktigin, was the slave of the slave of the slave of the caliph.[666] Mahmud, however, was to distinguish himself as one of the first Muslim leaders to earn the title of *al-ghazi,* bestowed on he who distinguished himself in war against the unbelievers.[667] Such was his aura, power and military prowess, he became the ruler of an independent eastern realm only paying nominal allegiance to the Abbasid Caliph al-Qadir (r. 991-1031), from whom he received the title of Yamin al-Dawla (the right arm of the state).[668]

Mahmud, who was an ardent Muslim, as well as an outstanding military and political leader, proved himself to be the scourge of the heterodox and the infidel.[669] `In this foreign narrative,' Gibbon says, `a volume would scarcely suffice to recapitulate the battles and sieges of his twelve expeditions. Never was the Muslim hero dismayed by the inclemency of the seasons, the height of the mountains, the breadth of the rivers, the barrenness of the desert, the multitudes of the enemy, or the formidable array of their elephants of war. The sultan of Ghazna surpassed the limits of the conquests of Alexander: after a march of three months, over the hills of Kashmir and Tibet, he reached the famous city of Kinnoge, on the Upper Ganges; and, in a naval combat on one of the branches of the Indus, he fought and vanquished four thousand boats of the natives.'[670]

From 1001 to 1024, Mahmud led about seventeen raids into India, the first being in the northern state of Punjab (28 November, 1001), near Peshawar, where he defeated and captured Jaipal, after a fearful massacre of the large Indian army.[671] Jaipal obtained his release by paying a ransom, but afterwards threw himself on a funeral pyre and burned to death to escape

---

[665] S.M. Ikram: *Muslim Civilisation in India;* Columbia University Press; New York; 1964; p. 24.
[666] E. Gibbon: *The Decline and Fall;* op cit; vol 6; p. 225.
[667] Mustawfi-Qazwini: *Ta'rikh-i-Guzida;* ed. E.G. Browne; Leyden; 1910-1913; vol 1; p. 396.
[668] Ibid; p. 395.
[669] H.U. Rahman: *A Chronology;* op cit; p. 166.
[670] E. Gibbon: *The Decline and Fall;* op cit; vol 6; p. 226.
[671] S.M. Ikram: *Muslim Civilisation in India;* op cit; p. 24.

the humiliation of defeat.[672] Nonetheless, the states of Ujjayn, Gwalior, Kalinjar, Kannawj, Delhi, and Ajmer formed an alliance against the Muslims, but were defeated between Peshawar and Waihind in 399H/1008; a victory which was a turning point in Mahmud's career.[673] Seeking to expand his dominion into these Indian states, his army gave battle to the Hindus and marched victorious into Nagarkot, Thanesar, Kannawj, Kalinjar and Somnath.[674]

Mahmud launched his most dramatic campaign in October 1024 against an extremely wealthy temple dedicated to the deity Shiva, situated at Somnath in the Kathiawar peninsula (now part of Gujarat state in India), on the shores of the Indian Ocean.[675] The dash to this distant goal, through an unknown and unfriendly area, across the deserts of Rajputana and marshes of Cutch, was a remarkable feat of courage, planning, resourcefulness, and tenacity of purpose.[676] Nearly a dozen Indian states had pooled their resources to protect the shrine and give him battle, and Mahmud had the disadvantage of being separated from his main base in Ghazna by nearly a thousand miles of enemy territory. Despite the reckless bravery of the Indian soldiers, fired with religious enthusiasm, Mahmud won the day after a fierce battle in which fifty thousand Indians were killed.[677] He returned in triumph to Ghazna in the Spring of 1026, laden with the extraordinary riches of the temple.[678] So much hatred had he for idol worship that in spite of a desperate plea by the Hindus, the deity image was destroyed and a part of it carried to Ghazna. Mahmud took great pride in professing to be an 'idol-breaker'.[679]

Mahmud, likewise, extended the western borders of his domains. He wrested places such as Rayy and Ispahan from the Buwaihids, who at a time had the caliph under their control.[680]

At their greatest extent, Mahmud's dominions, besides northern India and eastern Iraq, included Khurasan, Tukharistan, Transoxiana and Sijistan.[681]

A brave and resourceful general during thirty years of ceaseless warfare, Mahmud never suffered defeat. He was a cultured monarch and by his

---

[672] Ibid.
[673] Ibid; p. 25.
[674] I.R. and L.L. Al-Faruqi: *The Cultural Atlas*; op cit; p. 218.
[675] S.M. Ikram: *Muslim Civilisation in India;* op cit; p. 25.
[676] Ibid.
[677] H.U. Rahman: *A Chronology;* op cit; pp. 166-7.
[678] S.M. Ikram: *Muslim Civilisation in India;* op cit; p. 25.
[679] H.U. Rahman: *A Chronology;* op cit; pp. 166-7.
[680] P.K. Hitti: *History*; op cit; p. 464.
[681] Halal al-Sabi; *Ta'rikh* (supplement to Miskawayh, Tajarib); vol 3; ed. Amedroz; pp 340; 386.

mugnificence attracted great poets and scholars to his court, making Ghazni the rival of Baghdad in the splendour of the edifices and the number of men of culture and learning such as al-Biruni (973-c.1050) and the historian al-Utbi (d. 1036).[682] He lacked the constructive genius of Mohammed Ghuri (see chapter 9), but he made the work of that later conqueror easier.[683]

In 1029, shortly before the death of Mahmud, from the steppes of eastern Asia, appeared a tribe of Turkmen, the Ghuzz, who settled in the Bukhara region, where they embraced Sunni Islam.[684] Defeated by the Ghaznavid army, they did not return to the steppes, but, dispersed into small groups, and continued to migrate towards the west. The chiefs of the Ghuzz were members of the Seljuk family. A grandson of Seljuk, Tughril, ventured with his brother as far as Khurasan, and in 1037, the two brothers wrested Merw and Nyshapur from Ghaznavid hands, whilst Balkh, Jurjan, Tabaristan and Khwarizm, as well as Hamadan, Ray and Ispahan were speedily added.[685] In his own dominions, Tughril was the father of his soldiers and people; by a firm and equal administration, Persia was relieved from the evils of anarchy; and the Seljuk became the guardians of justice and the public peace.[686] The first of the Seljuk sultans was very religious, each day he repeated the five prayers; of each week, the two first days were consecrated by an extraordinary fast; and in every city a mosque was completed, before Tughril presumed to lay the foundations of a palace.[687]

Meanwhile, the endless futile family squabbles of the Buwaihid princelings in lower Iraq, Khuzistan and Fars had resulted in a certain rise in prestige on the part of the caliph. In 1044, Caliph Al-Qaim wrote to Tughril Beg, the Seljuk leader, who was in Ray, to arrange peace between him and the Buwaihid prince of Baghdad.[688] The Seljuk had conquered large territories, and in front of them the Buwaihid house trembled; and for a good reason; on December 18, 1055, Tughril Beg at the head of his armies stood at the gate of Baghdad.[689] Tughril was received by the Caliph

---

[682] S.M. Ikram: *Muslim Civilisation in India;* op cit; p. 26.
[683] Ibid.
[684] P.K. Hitti: *History*; op cit; p. 474.
[685] Ibid.
[686] E. Gibbon: *The Decline and Fall*; op cit; p. 232.
[687] Ibid; p. 233.
[688] J. Glub: *A Short History*; op cit; p. 129.
[689] P.K. Hitti: *History*; op cit; p. 474.

with elaborate ceremonies, and was hailed as 'king of the East and of the West.'[690]
Taking advantage of Tughril's temporary absence from Baghdad on an expedition to the north, Al-Basari, the general in command under the Buwaihid, who had espoused the Fatimid cause, at the head of his Daylamite troops, forced Caliph al-Qaim to sign a document renouncing his right and the rights of all other Abbasids in favour of the Fatimids in Cairo, to whom he sent the emblems of the caliphate.[691] On his return, however, Tughril reinstated al-Qaim, and made al-Basari pay with his life (1060). The Daylamite troops were disbanded and Buwaihid power was for ever crushed.[692]

The advent of the Seljuk Turks ushered a new and notable era in the history of Islam, Hitti correctly notes.[693] At their appearance from the east in the early part of the 11th century, the caliph held but a shadow of his former power and the Islamic land had been almost entirely dismembered. Such were the divisions, wars, each local prince 'waiting for an opportunity to fly at the throat of the other,' political and military anarchy prevailing everywhere, Shi'ite-Sunni conflict the order of the day, 'Islam seemed crushed.'[694]
It is into this chaotic realm that the Seljuks entered. Not only would they restore Islamic unity and strength, something most non-Muslim and Western historians never forgave them,[695] it was also the Seljuks who stood and fought the crusaders as the following chapter will show.

---

[690] Ibn al-Athir: *Kitab al-kamil*; op cit; vol ix; p. 436.
[691] P.K. Hitti: *History*; op cit; p. 474.
[692] Ibid; p. 475.
[693] Ibid; p. 473.
[694] Ibid.
[695] See, for instance:
-E. Ashtor: *A Social and Economic History of the Near East in the Middle Ages*; Collins; London; 1976; pp. 214 ff.
G. Wiet et al: *History of Mankind*; op cit; pp.243; 458; 663; etc.

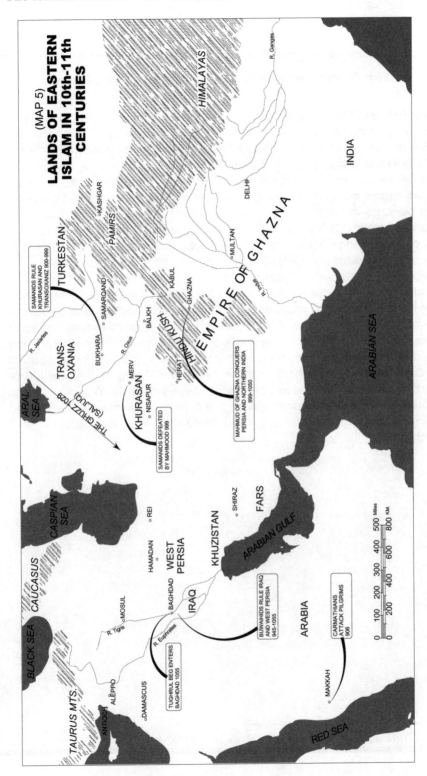

(MAP 5)

LANDS OF EASTERN ISLAM IN 10th-11th CENTURIES

SAMANIDS RULE KHURASAN AND TRANSOXANIZ 900-999

TURKESTAN

KASHGAR

PAMIRS

HIMALAYAS

R. Ganges

INDIA

DELHI

MULTAN

R. Indus

EMPIRE OF GHAZNA

MAHMUD OF GHAZNA CONQUERS PERSIA AND NORTHERN INDIA 999-1050

KABUL

GHAZNA

HINDU KUSH

HERAT

BALKH

SAMARQAND

BUKHARA

TRANS-OXANIA

R. Jaxartes

R. Oxus

KHURASAN

MERV

NISAPUR

SAMANIDS DEFEATED BY MAHMOOD 999

THE GHRUZZ 1029 (SALJUQ)

ARAL SEA

CASPIAN SEA

CAUCASUS

BLACK SEA

REI

HAMADAN

WEST PERSIA

BAGHDAD

IRAQ

MOSUL

R. Tigris

R. Euphrates

ALEPPO

ANTIOCH

DAMASCUS

TAURUS MTS.

TUGHRUL BEG ENTERS BAGHDAD 1055

KHUZISTAN

SHIRAZ

FARS

ARABIAN GULF

BUWAHHIDS RULE IRAQ AND WEST PERSIA 945-1055

ARABIA

CARMATHIANS ATTACK PILGRIMS 906

MAKKAH

RED SEA

ARABIAN SEA

0 100 200 300 400 500 Miles
0 200 400 600 800 KM.

141

The Great Sense of Justice of Mahmud of Ghazna

The name of Mahmud of Ghazna is still venerable in the East: his subjects enjoyed the blessings of prosperity and peace; and two familiar examples will testify his justice and magnanimity. As he sat in the Divan, an unhappy subject bowed before the throne to accuse the insolence of a Turkish soldier who had driven him from his house and bed. "Suspend your clamours," said Mahmud; "inform me of his next visit, and ourselves in person will judge and punish the offender." The sultan followed his guide, invested the house with his guards, and extinguishing the torches, pronounced the death of the criminal, who had been seized in the act of rapine and adultery. After the execution of his sentence, the lights were rekindled, Mahmud fell prostrate in prayer, and rising from the ground, demanded some homely fare, which he devoured with the voraciousness of hunger. The poor man, whose injury he had avenged, was unable to suppress his astonishment and curiosity; and the courteous monarch condescended to explain the motives of this singular behaviour. "I had reason to suspect that none, except one of my sons, could dare to perpetrate such an outrage; and I extinguished the lights, that my justice might be blind and inexorable. My prayer was a thanksgiving on the discovery of the offender; and so painful was my anxiety, that I had passed three days without food since the first moment of your complaint."[696]

****

---

[696] E. Gibbon: *The Decline and Fall*; vol 6; op cit; pp. 227-8.

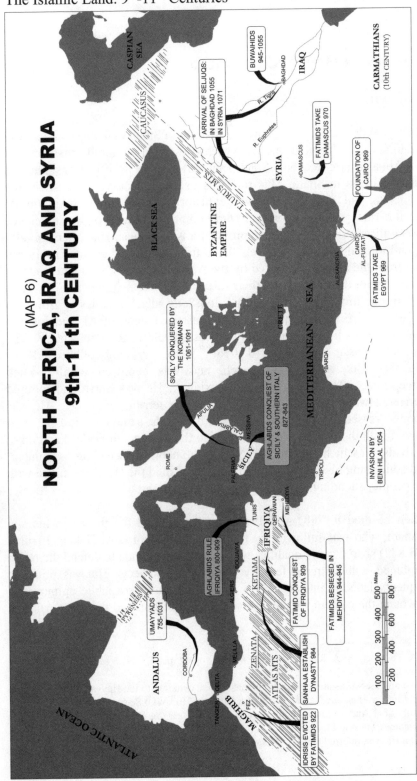

(MAP 6)

**NORTH AFRICA, IRAQ AND SYRIA
9th-11th CENTURY**

3. Spain and the Mediterranean:

a. Spain:

The establishment of an Umayyad dynasty in Spain took place under Abd Errahman ibn Muawiya in 755, who had escaped his family massacre by the Abbasid. He reached Spain, and after arduous efforts established Umayyad rule in Spain. This rule was to prove decisive not just for the Peninsula, but also for the whole history of humanity, Spain, under Muslim rule, was to become at some point the beacon of world science and civilisation. Abd Errahman proved himself to be an able ruler. Initially he had to deal not only with rebellions from within the country itself, but also from the attacks organised by the Abbasid Caliphs, who had made an alliance with the Franks, and their ruler, Charlemagne (emperor 742-814), to dethrone him (Abd Errahman.)[697] In a long rule, which lasted from 756 to 788, Abd Errahman became known as the Falcon of Al-Andalus, the man who established strong, united Muslim rule in the Peninsula.[698] The Muslim historian Ibn Hayyan (d.1076)[699] wrote this eulogy of him:
`He was eloquent in his speech, and was endowed with a quick perception..... He was active and stirring.... He was brave and intrepid warrior, always the first in the field; he was terrible in anger... He was always dressed in white, and wore a turban of the same colour... He often prayed with the people when he attended the mosque on Fridays and other festivals, on which occasions he was in the habit of ascending the minbar, and addressing his subjects from there. He visited the sick, and mixed with the people, attending their rejoicing and recreations.'[700]

When he died in 788, Abd Errahman bequeathed the throne to his son Hisham, who was followed by the inept Al-Hakem I. Al-Hakem I (ruled 796-822) shared many qualities with despots: ineptitude to defend the realm combined with extreme ferocity towards his subjects. He was prone to frequent alcoholic intoxication, a vice which outraged public opinion and provoked the contempt of the conscientious Muslim, and made the palace a

---

[697] A. Thomson; M.A. Rahim: *Islam in Andalus*; op cit; p. 32.
[698] Ibid; pp. 32-3.
[699] Among the works attributed with greater or less certainty to Ibn Hayyan, two titles stand out: *Kitab al-Muqtabis fi tarikh al-Andalus* (Book of Him Who Seeks Knowledge About the History of al-Andalus) in ten volumes, and *Kitab al matin (the Solid Book)* (the latter was in 60 volumes, but is lost today).
[700] Ibn Hayyan referred to by Al-Maqqari in *Nafh Al-Tib*; op cit; I.

scene of orgies that were the reproach and the scandal of the capital.[701] He was the first Spanish Muslim monarch to have his throne surrounded with splendour and a personal guard of six thousand men.[702] He had an exaggerated idea of his authority, an implacable spirit, and merciless severity in the infliction of punishment for even trifling offences.[703] He slaughtered countless thousands of his subjects who objected to his debauched lifestyle.[704] Al-Hakem even had the suburbs where Cordova first originated razed to the ground.[705] Al-Hakem was cruel, yet ineffective. The loss of Barcelona in 800 during his rule was the first great success for the Christians that revived their confidence that they could defeat the Muslims. Scott notes the surprising indifference or culpable neglect of al-Hakem in allowing the enemies of his faith and his dynasty to wrest from its brave defenders one of the most considerable and prosperous cities in his dominions.[706] From Barcelona, the Christians were going to take over the whole of Catalonia, completing this thorough colonization in 811 under the rule of Charlemagne. From Catalonia, the Christians would regroup to mount attacks to wrestle Spain from the Muslims.

The final years of al-Hakem's rule are told by Scott:

'The closing years of Al-Hakem were passed in the seclusion of the harem, where, diverted by the companionship of the beauties of his seraglio, amidst the excitements of intemperance and of every species of debauchery, he endeavoured to forget the sinister events of his checkered career and the manifold acts of cruelty which had avenged the crimes and errors of those who were unfortunate enough to incur his resentment. The controlling maxim of his policy had always been that mildness was synonymous with cowardice, and that the people must be governed by the sword alone.

Oppressed with the memory of his crimes, haunted by the groans and imprecations of his expiring victims, he became the prey of frightful hallucinations, the offspring of a disordered brain..... For four years Al-Hakem continued in this deplorable condition, until relieved by a painful and lingering death.'[707]

Al-Hakem was succeeded by Abd Errahman II (ruled 822-852), who brought substantial changes. Al-Andalus, with its mixed population, had now become a nation, where religious toleration was observed, but where

---

[701] S.P. Scott: *History of the Moorish Empire;* op cit; Vol 1; p.454.
[702] A. Thomson and M.A. Rahim: *Islam in al-Andalus*; op cit; p. 43.
[703] S.P. Scott: *History of the Moorish Empire;* op cit; Vol 1; p.454.
[704] A. Thomson and M.A. Rahim: *Islam in al-Andalus*; op cit; p. 43.
[705] Ibid.
[706] S.P. Scott: *History of the Moorish Empire;* op cit; Vol 1; p.452.
[707] Ibid; pp. 473-4.

many Goths and Spaniards had nevertheless converted to Islam.[708] Abd Errahman II ruled over a strong, not to say a glorious kingdom.

Abd Errahman was succeeded by Mohammed I, who like his father, ruled for more than 30 years. He extended the great mosque of Cordoba, fought off attacks by the Vikings, and by the northern Christians. He was succeeded for a short period by al-Mundhir, who himself was succeeded by Abd Allah, who is described by al-Maqqari as a very pious man.[709] Then came Abd Errahman III.

Burckardt notes how Abd Errahman III granted Muslim Spain its period of greatest unity and finest flowering.[710] He repelled the Christian kingdoms which had been gaining strength in the north of Spain, and halted the advance of the Fatimids in North Africa.[711] He built monuments of great stature, such as the famed al-Zahra, which at some points, in his very presence at the Friday prayer at the mosque, drew criticism from the religious circle, criticism the sovereign acknowledged but did not repress.[712] One of Abd Errahman III's early measures, noted later by Ibn Khaldun, was to suppress all taxes not in accordance with Muslim Tradition, and by causing justice to be fairly and equally delivered.[713]

On the military front, Abd Errahman led many military campaigns. In 914, the King of Leon laid waste the district of Merida and advanced to within a hundred miles of Cordova, the capital. Soon, under Abd Errahman, the tide began to turn. In 918, he defeated the combined armies of Leon and Castile at Tudela. In June 920, he routed the Christians at Val de Junqueras, forty-five miles from the Bay of Biscay.[714] In 924, he captured Pamplona, the capital of Navarre, and carried fire and sword throughout the kingdom. In 934, he took the city of Burgos. Years later, the King and Queen of Navarre and the King of Leon were received by him as suppliants in his palace in Cordova.[715]

The army of Andalus was one of the finest in the world, consisting of Arabs and Berbers and also of "Slavs", who were young boys bought as slaves in France, Germany or Italy, converted to Islam and enlisted as

---

[708] J. Glubb: *A Short History*; op cit; p. 148.

[709] A. Thomson and M.A. Rahim: *Islam in Andalus*; op cit; p. 51.

[710] T. Burckhardt: *Moorish Culture in Spain,* George Allen & Unwin, London; 1972; p. 34.

[711] Ibid.

[712] A. Thomson and M. A. Rahim: *Islam in Andalus;* op cit; p. 59.

[713] In Al-Maqqari: *Nafh Al-Tib;* op cit; vol I; Appendix; xlvii

[714] J. Glubb: *A Short History;* op cit; p. 149.

[715] Ibid.

soldiers.[716] This army had not been built up by means of heavy taxation, for Al-Andalus was extremely prosperous. Many industries were active, including weapons, wrought iron, enamel, jewellery, goldsmith's work, textiles and pottery.[717] The ships of Andalus were to be seen in every Mediterranean port, and agriculture thrived all over the country.[718] Science and art were fostered no less than commerce and industry. Philosophy, medicine and mathematics were actively studied and the Christians of the north, when in need of medical care, came to consult Muslim specialists in Cordova. The Muslims were then far in advance of Western Europe in all forms of knowledge.[719] Muslim Cordova was destined to remain the literary centre of the Middle Ages, the school of polite manners, the home of science and arts; to be regarded with awe by every Muslim, with affectionate veneration by every scholar, and with mingled feelings of wonder and apprehension by `the turbulent barbarians of Western Europe.'[720]

Abd Errahman was succeeded in 961 by another successful ruler, al-Hakem II. He personally led the Muslim armies, and repulsed combined attacks from the North by the Christians and from the south by the Fatimids, and from even further north, attacks by the Vikings.[721] Al-Hakem delighted in books. He amassed such a collection that was estimated at four hundred thousand volumes, causing works on all subjects to be conveyed to Cordova from every country, however remote, lavishing his treasures in their acquisition, and he was so fond of reading them, that he preferred the company of books to the pleasures of royalty.[722] Al-Hakem gave himself to the adornment of Cordova and other cities; built mosques, colleges, hospitals, markets, public baths, and asylums for the poor. He also made the University of Cordova the greatest educational institution of his time, besides helping hundreds of poets, artists, and scholars.[723] The University of Cordova was world famous and many Christians from Western Europe went there for their studies, as Arab

---

[716] See E. Levi Provencal: *Histoire de l'Espagne Musulmane*; 3 Vols; Paris, Maisonneuve, 1953.
[717] See, for instance, S.M. Imamuddin: *Some Aspects of the Socio-Economic and Cultural History of Muslim Spain;* Brill; 1965; T. Glick: *Islamic and Christian Spain in the Early Middle Ages*, Princeton University Press, New Jersey, 1979.
[718] See, T. Glick: *Islamic and Christian Spain.*
[719] See, for instance, T. Burckhardt: *Moorish Culture;* op cit.
[720] S.P. Scott: *History*; op cit; vol 1; p. 271.
[721] A. Thomson: M.A. Rahim: *Islam in Andalus;* op cit; p. 67.
[722] Al-Maqqari: *Nafh al-Tib*; op cit; vol 2; p. 169.
[723] Ibid; p. 146.

students do now to universities in the West.[724] Free primary schools were opened for poor children and even peasants could read and write, though in Christian Europe kings and nobles were often illiterate.[725] Al-Hakem was also a man of war. When counting on his mild disposition, Leon and Navarre repudiated their treaties with Al-Andalus, he invaded their countries and obliged them to sue for peace.[726]

Al-Hakem II died in 976 after a reign of fifteen years and was succeeded by his infant son, Hisham. Due to Hisham's young age, Mohammed ibn Abi Amir became vizier, and soon rose to power. In 981, the new vizier invaded Leon and defeated the Christians at Rueda. On his return, he assumed the title of Al Mansur, the Victorious, by which he was called from then on. Al-Mansur established his authority in the name of Hisham.[727] Al-Mansur's deeds were exemplary. He extended the Cordova mosque, built another palace, al-Zahira, on the banks of the *Wadi al-kebir* (Guadalquivir), and then spent the rest of his rule leading his armies into battle against the Christians in the north, two expeditions each year, even taking Santiago de Compostela on his fiftieth expedition.[728] On 6th July, 985, he sacked the great city of Barcelona; in 988, he overran Leon, taking the capital by assault, and in his twenty-five year rule, he reduced the Christian kingdoms to trembling subservience.[729]

Al-Mansur was not only a soldier but was also extremely active in promoting the material welfare of his country. Roads were constructed, irrigation extended and commerce and industry actively fostered. The judicial system was honest and impartial and every effort was made to encourage education.[730]

In the year 1002, during his fifty second military expedition, Al-Mansur died.

Al-Mansur was followed by the inept rule of his son. After six years, Muslim Spain entered a period of chaos. Civil war erupted throughout the territory, which soon disintegrated into thirty or so independent states, the Reyes of Taifas (1009-1091).[731] The Reyes of Taifas, with rare exceptions,

---

[724] J. Glubb: *A Short History*; op cit; p. 150.
[725] Ibid.
[726] Ibid.
[727] A. Thomson; M. A. Rahim: *Islam in Andalus*; op cit; p. 69.
[728] Ibid; p. 74.
[729] J. Glubb: *A Short History;* op cit; p. 150.
[730] Ibid; p. 151.
[731] J. Read: *The Moors in Spain and Portugal*, Faber and Faber, London, 1974.
D. Wasserstein: *The Rise and Fall of the Party Kings;* Princeton University Press; 1985.

such as Al-Mamun of Toledo, were inept and dissolute, and fought each other, making alliance with the Christians. These intrigues and civil wars amongst Muslims soon invited Northern Christian interventions.[732] Christian strength was enhanced by papal edict. In 1063, Pope Alexander II promised the remission of their sins to any Christians taking part in a 'holy war' against the Muslims of Spain.[733] This brought French knights and adventurers streaming across the Pyrenees. With these powerful reinforcements, Barbastro was taken in 1063 from the Muslims, followed by the massacre of its population.[734] Scott narrates:

'The atrocities practiced (at Barbastro) by these Christian barbarians seem incredible. Such was the amount of booty, that an inferior officer is said to have received as his share five hundred loads of merchandise and fifteen hundred maidens. In the general division, as was customary, the master with his households and possessions were delivered to the fortunate soldier, who at once proceeded, by ingenious tortures, to insult the distress of his victim and inflict upon him exquisite pain in order to compel the discovery of hidden treasure. The female members of his family were violated in his presence. His body was plunged into boiling oil. He was hacked with swords and battle axes and his limbs were slowly wasted by fire.'[735]

In 1085, Toledo fell to Alfonso VI of Castile,[736] a victory achieved with the help of al-Mu'tamid of Seville.[737] Al-Mu'tamid, himself, soon found himself threatened by the Christians. Swallowing his scruples, al-Mu'tamid took ship to North Africa and persuaded Yusuf ibn-Tashfin, the leader of the Berber Almoravids, to intervene.[738] The Almoravids, who had just established their rule in Morocco responded. In 1086, the Berber armies, manoeuvring en masse to the sound of drums, inflicted on the Christian knights a shattering defeat at Sagrajas near Bajadoz.[739] Alfonso made urgent demands for help across the Pyrenees, even threatening to ally himself with the Muslims and to break into France if he did not receive adequate support.[740] In the meantime, Ibn Tashfin had been prompted by local Spanish Muslim rulers to withdraw now the Christian danger had abated. Learning of Ibn Tashfin's withdrawal back to Africa, Alfonso resumed his offensive.[741]

---

[732] J.J. Saunders: *Aspects of the Crusades*, University of Canterbury, 1962. p.19.
[733] J. Read: *The Moors;* op cit; p.103.
[734] J. Read: *The Moors;* op cit.
[735] S.P. Scott: *History of the Moorish Empire;* op cit; vol 2; p. 156.
[736] J.J. Saunders: *Aspects of the Crusades;* op cit p.19.
[737] W. Durant: *The Age of Faith,* op cit; chap 19. p.460.
[738] J. Read: *The Moors in Spain and Portugal;* op cit; p.133.
[739] G. Wiet et al: *History of mankind;* Vol III: op cit; p.269.
[740] J. Read: *The Moors in Spain and Portugal;* op cit.p.128.
[741] Ibid.

Falling under renewed Christian threats the Muslim princes called again upon Ibn Tashfin, who landed in the Peninsula in 1088, then again in 1090. On the final occasion, he decided to take in charge the destinies of the country by himself, removing all princelings, and putting Muslim Spain under Almoravid control. A year after Ibn Tashfin had taken control in Spain, Sicily fell under total Norman control. This happened after an initial great period of Muslim expansion.

b. Muslim Rise and Fall in the Mediterranean:

The period between the 9th and 11th centuries witnessed many other changes around the Mediterranean. Having subdued Catalonia, a Muslim army marched straight into southeast France and joined ranks with the remnants of the Muslim forces that had retreated from Poitiers/Tours, and occupied Narbonne, Carcassonne, Lyons, Arles and Nimes.[742] Having occupied the islands of Majorca, the Muslims of Spain and those of Africa carried out a number of raids against Corsica and Sardinia in 806-808, aided by their co-religionists from Nice. But it was not until the end of the century that the Muslims made a serious advance into southeast France.[743] The Muslims chose another area east of Marseilles, around the bay of Grimaud, and established a base for their operations at Fraxinet (today's GardeFrainet) because of its strategic location: accessible by sea, guarded by a dense forest of ash (fraxini), and providing passage to the Alps. The Muslims seized the passages of the Alpine chains, one after another, and spread their dominion over the countryside.[744] By 288H/900, the regions of Provence, Dauphiné, Piedmont, Monferrat, and La Maurienne, and up the Rhine including St. Gall, Great St. Bernard, St. Rémy, and south to the Mediterranean slightly east of Nice, all came under Muslim control.[745] Gradually, though, the Muslims were forced out of these areas by the invading Huns from the north and Hungarians from the east. The Castle of Fraxinet was captured by the French in 365/975, and Muslim presence in France and Switzerland was over by the end of the 10th century.[746]

---

[742] P.K. Hitti: *History*; op cit; p. 501.
[743] I. Rand LL. Al-Faruqi: *The Cultural Atlas*; op cit; p. 217.
[744] Ibid.
[745] Ibid.
[746] Ibid.

An important place the Muslims gained and then lost over the same period was Sicily. In the year 668, a Muslim fleet of 200 ships sailed from Alexandria and plundered Byzantine Sicily, which was thus overrun for the second time-the first having been in 652.[747] This, however, did not lead to a permanent conquest of the island, which came much later, in 827. Control of Sicily implied a major role in the affairs of the Mediterranean world, and it is thus no wonder that during the Middle Ages possession of the island was a prize contested among the major Mediterranean powers.[748] In 827, the Aghlabid ruler of Tunisia, Ziyadat Allah I (817-838), mounted a seventy vessel expedition, led by Assad Ibn al-Furat, which succeeded in establishing a long term foothold on the island.[749] From their base in Mazara, on the west coast, taken in 827, the Muslim force of ten thousand men moved forward on Syracuse.[750] Palermo fell in 831, which gave vantage point to the Muslims for further conquest: Messina fell in 843, Enna in 859, Syracuse, after a nine month siege, was taken in 878.[751] The Muslim expeditionary force was 'an infinitely mixed lot of Arabs, Berbers, Spaniards, and Sudanese.'[752] And so was to be the island itself, ethnic and religious diversity the main feature of its population during the 250 years of Muslim rule. The monk Theodosius, brought thence from Syracuse with Archbishop Sophronius in 883, acknowledged the grandeur of the new capital, Palermo, describing it as:
'Full of citizens and strangers, so that there seems to be collected there all the Saracen folk from East to West and from North to South . . . Blended with the Sicilians, the Greeks, the Lombards and the Jews, there are Arabs, Berbers, Persians, Tartars, Negroes, some wrapped in long robes and turbans, some clad in skins and some half naked; faces oval, square, or round, of every complexion and profile, beards and hair of every variety of colour or cut.'[753]
A majority of the inhabitants retained their Christian religious allegiance and, in line with Islamic practice, were accorded the status of protected minorities (dhimmis); which meant, that in return for the payment of a poll tax (jizya) and adherence to certain regulations, they were guaranteed the

---

[747] Al-Baladhuri: *Kitab Futuh al-Buldan;* op cit; p. 235.
[748] A.L. Udovitch: Islamic Sicily; in *Dictionary of the Middle Ages*; J.R. Strayer Editor in Chief; Charles Scribner's Sons, New York; 1980 ff; Vol 11; pp. 261-3; p.261.
[749] Ibn al-Idhari: *Al-Bayan al-Maghrib;* op cit; vol 1; p. 95.
[750] Ibn al-Athir: *Kamil;* op cit; vol vi; p. 236.
Al-Idrisi: *Min Kitab Nuzhat al-Mushtaq fi Ikhtiraq al-Afaq;* ed. M. Amari and C. Schiaparelli; Roma; 1878; p. 32.
[751] Ibn al-Athir: *Kamil*; op cit; vol vii; p. 31.
[752] J. D. Breckenridge: The Two Sicilies; in *Islam and the Medieval West*; S. Ferber Ed; State University of New York; 1975; pp. 39-59; at p. 43.
[753] Ibid.

safety of their persons and property, and the freedom to follow the precepts of their own religion and maintain the institutions of their religious community.[754] The same status was accorded to the small Jewish community of the island, which seems to have been concentrated mainly in the coastal towns.[755]

After two or so centuries of prosperity, Muslim rule in Sicily ended. This happened in the 11th century. It began early in the century with open warfare between the Kalbid Emir of Palermo and the Zirid of Tunisia.[756] Fully aware of such internal quarrels among the Sicilian Muslims, the Christians, through the Normans, resolved to retake the island.[757] The initial Norman invasion followed a local Muslim invitation.[758] One of the Muslim emirs built links of intelligence with Roger I, the youngest of the Norman Hauteville brothers, who did not refuse the offer.[759] The Normans who swept across South Italy in the next few decades were a small band,[760] and had the Muslims not been divided, the Normans would have found no foothold; as it was, in the course of a generation, the small band of adventurers created for themselves a kingdom.[761] The Normans landed in Sicily and began to advance at the expense of the Muslims; which hardly seemed to bother the Muslims, as even when the Normans were half masters of the island, the Muslim chiefs continued to fight one another.[762] In fact, the Sicilian Christians were less supportive of the Norman invasion than the Muslim factions.[763] In 1061 Roger I succeeded in capturing Messina, Palermo in 1071, and Syracuse in 1085.[764] By 1091, the conquest of the Island was complete.

Muslim communities survived in Sicily for more than two centuries after the Norman conquest.[765] Then, in the 14th century, as chapter seven will show, the Muslims disappeared.

---

[754] A.L. Udovitch: Islamic Sicily; op cit; p.262.
[755] Ibid.
[756] See Ibn al-Athir: *Kamil*; op cit; vol viii.
[757] A.A. Vasiliev: The Struggle with the Saracens (867-1057): in *The Cambridge Medieval History*, Vol IV: Edited by J. R. Tanner, C. W. Previte; Z.N. Brooke, 1923; p.150.
[758] N. Daniel: The Arabs; op cit; p.144.
[759] M.L. de Mas Latrie: *Traites de paix et de Commerce,* Burt Franklin, New York, originally Published in Paris, 1866; p.42.
[760] J. D. Breckenridge: The Two Sicilies; op cit; 46-7.
[761] N. Daniel: *The Arabs*; op cit; p.145.
[762] G. Le Bon: *La Civilisation*; op cit; p.230.
[763] J. D. Breckenridge: The Two Sicilies; op cit; pp 46-7.
[764] P.K. Hitti: *History;* op cit; p. 606.
[765] A.L. Udovitch: Islamic Sicily; op cit; p.263.

The Muslim Legacy to Humanity in Civilisation

Scott writes:
`The genius of the Arabian people advanced rapidly in the path of civilisation, while the dense and sluggish intellect of the northern barbarians, who, in their origin, were not less ignorant, remained stationary. It took Spain, under the Moslems, less than half a century to reach a point in human progress which was not attained by Italy under the popes in a thousand years. The capacity of the Arab mind to absorb, to appropriate, to invent, to develop, to improve, has no parallel in the annals of any race. The empire of the khalifs included an even greater diversity of climate and nations than that of Rome. The ties of universal brotherhood proclaimed by the Koran; the connections demanded by the requirements of an extended commerce; the intimate associations encouraged by the pilgrimage to Mecca, awakened the curiosity and enlarged, in an equal degree, the minds of the Moslems of Asia, Africa and Europe. Yet more important than all was the effect of the almost incessant hostilities waged against the infidel. By its constantly varying events, its fascinations, its thrilling excitements, its dangers, its victories, defeats, and triumphs, war has a remarkable tendency to expand the intellectual faculties, and thereby to advance the cause of truth and promote the improvement of every branch of useful knowledge.'[766]

---

[766] S.P. Scott: *History;* op cit; vol 1; p. 324.

4. North Africa and Egypt:

The history of North Africa and Egypt during this period is very much intermingled, events very often shared by both. The most glorious page of the region was under the Tunisian Aghlabid, whose rule was also to have decisive impacts north of the Mediterranean.

a. The Greatness of the Aghlabid Dynasty:

In North Africa, by the 9th century, the local dynasties of the Rustamids and the Idrisids had already carved out independent domains for themselves. An army officer, Ibrahim ibn Aghlab, offered the Caliph to restore order in Ifriqiya and keep it under the control of Baghdad, provided governorship of the region with considerable autonomy was granted to him.[767] Ibn Aghlab made it easy for the Abbasid caliph by foregoing the subsidy which Tunisia had been receiving from Egypt, and undertaking to pay tribute to Baghdad.[768] Ibrahim, a man of exceptional ability and energy, established a new dynasty of rulers-the Aghlabids (r. 800-909) and started exercising independent rule from the capital at Al-Qayrawan in Tunisia, according only nominal recognition to the Caliph. To North Africa, a region, which had been torn apart by endless civil wars during the previous years, Aghlabid rule brought peace and prosperity. It was under Ziyadat Allah I (ruled 817-838), most particularly, that the dynasty's prestige was carried to its highest.[769]

It was under the Aghlabids that Al-Qayrawan, the greatest city of the Maghrib, underwent considerable expansion and reached the zenith of its prosperity.[770] The Aghlabid rulers vied with each other in enriching the city with monuments and multiplied the works of public utility.[771] Prince Ziyadat Allah I built a hospital in the city in 830, one of the most pioneering of its genre, called ad-Dimnah hospital, near the Great Mosque.[772] The Aghlabids

---

[767] Ibn al-Athir: *Kamil*; op cit; vol vi; pp. 106 ff. Ibn al-Idhari: *Al-Bayan al-Maghrib;* op cit; vol 1; p. 83.

[768] J.M. Abun Nasr: *A History of the Maghrib;* op cit; p. 76.

[769] S and N. Ronart: *Concise Encyclopaedia of Arabic civilization; The Arab West;* Djambatan; Amsterdam; 1966; p. 38.

[770] G. Iver: Kairawan; *Encyclopaedia of Islam*; first series vol 4; pp. 646-9; p. 647.

[771] Ibid.

[772] S. Hamarneh: *Health Sciences in Early Islam;* Noor Foundation and Zahra Publications; Texas, 1983; p. 102.

also constructed great engineering works, including water reservoirs, aqueducts and bridges, and complex sewerage systems.[773] Some such remarkable works were the reservoirs, one of which al-Bakri describes: `Is circular in form and of enormous size. In the centre rises an octagonal tower covered by a pavilion with four doors. A long series of arcades of arches resting one upon the other ends on the south side of the reservoir.'[774]

One of the glories of Islam, to be found in Al-Qayrawan, is the large mosque. Al-Qayrawan Mosque, also known as Jamii Uqba, was built sometime between 670 and 680 by Uqba ibn Nafi, the founder of that city.[775] It is the first mosque in the Maghrib, several times rebuilt and lavishly embellished in the course of centuries, and is still standing.[776] The Aghlabid ruler, Ziyadat Allah set up in the prayer hall the multitude of splendid columns, rich panelling of glazed tiles and ornamentations of sculptured wood.[777]

Al-Qayrawan, together with Kufa and Madinah, was one of the capitals of Muslim sciences and learning. Yahia Ibn Salam al-Basri (745-815) composed and taught there his tafsir; Assad Ibn al-Furat (759-828) made a synthesis of teachings of all his masters.[778] Al-Qayrawan attracted students from all parts, including Muslim Spain.[779] Women actively participated in the pursuit of learning there, and scholars, reigning monarchs and men from all walks of life supported eagerly the library of their town's grand mosque.[780] At the end of the 9th century, the Aghlabid established a Bayt al-Hikma (House of Wisdom)[781] rivalling its counterpart in Baghdad in the study of medicine, astronomy, engineering and translation.[782] Alongside these subjects, were also taught the Qur'an and jurisprudence, grammar and mathematics.[783] The study of medicine was well represented by Ziad. B.

---

[773] S and N. Ronart: *Concise Encyclopaedia;* op cit; pp, 37-8.

[774] Al-Bakri quoted by G. Iver: Kairawan; op cit; at p. 647.

[775] H. Saladin: *Tunis et Kairouan;* Librairie Renouard; Paris; 1908. p.100.

[776] P.K. Hitti: *History;* op cit; p. 452.

[777] S, and N. Ronart: *Concise Encyclopaedia;* op cit; p. 37-8.

[778] J. Fontaine and P. Gresser: *Le Guide de la Tunisie;* op cit; p.309.

[779] M. Talbi: Al-Qayrawan; *Encyclopaedia of Islam*, op cit, vol IV, p 829.

[780] M.M. Sibai; *Mosque Libraries: An Historical Study;* Mansell Publishing Limited: London and New York: 1987; p. 58.

[781] H H Abd al-Wahab, `*Bait al-Hikma al-Tunusi, Baht Tarikhi fi Awwal Musasa Ilmiya jamia fi al-Bilad al-Ifriqiya,*" Majallat Majma al-Lugha al-Arabiya (Cairo) 30 (1963-4), p 128.

[782] M. Al-Rammah: The Ancient Library of Kairaouan and its methods of conservation, in *The Conservation and Preservation of Islamic Manuscripts*, Proceedings of the Third Conference of Al-Furqan Islamic Heritage Foundation, 1995, pp 29-47. p. 29.

[783] H. Djait et al: *Histoire de la Tunisie*; (le Moyen Age); Societe Tunisienne de Difusion, Tunis;. p. 378.

Khalfun, Ishak B. Imran and Ishak B. Sulayman.[784] Their works were taken to Europe, and were translated by Constantine the African, thus helping establish the university of Salerno (in southern Italy), which was to become subsequently the first European university, with a specialisation in the study of medicine.[785] Constantine's translations, thus, revolutionised the whole of learning in Western Christendom courtesy of the medical learning of al-Qayrawan.[786]

A venerated sanctuary, and capital of a powerful state, Al-Qayrawan was also a great commercial city, the shops of the merchants stood on either side of a covered street about two miles in length.[787] Many monuments and sites witness the greatness of the city.[788]

It was under the Aghlabids that Islam expanded from the Maghrib in the direction of the Mediterranean islands.[789] The Aghlabid ruler, Ziyadat Allah I, granted al-Qayrawan the first role in the expansion of Islam, just as Uqba did centuries before him. He carried the dynasty's prestige to its highest, and set about a policy of Muslim expansion.[790] In 827 the mounted Muslim expedition succeeded in establishing a long term presence in Sicily.[791]

Aghlabid rule, however, became a prey to the rapidly growing power of the Fatimids. In 873, a man named Abdullah ibn Maimun al-Qaddah (d. circa 875) appeared on the scene and claimed for himself and his successors the position of a chosen legate of the *Mahdi*. He professed to be inspired and had the power to perform miracles.[792] He, soon, established a vast network of secret but active organizations in various parts of the Islamic land preaching a doctrine of revolution against the Sunni order and the Abbasid Caliphate.[793] In 893, a certain Abu Abdullah was sent out to Tunisia from Yemen with the task of propagating the Ismaili faith and inspiring the Berbers to rebel against their Sunni Aghlabid rulers.[794] Settling among the martial Kutama, south of Bejaia (modern Algeria), he converted them and became the principal man in the tribe. He was helped

---

[784] Al-Bakri, *Massalik*, 24; Ibn Abi Usaybi'a, *Uyun al-anba*, ed. and tr A. Nourredine and H. Jahier, Algiers 1958, 2.9, in *Encyclopaedia of Islam*, Vol IV, pp 29-30.

[785] D. Campbell: *Arabian Medicine and its Influence*; op cit; p. 123.

[786] W. Durant: *The Age of Faith*; op cit; P. 457

[787] G. Iver: Kairawan; op cit; at p. 647.

[788] J. Fontaine, and P. Gresser: *Le Guide de la Tunisie*; op cit; p. 3 06.

[789] Ibn al-Athir: *Kamil;* op cit; vol vi; pp. 235 ff.

[790] S and N. Ronart: *Concise Encyclopaedia*; op cit; p. 38.

[791] A.L. Udovitch: Islamic Sicily; op cit; p.261.

[792] H.U. Rahman: *A Chronology;* op cit; p. 143.

[793] Ibid.

[794] Ibid.

in his task by the fact that the ruling Aghlabid ruler happened, in 904, to be a drunken degenerate.[795] The Kutama, led by Abu Abdullah, rose in revolt. Promising the early arrival of the true Imam, who would bring in the age of peace and justice, Abu Abdullah captured Al-Qayrawan on 27th March, 909, from the last Aghlabid ruler, who took a flight without offering any resistance, and, thus, the Aghlabid dynasty came to an end.[796] This was the beginning of the Fatimid era

b. The Rise of the Fatimids:

In 902 and then 904, there were uprisings in Syria, where a claimant to the Imamate, Sa'id ibn Ahmad, had assumed the name of Ubaidulla. He sought to join Abu Abdullah, travelling in the south to Sijilmasa, but was captured and imprisoned by the Rustamids.[797] Meanwhile, Abu Abdullah, had been very active in the missionary work, and his promise of the imminent arrival of the Mahdi, overthrew the century-old Aghlabid dynasty in 909 with the help of his converts from the Kutama Berber tribes, and captured Al-Qayrawan.[798] He rescued Ubaidulla from Sijilmassa, overrunning and putting an end to the small principality of the Rustamids. The new dynasty called itself the Fatimid, claiming descent from Fatima, the Prophet's daughter.[799] The emergence of the Fatimids (909-1171) was a major event in Islamic history. At its peak, the Fatimid empire included north Africa, Sicily, the Red Sea coast of Africa, Hijaz (including Makkah and Madinah), Yemen, Palestine and Syria.

Once the first Fatimid ruler, Ubaidulla (r. 909-34), was in the saddle, he assumed the titles of both Mahdi and Caliph. Soon a rift developed between him and Abu Abdullah. Abu Abdullah questioned Ubaidulla's claim to be the expected Mahdi, and was consequently assassinated together with his brother in 911.[800] Abu Abdullah's killing led to revolts among the Kutama and the Kharijites of the Atlas, but these were eventually suppressed after two years of heavy fighting. Soon, Fatimid power was stretched from Morocco to the confines of Egypt. In 922,

---

[795] J. Glubb: *A Short History;* op cit; p. 142.
[796] Ibn al-Idhari: *Al-Bayan al-Maghrib*; op cit; vol 1; pp. 142-6; J. Glubb: *A Short History;* p. 142.
[797] J.M. Abun Nasr: *A History of the Maghrib;* op cit; p. 81.
[798] H.U. Rahman: *A Chronology;* op cit; p. 144.
[799] J. Glubb: *A Short History;* op cit; p. 142.
[800] J.M. Abun Nasr: *A History of the Maghrib;* op cit; p. 81.

Ubaidulla sent his army to the west, overran the Berber states and drove the Idrisids from their throne in Fez.[801] Ubaidulla regarded Ifriqiya as a mere stepping-stone to the replacement of the Abbasids as sole Caliphs of the Muslim world.[802] In 913, he sent his son Qaim with an army to conquer Egypt. Alexandria was seized in 914, and the Delta devastated two years later.[803] He failed, though, to take the capital, Fustat. To Sicily, the Fatimid ruler sent a new governor, and with the rebel leader Ibn Hafsun in Spain, he established friendly relations.[804] Malta, Sardinia, Corsica, the Balearic, and other islands felt the power of the fleet which he had inherited from the Aghlabids.[805] Across the straits in Al-Andalus, the Umayyad, Abd Errahman III, was alarmed by this Fatimid advance and seized the ports of Melilla and Ceuta, whence he supported Berber resistance to the Fatimids.[806]

North Africa, meanwhile, was a powder-magazine of religious passions. The Berbers of the Atlas were Kharijite puritans, the people of the coastal plains were Sunnis, the ruler and the government were Fatimid-Shiites. In 944, Abu Yazeed, a Berber Kharijite ascetic, preached a holy war against the Shiites. Sweeping irresistibly forward at the head of vast numbers of Berbers, he laid siege, in November 944, to the fortress of Mehdiya, where the Fatimids had taken refuge.[807] The dynasty was saved by the support of the Sanhaja, a nomadic tribe of the Sahara, under their chief Ziri ibn Manad. The Berbers of the Atlas grew tired, and, in September 945, Abu Yazeed was obliged to withdraw after a siege of ten months.

North African dislike of the Fatimids was not ended, though. The Tunisian population rose in anger against the Fatimids. Several Muslim theologians had been murdered under the Fatimid ruler al-Qasim (934-46); religious oppression, which was accompanied by economic extortion, and selling of government offices.[808]

In May 946, the Fatimid caliph Qaim died and was succeeded by his son Ismail. Ismail died in 953 and was succeeded by his son, Al Muizz li Deen Allah, "he who makes glorious the religion of God". Muizz at last found himself strong enough to return to the family ambition of conquering

---

[801] J. Glubb: *A Short History;* op cit; p. 142.
[802] Ibid.
[803] P.K. Hitti: *History;* op cit; p. 618.
[804] Ibid.
[805] Ibid.
[806] J. Glubb: *A Short History*; op cit; p. 142.
[807] J.M. Abun Nasr: *A History of the Maghrib*; op cit; p. 84.
[808] Ibid; p. 83.

Egypt. But before marching eastwards, he decided to re-establish Fatimid authority in all North Africa. In 958, a Fatimid army marched out of Al-Qayrawan and swept across North Africa to the Atlantic coast, capturing Fez and Tangier.[809] Then came the turn of Egypt. Egypt was taken in 969, and the Fatimid ruler Muizz established himself in Cairo.

When Muizz left Al-Qayrawan for Cairo, he left behind as his viceroy in North Africa the son of Ziri ibn Manad of the Sanhaja Berbers, who had relieved Mehdiya during the rebellion of Abu Yazeed. In 984, however, the Sanhaja, under their leader, Mansur, established an independent dynasty in Al-Qayrawan.[810] When the ruler Mansur died in 996, his son Badis, was only twelve years old. Mansur's brother, Hammad, refused to swear allegiance to a child and the dynasty divided into two parts, Beni Ziri and Beni Hammad. Further west, the Zenata, another Berber group which had replaced the Idrisids, also broke away.[811] From 996 onwards, therefore, North Africa was divided between three Berber dynasties, the Beni Ziri Sanhaja in Al-Qayrawan, the Beni Hammad Sanhaja (Eastern-central Algeria) and the Zenata. Henceforward the authority of the Fatimid Caliph extended no further west than Barqa, and was centred on Egypt.[812]

Egypt:

In 868, Ahmed Ibn Tulun, a young Turkish officer, whose father was a Turk from Farghanah, sent by the Samanid ruler of Bukhara as a present to the Abbasid caliph, Al-Mamun,[813] was made governor of Egypt. Thus was established the first local dynasty, the Tulunids (868-905), of Egypt, and later jointly of Egypt, Palestine and Syria, which he occupied in 877.[814] To maintain his hold on Syria, Ibn Tulun developed a naval base at Akka (Acre).[815]
During the rule of this enterprising soldier-politician, agriculture, commerce and industry were promoted, government finances reorganized and a large-scale public building programme undertaken, which made

---

[809] J. Glubb: *A Short History;* op cit; p. 144.
[810] Ibid.
[811] Ibid; p. 145.
[812] Ibid.
[813] Ibn Khaldun: *Kitab al-Ibaar;* Bulaq; 1868; vol 3; p. 295.
[814] P. K. Hitti: *History*; op cit; p. 453.
[815] Yaqut al-Hamawi: *Mu'Ajam al-Buldan*; Wustenfeld ed; op cit; vol 3; pp. 707-8.

Egypt enter an era of prosperity.[816] In this vast effort, Ibn Tulun improved the Nilometer, and adorned the capital, al-Fustat, with magnificent edifices.[817] Some such edifices were the famed sixty thousand dinar hospital, which bore his name,[818] and the mosque, which he had completed in 879. This mosque is remarkable for the use of brick piers and for the early use of the pointed arch, besides the inscription of one seventeenth of the Qur'an on the wooden frieze round the inside of the building just below the flat timbered roof.[819]

In 884, lbn Tulun died and was succeeded by his son, Khumarawayh (884-895). Khumarawayh was extravagant, his palace, with its golden hall, had its walls covered in gold, and decorated with bas relief of himself, his wives and his songstresses.[820] The new ruler indulged in great extravagances, which absorbed the country's wealth; his daughter's dowry at her wedding consisting of a million dirhams, whilst presents consisted of one thousand mortars of gold and other things, the Muslim chroniclers, Ibn Khallikan and Ibn Tahgri-Birdi, noting, `the like of which had never been seen before.'[821] Khumarawayh was also famed for his drunkenness, able to drink four rotls of wine at one sitting.[822] On the day of his burial, the seven Qur'an readers appointed to recite the sacred text happened to be chanting:
`Seize ye him and drag him into the mid-fire of hell.'[823]

Khumarawayh, just as his three subsequent successors, turned out to be ineffectual and wasteful, causing Egypt and Syria to fall into confusion. Egypt was rent with bloody clashes amongst the diverse factions.[824] Under such conditions, the Abbasid army had no difficulty in capturing the Egyptian capital, Fustat, after the Tulunid ruler had been assassinated by

---

[816] P. K. Hitti: *History*; op cit; p. 453.

[817] Al-Maqrizi: *Kitab al-Khitat,* ed. Bulaq; partial Fr tr. by U. Bouriant and P. Casanova: *Description topographique et Historique de l'Egypte*, Paris, 1895-1900; vol 1; pp. 313 ff.

[818] Ibn Taghri Birdi: *Al-Nujum al-Zahirah fi Muluk Misr wa'l Qahira;* ed. T.G.J. Juynboll; vol 2; Leyden; 1855; p. 11.

[819] Al-Maqrizi: *Kitab al-Khitat,* ed. Bulaq; vol 2; pp. 265 ff.

[820] Ibn Taghri Birdi: *Al-Nujum al-Zahirah*; op cit; vol 2; pp. 57-8.
Al-Maqrizi: *Kitab al-Khitat,* ed. Bulaq; vol 1; pp. 316-7.

[821] Ibn Khallikan: *Wafayat Al-Ayan;* op cit; vol 1; p. 310.
Ibn Taghri Birdi: *Al-Nujum al-Zahirah*; op cit; vol 2; p.55.

[822] Tanukhi: *Jami' al-Tawarikh;* ed. D.S. Margoliouth; vol 1; London; 1921; p. 261.

[823] In P. K. Hitti: *History;* op cit; p. 455.

[824] H.U. Rahman: *A Chronology;* op cit; pp. 129-130.

his own men; thus the Tulunid dynasty coming to an abrupt end after a short life of thirty-seven years.[825]

Abbasid rule over Egypt was not to last, either. The years of chaos which had distracted Baghdad after the murder of Mutawakkil had prevented the Abbasids from controlling Egypt. In August 969, a Fatimid army commanded by Jawhar, established its headquarters outside Fustat, and marked out in the vicinity the foundations of a new royal palace and city, first named Mansuriya but renamed Al-Qahira, the Victorious (Cairo).[826] In July 972, the Caliph Muizz made his state entry into his new capital where, seated on a golden throne, he received the homage of the notables of Egypt. Jawhar then led the Fatimid armies to occupy Syria in 975. For a brief moment, the Fatimids were acknowledged by an immense empire extending from the Maghrib to Syria.[827] Together with this vast empire, the wealth of' the Fatimids in the reign of' Azeez (975-996) was almost past belief. The golden thrones covered with precious stones and approached by silver steps, the marble pillars, and the roof beams covered with gold in their palaces, suggest a fairy story more than the world we know.[828]

The Banu Hilal Invasion and the End of North-Africa's Power and Prosperity:

From the departure of the Fatimids to Egypt in 972 until 1054, North Africa enjoyed a period of peace and prosperity.[829] The Banu Hilal invasion in 1057 changed this for ever. This invasion was the result of Fatimid revenge against their former Zirid allies for the latter abandoning their side.

'I give you,' said the Fatimid Caliph to the Banu Hilal tribes (unruly tribes of herdsmen), 'I give you, he said, 'the Maghrib with all its riches.' And to enhance his vow, he gave each warrior who crossed the western frontier of Egypt a dinar and a cloth of honour.[830] This, Saladin reckons, simply meant ruin and devastation of Ifriqya.[831] In wave after wave, the invaders, the Banu

---

[825] Ibid; p. 142.
[826] J.M. Abun Nasr: *A History of the Maghrib;* op cit; p. 84.
[827] J. Glubb: *A Short History;* op cit; p. 144.
[828] Ibid; p. 145.
[829] Ibid; p. 146.
[830] H. Saladin: *Tunis et Kairouan;* op cit; p. 106.
[831] Ibid; p. 107.

Hilal warriors followed by their families and herds, swept over Cyrenaica and Tripolitania into southern Tunisia, drawing others behind them, pilfering, burning, and destroying everything on their way.[832] The invaders spread havoc, the towns and cities were burnt down; the countryside devastated; the whole of Ifriqya was turned from its once prosperous condition into a vast empty and arid zone, only suitable land for herds, nomads, and shepherds.[833] The Hilali invasions of the mid-11th century ended Tunisia's role as an entrepot.[834] The Banu Hilal entered Al-Qayrawan, and wrought the most frightful havoc on it in 1057.[835] Al-Qayrawan, residence of the caliph's governors, the spiritual and intellectual metropolis of the Muslim West in the days of the Aghlabids and the Zirids, was thoroughly devastated.[836] Ibn Khaldun says:

`They destroyed all the beauty and all the splendour of the monuments of Qayrawan. Nothing that the Sanhadji princes had left in their palaces escaped the greed of the brigands. All that there was in the town was carried off or destroyed.'[837]

The population was scattered in all directions.[838] The capital of Ifriqya never recovered from this disaster.[839] Writing in the 16th century, Leo Africanus, who visited Al-Qayrawan in 1516, says:

`The inhabitant are at present all poor artisans, of whom some are curriers of the skins of sheep and goats, the others furriers whose handi work is sold in the cities of Numidia, where no European cloth is to be had. But of these traders, there is none who is able to make a decent living and those who follow them live a miserable existence and are in very great poverty.'[840]

The devastation caused by the Banu Hilal spread throughout the region. The Banu Hammad abandoned their capital for Bejaia, surviving in a helpless situation.[841] The whole of the Maghrib was in a state of anarchy, even the most prosperous regions had now become impoverished.[842] Talbi writes:

`On the first day of Ramadhan of 1057, they (the Banu Hilal) began their destruction and devastation. This half of the century symbolised not just the

---

[832] S and N. Ronart: *Concise Encyclopaedia;* op cit; p. 398.

[833] H. Saladin: *Tunis et Kairouan;* op cit; p. 107.

[834] T. Glick: *Islamic and Christian Spain;* op cit; p. 131.

[835] G. Iver: Kairawan; op cit; p. 648.

[836] S and N. Ronart: *Concise Encyclopaedia;* op cit; p. 368.

[837] Ibn Khaldun: *Histoire des Berberes;* Trans De Slane; i.37.

[838] Abd al-Wahid al-Marrakushi: *Al-Mu'djib fi Tarikh akhbar al-Maghrib;* ed. R. Dozy; 2; p. 259.

[839] G. Iver: Kairawan; op cit; at p. 648.

[840] Leo Africanus; quoted in G. Iver: Kairawan; op cit; at p. 648.

[841] J.M. Abun Nasr: *A History of the Maghrib*; op cit; pp. 85-6.

[842] Ibid; p. 86.

end of al-Qayrawan, but also the end of the whole brilliance of the Maghrib. It was the end of a prestigious period of civilisation. Urban life and urbanity retreated in front of the advance of the nomadic hordes, the Bedouinisation of the country spread down to the 19th century.'[843]

Following the Banu Hillal attacks, a Norman baron, Roger, the son of Tancred of Hauteville, landed in Sicily in 1061, and by 1091 won Sicily and Malta for Christendom.[844] Soon, the Normans and their Christian allies began to land and destroy what was left of a weakened North Africa.

Chaos in North Africa, followed by Christian victories and conquests there, came on top of the Christian gains in Sicily in 1091 and in Spain less than a decade before. These victories emboldened Western Christendom. Now that the Muslim world was in chaos and divided, this was the best opportunity to destroy the whole of its realm. Thus were launched the crusades in 1095.

---

[843] M. Talbi, quoted in J. Fontaine, and P. Gresser: *Le Guide de la Tunisie*; op cit; p. 310.
[844] J. Glubb: A Short History; op cit; p. 148.

SIX

THE CRUSADES AND THE GREAT MUSLIM HEROES
(1095-1291)

This chapter looks at the crusades in the East. It is a period of two halves, the first elapsing from the Crusader entry in the Holy Land in 1096 to the death of Salah Eddin el-Ayyubi (1193). The second half begins with Salah Eddin's successors, and ends with the Mamluks re-taking the last Crusade stronghold: Acre, in 1291.

1. From the First Crusade to Salah Eddin: 1096-1193:

The crusades resulted mainly from the state of chaos in the Muslim world, its divisions and collapsing strength, which encouraged the Church to launch attacks in Spain, Sicily, and now in the East. The Damascus Imam-Scholar, al-Sulami, rightly understood that the crusades were the outcome of the Frankish success in the West (Spain and Sicily), and a decision to pursue the fight in the Orient.[845] The capture of Sicily (1091), most particularly, was a very encouraging sign to the Christians that they could remove the Muslim presence everywhere. And so, the crusades were launched in the East.

Christendom, however, needed a justification for the crusades. Thus, prior to launching the crusades, Pope Urban II stirred Christian zeal by emphasising Muslim crimes against the Christians. In his speech to the Christian assembly meeting in the French town of Clermont Ferrant, he said:
`An accursed race, a race utterly alienated from God, a generation forsooth which has not directed its heart and has not entrusted its spirit to God, has invaded the lands of those Christians and has depopulated them by the

---

[845] Al-Sulami: Un traite Damasquin du debut du XIIem siecle, ed E. Sivan, *Journal Asiatique*, 1966, p. 207.

sword, pillage and fire; it has led away a part of the captives into its own country, and a part it has destroyed by cruel tortures; it has either entirely destroyed the churches of God or appropriated them for the rites of its own religion. They destroy the altars, after having defiled them with their uncleanness. They circumcise the Christians, and the blood of the circumcision they either spread upon the altars or pour into the vases of the baptismal font. When they wish to torture people by a base death, they perforate their navels, and dragging forth the extremity of the intestines, bind it to a stake; then with flogging they lead the victim around until the viscera having gushed forth the victim falls prostrate upon the ground. Others they bind to a post and pierce with arrows. Others they compel to extend their necks and then, attacking them with naked swords, attempt to cut through the neck with a single blow. What shall I say of the abominable rape of the women? To speak of it is worse than to be silent.... Accordingly undertake this journey for the remission of your sins, with the assurance of the imperishable glory of the kingdom of heaven.' [846]

This is the message relayed, and spread far and wide through the counties by priests and prelates. Hence, Balderic (Baldricus), archbishop of Dol, said: "We have heard, most beloved brethren, and you have heard what we cannot recount without deep sorrow how, with great hurt and dire sufferings our Christian brothers, members in Christ, are scourged, oppressed, and injured in Jerusalem, in Antioch, and the other cities of the East..... Base and bastard Turks hold sway over our brothers.' [847]

The Turks according to Fulcher of Chartres, `have killed and captured many, have destroyed the churches and devastated the Kingdom of God.' And they have according to Baldric, inflicted 'dire sufferings, scourging, and enslavements.' [848]

For Guibert of Nogent, unspeakable cruelty has been inflicted on the pilgrims; 'remember, I pray you, the thousands who have perished vile deaths.' [849]

Thus, oncoming Christian armed response was made to look in self defence, a response to the dangers of extermination facing Christians. `For the whole European community, it seemed a case of kill or be killed.' [850]

---

[846] In D. C. Munro, "Urban and the Crusaders", Translations and Reprints from the *Original Sources of European History*, Vol 1:2, 1895, pp. 5-8

[847] In A. C. Krey, *The First Crusade: The Accounts of Eyewitnesses and Participants*, Princeton University Press; 1921; pp 33-36.

[848] D.C. Munro: The Western attitude; op cit; at p.329.

[849] In N.Daniel: *The Arabs*; op cit; p. 253.

[850] N. Daniel: *The Cultural Barrier*, Edinburgh University Press, 1975; p.158.

In truth, there were no Turkish atrocities and defilements of the Holy sites; and far from being in danger of extermination, the Christians enjoyed a uniquely favourable status under Muslim rule. In 1047, the Church of the Holy Sepulchre was described as `a most spacious building, capable of holding 8000 persons, and built with the utmost skill. Inside, the church is everywhere adorned with Byzantine brocade, worked in gold.[851] This was but one of many Christian churches in Jerusalem. Christian pilgrims had free access to the holy places.[852] Christians (like Jews) also occupied all spheres of command inside the Islamic realm, and from the earliest times. Caliph Al-Mutasim (833-842), for instance, had two Christian ministers, one of whom was for finance.[853] Everywhere Christians were free to practice their faith, and keep property and wealth, hardly disturbed by the Muslims. In fact, the destruction of The Church of the Resurrection in Jerusalem, which the Pope used as the instance of Muslim desecration of Christian sites, was the work of the Fatimid king (Al Hakem) (b. 985), gone mad; and the paradox was that the king's chief secretary, who drew up the document of destruction of the Church was a Christian just like his vizier who signed it.[854] Even more importantly, this Fatimid ruler who persecuted Jews and Christians had put to death many of the respectable Muslim Sunnis.[855]

The real reason why the pope launched the crusades was precisely due to Muslim internal divisions and wars against each other. As the Muslim historian, Ibn al-Athir, observes:

When the Franks, `may God frustrate them, extended their control over what they had conquered of the lands of Islam and it turned out well for them that the troops and the kings of Islam were preoccupied with fighting each other, at that time opinions were divided among the Muslims, desires differed, and wealth was squandered.'[856]

And as Hillenbrand notes, `the timing of this devastating attack could not have been more auspicious for the Europeans.'[857] Had the First Crusade arrived even ten years earlier, it would have met strong, unified resistance from the state then ruled by Malik Shah, the last of the three so called Great

---

[851] G. Le Strange: *Palestine under the Moslems*; Alexander P. Watt; London; 1890; p. 202.

[852] W. Durant; The Age; op cit; p. 585.

[853] T.W. Arnold: The Preaching of Islam. in Y. Courbage, P. Fargues: *Chretiens et Juifs dans l'islam Arabe et Turc*, Payot, Paris, 1997; p. 53.

[854] R. Finucane: *Soldiers of the Faith*; J.M. Dent and Sons Ltd; London, 1983; p. 155.

[855] C.R. Conder: *The Latin Kingdom of Jerusalem;* The Committee of the Palestine Exploration Fund; London; 1897; p. 231.

[856] Ibn al-Athir: *Kamil;* X; op cit; p. 256.

[857] C.Hillenbrand: *The Crusades, Islamic Perspectives,* Edinburgh University Press; 1999; p.31.

Seljuk Sultans.[858] Instead, when the Crusaders arrived, in 1096, the East was divided in innumerable principalities, and worse, the two ruling groups, Seljuk and Fatimids were extremely hostile to each other. Egypt was in Fatimid hands; two rulers of Armenian origin, Badr and Afdal, father and son, ruled the Fatimid land successively from 1073 to 1121 as virtual dictators.[859] The news of the first Crusader assault in 1097 against the Seljuk in Anatolia was received with joy by the Fatimids who sent an envoy to the Crusaders in Antioch to congratulate them on their victory and to try and reach agreement with them.[860] The Arabs, Turks and Kurds who resolved to fight the crusades had also to contend with another internal enemy: the Ismaili who assassinated virtually every Muslim leader fighting the crusades. The medieval Egyptian historian, Al-Maqrizi, notes how the Ismaili took by ruse or bribery a number of other mountain citadels in Syria, from which they launched their assassinations, eight such castles they retained until towards the end of the Crusades, two centuries later, when Baybars re-took them from them in 1270-3.[861]

This Muslim disunity allowed the First Crusaders to succeed in their advance and conquer vast Muslim territory,[862] even threatening to annihilate the Muslims had it not been for Seljuk resilience, most particularly.

These briefly summed up points form the main focus of the following outline in two halves; the first which looks at Seljuk fight against the crusaders from 1096 to the death of Imad Eddin Zangi (1146); the second, from the rise of Nur Eddin Zangi to the death of Salah Eddin al-Ayyubi (1146-1193.)

---

[858] Ibid; p.33.
[859] J.J. Saunders: *Aspects of the Crusades*, University of Canterbury, 1962; p.31.
[860] W. Z. Haddad: The Crusaders through Muslim eyes: *The Muslim World.* Vol 73 (1983); pp 234-52; at p.235.
[861] Al-Maqrizi: *Khitat*; tr Broadhurst; Boston; 1980; p. 60.
[862] W. M. Watt: L'Influence de l'Islam sur l'Europe medievale in *Revue d'Etudes Islamiques;* Vol 41: pp. 127-56; at p.152.

a. Christian Onslaught and Seljuk Fight-Back (1096-1146):

Following Urban's Speech (1095) descended upon the Islamic East from throughout Europe hordes of armed men (and women); knights, and peasants, vagrants; murderers and priests, noble women and prostitutes; 'a big army and workmen of all sorts, thousands and tens of thousands without end.'[863] To encourage the crusades, the pope offered a remission of all sins. He said:

'To all those who will depart and die en route, whether by land or sea, or lose their life in fighting the pagans, the forgiveness of their sins will be granted. And this I grant to those who participate to this voyage in accordance with the authority that I hold from God.'[864]

The van of the Crusades consisted of two hundred and seventy five thousand men, accompanied by eight horses, and preceded by a goat and a goose, 'into which some one had told them that the Holy Ghost had entered,' says Draper.[865] Disappointment and famine drove the hordes to madness, and in their ignorance, that every town they came to must be Jerusalem- in their extremity they laid hands on whatever they could. Their track was marked by robbery, bloodshed and fire.[866] In Byzantium, their xenophobic, violent behaviour made Emperor Alexius only too glad to be rid of them; 'such a rabble at the gates of Constantinople was not a pleasant prospect.'[867] Once reaching the Muslim territory, in October (1096), they were met at Nicea by the Turks under Kilij Arslan, who drew this army (of over three hundred thousand) into an ambush, and then slaughtered them on the seashore, so that of all the host, barely three thousand-one man for every hundred who set out-escaped to tell the tale.[868] Their bones piled into mounds outside Nicea, and may have been used by a later wave of crusaders to build part of a fortification.[869]

---

[863] The First and second Crusades from an Anonymous Syriac Chronicle: Translated by A.S. Tritton; with notes by H.A.R. Gibb: pp 69-101; *Journal of The Royal Asiatic Society (JRAS)* 1933; p.69.

[864] A. Bouamama: l'Idee de croisade dans le monde Arabe hier et aujourd'hui, in *De Toulouse a Tripoli*, AMAM, Colloque held between 6 and 8 December, 1995, University of Toulouse; 1997; pp 211-9; at p.212.

[865] J.W. Draper: *A History;* vol ii; op cit; pp 22-3.

[866] Ibid.

[867] R. Finucane: *Soldiers of the Faith*; op cit; p.21.

[868] C.R. Conder: *The Latin Kingdom of Jerusalem;* op cit; p. 26.

[869] R. Finucane: *Soldiers of the Faith;* op cit; p.104.

The Turks of Anatolia who met the crusaders were fierce and effective fighters, but were few in number.[870] They could not prevail in fixed encounters against superior numerical forces, especially as the Franks kept pouring in across Asia Minor.[871] Many local Christians also offered assistance to the crusaders. The local Maronite of Mount Lebanon, Salibi notes, gave the Franks a good welcome,[872] and `great loyal support to their co-religionists from the West.'[873] Muslim local leaders, as a whole, also refused to fight back. As the Muslim medieval historian, imam, Al-Sulami notes, the Muslim rulers had themselves to blame for their crushing defeats, each of such rulers trying to leave the task to the others.[874]

The first major crusader victory was the capture of Antioch. The city was besieged in October 1097. Yaghi Siyan, who was ruler of the city protected the Christian families living under his protection in the city, not allowing `a hair of their heads to be touched.'[875] One such Christian subjects, though, was to cause the city to fall to the crusaders who surrounded it near the hill on the eastern side.[876] This Christian, Phirouz, had acquired the favour of the emir and the command of three towers, disguising in the words of Gibbon, his foul design of perfidy and treason.[877] A secret correspondence was kept by Phirouz and the crusader prince of Tarento,[878] to let the crusaders into Antioch. At night, the French and Normans ascended the scaling-ladders that were thrown from the walls by the Armenians. Soon the army rushed through the gates; and the Muslims inside quickly found, `that although mercy was hopeless, resistance was impotent.'[879] Yaghi Siyan, the ruler, fled the city, and when he saw him, his army commander did the same. Some three thousand men still fortified themselves in the citadel of Antioch and refused to move.[880] Needlessly; as the city was taken. The Muslim population was overwhelmingly massacred or mutilated.[881] The Crusaders `spared neither sex nor condition and paid no respect to age...

---

[870] C. Hillenbrand: *The Crusades*, op cit; p.42.
[871] Ibid.
[872] C. Cahen: *Orient et Occident au temps des Croisades*, Aubier Montaigne, 1983; p.73.
[873] K.S. Salibi: The Maronites of Lebanon under Frankish and Mamluk rule; 1099-1516; *Arabica* IV; 1957.
[874] Al-Sulami Fol. 174a-b; French tr. P. 215 in C. Hillenbrand: *The Crusades*, op cit; p.73.
[875] Ibn al-Athir: *Kamil*; op cit; X, 185-8.
[876] The First and second Crusades; op cit; p.71.
[877] E. Gibbon: *The Decline and Fall*; op cit; Vol 6; p. 301.
[878] Ibid.
[879] Ibid.
[880] Abu Shama: *Kitab al-rawdatayn;* ed. M.H. M. Ahmad; 2 vols; Cairo; 1954.; I; p. 175.
[881] Ibn al-Qalanisi: *Dayl Tarikh Dimashk;* ed. H.F. Amedroz; Leiden; 1908, p. 220.

killed the servants... mothers of families and the children of nobles.'[882] It is accepted that a total of ten thousand Muslims were massacred.[883]

In 1098, the crusaders took Ma'arrat an'Numan. The siege was valiantly sustained, until, as in Antioch, one night, some defenders began to desert their place, followed by others who saw them.[884] The crusaders seized their chance, and scaled the undefended walls; then entered the city. The terrified population hid in their homes, but to no avail. For three days the slaughter never stopped; the crusaders killed more than 100,000 people.[885] The chronicler of nearby Aleppo, Ibn al-Adim (d. 1262), speaks of the carnage:
`They (the Franks) killed a great number under torture. They extorted people's treasures. They prevented people from (getting) water, and sold it to them. Most of the people died of thirst... No treasure remained there that was not extorted by them. They destroyed the walls of the town, burned its mosques and houses and broke the minbars.'[886]
Christian sources had the same account. Robert the Monk writes:
`Our men walked through the roads, places, on the roofs, and feasted on the slaughter just like a lioness who had her cubs taken from her. They cut into pieces, and put to death children, the young, and the old crumbling under the weight of the years. They did that in groups... Our men grabbed everybody who fell in their hands. They cut bellies open, and took out gold coins. Oh detestable cupidity of gold! Streams of blood ran on the roads of the city; and everywhere lay corpses. Oh blinded nations and destined to death; none of that multitude accepted the Christian faith. At last Bohemond brought out all those he had first invited to lock themselves in the tower of the place. He ordered that all old women be put to death, and also old men, whose age had rendered useless; then all the rest he ordered to be taken to Antioch to be sold as slaves. This massacre of the Turks took place on 12 December; on Sunday; but on this day not all work could be accomplished; so the following day our men killed all the rest.'[887]
Radulph of Caen said how:
"In Maarra our troops boiled pagan adults in cooking pots; they impaled children on spits and devoured them grilled."[888]

---

[882] R. Finucane: *Soldiers of the Faith*; op cit; 1983.
[883] C.R. Conder: *The Latin Kingdom*; op cit; p. 47.
[884] Ibn al-Athir: *Kamil*; x; op cit; p. 190.
[885] Ibid.
[886] Y.Tabba: Monuments with a message, in *The Meeting of Two Worlds*; Ed V.P. Goss; Kalamazoo; Michigan; 1986; pp. 223-40; at p. 233.
[887] Robert the Monk, in G. Le Bon: *La Civilisation*, op cit; p. 248.
[888] In J Abu Lughod: *Before European Hegemony*; Oxford University Press; 1989; p. 107.

In fact, it was a common practice, as the chronicler, William of Tyre reports, for the crusaders to roast and eat the flesh of the Turks they slew.[889] At Ma'arrat, to avoid such a fate, many Muslims were said by a Christian writer to have jumped down wells to their deaths.[890] For Muslim chroniclers, the massacres of Ma'arrat were yet another sign of the ferocity of the enemy.[891]

On July 15, 1099, the crusaders, led by their French leader, Godfrey de Bouillon, entered the city of Jerusalem held for the Fatimids by Iftikhar ad-Daula (The pride of the Nation.) Iftikhar, his entourage and his army were allowed to leave the city under safe crusader conduct.[892] The population on the other hand was put to the sword. The crusaders slaughtered more than 70,000 Muslims.[893] Draper narrates:
'The capture of Jerusalem, as might be expected under such circumstances, was attended by the perpetration of atrocities almost beyond belief. What a contrast to the conduct of the Arabs! When the Khalif Omar took Jerusalem, A.D. 637, he rode into the city by the side of the Patriarch Sophronius, conversing with him on its antiquities. At the hour of prayer, he declined to perform his devotions in the Church of the Resurrection, in which he chanced to be, but prayed on the steps of the Church of Constantine; 'for,' said he to the patriarch, 'had I done so, the Musselmen in a future age would have infringed the treaty, under colour of imitating my example.' But, in the capture by the Crusaders, the brains of young children were dashed out against the walls; infants were thrown over the battlements; every woman that could be seized was violated; men were roasted at fires; some were ripped open, to see if they had swallowed gold; the Jews were driven into their synagogue, and there burnt; a massacre of nearly 70,000 persons took place; and the pope's legate was seen 'partaking in the triumph.[894]
A contemporary, Abbot Raymond of Agiles of the French town of Du Puy, present during the dramatic moments wrote with glee:
'When our men took the main defences, we saw then some astonishing things amongst the Saracens. Some were beheaded, and that's the least that could happen to them. Others were pierced through and so threw

---

[889] C.R. Conder: *The Latin Kingdom;* op cit. p. 45.
[890] R. Finucane: *Soldiers of the Faith;* op cit; p.106;
[891] A.M. Nanai: L'Image du croise dans les sources; op cit; p. 18.
[892] B. Z. Kedar: The Subjected Muslims of the Frankish Levant, in *Muslims under Latin Rule, 1100-1300,* ed J.M. Powell, Princeton University Press, 1990; pp 135-74; at p.143. On the dumping of corpses, see e.g., *Gesta Francorum et aliorum Hierosolimitanorum,* ed. K. Mynors, trans. R.Hill; London, 1962; p.92.
[893] Ibn al-Athir: *Kamil;* X, pp.193-95 in F. Gabrieli: *Arab Historians of the Crusades;* London; Routledge; 1957; p.11.
[894] J.W. Draper: *A History;* Vol II; op cit; pp. 22-3.

themselves from the heights of the walls; others after having suffered in length were thrown into the flames. We could see in the roads and in the places of Jerusalem bits and pieces of heads, hands, and feet. Everywhere we could only walk through cadavers. But all that was only little... The abbot's description moves onto the Mosque of Omar, where: there was so much blood in it that dead corpses swam in it. We could see hands floating and arms that went to glue themselves to bodies that were not theirs; we could not distinguish which arm belonged to which body. The men who were doing the killing could hardly bear the smoke from the corpses.'[895]

For seven days riot and carnage continued; `Men forgot their vows, forgot the Sepulchre and Calvary, hastening to gather spoil, revelling and exulting, and claiming for their own the empty houses which they seized.'[896] Even priests were not slow to take their share. Arnold, as Latin patriarch, claimed the treasures of the Mosque, which Tancred and Godfrey had shared between them.[897]

The Christian chronicler, Humbert of Romans, delighted on `the splendid occasion when the blood of the Arabs came up to the horses' knees, at the capture of Jerusalem in I099.'[898]

The city (Jerusalem) must have contained a sizeable population at the time of the Crusader siege, since, as well as its own inhabitants, it probably also housed refugees from other towns and villages who had sought asylum behind its walls.[899] The city was also a great centre of learning.[900] Following the taking of the city by the crusaders, all Muslims, regardless of status, age, and gender, were slaughtered, and the city's greatness dimmed for centuries. The Franks targeted most particularly Muslim scholars. Al-Rumayli, the most celebrated Palestinian hadith expert of his age and author of tracts on the merits of Jerusalem and Hebron, was stoned to death.[901] Such was the carnage, when the Christian Chronicler, Fulcher, visited Jerusalem in December 1099, five months after it was taken, he was disgusted by the stench of death inside and outside the city walls.[902] One of the first crusader deeds was to desecrate the Al-Aqsa Mosque. Pigs were installed in the sanctuary (Mirhab) of the sacred mosque, and a church was erected in place

[895] Abbot Raymond of Agiles; in G. Le Bon: *La Civilisation*; op cit; p. 249.
[896] C.R. Conder: *The Latin Kingdom;* op cit; p. 67.
[897] Ibid.
[898] In N. Daniel: *The Arabs,* op cit; p.253.
[899] C. Hillenbrand: *The Crusades,* op cit; p.66.
[900] Mudjir Eddin: *Al-Euns al-jalil bi Tarikh el-Qods wa'l Khalil,* tr. into French as Histoire de Jerusalem et Hebron, by H. Sauvaire; Paris; Ernest Leroux; 1875; and 1926; pp. 140 ff.
[901] B. Z. Kedar: The Subjected Muslims of the Frankish Levant, op cit.143.
[902] In R. Finucane: *Soldiers of the Faith;* op cit; p.104.

of one of its oratories.[903] Imad Eddin speaks of the mihrab of the mosque full of pigs and excrement.[904]

Following their taking of Jerusalem, the Crusaders pursued their advance, with the same results. In October 1101, they advanced on Saruj, captured it, and killed and enslaved all the inhabitants they found.[905] At the end of May 1102, the crusaders assisted by the Genoese, captured Qaisariya by assault, killed its population and plundered everything in it.[906]

Muslim contemporary scholars saw in the Crusade invasion and the mass slaughter of Muslims a terrible calamity upon Islam and the Muslims.[907] Amongst these scholars was al-Sulami, who preached in the Umayyad mosque of Damascus in the early years after the fall of Jerusalem that Muslims should rally against their enemy, the Crusaders.[908] Al-Sulami's solution to this dire predicament lies first in moral rearmament to end this process of Muslim spiritual decline. The Crusader attacks he saw as a punishment as well as a Divine warning to Muslims to return to 'the Right Path.' Jihad against the infidel, he insists, is a hollow sham if it is not preceded by the greater Jihad (al-Jihad al-Akbar) over one's baser self; personal spiritual struggle becoming an absolute requirement before conducting war against the Franks.[909] Muslim defeat, argues al-Sulami, was God's punishment for abandoning their religious duties, their indifference to the Frankish presence, and, above all, for their neglect of Jihad.[910] According to al-Sulami, the neglect of Jihad is not so peculiar to his own time, nor just to Syria but has existed since the caliphs first began to neglect their religious duty to conduct at least one campaign a year into infidel territory. In his view this forms part of a wider religious and moral decline amongst Muslims, which, he argues, has resulted in the fragmentation of Islam and has encouraged the enemies of Islam to take the offensive and seize Muslim territories.[911]

---

[903] Abu Shama: *Kitab al-rawdatayn*, ed. M. H. M. Ahmad; 2 vols Cairo; II, p. 96.
[904] In C. Hillenbrand: *The Crusades*, op cit; p.301.
[905] Ibn al-Qalanis: *The Damascus Chronicle of Ibn al-Qalanisi*, extracted and tr. by H.A. R. Gibb; London, Luzac and Co, Ltd, 1932, p.49.
[906] Ibid.
[907] Ibn Al-Qalanisi: *Dayl tarikh Dimashq*, Damascus, 1983, p.218.
[908] Al-Sulami In C.Hillenbrand: *The Crusades*, op cit; p.104.
[909] In E.Siwan: La Genese de la contre croisade; *Journal Asiatique*; 254 (1966); pp 199-204.
[910] Al-Sulami: Un traite Damasquin du debut du XIIem siecle, ed. E. Siwan, *Journal Asiatique*, 1966, p. 207.
[911] Al-Sulami in C. Hillenbrand: *The Crusades*, op cit; p.104.

In the winter of 1100-1101, four huge armies set off from Europe. The first great army, of tens of thousands of men, was composed largely of Lombards who left Italy in September 1100, an army led by Albert Count of Biandrate, Anselm of Buis, Archbishop of Milan, Guibert Count of Parma, and Hugh of Montebello.[912] The Arch-Bishop of Milan brought the arm of St.Ambrose, and the whole army numbered at least one hundred thousand souls.[913] Their aim was not Jerusalem, but Baghdad.[914] The second army was French, including no civilians, but made of well equipped fighting men, lead by Stephen of Blois, the Bishop of Soissons, and Conrad, constable of the Empire, who took with them picked bodies of knights and infantry.[915] These two armies were the first to set out, and were followed in February 1101 by an army belonging to William II, Count of Nevers, and fifteen thousand men, all professional soldiers, under his command, forming a compact and well disciplined army.[916] There was a fourth army, an extremely large one, estimated at sixty thousand persons, including a great many civilians, which was led by William IX, Duke of Aquitaine, Welf IV, Duke of Bavaria, and by the Margravine Ida of Austria, mother of Duke Leopold of Austria.[917]

The arrival of these four fresh Crusader armies united the Turks, and, together, Malik Ghazi and Qilij Arslan fought them back.[918] The first army was wiped out near Angora.[919] Fifteen thousand Latin, under the Counts of Nevers and Bourges perished near Erekli on the way to Tarsus;[920] and near the same town, the third division of William of Poitou, was also defeated.[921] The Franks, attacked by Qilij Arslan and Malik Ghazi met with a crushing defeat at Heraclea; whilst William IX of Acquitaine and Welf, Duke of Bavaria, were defeated by Qilij Arslan and Qaraja, the Emir of Harran, as they sought to reach Cilicia.[922] Thus, nearly half a million crusaders wiped out in the space of two years, a decisive Turkish victory considering that the

---

[912] Z. Oldenbourg: *The Crusades*; tr from the French by A. Carter; Weinfeld and Nicolson; London; 1965; p. 174.
[913] C.R. Conder: *The Latin Kingdom;* op cit; p. 71.
[914] Ibid.
[915] Z. Oldenbourg: *The Crusades*; op cit; p. 174.
[916] Ibid.
[917] Ibid; pp. 174-5.
[918] Ferdinand Chalandon: The Earlier Comneni: in *The Cambridge Medieval History,* Vol IV; op cit; pp 318-50 at pp.340-1.
[919] C.R. Conder: *The Latin Kingdom;* op cit; p. 71.
[920] Ibid.
[921] Ibid.
[922] Ferdinand Chalandon: The Earlier Comneni; op cit; p.340.

crusader aim was nothing other than destroying the Caliphate itself and Baghdad.[923]

Muslim resilience and bravery was hampered by extraordinary obstacles, though. Muslim rulers fought each other, some in alliance with the crusaders, despite the latter's massacres of Muslims. The effects of such infightings did not escape Al-Sulami, who rightly saw them as the main reason for the crusader success; and clearly the Franks knew the situation in advance:
'Examining the country of Syria, they (the crusaders) confirmed that the states there were involved one with another, their opinions diverged, their relationships rested on secret desires for vengeance. Their (the crusaders) greed was thereby reinforced, encouraging them to apply themselves (to the attack).'[924]
Furthermore, as Nanai observes, Muslim ruling elites showed 'a humiliating incapacity to understand the nature and the real objectives of the massive outbreaks of Franks in Syria and Palestine.'[925] As a general rule, Nanai insists, the Muslim lay man was always faster than his rulers to perceive the hate that the Frank had towards the Muslims.[926] And it is for this reason that the resistance to the invader in the first half of the 12th century was stronger and more effective from the people than from the rulers.[927] There was an outburst of popular resistance in the form of armed militia that were very effective along the roads of Palestine[928] as the European traveller Saewuff (1102-1103) had noted.[929]

Muslim fight back was also hampered by the murder of the leadership fighting the crusaders. Janah al-Dawla, Mawdud, Il-Bursuqi, Ibn al-Khashab the Qadi of Aleppo, and many others, all fell to the Ismaili daggers. On one such murder, Ibn al-Qalanisi, writes:
'In this year (1103), also news were received from Hims that its lord, the emir Janah al-Dawla Hussain Atabeg, on descending from the citadel to the mosque for the Friday prayer, surrounded by his principal officers with full armour, and occupying his place of prayer, according to custom, was

---

[923] Z. Oldenbourg: *The Crusades*; op cit; pp. 174-5; C.R. Conder: *The Latin Kingdom;* op cit; p. 71.
[924] Al-Sulami: Fol.174a-b (French trans); p. 215; in C. Hillenbrand: *The Crusades*, op cit; p.72.
[925] A.M. Nanai: L'Image du croise; op cit. p. 14.
[926] Ibid; p.19.
[927] Ibid; p. 19.
[928] `Awad Munis: *al-Rahhala al-awrubiyyun fi al-bayt al-maqdis*, Cairo, 1992, p. 44.
[929] A.M. Nanai: L'Image du croise; op cit; pp: 11-39; p. 19.

set upon by three Persians belonging to the Batinya (Ismailis). They were accompanied by a sheikh, to whom they owed allegiance and obedience, and all of them were dressed in the garb of ascetics. When the Sheikh gave the signal they attacked the emir with their knives and killed both him and a number of his officers.... The people of Hims were greatly perturbed by this event, and at once dispersed in panic. The city soon fell into confusion.... Soon the Franks arrived and camped in the vicinity of the city at al-Rastan, with the intention of cutting off supplies and besieging the city, but on hearing that Shams al-Muluk and Zahir al-Din Atabeg were advancing, the Franks lifted the siege and left.'[930]

Even Salah Eddin himself, later on, survived two attacks from the Ismailis, in 1175-1176, and in 1185.[931]

Divisions amongst Muslims contrasted with crusader unity. A constant supply of men and equipment kept arriving from the Christian West to boost the crusaders. The crusaders built up a strong coastal base, which ensured such free and easy access of supplies and soldiers. One such base was the city port of Haifa, which, in 1100, after a long siege, was stormed, and its population massacred.[932] Every year, the ranks of the Franks were swelled by large numbers of pilgrims, especially in the Spring and Summer season, when transport by sea was much more feasible.[933] Manpower came from all parts of Europe, even from as far as Norway; the sons of Magnus Barefoot were then kings in Norway, and of these Sigurd led a fleet of sixty ships to Palestine.[934]

As the crusaders kept pouring in, Muslim resistance kept mounting, too, the northern city of Mosul, and its Atabegs, playing the leading role in such resistance. In April 1110, the Atabeg Mawdud, the Seljuk commander of Mosul, began moving against Edessa with the support of the Ortoqid Il-Ghazi and the Emir of Mayyafaraqin, Soqman al-Qutbi.[935] Informed by their spies, the Franks hastened to meet Mawdud at the Euphrates with a superior army. The Franks were systematically crushed.[936] Mawdud led further campaigns before he fell to the daggers of the Ismaili Assassins, murdered at

---

[930] *The Damascus Chronicle of Ibn al-Qalanisi*; op cit; at pp. 52-3.
[931] Imad Eddin: *Sana al-Barq al-Shami*; summarised by al-Bundari; ed. F. al-Nabarawi; Cairo; 1979; p. 100.
[932] B. Z. Kedar: The Subjected Muslims; op cit; at p.146.
[933] C.R. Conder: *The Latin Kingdom;* op cit; p. 114.
[934] Ibid; p. 90.
[935] S. Runciman: *A History of the Crusades*; op cit; vol ii; p. 115.
[936] The First and second Crusades; op cit; p.83.

the Friday prayers in October 1113;[937] his death freeing the Franks of a formidable adversary.[938]

No sooner a Muslim leader fell, another rose, and registered great victories such as at Balat, in 1119, by the emir Il-Ghazi. This victory is recorded by the historian Kemal Eddin (or Ibn al-Adim) (1192-1262):
'Sir Roger, the crusade ruler of Antioch assembled the Frankish and Armenian armies and made straight for the iron bridge (over the Orontes) and went from there to take up his position at Balat, between the two mountains near the Sarmada Pass, north of al-Atharib. He camped there on Friday 20 June 1119. Il-Ghazi made all the emirs and commanders renew their oath to fight bravely, to stand form without retreating, and to offer their lives in Holy War. To this they cheerfully swore... At the head of the Muslim army was Ibn al-Khashab, the Qadi of Aleppo, mounted on a mare and carrying a lance, and urging the Muslims on to war. A soldier seeing the Qadi said: 'so we left home and come all this way to march behind a turban.'
But the Qadi at the head of the troops rode up and down the lines haranguing them and using all his eloquence to summon every energy and rise to the highest pitch of enthusiasm, until men wept with emotion and admiration. Then Tugha Arslan Ibn Dimlaj (emir of Arzan in the Jezira, and vassal of Il-Ghazi) led the charge, and the army swept down on the enemy tents, spreading chaos and destruction. God gave victory to the Muslims. The Franks who fled their camp were slaughtered. The Turks fought superbly, charging the enemy from every direction like a man. Arrows flew thick as locusts, and the Franks, with missiles raining down on infantry and cavalry alike, turned and fled.... Roger was killed, and so were 15,000 of his men... A signal of victory reached Aleppo as the Muslims were assembled for the noon prayer in the Great Mosque.'[939]

In the year 1127, Imad Eddin Zangi, the Atabeg of Mosul, was appointed commander of the east. Zangi began to make his imprint at al-Atharib in 1130, when he destroyed the citadel, and razed it to the ground. The chronicler Ibn al-Furat, centuries later, remarks that it has remained in ruins until his time.[940] Zangi, however, had first to survive the dangers of the Muslim internal foes, and was rescued by the Kurdish governor of Tikrit,

---

[937] Ibid; p.85.
[938] S. Runciman: *A History*; vol ii; op cit; p. 127.
[939] Kamal Eddin: *Zubdat al-Halab fi ta'arikh Halab;* S. Dahan edition; Damascus; 1954; II; pp. 187-90.
[940] Ibn al-Furat: *Tarikh al-Duwal wal Muluk;* ed. M. F. El-Shayyal; unpublished Ph.d.; University of Edinburgh; 1986. IV; p. 30.

Najm Eddin Ayyub, who saved him from the Abbasid Caliph Mustarshid who was bent on his capture and execution.[941] Zangi's ally, Taj al-Mulk, ruler of Damascus, was less fortunate, though, he, too, falling to the daggers of the Ismaili in 1132.[942] Zangi could hardly count on Egypt, which was still under the Fatimids, another Armenian: Vahram, at the helm of power there; his interest consisting in enriching his friends and fellow Christians, and not in fighting the crusaders.[943] Zangi was, however, dedicated to the war against the crusaders, and around his command began to grow the concept of jihad, and more dedicated forces coalesced around him.[944] In 1137, he besieged Castle Mont Ferrand; Pons of Tripoli was slain there, whilst King Fulk, shut up in the castle, was forced to cede it to Zangi.[945] The same year, Zangi recovered from the crusaders Kafartab, Maarat al-Numan, Bizaa, and Athareb.[946]

The call for Jihad by Zangi eventually rallied around him, and for the first time since the crusaders' arrival in 1096, a united Muslim army.[947] Now, Zangi was strong enough to mount a major offensive on Edessa. The defence of the city was entrusted to the Latin archbishop Hugh II with support of the Armenian Bishop John, and the Jacobite Bishop: Basil.[948] The siege lasted for weeks before, on Christmas Eve, of the year 1144, a wall collapsed and the Muslims penetrated the city. The panicked population sought to escape, but the gates of the citadel had been shut by orders of the Archbishop.[949] At the mercy of the Muslim armies, the Christians expected Muslim deeds of blood and cruelty as `they (the Muslims) might be apt pupils in the horrible school in which the Christians had attained a standard of ideal excellence.'[950] Instead Zangi had all the Franks rounded and executed but spared the lives of the local Christians, even allowing the local Armenians, Jacobites and Greeks a certain autonomy.[951] An anonymous Christian source said:
`Zangi visited our Syrian churches, examined their beauty, ordered two great bells to be given them and hung on them as was the custom in the time of the Franks.'[952]

---

[941] S. Runciman: *A History*; vol ii; op cit; p. 194.

[942] The First and second crusades; op cit; Part two: April; pp. 273-305; at p.273.

[943] Ibn al-Athir: *Kamil*; pp. 405-8; in S. Runciman: *A History*; op cit; vol ii; p. 196.

[944] See: Ibn al-Athir: *Ta'rikh al-Dawlah al-Atabakiya;* ed. Ab Al-Qadir Ahmad Tulaymat; Cairo; 1963.

[945] C.R. Conder: *The Latin Kingdom;* op cit; p. 99.

[946] S. Runciman: *A History*; op cit; vol ii; pp. 219-20.

[947] The First and second crusades: Part two; op cit; p.280.

[948] S. Runciman: *A History*; op cit; p.235.

[949] Ibid; p. 236.

[950] G.W. Cox: *The Crusades*; Longman; London; 1874; p.83.

[951] S. Runciman: *A History*; op cit; Vol ii; p. 236-7.

[952] The First and second crusades Part two; op cit; p. 291.

The fall of Edessa marked a significant turning point in Muslim fortunes, and soon the whole state of Edessa was regained for Islam. However, just as the fall of Edessa was deemed a major breakthrough for Islam, it was cause of distress in Christianity. The second crusade was launched shortly afterwards as a direct consequence.

Before the second crusade arrived, Zangi's career, just like that of all his leading predecessors, was once more interrupted by assassination; murdered on 14th September 1146 as he lay asleep during his army's siege to a Christian stronghold. His two murderers fled to the Christian castle.[953] Zangi's murder was a major reprieve for the crusaders, but succeeding him was his son Nur-Eddin. Imad legated to his son both spirit of jihad, and leadership qualities, qualities also found amongst the officers who served him, his most able general, the Kurd, Shirquh, and Shirquh's nephew, Salah Eddin (Saladin) who was to become 'the great protagonist of the Crescent against the Cross.'[954] Nur Eddin was to devote his life to the furtherance of his father's policy, and in a reign of nearly thirty years (1146-1174) was to shake the whole foundation of Frankish power in the East, says Saunders.[955]

---

[953] Ibid.
[954] H. M. J. Loewe: The Seljuqs; in *The Cambridge Medieval History*, Vol IV; op cit; pp 299-317; at p.317.
[955] J. J. Saunders: *A History of Medieval Islam*; Routledge; London; 1965; p. 162.

In Praise of the Turks

Al-Jahiz (ca. 776-868) credits the Turks with simple virtues.[956] `The Turks know not how to flatter or coax, they know not how to practice hypocrisy or backbiting, pretence or slander, dishonesty or haughtiness on their acquaintance, or mischief on those that associate with them. They are strangers to heresy and not spoiled by caprice, and they do not make property lawful by quibbles.'[957] Al-Jahiz is also quick to point out the skills, resilience, and determination in the face of adversity of the Turk:

`His patience for continuing in the saddle and for going on without stopping and for long night journeys and for crossing a country is remarkable... and supposing at the end of a Turk's life one were to number his days, it would be found that he had spent longer time sitting upon his beast than he had spent sitting upon the earth.'[958]

Equally Al-Ghazali (d.1111) argues:

`In this age of ours, from amongst the [various] kinds of human beings it is the Turks who possess force... If there should be an insurrection in any region of the earth against this resplendent state [the Seljuk] there is not one among them [the Turks] who on seeing strife beyond its frontiers would not fight in the way of God waging jihad against the infidels.'[959]

The admiration by the crusaders, themselves, for their Turkish adversaries is boundless, even if they fought them fiercely.[960] Such was their regard for their Turkish adversaries, the crusaders saw that the Turkish leaders: Qilij Arslan, Alp Arslan, Kerbogha, Imad Eddin Zangi... `could only be of Christian descent.'[961] Just as decades later, the same admiration was for the Kurd Salah Eddin, said to be the son of `a countess of Ponthieu who had been shipwrecked in Egypt by a storm.'[962]

---

[956] Al-Jahiz: *Tria opuscula*, ed. G. Van Vloten; Leiden, 1903, p. 46.

[957] Opuscula, pp 39-40 in G.E.Von Grunebaum: *Medieval Islam*; op cit; p.208.

[958] Al-Ghazali: *Manaqib al-Turk*; Tr Harley-Walker; p. 667.

[959] Ibid; p. 666.

[960] R. Finucane: *Soldiers of the Faith;* op cit; p.87.

[961] D.C. Munro: The Western attitude; op cit; pp. 329-43; p. 339.

[962] See G. Paris: La Legende de Saladin, *Journal des Savants*, 1893; pp 284-5 and others.

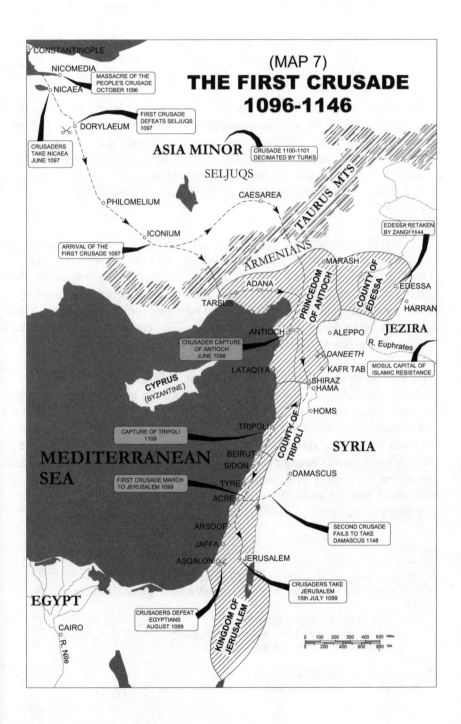

CONSTANTINOPLE

NICOMEDIA

NICAEA | MASSACRE OF THE PEOPLE'S CRUSADE OCTOBER 1096

DORYLAEUM | FIRST CRUSADE DEFEATS SELJUQS 1097

CRUSADERS TAKE NICAEA JUNE 1097

(MAP 7)

THE FIRST CRUSADE
1096-1146

ASIA MINOR | CRUSADE 1100-1101 DECIMATED BY TURKS

SELJUQS

PHILOMELIUM

CAESAREA

ICONIUM

TAURUS MTS.

EDESSA RETAKEN BY ZANGI 1144

ARRIVAL OF THE FIRST CRUSADE 1097

ARMENIANS

MARASH

ADANA

PRINCEDOM OF ANTIOCH

COUNTY OF EDESSA

EDESSA

TARSUS

HARRAN

ANTIOCH

ALEPPO

JEZIRA

R. Euphrates

CRUSADER CAPTURE OF ANTIOCH JUNE 1098

DANEETH

LATAQIYA

KAFR TAB | MOSUL CAPITAL OF ISLAMIC RESISTANCE

CYPRUS (BYZANTINE)

SHIRAZ

HAMA

HOMS

TRIPOLI

CAPTURE OF TRIPOLI 1109

COUNTY OF TRIPOLI

SYRIA

MEDITERRANEAN SEA

BEIRUT

SIDON

DAMASCUS

FIRST CRUSADE MARCH TO JERUSALEM 1099

TYRE

ACRE

ARSOOF

SECOND CRUSADE FAILS TO TAKE DAMASCUS 1148

JAFFA

ASQALON

JERUSALEM

CRUSADERS TAKE JERUSALEM 15th JULY 1099

EGYPT

KINGDOM OF JERUSALEM

CRUSADERS DEFEAT EGYPTIANS AUGUST 1099

CAIRO

R. Nile

0 100 200 300 400 500 Miles
0 200 400 600 800 KM.

181

b. From Nur-Eddin Zangi to Salah Eddin Al-Ayyubi (1146-93):

The Muslim success at Edessa spread consternation in Europe. Preaching for a new crusade was St. Bernard of Clairvaux, who promised absolution and a heavenly reward to all those who took up the cross.[963] He proclaimed that:

`The soldier of Christ carries a sword not without reason; for he is the minister of Christ for the punishment of evil-doers, as well as for the praise of good men. Clearly when he kills a malefactor he is not a homicide but as I should say a malicide, and he is simply considered the avenger of Christ on those who do evil and the protector of Christians.....
The Christian glories in the death of the pagan, because Christ is thereby glorified.'[964]

Hundreds of thousands responded, so many, according to a contemporary, it left the cities and castles empty, and scarcely one man for seven women.[965] Three hundred and ninety five thousand men reached the capital of the Greeks, Constantinople.[966] The Greeks, `tainted with perjury' as one Latin wrote, `shut their cities and fortresses and sent their merchandise down to us on ropes suspended from the walls.'[967] The crusaders responded by plundering the countryside and local villages for their food.[968]

The multitude soon arrived at Dorylaeum, where the first crusade had defeated Qilij Arslan; this time Emperor Conrad's army meeting a large Turkish force was so badly beaten that hardly any one Christian in ten survived.[969] The French King's army was severely checked, too, constantly attacked by Turkish archers on its march. Two days beyond Laodicea, the French met a greater disaster at a pass following a Turkish attack that caused them terrible losses, and nearly claimed the life of the French King himself.[970] The remnants of the crusader armies reached the land of conflict, considerably weakened, to join in with the local crusader forces.

---

[963] R. Payne: *The Crusades*; Wordsworth Editions; 1986; p. 156.
[964] St Bernard: *Opera*; ed Mabillon; Vol I; col. 549. Also in Milman *Latin Christianity*, IV, p. 251.
[965] G.W. Cox: *The Crusades*; op cit; p.93.
[966] The First and second crusades; Part two: op cit; p.298.
[967] R. Finucane: *Soldiers of the Faith*; op cit. p.59.
[968] Ibid.
[969] W. Durant: *The Age of Faith*; op cit; p. 595.
[970] R. Payne: *The Crusades*; Wordsworth Editions; London; 1994; pp 157-8.

Damascus, it was decided, was the target for attack. The crusade armies, which advanced on Damascus were led by three rulers, the French King, Louis, Emperor Conrad, and King Baldwin slaughtering their way to the outskirts of the city. The Muslims had retreated into the city walls, letting the crusaders establish themselves in the orchards, which they chopped down to build defences. The Muslim historian Ibn al-Qalanisi, in his Damascus Chronicles, offers the best account of the crusader siege of the city.[971] The Muslims inside were reinforced by Nur Eddin Zangi's men, and organised sorties, and in the end, gained the upper hand.[972] Disheartened, the Christian armies fearing the sudden fall on them by Nur-Eddin retreated, under continuous attacks of Turkish light horsemen, who inflicted considerable losses on them, the stench of their corpses polluting the plains for many months to come.[973] The attack on Damascus had not just failed it had also proved to the Muslims, and to the Damascenes (who had a peace treaty with the crusaders), most particularly, that the Franks were not to be trusted.[974] Following this fiasco, the two Western sovereigns, Louis and Conrad, left the East back for home in 1148, soon to be followed by the rest of the nobility, including Queen Eleonor and most of the French knights.[975]

Europe was stunned once more by both defeat and the scale of losses; the fathers, husbands and sons or the brothers of many women would see their homes no more.[976] People began to ask how it was that the Almighty allowed His defenders to be so humiliated. St Bernard who preached the second crusade was attacked as a reckless visionary who had sent men to their death, and sceptics even called in question the most basic tenets of the Christian faith.[977] St-Bernard himself lamented:
`He (the Lord) has not spared His people; He has not spared even His own name, and the gentiles say: `Where is their God?' We promised success, and behold desolation!'[978]
He went on:
`It seems that the Lord, provoked by our sins, has forgotten His pity and has come to judge the earth before the appointed time.'[979]

---

[971] Ibn Al-Qalanisi: *Dayl tarikh Dimashq*, Damascus, 1983.
[972] S. Runciman: *A History;* op cit; p. 282.
[973] Ibid; p. 284.
[974] R. Finucane: *Soldiers of the Faith*; op cit; p. 23.
[975] W. Durant: *The Age of Faith;* op cit; p. 595.
[976] G.W. Cox: *The Crusades*; op cit; p.93.
[977] W. Durant: *The Age of faith,* op cit; Chapter 23; p.595.
[978] St Bernard in R.H.C. Davis: *A History of medieval Europe*; Longman; London; second edition; 1988; p. 277.
[979] Ibid.

Failure, which St Bernard also attributed to the iniquity of allowing thieves and murderers to take part in an enterprise that ought to be for the devout alone.[980]

The Muslims, for their part, had now a great leader, under whom they could unite to large measure: Nur Eddin Zangi. 'In the Sultan of Aleppo (Nur Eddin Zangi), as in the general (Shirquh), who had risen through his favour,' Cox notes, 'we have a man to whom the chronicles of the time and of later ages delighted to ascribe the magnanimity and simplicity of Omar.'[981] Nur-Eddin's career at war and peace, of all the rulers and leaders of Islam, came the nearest to that of the first four Caliphs. Nur-Eddin gradually united the once shattered Muslim land, added the kingdom of Damascus to that of Aleppo, and waged a long and successful war against the Crusaders, spreading his rule from the Tigris to the Nile, and forcing the crusaders 'to own the wisdom and courage, and even the justice and piety, of this implacable adversary,' says Gibbon.[982] Nur Eddin also believed in Jihad as the weapon for resistance, and like Baybars later, he was a strict upholder of public morals.[983]

Nur Eddin was a great general, too, leading from the front, mounting military campaigns against the foe relentlessly. Thus, following his success at Damascus, in 1148, Muslim armies attacked the castle of Araima, which was instantly destroyed, and Bertram, its lord, carried prisoner to Aleppo by Nur Eddin.[984] Later in the year, Nur Eddin attacked Antioch, and strongholds of Basuta and Hab were added to his captures.[985] However, just before the year ended, Nur Eddin suffered defeat at the hands of the armies of Raymond, which prompted the crusaders to take the offensive against him.[986] Nur Eddin recovered, and was able to defeat them at Bagras or Yagra, to the north of Antioch, and after being joined by the troops of Damascus, he laid siege to the castle of Anab, not far from Sarmin.[987] On 30 of June 1149, attacked by the forces of Raymond of Antioch, he crushed them, took countless prisoners, whilst Raymond, himself, was slain, it is said by the hands of Shirquh (a Muslim Kurdish

---

[980] G.W. Cox: *The Crusades*; op cit; p.93.

[981] Ibid; p.100.

[982] E. Gibbon: *The Decline and Fall*; op cit; Vol 6; p. 336.

[983] Ibn al-Athir: *Kamil;* XI; op cit; p. 73.

[984] Abu Shama: *Kitab al-rawdatayn;* ed. M.H. M. Ahmad; 2 vols; Cairo; 1954; p. 55.

[985] Abu Shama: *Kitab* (Cairo ed); p. 55; and W.B. Stevenson: The *Crusades*; op cit; p. 165.

[986] Abu Shama: *Kitab*; op cit; p. 55.

[987] Ibn al-Athir: Kamil; op cit; in *Receuil des Historiens des Croisades (Historiens Orientaux)*; Paris; 1967 ed; vol I; p. 476.

general, who was to play a leading role in the ensuing phase (the capture of Egypt.)[988]The death of one of the leading crusader leaders was soon followed by the removal of yet another: Joscelin of Tell Bashir. This occurred probably towards early 1150, during a fresh attempt by Joscelin and his army on Edessa.[989]

Joscelin's army was annihilated, and Joscelin fell in the hands of Nur Eddin's viceroy in Aleppo, Ibn al-Daya.[990] Nur Eddin who had a deadly grudge against Joscelin, probably since the Edessa days, had him blinded and left to languish in a dungeon at Aleppo till his death nine years later.[991] Joscelin's captivity was soon followed by the loss of all that remained of his once prosperous county.[992] Nur-Eddin made gains in the districts neighbouring Aleppo, and Ezaz, his first objective, was captured after a long siege on 15th July 1150.[993] In October-November he besieged Tell Khalid and defeated a crusader relieving force near Tell Bashir; Tell Bashir itself falling to him after a series of attacks in July 1151.[994]

Aware of Zangi's power, the crusaders kept arriving into Palestine from all parts of Europe. In 1153, new Flemish forces under Theodoric came to reinforce Antioch.[995] Zangi, however, had under his command the able and loyal Kurdish general, Shirquh, and his nephew Salah Eddin, a united leadership, ever animated by the chief desire 'to rid the land of the infidels.'[996] More importantly, Jihad had become a rallying cry for the Muslims, and the alliance between the religious classes and the military leadership became powerful.[997] The army of Nur Eddin included religious men, who were actually prepared to fight in the ranks.[998] Also in the ranks were prayer leaders, Qur'an's readers, preachers, judges, who enhanced the religious dimension of the military conflict.[999] Nur Eddin also kept cast iron discipline amongst his troops.[1000] With all this, he combined good strategic

---

[988] Kemal Eddin: Zubdat al-Halab fi ta'arikh Halab; tr into Fr as Histoire d'Alep; with additional notes by E. Blochet; Ernest Leroux; Paris; 1900; p. 13..

[989] T.A. Archer: The Crusades; T. Fisher Unwin; London; 1894; p. 205.

[990] T.A. Archer: The Crusades; op cit; p. 205; Kemal Eddin: Zubdat; (Blochet); p. 16.

[991] T.A. Archer: The Crusades; op cit; p. 205.

[992] Ibid.

[993] Kemal Eddin: Zubdat; (Blochet); op cit; p. 16.

[994] Ibid.

[995] C.R. Conder: The Latin Kingdom; op cit; p. 115.

[996] J.H. Lamonte: Crusade and Jihad: in N.A. Faris ed: The Arab Heritage, Princeton University Press, 1944; pp 159-98; p.171.

[997] C. Hillenbrand: The Crusades, op cit; p.131.

[998] N. Elisseeff: Nur al-Din: Un GrandPprince Musulman de Syrie au temps des croisades; Damascus; 1967; Vol 3; p. 735.

[999] C. Hillenbrand: The Crusades, op cit; p.120.

[1000] Ibid; p.113.

skills knowing when and how to strike. Thus, before he lent his full attention to Fatimid Egypt, itself threatened by crusader greed, he spent the years 1165-6 grinding into Christian territory, attacking fortresses on the eastern slopes of the Lebanon, whilst Shirquh busied himself destroying the Templars' defences south of Amman,[1001] which diverted Frankish attentions on his real aim, that was to counter them in Egypt

In October 1163, Shawar, the evicted Egyptian Wazeer, appealed to Nur Eddin to reinstate him against his rival Dirgham, promising to pay the cost of the campaign. In response, in April 1164, a column left Damascus commanded by Shirquh. Reaching Egypt, it swiftly eliminated Dirgham and had Shawar reinstated. Having achieved his first aim, Shawar sought to achieve his second that was to rid himself of Shirquh. Throughout the subsequent years, until 1169, Fatimid Egypt and the crusaders remained in alliance against Shirquh's repeated attempts to gain Egypt. At one point, in secret, Shawar invited the crusader King Amaury of Jerusalem to drive Shirquh out.[1002] Amaury was to receive 400,000 gold pieces, half to be paid immediately, and another half to be paid once Shirquh was eliminated with his army.[1003] That seemed little amount for the crusader ruler, who had in his sight the country itself and the much greater wealth and treasures of the Fatimid. The Christian envoys knew of, and had been bewildered by the sight of luxurious display in the Great palace of the Fatimid in Cairo; the inner part of the palace described here by the Christian Ambassador/chronicler, William of Tyre (1130-90):
`Curtains embroidered with pearls and gold, which hung down and hid the throne, were drawn aside with marvellous rapidity, and the caliph was revealed with face unveiled. (The caliph) seated on a throne of gold, surrounded by his privy counsellors and eunuchs.'[1004]
At one point, Crusaders and Fatimids signed a pact, which put Egypt directly under the Crusader protectorate for the first time in the history of the crusades.[1005] Soon after, in Alexandria, banners of Amaury and the Fatimids waved together on the city walls in a common effort against Shirquh.[1006] `We can see' Lamarque notes, `this stupefying spectacle for the era, a Muslim

---

[1001] William of Tyre: *A History of Deeds Done Beyond the Sea*; 2 Vols; tr and ed by E. Babcock and A.C. Krey; New York; Columbia University Press; 1943; repr 1976; xix, ii; pp. 901-2.
[1002] J. Glubb: *A Short History;* op cit; p.172.
[1003] G.W. Cox: *The Crusades*; op cit; p.97.
[1004] W of Tyre: *A History of Deeds done*; op cit; 319-21.
[1005] A.S. Atiya: *Crusade, Commerce and Culture*; Oxford University Press; London; 1962; p. 74.
[1006] G.W. Cox: *The Crusades*; op cit; p. 97.

army fighting alongside a Christian army another Muslim army.'[1007] The crusader-Fatimid coalition managed to force Shirquh out of Egypt on two occasions, before, in January 1169, he fell on the crusaders with devastating consequences, forcing them to retreat, and making a triumphal entry in Cairo.[1008]

In 1171 the Fatimid Caliph died. The mass of the Egyptian population hardly mourned the end of Fatimid rule, although there were a few sporadic revolts in favour of the Fatimid house, one of which involved the Christians, who brought a crusade from Sicily, but which failed to take Alexandria.[1009] Now, the religious schism between the Sunnite and Shi'ite caliphs, which had materially aided the Christians in their earlier conquests, was ended, and Christendom was now confronted with a technically united Islam.[1010] Following the death of Shirquh, his nephew, Salah Eddin became governor of Egypt, representing Nur Eddin. Nur-Eddin himself was soon to die, at last having unified, and for the first time in centuries, a wide stretch of Muslim territory from Egypt to Damascus, and large Muslim populations brought together in the fight to repulse the Franks.

[1007] Henri Lamarque: La Premiere Traduction Latine du Coran; op cit; p.239.
[1008] W.B. Stevenson: *The Crusades in the East*; Cambridge University Press; 1907; p.194.
[1009] J.H. Lamonte: Crusade and Jihad: op cit; pp 159-98; at p.176.
[1010] Ibid.

The Character of Nur Eddin Zangi

According to Gibbon:

`In his life and government the holy warrior revived the zeal and simplicity of the first caliphs. Gold and silk were banished from his palace; the use of wine from his dominions; the public revenue was scrupulously applied to the public service; and the frugal household of Noureddin was maintained from his legitimate share of the spoil which he vested in the purchase of a private estate. His chamber of justice was the terror of the great and the refuge of the poor. Some years after the sultan's death, an oppressed subject called aloud in the streets of Damascus, "O Noureddin, Noureddin, where art thou now? Arise, arise, to pity and protect us!" A tumult was apprehended, and a living tyrant blushed or trembled at the name of a departed monarch.'[1011]

Archer writes:

`Nur Eddin was one of the greatest princes that ever ruled in Syria. The Christians themselves acknowledged his valour and success; to the Muslims of this century and the next he was a model of every virtue. "Though so great a persecutor of Christians," writes William of Tyre, "he was a just ruler, wise, and religious, so far as the traditions of his race permitted." It was for his justice above all that his subjects loved him; he would take no unjust tax from his vast dominions, but like any private man lived of his own; when his wife complained of her poverty, and slighted a gift of three shops in Emesa as insignificant, "I have nought else, for all I have I hold only as treasurer for the faithful," was his reply. He once left his game of ball to appear before the cadi at the suit of a private person, and when the decision was given in his favour, resigned his claim in favour of his opponent. His justice enticed strangers to his dominions, one of whom, after his death, having appealed to Salah Eddin in vain, went in tears to the tomb of Nur-Eddin. The popular sympathy forced Salah Eddin at last to make recompense; the man then wept again, and when Salah Eddin asked his reason, the man replied that he wept for a ruler who could do justice even in the grave. When an emir slandered a learned doctor from Khorassan, Nur-Eddin replied, "If you speak ill of him, I shall punish you severely, even though you tell the truth. His good qualities are enough to cover his faults, whereas you and your like have vices many times greater than your virtues."[1012]

[1011] E. Gibbon: *The Decline and Fall;* op cit; Vol 6; p. 336.
[1012] T.A. Archer: The Crusades; op cit; pp. 239-41.

c. Salah Eddin (d.1193):

Just as under Zangi, the Muslim armies were now regularly accompanied by the `ulama' who read them and preached to them. Salah Eddin himself was personally and publicly committed to jihad.[1013] The call for Jihad was extremely powerful in uniting the Muslims at war as in peace.[1014] Jihad was also an expression of the yearning for Jerusalem, especially as the Muslims had to suffer the pain and humiliation of seeing it in Christian hands with mosques and Muslim shrines turned into churches or secular buildings,[1015] often sullied with pigs and excrement. Salah Eddin had himself, during a serious illness, pledged that he would devote himself to recovering Jerusalem whatever the cost, an illness, which according to his biographer, Imad Eddin, was sent by God to Salah Eddin to wake him from the sleep of forgetfulness'.[1016]

The road to Jerusalem passed by the Battle of Hattin. This battle came as a direct result of the crusader leader, Reynald (Reginald) of Chatillon's, attack on a Muslim caravan, which broke the truce, and resulted in many Muslim prisoners, including Salah Eddin's sister.[1017] `Since they trusted in Mohammed,' said Reginald `let him come and save them.' Salah Eddin, infuriated, swore to kill Reginald with his own hand,[1018] which he would eventually do after the Battle of Hattin. This battle was fought on the 4th of July 1187. In the battle, Salah Eddin was joined by his son, al-Afdal, and also his nephew, Taki Eddin, who both played their part.[1019] In a clean sweep, Salah Eddin defeated the Christian armies assembled in front of him. These lines from the Muslim chronicler, Imad Eddin, give an account of battle:
`The fire of (Muslim) arrows burned and wounded them (the crusaders), the fierce grip of the bows seized tenaciously upon them and struck them dead. They were impotent, driven off pushed to extremes and driven back, every charge thrown off and destroyed, every action or attack captured and put in chains. Not even an ant could have escaped, and they could not defend themselves by charging. They burned and glowed in a frenzied

---

[1013] C. Hillenbrand: *The Crusades,* op cit; p.191.

[1014] W.M. Watt: *Muslim Christian Encounters*; op cit; p.81.

[1015] C. Hillenbrand: *The Crusades*, op cit; p.150.

[1016] Abu Shama: *Kitab al-rawdatayn;* ed. M.H. M. Ahmad; 2 vols; Cairo; 1954.; II; p. 65.

[1017] W. Durant: *The Age of Faith*, op cit; p.597.

[1018] Ibid.

[1019] See: S. Runciman: *A History;* op cit; vol ii; pp. 456-60; and appendix pp. 486-91 for details on the battle, although Runciman, understandably stresses the Crusader valiant fighting.

ferment. As the arrows struck them down those who had seemed like lions now seemed like hedgehogs. The arrows beat them down and opened great gaps in their ranks. They sought refuge on the hill of Hattin to protect them from defeat, and Hattin was surrounded by the flags of destruction. The sword-blades sucked away their lives and scattered them on the hillsides; the bows found their targets, the wild fates stripped them, disasters crushed them, destruction picked them out, they became death's target and fate's prey.'[1020]

Only 200 of the knights and foot-soldiers escaped together with the count of Tripoli, the lord Bailan, and Reynald of Sidon.[1021] Amongst the prisoners was the king, the master of the Temple, Prince Reynald, the Marquis William, Aimery the constable, Humphrey of Toron, Hugh of Jubail, Pilvain Lord of Botron, and many other barons and knights.[1022] As he had vowed, Salah Eddin struck the head of Reynald of Chatillon, and then had all the knight Templars and Hospitallers slain. The lives of the countless others he spared. At the Horns of Hattin, Runciman concludes, the greatest army that the crusaders had ever assembled was annihilated, and the victor, was now the ruler of the united Muslim world.[1023]

The castle of Tiberias surrendered the following·day after Hattin; Acre opened its gates within five days of the victory; three weeks later the strong castle of Toron in Upper Galilee surrendered.[1024] The Muslims took Jaffa and Mejdel Yaba, whilst Haifa, Caesarea and Arsuf, Nazareth, Sebastieh and Nablus submitted to Muslim detachments sent against them.[1025] The forts south of Seffurieh were taken, including Fuleh and Deburieh, Lejeun, and Beisan. Then from Toron, Salah Eddin marched on Sidon, and took it after subduing Sarafend. Beirut fell on 8th of August, whilst Gebal was given up to a Muslim force a week later.[1026] By the end of the Summer of 1187, only Tyre, Tripoli and Antioch were remaining seaports in Christian hands.[1027]

[1020] Imad Eddin al-Isfahani: *Al Fath al-Qusi fi 'l fath al-Qudusi*; Landberg Ed; Leiden; 1888. I. F. Gabrieli: Arab Historians; op cit; pp. 132.
[1021] P. W. Edbury: *The Conquest of Jerusalem and the Third Crusade*, Scolar Press, 1996; p.161.
[1022] Ibid; p.47.
[1023] S. Runciman: *A History*; op cit; vol ii; p. 460.
[1024] C.R. Conder: *The Latin Kingdom;* op cit; p. 154-5.
[1025] P. W. Edbury: The Conquest; op cit; p.161; C.R. Conder: *The Latin;* op cit; pp 154-5.
[1026] C.R. Conder: *The Latin Kingdom;* op cit; p. 155.
[1027] A.S .Atiya: *Crusade, Commerce and Culture*; Oxford University Press; London; 1962; p. 80.

On 2 October 1187, after a short siege, Jerusalem surrendered to the Muslims; that was nearly a century after it was first taken from them. Salah Eddin's terms were accepted, says a learned Christian, `with gratitude and lamentation"; perhaps some learned Christians compared these events of 1187 with those of 1099.[1028] No massacre or violence were perpetrated, the entry of Salah Eddin more `(peaceful) like that of Omar rather than (murderous) like that of Geodfrey.'[1029] Salah Eddin's brother al-Adil asked for the gift of a thousand slaves from the still un-ransomed Christian poor; it was granted and he freed them.[1030] Following the retaking of Jerusalem, Ibn Al-Athir writes:

`He (Salah Eddin) commanded that the buildings should be put back to their ancient usage. Now the Templars had built to the west of the Aqsa a building for their habitation, and constructed there all that they needed of granaries, and also latrines, with other such places, and they had even enclosed a part of the Aqsa in their new building Salah Eddin commanded that all this should be set back to its former state, and he ordered that the Masjid (or Haram area) should be cleansed, and also the Rock from all the filth and the impurities that were there. All this was executed as commanded.'[1031]

Later on, when Richard's vowed that he would not abandon Jerusalem, Salah Eddin answered:

`Al-Quds is to us just as much as to you, and is more precious in our eyes than in yours, for it is the site of our Prophet's nocturnal departure and the place where people will assemble on Judgment Day. Therefore do not imagine that we can waver in this regard.'[1032]

The news of the fall of Jerusalem struck the hearts of Christendom. It was in the time of the papacy of Urban II that Jerusalem was taken from the Muslims, and it was in the time of Urban III that it was retaken by the Muslims. Pope Urban III who was at Ferrara died of grief when he heard the news.[1033] The new pope, Clement III, sent his messengers to all the great men of Christendom- emperors, kings, counts, and marquises- and to the knights and sergeants telling them that `he would take upon himself and acquit before God all the sins of those who would bear the sign of the cross to go to recover the Promised Land provided that they had confessed and were truly

---

[1028] W. Durant: *The Age of Faith,* op cit; p.598.
[1029] C.R. Conder: *The Latin Kingdom;* op cit; p. 156.7.
[1030] W. Durant: *The Age of Faith,* op cit; p.598.
[1031] Ibn al-Athir: *Al-Kamil;* op cit; vol ix; p. 364.
[1032] Ibn Shadad: *Al-Nawadir al-Sultaniya wa'l Mahassin al-Yussufiya;* in *Receuil des Historiens des Croisades; Historiens Orientaux;* Paris; 1884; III; p. 265.
[1033] P. W. Edbury: *The Conquest;* op cit; p.47.

penitent.'[1034] He also announced that he would grant the tithe to all those who wished to have it so that they might do God's service.[1035] And so was launched the third crusade in 1189.

The third crusade brought three large armies led by the principal rulers of Europe, Richard Coeur de Lion of England, Philip August of France, and Conrad of Germany. Before it even reached its destination, the army of Conrad which came overland was decimated nearly entirely by the Turks in Asia Minor, and Conrad himself drowned in a river.[1036] Richard and Philip came by sea in the year 1191, Richard capturing for himself Cyprus on his way. Then a fleet arrived, bringing ten thousand men, mostly from Flanders and Denmark.[1037]

Acre, in Muslim hands, and on the coast, was the focus of attack of the incoming crusaders. When he heard the news that the emperor of Germany, the king of France and the king of England and all the high barons overseas were coming against him, Salah Eddin had Acre strongly garrisoned and fortified in every way necessary, pledging to support the town in case of Christian attack.[1038] Acre was soon besieged by land and sea by huge Christian armies. The Muslim garrison resisted aware that Salah Eddin's army was in the field helping them. Salah Eddin made repeated attempts to relieve the city, seeking to draw out the Christians in his direction, and causing them considerable casualties,[1039] but failing in his purpose. In 1191, Acre was retaken by the crusaders; and Richard of England, devious and greedy,[1040] had 2700 chained Muslims beheaded, sending a signal by this to Salah Eddin as 'a hint to hurry' to meet his terms in paying the prisoners' ransom.[1041] On that day, the 15th of August, the 2700 Muslims were killed by Richard's order, the chronicler says: 'his (Richard's) soldiers came forward with joy to fulfil his commands, and to retaliate, by Divine Grace, taking revenge on those who had destroyed so many Christians with missiles from bows and arbalists.'[1042]

Acre remained one of the rare exploits of the third crusade, which

---

[1034] Ibid; p.75.
[1035] Ibid.
[1036] R.C.H. Davis: *A History*; op cit; vol 2; p. 280.
[1037] J. Glubb: *A Short History*; op cit; p.178.
[1038] P. W. Edbury: *The Conquest*; op cit; p.76.
[1039] Ibid; p.95.
[1040] Ibid; p.97.
[1041] W. Durant: *The Age of Faith;* op cit; p. 599.
[1042] Jeoff de Vinsauf, IV, 4; in C. R. Conder: *The Latin*; op cit; p. 273.

eventually failed in its aim to recapture Jerusalem. Its two leaders, the French king and Richard fell out with each other; both eventually withdrawing back to their countries.[1043]

The reputation of Richard the Lion Heart suffers in comparison with that of his rival, Salah Eddin. On one occasion, he, Richard, dropped his loot and ran off with his soldiers when he learnt of Salah Eddin's approach.[1044] The testimony of Salah Eddin by outsiders, however, does corroborate the statements of those close to him.[1045] In 1193, just like Caliph Omar centuries before him, building walls and digging trenches round Jerusalem, he carried stones on his own shoulders, so that all, rich and poor, strong and weak, followed his example, even including the scribe `Imad Eddin and the Qadi al-Fadil.[1046] Like Omar, his chief garment was a coarse woollen cloth, his only drink was water.[1047] And like Caliph Omar, all wrongs that came to his knowledge were speedily redressed; and taxes were lowered at the same time that public works were extended and the functions of government were carried on with efficiency and zeal.[1048] Following Nur-Eddin's example, he also built several mosques, hospitals, monasteries, and madrasas, and encouraged architecture.[1049] And just as his predecessor, he esteemed money `as little as dust,' and left only one dinar in his personal treasury.[1050] When he entered the Fatimid caliph palace in Cairo, he found there 12,000 occupants, all women except the male relatives of the Caliph; and such wealth of jewellery, furniture, ivory, porcelain, glass, and other objects of art as could hardly be rivalled by any other dignitary of that era.[1051] He kept nothing of all this for himself, gave the palace to his captains, and continued to live in the vizier's chambers, a life of fortunate simplicity.[1052] The sum of money he left at his death was not large enough to be submitted to tax; his private charities had absorbed everything. `He who possessed such abundant wealth left in his treasury,' Beha Eddin said, `when he died, but seven and forty Nasri dirhems,

---

[1043] W.B. Stevenson: *The Crusades*; op cit; pp. 273 ff.

[1044] A.M. Nanai: L'Image du croise; op cit; p. 24.

[1045] Such as Beha Eddin: *The Life of Saladin*; London, Palestine Pilgrim's Text Society, 1897.

[1046] Abd al Latif quoted in Abu Usaybia: *Kitab uyun al-anba fi tabaqat al-atiba; ed*, A. Muller, 2 vols, Konigsberg, 1884.II; p. 206.

[1047] W. Durant: *The Age of Faith*, op cit; p.310.

[1048] Ibid; p.311.

[1049] Ibid.

[1050] Baron Carra de Vaux: *Les Penseurs de l'Islam,* Vol 1; Geuthner; Paris; 1921; p. 27.

[1051] W. Durant: *The Age of Faith*, op cit; p.311.

[1052] Ibid.

and a single Tyrian gold piece.'[1053] He left neither goods, nor house, nor real estate, neither garden, nor village, nor cultivated land, nor any other species of property.[1054]

Not long before his death (1193), Salah Eddin gave his son Ez-Zahir instructions:
'My son, I commend thee to the most high God... Do His will, for that way lies peace. Abstain from shedding blood.... for blood that is spilt never sleeps. Seek to win the hearts of thy people, and watch over their prosperity; for it is to secure their happiness that thou art appointed by God and me... If I have become great it is because I have won men's hearts by kindness and gentleness.'[1055]
After his death, one of his contemporaries,' Abd al-Latif, says: 'men grieved for him as they grieved prophets. I have seen no other ruler for whose death the people mourned, for he was loved by good and bad, Muslim and unbeliever alike'.[1056]
Islam gloried in the integrity and justice of his rule, and Christendom acknowledged in him an 'infidel gentleman.'[1057]

Soon, though, after the death of Salah Eddin, the Muslim world returned to its usual woes and divisions and alliances with the enemies of the faith, which, once more, had it not been for the Mamluks, this time, would have caused the extinction of Islam. This is seen in the following

---

[1053] Beha-Eddin: The Life of Saladin; op cit; reprinted in The Islamic World and the West; Edited by A.R. Lewis; pp. 53-61; at p. 55.
[1054] Ibid.
[1055] S. Lane Poole: Saladin and the Fall of the Kingdom of Jerusalem; Beirut; Khayats; 1964; p. 367.
[1056] Cited by B. Lewis: Islam; vol I; The Mac Millan Press; Ltd; London; 1974; p. 67.
[1057] W. Durant: The Age of Faith, op cit; p.311.

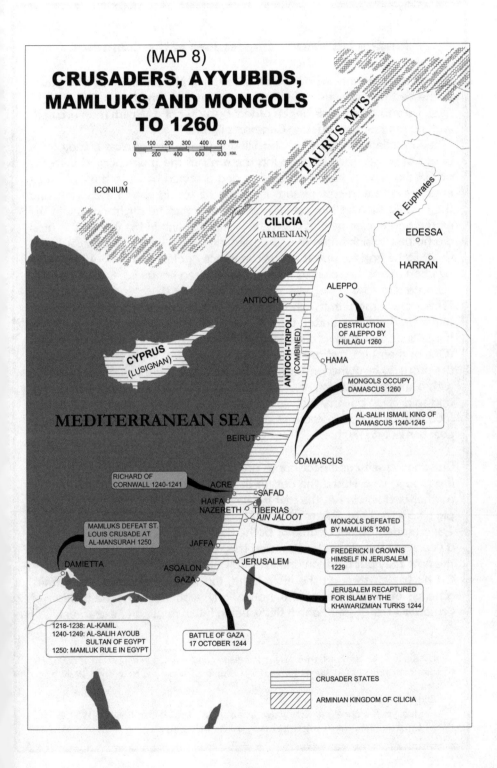

(MAP 8)
CRUSADERS, AYYUBIDS, MAMLUKS AND MONGOLS TO 1260

TAURUS MTS

| 0 | 100 | 200 | 300 | 400 | 500 | Miles |
| 0 | 200 | 400 | 600 | 800 | KM. |

ICONIUM

CILICIA
(ARMENIAN)

R. Euphrates

EDESSA

HARRAN

ANTIOCH

ALEPPO

DESTRUCTION OF ALEPPO BY HULAGU 1260

ANTIOCH-TRIPOLI (COMBINED)

CYPRUS
(LUSIGNAN)

HAMA

MONGOLS OCCUPY DAMASCUS 1260

AL-SALIH ISMAIL KING OF DAMASCUS 1240-1245

MEDITERRANEAN SEA

BEIRUT

DAMASCUS

RICHARD OF CORNWALL 1240-1241

ACRE

SAFAD

HAIFA

NAZERETH

TIBERIAS

AIN JALOOT

MONGOLS DEFEATED BY MAMLUKS 1260

MAMLUKS DEFEAT ST. LOUIS CRUSADE AT AL-MANSURAH 1250

JAFFA

JERUSALEM

FREDERICK II CROWNS HIMSELF IN JERUSALEM 1229

DAMIETTA

ASQALON

GAZA

JERUSALEM RECAPTURED FOR ISLAM BY THE KHAWARIZMIAN TURKS 1244

1218-1238: AL-KAMIL
1240-1249: AL-SALIH AYOUB
SULTAN OF EGYPT
1250: MAMLUK RULE IN EGYPT

BATTLE OF GAZA
17 OCTOBER 1244

CRUSADER STATES

ARMINIAN KINGDOM OF CILICIA

195

Muslim Historians' Impressions of the Crusaders

One of the historians who lived at the time of Nur-Eddin, and who gave us the best descriptions of the Franks was Usama Ibn Munqhid (fl. 1138-1188). Usama describes Frankish ordeal by water of a Muslim man accused with his mother of murdering Christian pilgrims:

`They installed a huge cask and filled it with water. Across it they set a board of wood. They then bound the arms of the man charged with the act, tied a rope around his shoulders and dropped him into the cask; their idea being that in case he was innocent, he would sink in the water and they would then lift him up with the rope so that he might not die in the water; and in case he was guilty, he would not sink in the water. This man did his best to sink when they dropped him in the water, but he could not do it. So he had to submit to their sentence against him—may Allah's curse be upon them! they pierced his eyeballs with red hot awls.'[1058]

Usama also says:

`There are some Franks who settled in our land and taken to living like Muslims. These are better than those who have just arrived from their homelands, but they are the exception, and cannot be taken as typical. (One of them) had retired from the army, and was living on the income of the property he owned in Antioch. He had a fine table brought out, spread with a splendid selection of appetising food. He saw that I was not eating, and said: `Don't' worry please, eat what you like, for I don't eat Frankish food. I have Egyptian cooks and eat only what they serve. No pig's flesh ever comes into my house!'[1059]

Crusaders cruelty and poor habits are depicted by many Muslim historians. Ibn Jubayr, who visited the East in the 1180s, calls Agnes of Courtenay, the mother of Baldwin IV, `the sow known as Queen who is the mother of the pig who is the Lord of Acre'.[1060]

The crusaders do not cleanse or bathe themselves more than once or twice a year, and then in cold water, and they do not wash their garments from the time they put them on until they fall into pieces.[1061]

On his travels through the Holy Land, Ibn Jubayr speaks of the Franks' absence of cleanliness, and is particularly scathing in his description of Crusader Acre: `It stinks and is filthy, being full of refuse and excrement.'[1062]

[1058] Usama in P. K. Hitti: *An Arab-Syrian gentleman and warrior in the period of the Crusades. Memoirs of Usamah ibn Munqidh*, Columbia University, New York, 1929; p. 168.
[1059] Ibid; pp. 103-4.
[1060] Ibn Jubayr: *The Travels of Ibn Jubayr*; Trans; R.J.C. Broadhurst; London; 1952; p.316.
[1061] Al-Qazwini: *Athar al-Bilad*; Tr B. Lewis; Islam; op cit; II; p.123.

`Mysterious are the works of the Creator, the author of all things!' says Usama, `when one comes to recount cases regarding the Franks, he cannot but glorify Allah (exalted is He!) and sanctify him, for He sees them as animals (bahaim) possessing the virtues of courage and fighting, nothing else; just as animals have only the virtues of strength and carrying loads.'[1063]
The chronicler Ibn Shaddad, a very close advisor to Salah Eddin, held that: `Mixing with the Franks and to be honest and cordial with them is an impossibility, their company is never secure or productive.'[1064]
The Muslims have also noted how the Western Christian lacks in marital jealousy, whilst his women are sexually loose.[1065]
Frankish ferocity was evident in their mass slaughter, rape, and eating of Muslim corpses. Ferocity that was so enduring, that even after their defeat by Salah Eddin, the Franks never ceased to spread fear and insecurity, and so much so that a chronicler travelling in Palestine in 1210 could state that `even birds did not, from the fear of the Franks, fly some country roads.'[1066]

[1062] Ibn Jubayr: *Travels*; ed Broadhurst; op cit; pp 318-25 .
[1063] Usama Ibn Munqidh: *Kitab al'Itibar;* tr P.K. Hitti; Beirut; 1964; p. 161.
[1064] Ibn Shaddad: *Al-Nawadir al-sultaniyya,* ed J. El-Shayyal; Cairo; 1964; p. 203.
[1065] In C. Hillenbrand: The Crusades, op cit; p.273.
[1066] Abu Shama: *Al-Dayl al-Rawdatayn*, Beirut, 1974, p. 70.

2. From Salah Eddin to the Recovery of Acre: 1194-1291:

Just before he died, Salah Eddin crowned his life achievements with the common error: to legate power and the Muslim realm to his heirs. Before he expired, he had his officers and high officials swear allegiance to his children and his successors,[1067] and to each child he assigned a certain portion of the Muslim land.[1068]

a. Ayyubid Ineptness:

Just to prove the point that great men, with few exceptions, leave behind inept heirs, Salah Eddin's heirs proved so greedy, corrupt, and all round dreadful rulers, that in the early 13th century, just a few years after Salah Eddin's death, the Muslim land found itself in the same state of chaos as it was a century before when the crusaders first arrived. Salah Eddin's Ayyubid successors did not just fail to follow on the impetus he gave them to eliminate the crusaders,[1069] but instead after his death, and that of his brother, the unity of the Muslim world, which took tens of battles, and decades to rebuild, again broke into a series of infighting kingdoms and principalities. The Ayyubid princes spent their energies fighting each other and capturing territory from each other rather than fighting the Franks.[1070] The Ayyubids, unlike Nur Eddin and Salah Eddin, were not interested in Jihad either.[1071] Rather, their policies allowed the continued survival of the Crusaders states.[1072] Two of the Ayyubid rulers went as far as to be ready to hand back Jerusalem to the Franks.[1073] During the sixth crusade, as the crusaders besieged Damietta, Malik al-Kamil offered to give up Jerusalem to the Crusaders, to free all the Christian captives, and to pay a large sum of

---

[1067] R.S. Humphreys: *From Saladin to the Mongols;* State University of New York Press Albany; 1977; p.57.

[1068] Ibn Wasil: *Mufarrij al-Kurub fi Akhbar bani Ayyub;* Ed. G. Shayyal, S.Ashur, and H. Rabi'; 4 vols; Cairo; II; 172-3.

[1069] J.H. Lamonte: Crusade and Jihad: op cit; pp. 159-98; at p.183.

[1070] R.S. Humphreys: Legitimacy and instability in Islam, in the *The Jihad and its times*, ed. Dajani Shakeel and R.A. Messier, Ann Arbor, 1991; pp. 10-11.

[1071] R.S. Humphreys: *From Saladin to the Mongols;* op cit; p.7.

[1072] R.S. Humphreys: Legitimacy and instability in Islam, op cit, 10-11.

[1073] C. Hillenbrand: *The Crusades,* op cit;.p.249.

money, only for the offer to be rejected by the Pope legate, Cardinal Pelagius.[1074]

It was in the midst of this Muslim ineptness that the 4th crusade was launched early in the 13th century (1204). The good fortune of Islam was that this crusade was deviated onto Constantinople. This fourth crusade, which could have finished off the Muslims at their most divided, found the crusaders more corrupt than their Muslim adversaries. Indeed, having heard that the Doge of Venice sought to capture Zara (the most important port after Venice,) now in Hungarian hands, the Crusaders rushed to his financial offer.[1075] Pope Innocent III denounced the proposal as villainous, and threatened to excommunicate all participants, but as Durant notes, the greatest and most powerful of the popes could not make his voice heard above the clamour for gold.[1076] The Pope was particularly incensed at this as the Hungarian King himself had assumed the cross.[1077] The combined crusader fleets attacked Zara, took it in five days, and divided the spoils; apologised to the Pope, ignored the excommunications, and proceeded to the second part of the Venetian plan: the conquest of Constantinople.[1078] The Venetians had as an aim to restore to the throne the ousted Byzantine emperor, which they eventually achieved.[1079] However, by the time this was done, their boats could not sail to attack the Muslims without danger on the sea.[1080] Thus they waited in Constantinople for conditions to improve before launching their crusade. Horrified to find Muslims worshiping in a mosque in a Christian city (Constantinople), the crusaders slew the worshipers, and set fire to the mosque. The fire spread through three miles of the city, raged for eight days, and laid a considerable section of Constantinople to ashes.[1081] The Greeks rose in rebellion against the outrage, just to be crushed by the crusader army, which had been toughened in wars and destruction, which Durant notes, passed like consuming locusts through the capital (1204).[1082] The Crusaders entered homes, shops, churches, and took whatever caught their fancy. Churches were ripped off gold, silver, and jewels accumulated for a millennium, and also of sacred relics that would later be peddled in Western Europe at good prices. St Sophia suffered on that occasion more

---

[1074] C.R. Conder: *The Latin Kingdom;* op cit; p. 310.

[1075] G.W. Cox: *The Crusades*; op cit; pp. 147-8.

[1076] W. Durant: *The Age of Faith*, op cit; p.603.

[1077] G.W. Cox: *The Crusades*; op cit; p. 149.

[1078] W. Durant: *The Age of Faith*, op cit; p.603.

[1079] G.W. Cox: *The Crusades*; op cit; p.155.

[1080] Ibid.

[1081] W. Durant: *The Age of Faith*, op cit; p.604.

[1082] Ibid.

damage than the Turks would inflict upon it in 1453.[1083] Some attempt was made to limit rape, but the crusaders spared neither age nor sex nor religious profession.[1084] Libraries were ransacked, and precious manuscripts were ruined or lost; museums as well as churches and homes were burnt down; great works of literature lost for-ever, and thousands of art masterpieces were stolen, mutilated or destroyed. The Byzantine Empire would never recover from the blow.[1085]

The Muslims further south, in their ineptness, could breathe.

A fifth crusade, aimed at Egypt took place in 1219, and failed in its aims. The Muslim ruler, al-Kamil granted the crusaders free passage to leave the country in August 1221.[1086]

In 1228 Frederick II of Sicily arrived in Palestine on a Crusade, the sixth. Worried about his own realm, and without a blow, the Ayyubid sultan al-Kamil concluded a treaty with Frederick, which in the words of Muslim chroniclers was a supplication on the part of the Muslim ruler.[1087] In such a treaty, al-Kamil surrendered the whole of Jerusalem, except the Mosque of Omar, the keys of which were to stay with the Muslims, but Christians under certain circumstances could enter it for prayer; and the treaty further restored Bethlehem, Jaffa and Nazareth to the Crusaders.[1088] So pleased was Frederick he decorated with the order of knighthood the Sultan's chief ambassador.[1089] This Muslim capitulation over Jerusalem caused widespread indignation and outrage amongst Muslims. In 1229, the chronicler Sibt al-Jawzi wrote: `In it (this year) al-Kamil gave Jerusalem to the emperor... the news of the handing over of Jerusalem to the Franks arrived and great anger broke loose in all the lands of Islam.'[1090]

Al-Kamil was not the only Ayyubid who sold out Jerusalem and other territories for the sake of his own realm. On hearing that the Franks had designs on Jerusalem, another Ayyubid with the name of al-Mu'azzam, i.e

---

[1083] Sir T.C. Jackson: *Byzantine and Romanesque Architecture*; 2 Vols; Cambridge University Press; Vol I; p. 101.

[1084] E. Gibbon: *The Decline and Fall*; Vol 6; op cit; p. 171.

[1085] W. Durant: *The Age of Faith*, op cit; p.605.

[1086] For the fifth crusade, and al-Kamil granting free passage to the crusaders, see: Ibn Iyas: *Bada't al-Zuhur fi waqai al-Duhur*; (Bulaq; 1311 H); vol I; pp. 79-80. Ibn Khaldun: *Kitab al-Ibar*; op cit; vol v; pp. 349-50; Ibn Khallikan: *Wafayat al-Iyan*; op cit; vol ii; pp. 451.

[1087] See Ibn al-Athir: *Kamil*; op cit; vol xii; p. 315.G.W. Cox: *The Crusades*; op cit; p. 189.

[1088] G.W. Cox: *The Crusades*; op cit; p. 189.

[1089] A.S. Atiya: *Crusades;* op cit; p. 89.

[1090] Sibt al-Jawzi: *Al-Muntazam fi tarikh al-muluk wa'l umam*; X; Hyderabad; 1940; VIII/2; p. 653.

The Grand, who initially had patronised building projects in the city, found himself dismantling its fortifications. According to Sibt al-Jawzi, al-Mu'azzam justified this very unpopular act by saying: `If they (the Franks) were to take it (Jerusalem), they would kill those in it and rule over Damascus and the countries of Islam. Necessity demands its destruction.[1091]

Weak Ayyubid rule was soon compounded by the greatest threat on the Islamic realm: the Mongols.

---

b. The Rising Mongol Threat, and Persistent Muslim Divisions:

In 1219, the Mongols descended on Eastern Islam, lands of great urbanity and civilisation, such as Khwarizm, the most populous, the most beautiful, and the best cultivated parts, whose inhabitants excelled in character and urbanism,[1092] and they devastated them. In three years, 1219-1221, they slaughtered more people than in any similar conflict of such duration notes Saunders.[1093] An army under Genghis' (Chingis) son Jagtai, captured and sacked Otrar, whilst another under Genghis himself, burned Bukhara to the ground, raped thousands of women, and massacred 30,000 men.[1094] A historian of Bukhara, a man fortunate, indeed, to have escaped with his life when his city was devastated in 1220, wrote:
`They came, they uprooted, they burned, they slew, they despoiled, they departed.'[1095]
The same they did elsewhere. In five days, (March 1220) Samarkand capitulated; the inhabitants were ordered to evacuate the city, which was more easily plundered in their absence.[1096] The Turkish garrison was put to the sword, the artisans in the number of 30,000 were deported to Mongolia, and a great deal of indiscriminate killing went on, and only a quarter of the place was reoccupied when the survivors were permitted to return.[1097] Such was the tenor of destruction, a century later Ibn Battuta

---

[1091] Ibid; p. 601.

[1092] B. Spuler: *History of the Mongols;* London, Routledge& Kegan Paul, 1972; p.31.

[1093] J.J. Saunders: *The History of the Mongol Conquests;* Routlege & Kegan Paul; London; 1971; p. 55-6.

[1094] W. Durant: *The Age of Faith,* op cit; p.339.

[1095] W. Blunt: *Splendours of Islam;* Angus and Robertson; London; 1976; p. 50.

[1096] J.J. Saunders: *The History of the Mongol Conquests;* op cit; p. 57.

[1097] Ibid.

described Samarkand and Balkh, too, as still largely in ruins.[1098] In February 1221, the Mongols totally annihilated Hamadan and its population.[1099] Through Khurasan, the Mongols ravaged every town on their march, placing captives in their van, giving them a choice between fighting their fellow men in front or being cut down from behind.[1100]

Genghis proceeded with the methodical destruction of the Khwarizmian kingdom.[1101] Merw fell in February 1221 to the Mongol leader Tolui; the city was burned to the ground; its libraries, the glory of Islam, were consumed in the conflagration.[1102] The Mongols butchered 700,000 persons,[1103] only eighty craftsmen were spared. The total slaughter there is put by Browne at 1.3 million lives.[1104] When the city of Gurganj fell in April 1221, the Mongols broke the dams and flooded the town, enslaved the women and children, deported the artisans to the number, it is said of 100,000, and slew the rest.[1105] Gurganj was completely ruined; the dams were never repaired, and the Oxus, having been diverted from its normal course, flowed into the Caspian for 300 years.[1106] Nishapur, taken in 1221, became a scene of a carnival of blood scarcely surpassed in Mongol annals, as separate piles of heads of men, women and children were built into pyramids, and even the cats and dogs were killed in the streets.[1107] In November 1221, Herat was levelled to the ground, after a full week had been devoted to killing the inhabitants. In this city, about one and half million people were massacred, and neighbouring cities met with a similar fate.[1108] The stench of the dead hung over the stricken land.[1109] Figures of Mongol massacres amounted to 747,000 at Nishapur; 1.3 million at Merw; and 1.6 million at Herat.[1110] On the dreadful depopulation of eastern Persia, Juwaini says:

[1098] Ibn Battuta: *Travels in Asia and Africa;* tr and selected by H.A.R. Gibb; George Routledge and Sons Ltd; London, 1929.
[1099] J.J. Saunders: *The History of the Mongol Conquests;* op cit; p. 59.
[1100] W. Durant: *The Age of Faith,* op cit; p.339.
[1101] J.J. Saunders: *The History of the Mongol Conquests;* op cit; p. 59.
[1102] W. Durant: *The Age of Faith,* op cit; p.339.
[1103] Ibn al-Athir; in J. J. Saunders: *The History;* op cit; p. 60.
[1104] E.G. Browne: *Literary History of Persia;* Cambridge University Press; 1929; 3 Vols; Vol 2; p. 439.
[1105] J.J. Saunders: *The History of the Mongol Conquests;* op cit; p. 60.
[1106] On the changing course of the Oxus, consult Le Strange: *Lands of the Eastern Caliphate;* op cit; pp. 455-8.
[1107] J.J. Saunders: *The History of the Mongol Conquests;* op cit; pp. 60-1.
[1108] M. Levey; N. Al-Khaledy: Chemistry in the Medical Formulary of al-Samarqandi; *Chymia;* vol 11; pp. 37-44; p.37.
[1109] J.J. Saunders: *The History of the Mongol Conquests;* op cit; p. 61.
[1110] R.W. Bulliet: *The Patricians of Nishapur; A Study of Islamic Medieval Social History;* Cambridge; mass; 1972; pp. 9-10; I.P. Petrushvskii: The Socio economic Conditions of

'Even though there be generation and increase until the Resurrection, the population will not attain a tenth part of what it was before.'[1111]
Extracts from Ibn al-Athir read:
'A tremendous disaster such as had never happened before, and which struck all the world, though the Muslims above all. If anyone were to say that at no time since the creation of man by the Great God had the world experienced anything like it, he would only be telling the truth. In fact nothing comparable is reported in past chronicles. The worst they recall is the treatment and extinction of the Israelites and the destruction of Jerusalem by Nebuchadnezzar. But what is Jerusalem compared with the areas devastated by those monsters, where every city is twice the size of Jerusalem? what are the Israelites in comparison with [the number of] those they massacred, for a single city whose inhabitants were murdered numbered more than all the Israelites together. It may well be that the world from now until its end... will not experience the like of it again..... Dadjdjal (the Antichrist) will at least spare those who adhere to him, and will only destroy his adversaries. These (the Mongols), however, spared none. They killed women, men and children, ripped open the bodies of the pregnant and slaughtered the unborn.'[1112]

Whilst the Mongol threat mounted, Muslim armies, as by now customary, were busy fighting each other. Sultan al-Kamil faced constant family rebellions in Syria.[1113]
The Ayyubid folly was to reach greater heights, for they allied themselves to the crusaders to fight against other Muslims, the Mamluks and their Khwarizmian Turkish allies.[1114] The Khwarizmian Turks were horsemen who swept west from Harran.[1115] They lived on little, boiled herbs, milk and little meat, but were admirable with the bows and lances.[1116] On July 11, 1244, after crossing the Galilee, they erupted into Jerusalem, now in crusader hands (after it had been ceded to them by al-Kamil in 1229) and literally, in the space of days slaughtered their way through crusader ranks, decimating the whole of the two crusader armies of Hospitallers and Templars; leaving

---

Iran under the Il-Khans; In *Cambridge History of Iran*; v; Cambridge; 1968; pp. 483-537; p. 485.
[1111] Boyle's translation; I, 97; in J.J. Saunders: *The History of the Mongol Conquests*; op cit; Note 42; p. 215.
[1112] Ibn al-Athir: *Chronicon, quod perfectissimum inscribitur*, (Al-Kamil) ed. K.J. Tornberg, XII, op cit; pp. 233-5.
[1113] J. Glubb: *A Short History*; op cit; p.201.
[1114] G.W. Cox: *The Crusades*; op cit; p. 195.
[1115] Including most sources referred to here, which, like other writing regard them just as the Mamluks, Seljuks, Almoravids and Almohads as barbaric fanatics.
[1116] R. Payne: *The Crusades;* op cit; p. 330.

barely fifty survivors.[1117] Thus was recaptured for Islam Jerusalem that had been ceded by the Ayyubid to the crusaders, and so ended Christian hegemony there until modern times.[1118]

This Turkish victory brought into alliance the crusaders and the Ayyubid sultans of Damascus and Hims against the Turks and their Egyptian allies at the Battle of Ghaza in October 1244. The Muslim chronicler, Sibt b. al-Jawzi narrates:

`Crosses were above their (the Muslim) heads and priests with the battalions were making the sign of the cross over the Muslims and offering them the sacrament. In their hand were chalices and drinking vessels from which they gave them to drink.... As for the lord of Hims... he began to weep, saying `I knew when we departed under the crosses of the Franks that we would not prosper.'[1119]

This Crusader-Muslim coalition was faced by the Mamluk-Turkish armies led by Baybars.[1120] This decisive battle took place near Ghaza, and lasted two days, beginning on the morning of October 17, 1244. The first day, the brunt of the battle was sustained by Baybars' troops, which stood firm against the repeated attacks of crusader-Sultan of Hims' coalition. The second day, the Khwarizmians went on the counter attack, first slaughtering the whole army of the sultan of Hims, and other Bedouin allies of the crusades, before turning onto the Christians `with the relish of men, who, having feasted well, look forward to the sweetmeats at the end of dinner.'[1121] They charged into Christian ranks, and every charge produced `a mountain of dead horses and dead riders.'[1122] The Battle of 1244 was furiously waged, and thirty thousand crusaders and their Muslim allies were killed; only the patriarch and the Prince of Tyre escaped with thirty three Templars, twenty six Hospitallers, and three Teutonic Knights.[1123] More Christians died in this battle than at Hattin; and hundreds were carried prisoners to Egypt.[1124] Following this success, Baybars went on the offensive, and in just a year, with his forces, he retook most of the territory that the Ayyubid had ceded to the Crusaders.[1125]

[1117] G.W. Cox: *The Crusades*; op cit; p. 195.

[1118] Al-Maqrizi: *Khitat;* op cit; vol ii; pp. 236-7; R. Finucane: *Soldiers of the Faith*; op cit. p.28.

[1119] Sibt al-Jawzi; *Al-Muntazam*;VIII/2; op cit; pp.746-7.

[1120] W. Durant: *The Age of Faith*, op cit; p.607.

[1121] R. Payne: *The Crusades;* op cit; p. 331.

[1122] Ibid.

[1123] C.R. Conder: *The Latin Kingdom;* op cit; p. 318.

[1124] R. Payne: *The Crusades;* op cit; p. 331.

[1125] A.S. Atiya: *Crusades;* op cit; p. 90.

Baybars and his Mamluks won another decisive battle over the crusaders at al-Mansurah (Egypt) in 1250. Following the successful landing of the seventh crusade, the French army began to march from Damietta towards Cairo. The crusade rash entry into al-Mansurah was by the infantry, led by the French King's brother, Robert of Artois.[1126] After surprising the Muslim camp and slaying the Muslim leader Fakhr Eddin, he hunted down the fleeing Muslims, attacking impetuously, spreading fear and terror, until he reached the outer walls of the citadel.[1127] Robert was determined to capture al-Mansurah and finish off the Egyptian army.[1128] In al-Mansurah, however, Robert came up against the Bahriyya and Jamdariyya Mamluk formations who had not been seized by the general panic.[1129] The ablest of the Mamluks, Baybars took control of the situation. He stationed his men at crucial points within the town itself, then let the Frankish cavalry come pouring through the open gate.[1130] When the French knights with the Templars close behind them swept up the very walls of the citadel, the Mamluks rushed out from the side streets, and attacked them.[1131] The crusaders were not able to deploy their heavy cavalry in the narrow alleys, and the Mamluks cut them to pieces, only a few knights escaped the blood-bath to bring King Louis the news of the disaster.[1132] The Templars were all but for five of them slaughtered; Robert of Artois barricaded himself and his bodyguards in a house, but the Egyptians soon burst in and slaughtered them all.[1133] Amongst the knights who fell in the battle were the Earl of Salisbury, and almost all his English followers, the Lord of Coucy and the Count of Brienne.[1134] The Mamluks in al-Mansurah had obtained a complete victory, which guaranteed the survival of the state, which subsequently legitimised Mamluk sovereignty over Egypt.[1135]

Following this crusader disaster, the French King, Louis IX, was captured then released after payment of a ransom. Following his release, he reorganised the forces of Christendom. Lebanese historians tell us that the Maronites had the privilege to be the only ones to welcome the king of

---

[1126] P Thorau: *The Lion of Egypt:* tr by P.M. Holt; Longman; London; 1992; p. 34.

[1127] Ibid.

[1128] S. Runciman: *A History*; op cit; p. 266.

[1129] P Thorau: *The Lion of Egypt*; op cit; p. 34.

[1130] S. Runciman: *A History*; op cit; p. 267.

[1131] Ibid.

[1132] P Thorau: *The Lion of Egypt*; op cit; p. 34.

[1133] S. Runciman: *A History*; op cit; p. 267.

[1134] Ibid.

[1135] P. Thorau: *The Lion of Egypt*; op cit; pp. 34-5.

France, Louis IX, on visit to Acre in 1250.[1136] The Maronites rushed to put at his service between twenty and twenty five thousand fighters.[1137] Louis, in a letter to the Maronite chief dated from 21 May 1250, declared his sympathy and praise for the Maronite faith as well as their union with the successors of Peter, recognising that the `Maronite nation' was part of the `French Nation'.[1138] The French king also built alliance with another, fiercer anti Muslim ally: the Mongols.

c. The Crusade-Mongol Alliance, and the Mamluk Response:

By the mid 13th century, it became harder to draw men from Europe to fight. Not only have the Muslims inflicted terrible losses on the crusaders, Muslim resilience, proved too much for the Christians. Indeed, in nearly two centuries of crusade attacks, despite divisions, betrayal, assassinations of leadership, mass slaughter carried out by the crusaders, no sooner one Muslim group was eliminated, another rose to fight. In crusader minds: `the hated Saracens had proved to be much more powerful than was first suspected, but perhaps it would be possible to defeat them with eastern allies; `the Saracens would then be caught between two fires?'[1139] The Mongols were such an eastern ally who could help crush the centuries old enemy by an attack from the rear.[1140]

There was, very importantly, a distinct factor, which brought the Mongols in direct alliance with the Christians: Christianity, as a faith, held a great place amongst Mongol beliefs.[1141] The Christian influence reached to the highest echelons. Simeon, a Nestorian monk, surnamed Rabban (Master) Ata (Father), had a great influence on the Grand Khan Ogtai. It was he who sent a letter to Pope Innocent IV of the Nestorian Katholikos.[1142] Simeon lived in Armenia and Tabriz, where he built many churches despite the local inhabitants' hostility, and he baptised many Mongols.[1143] Alongside Simeon,

---

[1136] A. Hoteit: Les Communautes de Tripoli et les Croises; in De Toulouse; op cit; pp. 41-58; p.56.
[1137] Ibid.
[1138] Ibid.
[1139] G. Sarton: Introduction to the History of Science; 3 vols; The Carnegie Institute of Washington; 1927-48. Vol II, p.37.
[1140] B. Spuler: History of the Mongols; London, Routledge& Kegan Paul, 1972; p.1.
[1141] Ibid; p.2.
[1142] S. Giami: Genuinae relations inter Sedem Apostolicam etc... Roma; 1902.
[1143] J.M. Fiey: Chretiens Syriaques sous les Mongols; Louvain; 1975; p. 7.

the Armenian Hethum (Hethoum) the First also had great favours of Mongol rulers.[1144] Via him, the Armenian influence amongst the Mongols was extremely strong, and Hethum, himself, acted as an ecclesiastic adviser to the Great Khan.[1145] Hulagu, the Mongol leader who was to take Baghdad in 1258, and his general Kitbuka (Kitbuqa and other spellings) had affinities with Nestorian Christianity.[1146] Hulagu's wife, Doquz (Dotuz) Khatun, was also Christian, and she ferociously loathed Islam.[1147] In fact the wives of Mangu (Mongke), Kubilai and Hulagu, all of them Christians, played the leading part in the favours shown by the Mongols to the Christians.[1148] And the Popes in Rome, aware of this, in order to achieve their wished aims, worked very hard to stimulate the zeal of these Christian wives.[1149] There were also Christian soldiers employed as archers, or sailors, and also adventurers in the Mongol court.[1150]

In order to cement the Christian alliance with the Mongols, a number of Christian envoys were sent to the Mongols by Louis IX (St Louis), King of France, and the Popes.[1151] In 1245, Pope Innocent IV commissioned Giovanni de Carpini to explore the alliance with the Mongols against Islam.[1152] Likewise, in 1253, Louis sent the Franciscan William of Rubrouck to the Mongols.[1153] Rubrouck was then sent to meet the great leader himself, Mangu Khan further to the east.[1154] These envoys were mainly Franciscan and Dominican missionaries.[1155]

The Mongols acknowledge the Christian messages for an anti Muslim alliance, and sent back their replies. In 1249, in Cyprus, on his way to attack

---

[1144] St Martin; Brosset etc in W. Heyd: *Histoire du commerce du Levant*; Leipzig; 1885-6; reedit; Amsterdam 1967; Vol II; p. 67.

[1145] J.M. Fiey: Chretiens; op cit; p. 7.

[1146] B Spuler: *Les Mongols dans l'Histoire*, Payot, Paris, 1961.

[1147] A.Mieli: *La Science Arabe et son role dans l'evolution scientifique mondiale*. Leiden: E.J. Brill. 1938; p. 147.

[1148] Hayton, Saint Martin Brosset quoted in W. Heyd: *Histoire du Commerce;* op cit; vol II; p. 66.

[1149] Jean Richard: *La Papaute et les Missions d'Orient au Moyen Age*; Ecole Francaise de Rome; Palais Farnese; 1977; p. 104.

[1150] Ibid.

[1151] Innocent IV: *Statuta capitulorum generalium ordinis Cisterciensis*, ed. J. Canivez, Vol II, Louvain, 1934, ad. ann.1245, & 28, p. 294. in J. Richard: La Papaute et les Missions d'Orient; op cit; p.66.

[1152] G. Sarton: *Introduction*; Vol II; op cit; p.37.

[1153] *William of Rubrouck, envoye de Saint Louis, Voyage dans l'empire Mongol (1253-1255)*, Payot, Paris; 1985.

[1154] C.R. Conder: *The Latin Kingdom of Jerusalem;* op cit; p. 372.

[1155] C. Cahen: *Orient et Occident au temps des Croisades*, Aubier Montaigne, 1983; p.200.

Egypt, Louis received Mongol envoys offering alliance against the Muslims.[1156]

Three years after the return of the Pope's envoy, in 1258, Hulagu crossed Persia and attacked Baghdad.[1157] The Mongols had already slaughtered millions in the east by the time they reached the capital of the Caliphate, Baghdad in early 1258.[1158] Mostassim was the ruling caliph. When his father died, the leading clique put Mostassim as Caliph in preference of his brother whose energies they feared.[1159] Mostassim, in the words of Baron d'Ohsson:

'Lacked good judgment and energy; and left to his ministers the levers of power, whilst he spent his time in frivolities, passionate for music, the spectacles offered by passing singers, mimes, and other games of the sort. His pride matched his poor mental state. The princes who came to pay homage to him were not admitted to his presence, but could only kiss a piece of cloth of black silk, representing a piece of the Caliph's robe, which was suspended to the palace door. And they had to prostrate themselves to kiss it. This way the Caliph sought to imitate the pilgrims kissing the black stone of the Kaaba. And whenever he ventured outdoors, the caliph did so in a luxurious suite, his face covered by a black veil.'[1160]

The weakness of the caliph was compounded by betrayal around him, in the person of his vizier, Ibn al-Alqami, who sent many secret letters to Hulagu informing him of both his loyalty, and talking down the character of the Caliph, insisting to Hulagu that the conquest of Baghdad would be very easy. Whilst Hulagu was reticent, Ibn al-Alqami pressed him to advance on Baghdad.[1161] The same minister pressed the Caliph, against Turkish officers' advice, to cut down the numbers of the military to save on expenses, and the Caliph gave him all powers to do so.[1162] The Turkish general, Suleiman Shah, and other officers became incensed at the Caliph's attitude, and his trivial occupations:

'If he does not take,' said Suleiman Shah, 'the most rigorous measures, we will soon see the enemy at the doors of Baghdad, and the city will then suffer the same fate as all other cities. Neither the old, nor the young, neither the poor, nor the rich, will escape slaughter; and our women will fall into the arms of these barbarians. If we can raise an army we can go

---

[1156] C.R. Conder: *The Latin Kingdom*; op cit; p. 350.
[1157] Ibid; p. 381.
[1158] E.G. Browne: *Literary History of Persia*, op cit; p.439.
[1159] Baron G. d'Ohsson: *Histoire des Mongols;* La Haye et Amsterdam; 1834; Vol 3; p.207.
[1160] Ibid; pp. 207-8.
[1161] Ibid; p. 212.
[1162] Ibid; p. 213.

and surprise the Mongols. And even if we are beaten, at least we will die with honour.'[1163]
The Caliph heard of this, and supported the idea of raising an army, but Al-Alqami intercepted the officer charged with implementing the mission and made him act with as much slowness as possible, and delay the measure as much as possible. By the time the army was ready, five months, the Mongols were already about to strike.[1164]

Before advancing on Baghdad, Hulagu asked his Muslim astrologer, Nasir Eddin al-Tussi, for his recommendation. Al-Tussi recommended the advance on Baghdad. Hussam Eddin, another Muslim astronomer sought to dissuade Hulagu, but Al-Tussi was the more convincing of the two, and Hulagu moved on Baghdad.[1165] (Incidentally, Al-Tussi's role in the massacre of the population of Baghdad, rather than his scholarship, is the main reason for his over-inflated popularity amongst non-Muslim scholars.)

On 30th January, 1258, Hulagu opened a massive bombardment with his mangonels against the capital. Within three days, the defences of Baghdad were in ruins. On 5th February, the Mongols mounted a long stretch of the walls.[1166] For a week the Mongol army waited on the walls, no soldier entering the city.[1167] On their arrival, the Mongols, understandably, following the Christian Mongol alliance explained above, favoured Christianity.[1168] This prompted the Caliph to choose a Nestorian Christian, Patriarch Machida II, to negotiate the surrender of Baghdad. Hulagu, thereupon, ordered the Caliph's army to assemble on the plain outside the walls, where all were massacred.[1169] Hulagu summoned the Caliph, and asked for him to surrender his wealth; the Caliph offered two thousand costumes, ten thousand Dinars in gold, and a quantity of precious stones. Hulagu refused to take them, and gave them to his officers. Turning to the Caliph, he said:
'This petty fortune is easily found, and is for my servants; what I want are the treasures hidden under ground, which I must have.'[1170]

[1163] Ibid; p. 220.
[1164] Ibid; pp. 220-1.
[1165] Ibid; pp. 225-6.
[1166] J. Glubb: *A Short History;* op cit; p.207.
[1167] Ibid.
[1168] Y. Courbage, P. Fargues: *Chretiens;* op cit; p. 29.
[1169] J. Glubb: *A Short History;* op cit; p.207.
[1170] Baron G. d'Ohsson: *Histoire des Mongols; op cit;* pp. 239-40.

The Caliph showed a spot in the courtyard, which was dug out, and there was found a whole well of riches, gold pieces, each weighing one hundred mithcals; then a large quantity of vases of gold and silver was dug out.[1171] Then Hulagu gave the order to count the number of women in the Caliphs' harem; there were found 700 women and slave girls, and a thousand enuchs to serve them.[1172]
Hulagu had the Caliph executed with his whole family.

In the meantime, the fate of the Muslim population of the city, over a million people, was also decided, and again betrayal played a major part. Ibn Al-Alqami went to the camp of Hulagu, then returned to the population of Baghdad, announcing to the nobles and officials, to come out of the city to attend the wedding between the daughter of Hulagu and the Caliph. As they came out they were slaughtered en masse.[1173] The whole Muslim population, between 800,000 and one million, was then entirely exterminated.[1174] 800,000 of the inhabitants, Arnold says, were brought out in batches from the city to be massacred, and the greater part of the city itself was destroyed by fire.[1175] The account by Glubb gives further details:
`On 10th February (1258), the Khalif Mustassim gave himself up. Hulagu ordered him to instruct the whole population to gather on the plain outside the walls, where they were slashed and hacked to death in heaps, regardless of age or sex.... The city was then systematically looted, destroyed and burnt. Eight hundred thousand persons are said to have been killed.'[1176] Christian quarters, on the other hand, were spared.[1177]
For five hundred years, Baghdad had been a city of palaces, mosques, libraries and colleges; its universities and hospitals the most up to date in the world, now nothing remained but heaps of rubble and a stench of decaying human flesh.[1178]

Following Baghdad, the Mongols moved in the direction of Syria. On 20th January, 1260, the Mongols took Aleppo by assault. One hundred thousand

---

[1171] Ibid.

[1172] Ibid; p. 240.

[1173] Ibn Tagri-Birdi: *Al-Nujum al-Zahirah*; op cit; vol 3; in Baron. G. d'Ohsson: Histoire; p. 259.

[1174] 800, 000 people according to H.H. Howorth: *History of the Mongols,* London, 1927 in Y. Courbage and Fargues: *Chretiens;* op cit; p. 29.

[1175] Sir Thomas W. Arnold: Muslim Civilisation during the Abbasid Period; in *The Cambridge Medieval History,* Vol IV; op cit; pp 274-98; at p.279.

[1176] J. Glubb: *A Short History;* op cit; p. 207.

[1177] Y. Courbage, P. Fargues: *Chretiens et Juifs;* op cit; p. 29.

[1178] J. Glubb: *A Short History;* op cit; p.207.

young women and children were taken as slaves, the remainder of the inhabitants were systematically exterminated.[1179] Malik al-Nassir, ruler of Damascus, abandoned the city and fled, but was subsequently captured by the Mongols and executed.[1180] Damascus gave in without a fight. At the taking of Damascus, three Christian leaders (the Mongol commander Kitbuqa, the King of Armenia and the Frankish Count Bohemund VI of Antioch) rode through the streets and forced the Muslim population to bow to the cross.[1181] Bohemond VI, whose father in law, the king of Armenia, had convinced him to join with the Mongols, had Mass sung in the Mosque of the Umayyads; the other mosques he had defiled by donkeys, wine was scattered on the walls, with grease of fresh pork, and salt, and the excrement of his men.[1182]

Only Egypt was left. Should Cairo fall, it was the end of Islamic power, and the final extermination of Muslims as elsewhere, as the Crusaders and Mongols had agreed. A Mongol embassy of forty people was sent by Hulagu to Cairo, with a letter,[1183] which says that `God had raised the house of Genghis Khan, and whoever resisted has been wiped out. The glory of our armies is invincible. If you do not submit, and do not bring tribute in person to my camp, prepare for war.'[1184] Cairo was, however, in the hands of the Mamluks. To Hulagu's summons for surrender, they responded with war. They began by decapitating Hulagu's envoys. And then, at the meeting of the leadership, which included Kuttuz, Baybars, the Turkish general Nassir Eddin, as well as the princes of Irbil and Acca, they decided for war. Kuttuz, the Mamluk leader then declared:
`Well then, we will go to war; victorious or losers, we would have done our duty, and the Muslim nation will not call us cowards.'[1185]
When they approached the Mongol army, Kuttuz reminded his generals how many populations had been slaughtered by the Mongols; that they must free Syria and save Islam, and that if they failed in their duty, God would inflict his retribution. The generals were in tears, and vowed to do all it takes to defeat the enemy.[1186] As the fighting began, Kuttuz shouted:
`Oh God, give your servant Kuttuz victory over the Mongols!'
Barron d'Ohsson sums up the battle:

[1179] Ibid.
[1180] Ibid.
[1181] J. J. Saunders: *A History;* op cit; p. 182.
[1182] Jean Richard: *La Papaute et les Missions d'Orient au Moyen Age*; op cit; p.99.
[1183] Baron G. d'Ohsson: *Histoire des Mongols*; op cit; vol 3; Note 2; p. 332.
[1184] Ibid; p. 332.
[1185] Ibid.
[1186] Ibid; p. 338.

`Kuttuz led the charge in person, pushing through Mongol ranks, encouraging his army to follow suite. The left wing of the Mamluk army that had first weakened, seeing its leaders, rallied to fight, and the Mongols, instead, began to lose ground, especially after losing many of their leaders. Kitbugha himself was killed in the fighting by a certain Djemal Eddin Accoush. A Mongol division that had remained entrenched in a neighbouring hill was cut to pieces, and Baybars himself led in the chase of the fleeing Mongols, only allowing a small number to get away with their lives. Some hid in the surrounding thick vegetation. Kuttuz ordered the place to be set alight; all the Mongols hidden there expired. The victory secure, Kuttuz dismounted his horse, and prayed two rakaas (prostrations) to thank God.'[1187]

The Mamluks had just crushed the Mongol army, and more than that, had just saved the land of Islam.[1188] One of Kitbuqa's lieutenants gathered the remnants of the Mongol army and fled north to Armenian territory, where he was received and soon re-equipped for further campaigns.[1189]

[1187] Ibid; p. 339.

[1188] See Al-Maqrizi: *Al-Suluk fi Ma'rifat Duwal al-Muluk;* tr. M. Qatremere as *Histoire des sultans Mamluks de l'Egypte*; Paris; 1845; vol I; pt. 1; pp. 98; 104.

[1189] J. Richard: *The Crusades c.1071-c.1291;* Cambridge University Press; Tr from the French; 1999; p. 415.

An Outline of the Battle of Ain Jalut

The modern scholar, A. A. Khowaiter, wrote an attractive book on the life and deeds of Baybars, and from a collection of sources, he outlined the battle of Ain Jalut, of which extracts are given here:

`Qutuz left Cairo about the middle of Sha'ban 658 A.H. (end of July, A.D. 1260) and sent Baibars as scout with a contingent to Gaza. On hearing of his approach, the Mongols, who were encamped there, moved to a place in al-Ghaur, presumably considering their position at Gaza was not favourable for a battle. Baibars at once occupied Gaza and was soon joined by Qutuz with the main army. Before Qutuz could engage the Mongols, he had to make sure the Franks would not take the opportunity to attack him while he was thus occupied.

The exact position of the Mongols was not known to the Muslim army, so Qutuz despatched Baibars with the vanguard to locate the enemy. Baibars left the region of Acre, riding continuously until he came upon the Mongols' vanguard which he attacked and defeated. Then, finding the main Mongol army at 'Ain Jalut, he sent word to Qutuz. During the night while waiting for Qutuz to join him with the rest of the Muslim troops, he took up a position on the mountain overlooking the plain where the Mongol camp was, and kept watch, coming down during the day to engage in skirmishes. Qutuz with the main army soon joined him. Early in the morning of Friday, 25th of Ramadhan, 658 A.H. (3rd of September, A.D. 1260), the two armies were drawn up in order of battle on the plain facing one another, the Mongols having positioned themselves at the foot of the mountain. A fierce battle began, and soon the left wing of the Muslim army began to lose formation. Qutuz noticed this, encouraged and drove on his troops, and himself fought desperately. In the end he was able to rally them and restore their order. The biographer of Baibars singles out the courage displayed by Baibars on this occasion: his bravery and determination inspired the troops to press against the enemy. The Muslims finally won the day: the Mongols were heavily defeated and forced to flee, hotly pursued by the Muslims headed by Baibars.

This victory over the Mongols brought a certain amount of confidence to the Muslims, and their rulers were perhaps convinced that, given unity, a better organisation and improved techniques, their armies could at least hold the Mongols in any future battle. Baibars in particular, ambitious as he had always been, must have felt confident that a Muslim force equipped and trained in accordance with his own ideas could restore their lost territories to the Muslims. The victory brought renewed assurance also to the inhabitants of the Muslim lands, especially to Syria, where people now began to return to their homes.

The battle of 'Ain Jalut was by no means the end of the struggle against the Mongols, but it lifted the despair which had up till then hung over the Muslims. The Mongols soon tried to avenge themselves with a larger force, and the Muslims, with individual and with collective forces, met them from different quarters."[1190]

[1190] A.A. Khowaiter: *Baibars the First*; The Green Mountain Press; London; 1978; pp.20-3.

d. The Mamluk Liberation of the Muslim Land:

The Mongol threat remained until the early 14th century, but the scale of the Mongol defeat at Ain Jalut was such that it showed they were not invincible. The defeat also convinced many Mongols that 'heaven was fighting for Islam and that it would be prudent to submit to Allah.'[1191] Many were now convinced that Islam was to be preferred to Christianity, and many converted en masse to Islam to the great chagrin of Christianity.[1192] Berke, the ninth ruler of the Golden Horde, based to the north, was the first Mongol ruler to convert to Islam.[1193] But the Mongols based in Iran remained terrible foes of Islam, and the greatest allies of the crusaders. In Baybars, though, Islam had now the greatest leader it ever had, the man who fought and defeated all enemies of Islam leagued against him.[1194]

Through the major part of the late 1260s and the 1270s, without relapse, Baybars, the new Mamluk leader, fought countless battles against the Crusade-Armenian-Mongol alliance.[1195] The campaigns of Baybars are well caught by Muslim historians such as Ibn Abd al-Zahir,[1196] Ibn al-Furat,[1197] and also by the scholar fighter Abu'l Fida.[1198] In 1263, Baybars took Karak, followed two years later by his victorious captures of Caesarea and Arsuf from the Hospitallers.[1199] In 1266, he forced the Templars of Safad to capitulate, and two years later, he took Jaffa.[1200] In 1268, that same year, he captured Antioch, a city which had kept close alliance with the Mongols; there, Baybars put the whole garrison, 16,000, to death as retribution.[1201]

[1191] J.J. Saunders: *Aspects of the Crusades;* op cit; p.64.

[1192] Ibid; p.63.

[1193] Berke, after the death of Baybars, was for three years (1277-80) the titular sultan of the Bahri Mamluk state of Egypt.

[1194] See Ibn al-Furat: *Tarikh al-duwal wal Muluk;* ed M.F. El-Shayyal; unpublished Ph.d., University of Edinburgh; 1986.
A.A. Khowaiter: *Baibars the First*; op cit.

[1195] Baron G. d'Ohsson: *Histoire des Mongols*; op cit; pp. 458-500.

[1196] Ibn Abd al-Zahir: *Al-Rawd al-Zahir fi sirat al-malik al-Zahir*; ed A. A. Al-Khuwaiter; Ryad; 1976.

[1197] U. and M.C. Lyons: *Ayyubids, Mamluks and Crusaders, selection from the Tarikh al-Duwal wal Muluk of Ibn al-Furat*; 2 vols, W. Heffer and Sons Ltd, Cambridge, 1971.

[1198] J. Reiske: *Abilfedae Annales Moslemici*, Lat. Ex. Ar. Fecit. J. J. Reiske; Leipzig; 1754; Arabic text published in 1789.
Abu'l Fida in *Receuil des historiens des croisades, Historiens Orientaux*; Vol 1; Paris; 1872; pp. 1-186.

[1199] P. K. Hitti: *History*; op cit; p. 656.

[1200] Al-Maqrizi: *Al-Suluk;* Tr Qatremere; op cit; vol I; pt. 2; pp. 29-30.

[1201] Ibid; pp. 52-4.

Baybars took a break to make his pilgrimage to Makkah, and then, no sooner he returned in the summer of 1269, he went north to Syria to check Mongol invasions.[1202] Then, he turned his attention to the Ismailis in an effort to finish them once for all.[1203] In the year 1270, he returned to Egypt to face the new crusade launched by the French king Louis IX. Louis having decided to invade Tunisia, instead, Baybars returned north in 1271 to take *Hasn al-Akrad* from the Hospitallers.[1204] Baybars repeated attempts to suppress the kingdom of Armenia to the north were, however, thwarted by the Mongols.[1205] In 1270-1 a combined force of Templars, Knight Hospitallers, and papal troops managed to drive back Baybars from Acre, and to march on Nazareth, which was pillaged, and all Muslims found there slain.[1206] Baybars' last action was in Asia Minor, where he defeated a Mongol army at Albistan, in 1277, the year he died.[1207]

Three years after Baybars' death, a large offensive against the Mamluks was launched. The Mongols, Armenians, and the Georgians advanced from the North but were met by Baybars' successor, Qala'un, at Emesa, and forced to retreat.[1208] Neither the Hospitallers, nor Bohemund VII of Antioch, nor the King of Cyprus (Hugh III) had been able, as intended, to join the invaders, for Qala'un held the road by which the Christians might have advanced from Tripoli on Emesa.[1209] Qala'un, who had risen to power in 1279, two years after Baybars' death, and like Baybars, was a Qipchak Turk, who had been brought to Egypt as a slave boy and sold to the Sultan Malik al-Salih Ayyub.[1210] As soon as he ascended the throne Qala'un vigorously prosecuted the war began by his predecessor.[1211] His first great victory was in 1280 over a Mongol army, which had invaded Syria, and which he wiped out at Hims.[1212] Three years later, in 1283, Qala'un removed the Maronite obstacle by taking their stronghold: Ehden et Hadat.[1213] After this success, all Christian lords of the southern Latin cities hastened to make treaties with him, but Qala'un took no risks.[1214] He eliminated them one after the other,

---

[1202] W.B. Stevenson: *The Crusaders;* op cit; p. 344.
[1203] Ibid; p. 345.
[1204] Ibid.
[1205] B. Spuler: *The Muslim World:* op cit; p. 27.
[1206] C.R. Conder: *The Latin Kingdom.* op cit; p. 391.
[1207] J. Glubb: *A Short History;* op cit; p.213.
[1208] C.R. Conder: *The Latin Kingdom;* op cit; p. 396.
[1209] Ibid; pp. 397-8.
[1210] J. Glubb: *A Short History;* op cit; p.213.
[1211] J.H. Lamonte: Crusade and Jihad; op cit; p.195.
[1212] Ibid.
[1213] Duwayhi in p. 146. in A. Hoteit: Les Differentes communautes; op cit; p. 52.
[1214] J.H. Lamonte: Crusade; op cit; p.195.

and like his predecessor, was not mean handed. He came to Tripoli, and by the time he left, there was nothing left in it.[1215]

In face of Mamluk successes, Christian hopes remained with the Mongols. From 1288 onwards, Pope Nicolas IV remained in constant touch with the new Mongol leader Argun for further allied attacks against the Muslims.[1216] The alliances against the Muslims were doomed, though. The Mamluk military, as the historian Ibn al-Furat notes, was characterised by cohesion and unity.[1217] The Mamluks had also a great source of inspiration, the Muslim scholar, Ibn Taymiyya.

Qala'un died in 1290, leaving to his successor, al-Ashraf Khallil, the task to capture the last Crusader stronghold, Acre, in May 1291.[1218] After the fall of Acre the other crusader towns surrendered; the kingdom of the Crusaders was ended.[1219] Al-Ashraf ended his campaign where it had begun, giving thanks at his father's tomb in Cairo, a campaign, culminating in the final removal of the crusaders from Muslim soil. The religious dimension of the war and the victory was stressed at every stage of the way.[1220] It was seen and celebrated as the removal of the infidel from Muslim soil and the triumph of Islam over Christianity.[1221] Immediately after the conquest of Acre, Al-Ashraf declared the Armenian Kingdom of Cilicia and the Mongols as his next targets.[1222]

Ricoldo da Monte Croce, the Dominican missionary, was in Mongol held Baghdad in 1291 when the news of the loss of Acre by the Franks reached him. His despair was all too great. The Mongols, as he now could see, were beginning to turn not to Christendom, as earlier generations had hoped and believed, but to Islam, because, as he explains, they found it easier to practice and easier to believe.[1223] These Tartars, he notes, who had at first killed the Muslims without mercy and spared the Christians, have become Muslims.

[1215] Ibid.

[1216] C.R. Conder: *The Latin Kingdom*; op cit; p. 403.

[1217] U. and M.C. Lyons: *Ayyubids, Mamluks;* op cit.

[1218] See account by Abu'l Fida who took part in the siege in vol 4 of his *Mukhtasar Tarikh al-Bashar;* Maqrizi: Al-Suluk; (tr. Qatremere); vol 2; prt 3; pp. 125-9; J.H. Lamonte: Crusade; op cit; p.195.

[1219] J.H. Lamonte: Crusade; op cit; p.195.

[1220] C. Hillenbrand: *The Crusades,* op cit; p.240.

[1221] Ibid.

[1222] Ibid; p.241.

[1223] The text of Ricoldo's *Liber Peregrinationis*, on which the account is based, together with a survey of his life is in U. Monneret de Villard, *Il libro della Peregrinazione nelle Parti d'Oriente*, 1948.

Even more depressing for him was, as he questioned, `how could God give the victory to Muslim armies.' Unless, he says:

`We were astonished how works of such perfection could be found in a religion so far from the truth' (*lex tantae perffidiae*).

Ricoldo also says:

`We have been amazed that among the followers of so perfidious a law works of so great perfection are found....But who is not amazed by their zeal, devotion in prayer, mercy to the poor, reverence for the name of God, the prophets and holy places, their courtesy in manners, their affability to strangers, their concord and love for one another?'[1224]

[1224] In D.C. Munro: The Western; op cit; p.343.

A Final Story from the Crusades

Odo of Deuil, a monk of St. Denis and chaplain to Louis VII, accompanied his patron on the Second Crusade and gave a moving account of the conversion to Islam of a large number of crusaders. Following a fierce attack by the Muslims in Phrygia (543/1148), the wealthy and influential crusaders satisfied the exorbitant demands of Greeks and Venetians and took to the sea, leaving behind thousands of poor, wounded, or exhausted crusaders. Their misery moved the Muslims to pity and compassion. They tended to the sick and wounded and fed the hungry, and this kindness and liberality caused the crusaders to abandon the crusade as well as their faith and join their enemies both in rank and in faith. "Avoiding their co-religionists who had been so cruel to them," wrote Odo of Deuil, "they went in safety among the infidels who had compassion upon them, and, as we heard, more than three thousand joined themselves to the Turks when they retired. Oh kindness more cruel than all treachery! They gave them bread but robbed them of their faith, though it is certain that contented with the services they performed, they compelled no one among them to renounce his religion."[1225]

[1225] Odo de Diogilo, De Ludovici vii, Itinere. Migne, *Patrologia Latina;* quoted in T. Arnold: *The Preaching of Islam,* op cit; pp. 89-90.

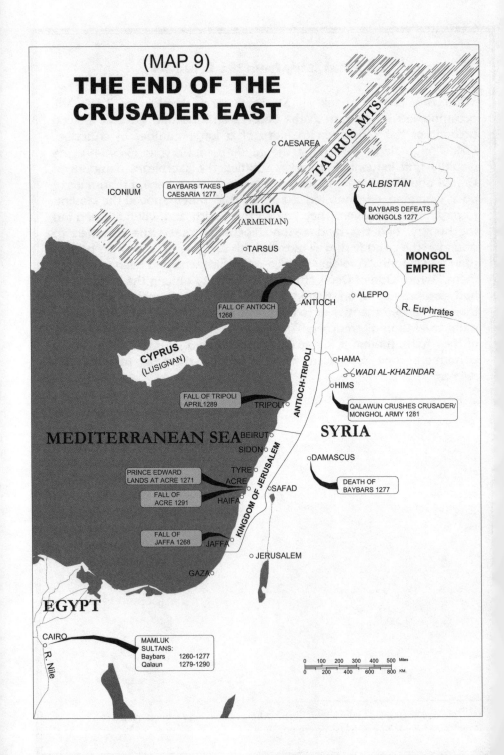

(MAP 9)
THE END OF THE CRUSADER EAST

CAESAREA

TAURUS MTS.

ALBISTAN

ICONIUM

BAYBARS TAKES
CAESARIA 1277

BAYBARS DEFEATS
MONGOLS 1277

CILICIA
(ARMENIAN)

MONGOL
EMPIRE

TARSUS

ALEPPO

ANTIOCH

R. Euphrates

FALL OF ANTIOCH
1268

CYPRUS
(LUSIGNAN)

HAMA

WADI AL-KHAZINDAR

HIMS

FALL OF TRIPOLI
APRIL 1289

ANTIOCH-TRIPOLI

TRIPOLI

QALAWUN CRUSHES CRUSADER/
MONGHOL ARMY 1281

MEDITERRANEAN SEA

BEIRUT

SYRIA

SIDON

DAMASCUS

PRINCE EDWARD
LANDS AT ACRE 1271

TYRE

ACRE

KINGDOM OF JERUSALEM

SAFAD

DEATH OF
BAYBARS 1277

FALL OF
ACRE 1291

HAIFA

FALL OF
JAFFA 1268

JAFFA

JERUSALEM

GAZA

EGYPT

CAIRO

R. Nile

MAMLUK
SULTANS:
Baybars   1260-1277
Qalaun   1279-1290

0   100 200 300 400 500 Miles
0   200   400   600   800 KM.

220

SEVEN

THE END OF MUSLIMS IN SICILY AND SPAIN
(12th-17th Centuries)

This chapter focuses on the end of the Muslim presence in Spain. It covers five centuries of history, charting the uninterrupted decline and phasing out of Muslims from Spain. Before this, it looks briefly at the fate of the Muslims in Sicily following the Muslim loss of the island in 1091.

1. The Fate of the Muslims in Sicily:

During the Muslim rule of Sicily (9th-11th centuries), the condition of the Christians on the Island was, on the whole, far more agreeable and prosperous under the Muslims than it had been under the Greeks. Relieved from arbitrary taxation, their trade prospered; every branch of commerce was also open to those amongst them who were enterprising.[1226] When the Normans conquered the island, they found Christians who have lived for over two centuries under Islamic rule well, and fairly, governed, prosperous, and practicing their faith.[1227] This, normally, would induce the Normans to show the same regards to Muslims.

Under the early Norman rulers (Roger I and II), the Muslims survived, and Muslim support was exploited to keep the island functioning as before.[1228] Gradually, though, the condition of the Muslims deteriorated, especially during the reign of William the Bad (1154-1166). Massacres of Muslims

---

[1226] S.P. Scott: *History of the Moorish Empire;* Vol II, op cit; p.189.
[1227] N. Daniel: *The Arabs;* op cit; D. Mathew: *The Norman Kingdom of Sicily*: Cambridge University Press; 1992.
[1228] N. Daniel: *The Arabs*; op cit; p.140.

became frequent.[1229] Muslim merchants of Palermo were massacred in 1160 in the marshes of Papiretum.[1230] In March 1161, following a palace revolt, the Muslims were slaughtered wherever they could be found; many were killed in the streets, others in their warehouses, and countless more in their offices.[1231] After that the Muslims judged it unsafe to live in the city centre. In 1161, the Lombard settlers were easily raised 'to invade the royal domain and to slaughter the Arabs wherever they found them.'[1232] Under their leader Roger Sclavus, the Lombards launched a series of Pogroms against the Muslims, forcing them to flee westward to safer areas, where the population was still predominantly Arab.[1233] They destroyed Muslim communities both those who lived mixed up with Christians in different towns, and those, who, living apart, possessed their own villages, with no distinction for sex or age.[1234] A few escaped disguised in Christian dress to the temporary safety of Muslim towns in the south, but felt such a horror of the Lombard areas that for generations they would only unwillingly pass through them.[1235] Muslim caught prisoners were liable to be singled out for exemplary punishment; and it used to be said that such things 'would not be done to Jews, not even to Arabs.'[1236]

In the reign of William II (The Good) (1166-1189), there was an improvement to the condition of Muslims. The Muslim eunuch pages at the court enjoyed the king's favour, and openly practised their religion, kept Ramadan, and would pray almost in the presence of the king, who himself wrote Arabic, but they went in fear and would not speak freely in front of the servants.[1237] The situation outside Palermo and direct royal protection does betray Islamic anxieties. At Messina the civil servant 'Abd al-Massih told Ibn Jubayr, the Muslim traveller from Spain,[1238] who visited Sicily then:

[1229] In B.Z. Kedar: *Crusades*; op cit; p. 52.

[1230] F.Falcand: Liber de Regno Sicilae, p. 52; in H. Bercher, A. Courteaux, J. Mouton: Une abbaye latine dans la societe Musulmane: Monreale au XIIem siecle. *ANNALES* Vol 34: 1979; pp. 525-47; p.538.

[1231] N. Daniel: *The Arabs;* op cit; p. 149.

[1232] Ibid; p. 151.

[1233] D. Abulafia: *Commerce and Conquest in the Mediterranean, 1100-1500*, Variorum, 1993; p. 108.

[1234] N. Daniel: *The Arabs;* op cit; p.151.

[1235] Ibid.

[1236] Ibid; p.155.

[1237] Ibid; p.147.

[1238] Ibn Jubayr: *Rihla*, (*Voyages*), tr. with notes by M. G. Demombynes, Paris, (1949-65). -*The travels of Ibn Jubayr;* tr from the original Arabic with introduction and notes, by R.J. C. Broadhurst; J.Cape, London, 1952.

`You can boldly display your faith in Islam... But we must conceal our faith and, fearful of our lives, must adhere to the worship of God and the discharge of our religious duties in secret.'[1239]

Ibn Jubayr talks about Caid Abu Kassim ibn Hammud, surnamed Ibn al-Hagar, as: `One of the nobles of this island who have inherited the quality of lordship from father to son... greatly praised for his virtues and charity towards the Muslims, ransoming prisoners and giving largess to poor wayfarers and pilgrims so that the whole town rejoiced at his coming. This man had lost the favour of the tyrants through intrigues, had been imprisoned in his house, and had all his palaces confiscated and also the possessions inherited from his ancestors....'[1240]

He expressed a wish to meet Ibn Jubayr and they had a talk, and the great man said that he and all his relatives only desired to sell all they had and thus be liberated from their woes and be free to live in Muslim lands. When our pilgrim parted from Ibn Hammud, he wept and made them weep.[1241]

Ibn Jubayr also noted other forms of persecution. He says:

`Thus it is told that when a man loses his temper with his wife or his son, or a woman with her daughter, and they in a fit of anger throw themselves into a church, they are made Christians and baptised, nor can a man see his son again nor a woman her daughter in any other guise, so that those with insight fear that it then happen to the Muslims of Sicily as it happened to those of the island of Crete (when all the inhabitants, what with one thing, and what with another, were all forced to become Christians.) May the world of damnation fall over the infidel!'[1242]

Another piteous case recounted is that of a leading man in the city who sent his own son to one of Ibn Jubayr's party asking him to accept his young daughter for his wife if she pleased him, or to give her in marriage to one of his countrymen, but in any case to take her away with him, she being gladly willing to leave father and brothers if she could only remain in the faith.[1243]

Muslims, gradually, lost all their wealth, through heavy taxation, or by having their property taken. Generally the Muslims were given the choice to be sold into slavery or settled on the land as serfs.[1244] The tenants of Montreale estate seem to have been bound to the soil; in a deed of 1177 three

---

[1239] Ibid; p. 342.
[1240] Ibn Jubayr in C. Waern: *Medieval Sicily;* Duckworth and Co; London; 1910; pp.74-5.
[1241] Ibid.
[1242] Ibid.
[1243] Ibid; p. 75.
[1244] Ibid; p. 86.

Muslims acknowledged themselves to be serfs of the Abbot Theobald.[1245] Outside Palermo, squatting in all the wasted places in miserable hovels were the enumerable serfs, generally Muslims.[1246]

Mistreatment of Muslims was not due to the fact that the Muslims were hostile to the Christian realm; far from it. They were some of the most faithful and loyal servants any Christian Sicilian lord or ruler could hope for.[1247] So loyal, they fought against their own co-religionists and fiercely. North African sages could hardly believe the presence of Sicilian Muslims in the armies and navies of the Norman kings during the attack on Alexandria in 1174, or, later, with Frederick II during his crusade.[1248] The fact is, as noted by Daniel, `the mercy that Europe would always offer the Muslims is conditional on the destruction of their religion, and, ultimately of their separate identity.'[1249]

Frederick II (1194-1250), just mentioned, was ready to accommodate a distinct Muslim presence in his realm. He himself preferred to be surrounded by Muslims rather than Christian influence, and was half Muslim in his own ways, according to Sarton.[1250] His court bore a very strong Islamic influence, even stronger after his visit to the East.[1251] This sympathy for Islam, however, caused Frederick and his successors great difficulties. Abu'l Fadail who wrote *Tarikh al-Mansuri*, speaks of a letter sent by Frederick telling of the problems he encountered with the Papacy on his return to his country after his sojourn in the East due to his closeness to Muslims. In the year 1229, an ambassador to Sultan al-Kamil carried from the Emperor to the Sultan a letter, extracts of which went:
`In the name of God the merciful, the forgiving....
We inform you that as we explained in Sidon, the Pope has treacherously and deceitfully taken one of our fortresses, called Monte Casino, handed over to him by its accursed Abbot. He has promised to do even more harm but could not because our faithful subjects expected our return. He was forced, therefore, to spread false news of our death, and made the Cardinals swear to it and to say that our return was impossible. They sought to deceive the population by these tricks and by saying that after us no one could administer

---

[1245] Ibid; p. 89.
[1246] Ibid; p. 97.
[1247] A. Lowe: *The Barrier and the Bridge*, G. Bles; London; 1972; p. 92.
[1248] D. Abulafia: *Commerce and Conquest;* op cit; p.112.
[1249] N. Daniel: *The Arabs;* op cit; p. 148.
[1250] G. Sarton: *Introduction,* vol 2; op cit, P. 575.
[1251] C.H. Haskins: *Studies in the History of Mediaeval Science.* Frederick Ungar Publishing Co. New York. 1967 ed. p. 244.

our estates and look after them for our son so well as the Pope. So on these men's oaths who should be High priests of the Faith and successors of the Apostles, a rabble of louts and criminals was led by the nose. When we arrived at the gates we found that King John (of Brienne who during Frederick's absence in the East had invaded and devastated his kingdom) and the Lombards had made hostile raids into our domains, and doubted even the news of our arrival because of what the Cardinals had sworn to them......
Meanwhile we had collected a large army of Germans who were with us in Syria and of those who left the Holy Land before us but whom wind had cast upon our shores, and of other loyal men and officials of our state; with these we have marched off by long stages towards our enemy's territories.
Finally, we inform your Highness of our desire for frequent letters from you revealing your happy state, your interests and your needs, and of the salutations that we have transmitted to the commanders of your army and to all your pages, Mamluks and courtiers. On your health be God's blessing and mercy.'
Written at Barletta 23 August 1229.[1252]

Despite his affection for Islam, Frederick had in the end to cut his links with his Muslim subjects due to papal pressure on him. For the Catholic clergy it was a scandal that Islam should be freely practised in the heart of Christendom, and that so many souls should be lost.[1253] In 1200, directives by Pope Innocent III clearly threatened the Muslims of Sicily with a crusade.[1254]

Muslims rose in rebellions to a large extent as a result of the repressive measures, which Frederick passed in order to please the Popes.[1255] The rebellion under Ibn `Abbad (1220s) was so widespread, that at some point, he even had his own coins minted probably at his stronghold of Entella.[1256]
The rebellion abated, but pressure from the Pope induced Frederick to mass transfer all his Muslim subjects deep into the Italian hinterland, to Lucera.[1257]
Possibly in hope, or good faith, these `Saracens' of Lucera still provided some of the bravest and most loyal of his (Frederick) and his successor's

---

[1252] Abu al-Fadail: *Tarikh al-Mansuri* in *Bibliotheca Arabo-Sicula*; Second Appendix; Leipzig; 1887; pp. 34-7.
[1253] N. Daniel: *The Arabs*; op cit; p.154.
[1254] E. Baluze: Epistolae Innocenti III, Leyden. 1682, 2 vols, epist. 226 in H. Bercher et al: Une abbaye latine; op cit; p. 527.
[1255] A. Lowe: *The Barrier and the Bridge*, op cit; p. 92.
[1256] D. Abulafia: *Commerce and Conquest*, op cit; p. 113.
[1257] A. Lowe: *The Barrier*; op cit; p.92.

guards.'[1258] 30,000 Muslim soldiers, with whom it was impossible for Frederick's enemies to tamper,[1259] and which he even took with him on his crusade in 1228 to conquer Jerusalem for Christianity.[1260]

Muslims were still not allowed to remain as a distinct people, observing their faith. In 1239 Pope Gregory wrote to the Archbishop of Canterbury, slightly paraphrasing the Book of Revelation, or perhaps misquoting from memory: `A beast arose out of the sea filled with the names of blasphemy... it opened its mouth to utter blasphemies against God.' The beast was Frederick II, and his blasphemies were often associated with his Islamic connections; legend collected round the Emperor and round Islam, and the two were associated.[1261] Pope Gregory IX urged Frederick to `shatter' the `presumptions' of these Muslims so that they would dare not disturb the hearts of God's faithful even a little, `especially since particular injury will seem to be done to our Redeemer if the sons of Belial, who are bound by the shackle of perpetual servitude, assail the sons of light within our borders or damnably imagine themselves to be equal to them in privileges.'[1262]

The pope sought to evangelise the Muslims in Lucera, and to that end, he announced he was directing Dominican friars to do so. Gregory urged Frederick to support the Dominicans `with the material sword, without which their mission might fail; indeed, to `drag this people, who are openly deceived by the error of perdition, to the font of regeneration and renewal by means of terror, because then their servitude will be more fruitful, since the one God shall have come to you and to them.'[1263]

In face of resistance by Frederick, and subsequently by his son Manfred, to remove the Islamic presence, the Papacy, in alliance with the French, launched a crusade. The Muslim historian, Ibn Wasil (b. 1207-8), sent by the Mamluk Sultan Baybars (ruled 1260-1277) as an envoy to King Manfred of Sicily (ruled from 1258 to 1266),[1264] offers an account of the situation:

`The Emperor, Frederick, died in 1250, and was succeeded by his son Conrad. When he too died, his brother Manfred came to the throne. All three

---

[1258] Ibid.

[1259] J.W. Draper: *History;* op cit; Vol II; p.69.

[1260] D. Abulafia: *Commerce and Conquest;* op cit; p.112.

[1261] N. Daniel: *The Arabs;* op cit; p.158.

[1262] MGH (Monumenta Germaniae Historica) Epist. Saec. XIII 1:398-9; No 494 in J.P. Lomax: Frederick II, His Saracens, and the Papacy, in *Medieval Christian Perceptions of Islam,* Edited by J.V. Tolan; Routledge; London; op cit; pp. 175-97; at p. 180.

[1263] M.GH Epist. Saec. XIII 1:447-8; No 553 in J.P. Lomax: Frederick II,; pp. 182-3.

[1264] See Adolf Friedrich von Schack: *Poesie und Kunst der Araber in Spanien und Sizilien;* 2 Vols; Berlin; 1865.

were hated by the Pope because of their sympathy for the Muslims; the Pope and Emperor Manfred went to war. Manfred was at first victorious. Then, as Qadi Jamal Eddin (Ibn Wasil), Chief Qadi of Hama, says in his history:
`I went as ambassador to Manfred from Sultan Baybars of blessed memory in Ramadhan 1261, and was entertained by him in the highest honour in a city called Barletta in Apulia.... Near where he lived was a city called Lucera, whose inhabitants were all Muslims from the Island of Sicily; they hold public prayer on Friday and make open professions of the Muslim faith. This has been so since the time of the Emperor's father, Frederick. He had undertaken the building of a scientific institute there for the study of all the branches of speculative sciences; most of his officials and courtiers were Muslims, and in his camp the call to prayer, and even the canonic prayers themselves, were openly heard.

When I returned home, news came that the Pope, together with the brother of the King of France (Charles of Anjou, brother of St Louis), was gathering an army to attack him. Rome was five day's journey from the town where I had stayed. The Pope had already excommunicated Manfred for his Muslim leanings and for having dishonoured Christian religious Law. His brother and his father, the emperor, had also been excommunicated by the Pope of Rome for the same reason. They say that the Pope of Rome is for them the vicar of the Messiah, and his representative, with authority to decide what is permitted and what is forbidden, to cut off and to separate. It is he who crowns their kings and sets them on the throne, and everything in their law needs his approval. He is a priest, and when he dies he is succeeded by the man who is endowed as he was with this sacerdotal quality....

The Pope and the King of France's brother attacked Manfred and in a pitched battle destroyed his army and took him captive. The Pope ordered that he should be killed, and it was done. The King of France's brother reigned over the lands that had belonged to the Emperor's son and held possession of them.'[1265]

Following the papal-French success, Islam, as religion and culture, and the Arabs and Berbers as distinct peoples, were eliminated from Italy.[1266] How the Muslims were completely eradicated, and how many Muslims were eliminated in Sicily, remain on the whole unanswered questions. Bresc says that the Muslim colony of Lucera survived for another generation before they were sold as slaves in Sicily after the colony was disbanded by Charles II of

---

[1265] Ibn Wasil: *Mufarrij al-Kurub*; from the Arabic manuscript; 1702; Caetani collection; pp. 121-3.
[1266] N. Daniel: *The Arabs;* op cit; p.140 ff.

Anjou in 1300.[1267] The Muslims constituted more than half the population of Sicily (the rest was largely Greek, with some Jews).[1268] Setting aside those who were deported to Lucera (10% of the population), and even though some stayed on in Sicily and its dependent islands, Abulafia states, this 90% reduction in a century and a half raises the question of where did most of the Muslims go.[1269] Abulafia points out that history is indeed silent on the issue of whether the Muslims either left the island for Africa, or were slaughtered, or were converted.[1270]

[1267] H.Bresc: *Un Monde Mediterraneen: Economies et Societe en Sicile*, 1300-1450: 2 vols, Rome-Palermo, 1986; vol 2: p.583.
[1268] D. Abulafia: *Commerce and Conquest*; op cit; p.4.
[1269] Ibid.
[1270] Ibid; p.109.

The Islamic Impact on the Christian West Through Sicily

Scott writes:

`The traders who visited the remote and semi-barbarous courts of Europe, the Crusaders who from time to time enjoyed the hospitality of the Sicilian cities, the returned adventurers who had served in the armies of the princely House of De Hauteville, all spread, far and wide, exaggerated and romantic accounts of the strange and sacrilegious customs of the Norman monarchy. Ecclesiastics crossed themselves with dismay when they heard of the honours lavished upon infidels (the Muslims), whose co-religionists had profaned the Holy Sepulchre, evoking gigantic expeditions which had depopulated entire provinces and drained the wealth of credulous and fanatic Europe. Others, whom study and reflection had made wise beyond the age in which they lived, saw, with open indifference and concealed delight, in this defiance and contempt of Popish tyranny, the dawn of a brighter era, the prospect of the ultimate emancipation of the human mind. The progress of the mental and moral changes which affected European society, acting through the intervention of Norman influence in the political and religious life of the continent, was gradual, indeterminate, and long imperceptible, but incessant and powerful. The universal deficiency of the means of information, the dearth of educational facilities, which promoted the dependence of the masses upon the only class capable of instructing and improving them, the terrible penalties visited upon heresy, deferred for nearly three hundred years the inevitable outbreak of an intellectual revolution. The principles on which that revolution was based, although at first discussed furtively and in secret, in time became so popular as to endanger the empire of the Church and to seriously impair its prestige.

The influence of the royal House of De Hauteville was extended, magnified, perpetuated, by the imperial House of Hohenstaufen. The traditions of the Arab, inherited by the Norman, were transmitted to and became the inspiration of the German. The genius of Frederick II impressed itself indelibly upon the entire Teutonic race. It must not be forgotten that the most formidable revolt against Papal tyranny and corruption broke out in Saxony. The new German Empire owes largely its commanding position in Europe and its exalted rank in the scale of civilization to the talents, the energy, and the transcendent wisdom of the greatest monarch of medieval times.'[1271]

[1271] S.P. Scott: *History;* op cit; vol 3; pp. 28-9.

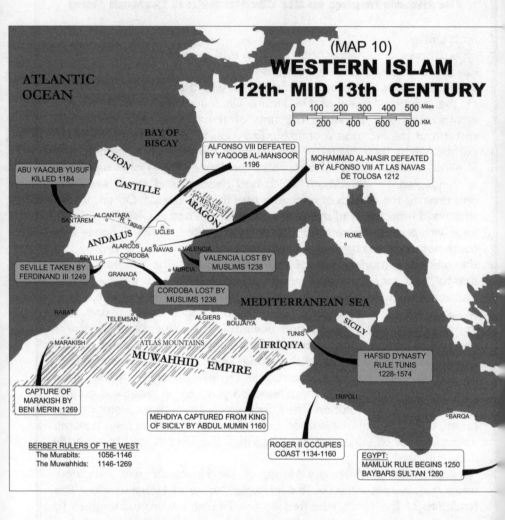

(MAP 10)
WESTERN ISLAM
12th- MID 13th CENTURY

ATLANTIC OCEAN

BAY OF BISCAY

0 100 200 300 400 500 Miles
0 200 400 600 800 KM.

ALFONSO VIII DEFEATED BY YAQOOB AL-MANSOOR 1196

MOHAMMAD AL-NASIR DEFEATED BY ALFONSO VIII AT LAS NAVAS DE TOLOSA 1212

ABU YAAQUB YUSUF KILLED 1184

LEON

CASTILLE

PYRENEES

ARAGON

ALCANTARA
SANTAREM
R. Tagus
UCLES

ANDALUS

ALARCOS LAS NAVAS VALENCIA
SEVILLE CORDOBA

ROME

VALENCIA LOST BY MUSLIMS 1238

SEVILLE TAKEN BY FERDINAND III 1249

GRANADA

MURCIA

CORDOBA LOST BY MUSLIMS 1236

MEDITERRANEAN SEA

RABAT

TELEMSAN ALGIERS
BOUJAIYA

SICILY

TUNIS

MARAKISH

ATLAS MOUNTAINS

IFRIQIYA

MUWAHHID EMPIRE

HAFSID DYNASTY RULE TUNIS 1228-1574

CAPTURE OF MARAKISH BY BENI MERIN 1269

TRIPOLI

BARQA

MEHDIYA CAPTURED FROM KING OF SICILY BY ABDUL MUMIN 1160

BERBER RULERS OF THE WEST
The Murabits: 1056-1146
The Muwahhids: 1146-1269

ROGER II OCCUPIES COAST 1134-1160

EGYPT:
MAMLUK RULE BEGINS 1250
BAYBARS SULTAN 1260

2. The End of Muslim Spain:

The beginning of the end of Muslim power in Spain began in the 11th century when Muslim Spain disintegrated into thirty independent republics (Reyes de Taifas) fighting each other.[1272] Muslim historians, such as Ibn Hayan, and Ibn Bassam, have given excellent accounts of the break up of the country and its disastrous effects.[1273] The break up of the Muslim kingdom emboldened Christian princes in North West Spain to sweep south. They saw their opportunity, and they made the most of it, observes Lane Poole.[1274] The Christian re-conquest of Spain proceeded `as rapidly as the fraternal chaos of the Spanish kings would permit,' notes Durant.[1275] Alfonso VI, who had united under his sway the three kingdoms of the Asturias, Leon, and Castile, understood `that he only had to allow the various Muslim princes rope enough, and they would proceed to hang themselves with the utmost expedition. These short sighted tyrants, indeed, caring only for their petty individual power, and eagerly aiding in anything that could weaken their rivals, threw themselves at Alfonso's feet, and implored his assistance whenever they found themselves overmastered by a mere powerful neighbour.'[1276]

This Muslim corruption and infighting is likewise captured by Muslim scholars of the time such as Ibn Hazm and Ibn Bassam. They blame the rulers for their indolence and preoccupations with their own pleasures, and they also blame the Muslim community which has lost touch with the practices of its faith.[1277] Ibn Hazm was sharp in his denunciation of the Taifa kings:

[1272] For the various principalities, their rulers, etc, see:
-Ibn Khaldun: *Kitab al-Ibar*; op cit; vol iv; pp. 160-1.
-Al-Maqqari: *Nafh al-Tib;* op cit; vol I; p. 288;
-Ibn al-Athir: *Al-Kamil;* op cit; vol ix; pp. 203-4.
[1273] The third part of the *Mukttabis* of Ibn Hayan has been published by M. M. Antuna, under the title: *Chronique du regne du calife umayyade Abd Allah a Cordoue*, Paris 1937, and has been translated into Spanish by Kh. Ghorayyib, in *Cuadernos de historia de Espana*, Buenos Aires 1952; E. Levi-Provencal and E. Garcia Gomez have published the Textos ineditos del "Muqtabis" ... sobre las origenes del reino de Pamplona, in *Al-Andalus*, xix (1954).
Ibn Bassam: *Kitab al-Dhakhira fi Mahasin ahl-Jazira*; ed. Fuad University, Cairo, 1939-44; a more up to date edition by I. Abbas; Beirut; 1978-9; (8 volumes).
[1274] S. Lane-Poole: *The Moors in Spain;* Fisher Unwin; London; 1888; pp. 176-7.
[1275] W. Durant: *The Age of Faith,* op cit; p.697.
[1276] S. Lane-Poole: *The Moors;* op cit; pp.176-7.
[1277] C. Melville and A. Ubaydli: *Christians and Moors in Spain;* vol 3; Arabic sources; Aris and Phillips Ltd; Warminster; UK; 1992; p. 90.

231

`By God, I swear that if the tyrants were to learn that they could attain their ends more easily by adopting the religion of the Cross, they would certainly hasten to profess it! Indeed, we see that they ask the Christians for help and allow them to take away Muslim men, women, and children as captives to their lands. Frequently they protect them in their attacks against the most inviolable land, and ally themselves with them in order to gain security.'[1278]

Ibn Bassam quotes a verse describing the Andalusian rulers:

`Their minds were occupied with wine and song, and listening to music.'[1279]

Ibn Bassam pours vindictive on these rulers, whose betrayal was to cause the loss of Muslim Spain, and eventually, centuries down the line, the extermination of millions of Muslims. Hence, he says:

`Call the kings and say to them,
What have you brought about?
You have handed over Islam into enemy captivity
And (yourselves) remained seated (and inactive)
We should rise up against you
Since you have given support to the Christians
You take no account of the breaking of the bonds of community of the Prophet.'[1280]

The Muslims, as a whole, were also blamed for their laxness and falling away from the ideals of Islam. In a poem mourning the fall of Toledo to Christendom (in 1085), an anonymous Muslim poet wrote:

`If we say, punishment has reached them,
And rejection by God has come to them,
Then we, too, like them, and more than they,
Deviate (from religion), and can one who deviates be safe?
Can we be sure that vengeance will not fall upon us,
When corruption has combined with licence amongst us?
….
The Veil is stripped from a people whenever
Free rein is given to disobedience.'[1281]

This Islamic generalised weakness and decadence was seized upon by the Christians.[1282] They now realised they could wrest Spain from the Muslims.

[1278] Quoted by MacKay: Spain in the Middle Ages; 27 from M. Asin Palacios: Un Codice inexplorado del cordobes Ibn Hazm; *Al Andalus;* 2; 1934; p. 42; in D. Wasserstein: *The Rise and Fall of the Party Kings;* Princeton University Press; 1985; p. 280.

[1279] Ibn Bassam: Dhakhira; I; part ii; p. 430 in D. Wasserstein: *The Rise*; p. 280.

[1280] Ibn Bassam: *Dhakhira;* I; part ii; p. 374; in D. Wasserstein; p. 280.

[1281] Anonymous quoted by Al-Maqqari: Analectes; ii; p. 778 in D. Wasserstein; p. 281.

Christian Spanish princes welcomed the reinforcements brought to them by French nobles from Aquitaine and Bourgogne, in general recruited by propaganda and under the religious order of Cluny.[1283] Then, they mounted a ferocious onslaught on the Muslims, which began with the Christian victories at Barbastro in 1063, and Toledo (1085). When the Christians threatened other cities, only then, did it become clear to everyone, Lane Poole observes, that Alfonso (the main Christian leader) meant nothing less than re-conquest of all Spain, and the extermination of all Muslims.[1284] Threatened with extinction by these very Christian allies they were fighting alongside against other Muslim neighbours, the Reyes called the Almoravids to come and help.

The Almoravids of Morocco, in power in North Africa, responded to the call. In 1086, the armies of Yusuf Ibn Tashfin, manoeuvring en masse to the sound of drums, inflicted on the Christian knights a shattering defeat at Sagrajas (Zallaqah) near Bajadoz.[1285] The Christian forces were awed and intimidated by the continuous drumming, which accompanied the swiftly executed manoeuvres of the Almoravid army.[1286]
'This weird drum beating, who so dumbfounded the Christians, is an indication in itself of the new tactics brought into play by the Almoravid, whereby compact masses, trained to regular, rhythmic and unfaltering action, moved with one accord in obedience to successive orders... at the same time as the drum, and the employment of bodies of Turkish archers, who fought in regular, parallel ranks, provide further evidence of this new method of warfare.'[1287]
Ibn Tashfin slaughtered the Spaniards so much so that Alfonso barely escaped with some five hundred horsemen. Many thousands of the best sword-arms in Castile 'lay stiff and nerveless on that fatal field.'[1288] Ibn Tashfin took with him back to North Africa 40,000 Christian heads as trophy,[1289] whilst Ibn al-Khatib estimates the numbers of Christian losses

---

[1282] E. Levi. Provencal: Toledo; in *Encyclopaedia of Islam;* vol 3; first series; pp. 809-12; p. 811.
[1283] C. Cahen: *Orient et Occident;* op cit. p.55.
[1284] S. Lane-Poole: *The Moors;* op cit; p.178.
[1285] Ibn Khaldun: *Kitab al-Ibar;* part translated as Histoire des Berberes; by De Slane; ed. P. Casanova; Paris; 1927; vol ii; pp. 78-9. Ibn Khallikan: *Wafayat al-Iyan;* op cit; vol ii; p. 415; Ibn al-Athir: *Kitab al-kamil;* op cit; x; pp. 101-2; G. Wiet et al: *History;* op cit; p.269.
[1286] A.Thomson; M.A. Rahim: *Islam in Andalus;* op cit; p. 90.
[1287] R.Menendez Pidal: *The Cid and his Spain;* Madrid; 1934; p. 219.
[1288] S. Lane-Poole: *The Moors in Spain;* op cit; p.179.
[1289] P.K. Hitti: *History;* op cit; p. 540.

at 300,000.[1290] Prior to battle, the Christian monarch, Alfonso as he looked upon his own splendid army, exclaimed: 'with men like these I would fight devils, angels, and ghosts!'[1291]

Twice the Almoravid were asked to intervene before being summoned to depart, their puritan faith hardly of the taste of the Reyes. Some Reyes even plotted to have Ibn Tashfin poisoned so as to rid themselves of an incumbent guest.[1292] The third time he was invited, in 1090, he crossed the straight of Gilbraltar from Morocco, removed the Reyes, and installed Almoravid rule over the country. Under Almoravid rule was not just restored the unity of the Muslim Peninsula, but also 're-appeared in the West a combative form of Islam that responded to the Christian combativeness,' says Cahen.[1293]

War between Muslims and Christians now reached a savagery equal to that of the East under the crusaders.[1294] Under cover of religious duty was justified Christian collection of booty.[1295] The popes had given the same privileges as the crusaders in the East to Christians who would help drive back the Muslims in Spain.[1296] In fact, from the Concile of Clermont (1095) (which also launched the crusades), the papacy placed the Spanish wars and the Crusade on the same level, and banned Spanish Christians from the Crusades in the East.[1297] Sharing in aim and methods, knight Templars came from France to help Spanish military religious orders, the Knights of Calatrava, of Santiago, of Alcantara, which had been formed in the 12th century.[1298]

The coalesced Christian forces met their match with the formidable Almoravids, who were animated by immense religious fervour, and also a unique mastery of the art of war.   A bloody war of attrition followed. In 1101, Yusuf ibn Tashfin ordered his general Mazdali to besiege the city of Valencia, which was recaptured in May of the following year, a city left in

---

[1290] Ibn al-Khatib: *Al-Hulal al-Mawshiyah fi Dhikr al-Akhbar al-Marrakushiyah*; Tunis (1329 H); p. 43.

[1291] S. Lane-Poole: *The Moors in Spain*; op cit; p.179.

[1292] A. Thomson; M.A. Rahim: *Islam in Andalus;* op cit; p. 92.

[1293] C. Cahen: *Orient et Occident au temps;* op cit.p.21.

[1294] N. Daniel: *The Arabs;* op cit; p.86.

[1295] Ibid.

[1296] W. Durant: *The Age of Faith*, op cit; p.697.

[1297] See the message of Pope Urban II to the Count of Barcelona and the Catalan knights: 'There is no merit in freeing Christians from under the Saracens in one place and deliver them to tyranny in another,' cited in A. Leman: l'Origine de l'idee de Croisade, *Hesperis*, XXIV, Paris, 1937, 3rd Trimester, pp 205-15; p. 213.

[1298] W. Durant: *The Age of Faith*, op cit; p.697.

ruins by its previous Christian occupiers.[1299] The Almoravids then progressed to take the whole of southern Spain and Portugal, overrunning the remaining Reyes and inflicting a shattering defeat on Alfonso VI at Ucles, west of Cuenca, in 1108.[1300] The Christian alliances suffered further crushing defeats, one of which claimed the life of their army chief, Garcia Ordonez. Alfonso VI himself died shortly afterwards, worn out and disappointed by failures.[1301] All the fortresses as far afield as Cuenca fell to the Muslims before the decade was out.[1302] In 1110 Tamim, a son of Yusuf Ibn Tashfin, captured Saragossa, and at the other side of the Peninsula the veteran Sir ibn Abu Bekr occupied Bajadoz, Santarem and Oporto.[1303] Only Toledo stood safe in Christian hands.

Almoravid power could not last, though. When Ibn Tashfin died, he was replaced by his son Ali. Unlike his father, a tough man of the southern Morocco desert, Ali was raised in the indolent, poet filled surrounding of urban Andalusia.[1304] He was also very much under the influence of his wife, Qamar, a former captive of Christian origin;[1305] so much influence she had, in Ali's latter years, the country was virtually ruled from the harem.[1306] To compensate for his weakness, the king surrounded himself with a powerful Christian militia devoted to him alone, with their priests and churches.[1307] The whole Almoravid rule has now fallen in decadence, in fact, not just the king. `They came to Spain hardy, rough warriors, unused to ease or luxuries, delighting in feats of strength and prowess, filled with a fierce but simple zeal for their religion,' says Lane Poole, now `they lost their martial habits, their love for deeds of daring, their pleasure in enduring hardships in the brave way of war... In twenty years, in place of the former Berber army now was a disorganised crowd of sodden debauchees, miserable poltroons, who had drunk and fooled away their manhood's vigour and become slaves to all appetites that make men cowards.'[1308] The Almoravids, who were at first welcomed by the common people, now behaved with the same flamboyant libertinism of their predecessors.[1309] And

---

[1299] J. Read: *The Moors in Spain and Portugal*; Faber and Faber, London, 1974; p.143.

[1300] Ibid; p.147.

[1301] Ibid.

[1302] Ibid.

[1303] A.Thomson; M.A. Rahim: *Islam;* op cit; p. 97; J. Read: The Moors; op cit; p. 147.

[1304] S and N. Ronart: *Concise Encyclopaedia of Arabic Civilization; The Arab West*; Djambatan; Amsterdam; 1966; p. 81.

[1305] Ibid.

[1306] J. Read: *The Moors;* op cit; p.147.

[1307] S and N. Ronart: *Concise Encyclopaedia*; op cit; p. 81.

[1308] S. Lane-Poole: *The Moors in Spain;* op cit; p.183.

[1309] J. Read: *The Moors*; op cit; p.147.

as moral decadence set in, their fortunes declined in the field of war.[1310] Soon followed the usual infighting between the various factions: Almoravid against Almoravid, Almoravid against Andalusian, Arab against Berber...[1311] Muslim Spain disintegrated into a multitude of hostile city states just like those of decades before. Every governor, chief, or man of influence, who could command a few followers and had a castle to retire to in case of need, Lane Poole says, styled himself Sultan, and assumed the insignia of royalty.[1312] Thus Muslim Spain had as many kings as there were towns in it: Ibn Hamdi rose at Cordova; Ibn Maymun at Cadiz; Ibn Kasy and Ibn Wezir Seddaray held the west; Lamtuny Granada...[1313]

These divisions were hardly lost to the Christians. They resumed their assaults under the conduct of King Alfonso I of Aragon, named El-Batallador (The Fighter) because of his deep thrusts into Muslim territory.[1314] Tudela was lost by the Muslims in 1114, then Saragossa, in 1118, when Alfonso, helped by local Christians under Muslim rule, was able to take the city, and make further incursions in Muslim territories.[1315] In 1121 he was even able to reach the walls of Grenada.[1316] In 1125, Alfonso crushed the Muslim army at Armisol, and in the same year, Christian armies harried the south for the whole year.[1317] In 1133 they burnt the very suburbs of Cordova, Seville and Carmona, and sacked Xeres and set it ablaze.[1318] In 1147 Lisbon was lost by the Muslims. It followed a diversion of northern crusaders (English, Germans, and Flemish) to assist the Portuguese siege of the city. On their way to the Levantine crusades, these Northerners had `stopped en route to wrest a town or castle.'[1319] The attraction of the booty was ever so powerful. Once the city fell, fierce rioting broke out among the crusaders over the loot of the city.[1320] Despite assurances given to the Muslims, pillage and rape followed, and when the starving and despoiled inhabitants began filing through the city's three gates, even the English priest was constrained to write: `we are inclined to feel pity for our enemies in their evil fortunes, and to feel sorry that the lashes of divine justice are not yet at an end.'[1321]

[1310] Ibid; p.150.

[1311] A.Thomson; M.A. Rahim: *Islam;* op cit; p. 97.

[1312] S. Lane-Poole: *The Moors in Spain*; op cit; p.184.

[1313] Ibid.

[1314] J. Read: *The Moors*; op cit.p.150.

[1315] A. Thomson; M.A. Rahim: *Islam*; op cit; p. 97.

[1316] Ibid.

[1317] S. Lane-Poole: *The Moors in Spain*; op cit; p.184.

[1318] Ibid.

[1319] Felipe Fernandez Armesto: *Before Columbus*: MaCMillan Education; London, 1987; p.64.

[1320] J. Read: *The Moors in Spain;* op cit; p .161.

[1321] Ibid.

In October 1147, the Muslim city of Almeira, besieged by land and sea, so 'tightly, that not even an eagle could find its way in or out, surrendered.'[1322] This presaged once more the end of the Muslim presence in the Peninsula. The arrival of the Almohad delayed the take over for another century, though.

Almohad rule typifies exactly the manner Islamic dynasties evolved. First they started brilliantly under powerful, devout, fighting rulers, before their sons and successors fell in for the usual attractions of luxury and palace life; followed by harem intrigues, plots, infighting, and alliances with the Christians, which ended in the collapse of the dynasty.

Almohad rule began with the elimination of the by now inept Almoravid, who had become reliant on Christian militias to guard rulers, to collect taxes, and to perform police duties in their very centre of birth: The Moroccan Atlas, and other African provinces.[1323] It was in the very foundations of the Almoravid power in the Atlas Mountains of Morocco, where a new leader Ibn Tumart (ca 1078-ca 1130), of the Berber Masmuda tribe, rose against the Almoravids.[1324] Ibn Tumart died, but his Algerian born disciple, Abd Al-Mumin, led the new power, and by 1147, he had put an end to Almoravid rule in Morocco, Algeria, Tunisia, and Libya.[1325]

Once they came to Spain, the Almohads obtained the submission of the weak local rulers who were fearful of the renewed Christian onslaught from the North. In 1145, the Almohads took Algeciras; in 1146 Seville and Malaga, and the next four years saw Cordova, Jaen and the rest of southern Spain united under their sway.[1326] Soon after, Abd al-Mumin, and his son, Abu Yaqub Yusuf led their armies and pushed back the Christian threat. The most decisive victory against the Christians came later at the hands of Abu Yaqub (ruled 1184-1199), who like the famous Ibn Abi-Abi Amir, was to take the honorific title of Al-Mansur (The Victorious).[1327] On 18th July, 1196, he inflicted a crushing defeat on Alfonso VIII of Castile at

---

[1322] M. Defourneaux: *Les Francais en Espagne aux 11 et 12em siecles;* Presses Universitaires Francaises; Paris; 1949; p.176.

[1323] S and N. Ronart: *Concise Encyclopaedia;* op cit; p. 81.

[1324] Ibn Khaldun: *Kitab al-Ibar;* op cit; vol vi; p. 225; Ibn al-Athir: *Kamil;* op cit; vol x; p. 400.

[1325] Al-Marrakushi: *Kitab al-Mujib fi talkhis akhbar ahl al-Maghrib;* 2nd ed; R. Dozy; Leyden; 1881; pp. 145-6.

[1326] S. Lane-Poole: *The Moors in Spain;* op cit. p. 214; A. Thomson; M.A. Rahim: *Islam;* op cit; p. 101.

[1327] See Al-Marrakushi: *Kitab al-Mujib*; op cit; p. 189.

Alarcos, the Christian army being virtually exterminated.[1328] So generous in victory was Abu Yaqub, he freed twenty thousand Christian prisoners without ransom.[1329] All Spain was at the mercy of Abu Yaqub, but he was obliged to cut short his operations to return to Africa, where a rebellion, sponsored and encouraged by the Ayyubids, the successors of Salah Eddin, was threatening him from the rear.[1330] Abu Yaqub quelled the rebellion, but by the time he returned to Spanish matters, his forces had been drained, and considerably, to maintain his momentum.

The Almohad checked for a while Christian advances, yet, soon, their rule was to fall to the same exertions as their predecessors. Some of the local lords, Ibn Mardanish of Murcia and Valencia, went into open rebellion against the Almohad in alliance with the Catalan Lord of Barcelona.[1331] Almohad energy and effort were spent fighting rebellions and defections of Andalusian Emirs, always ready to submit to the Christian princes to secure their possessions.[1332]

Then, as most often happens, at his death, the illustrious victor at Alarcos, Abu Yaqub (1184-99) (Al-Mansur), was succeeded by his son Al-Nasir (1199-1214), who was of a very different mould. Al-Nasir cared neither for science nor for religion, neglected government, and specialised in pleasure.[1333] At the very decisive battle of Las Navas de Tolosa, in 1212, Al-Nasir's much superior army, of over 600,000 Muslim men, drawn from both Al-Andalus and North Africa, was too disunited and badly led by al-Nasir, to face effectively a smaller, and yet united Christian army.[1334] Al-Nasir's army was crushed. In the wake of the battle, 70,000 Muslim prisoners were slaughtered at the order of the Bishops of Toledo and Narbonne who were at the scene.[1335]

The Muslim historian Al-Maqqari captures perfectly the gravity and consequences of this defeat. He says:

`The result (of this defeat) was that the greater part of the Maghrib was deserted and that the Franks conquered the greater part of al-Andalus. Out of the 600,000 (Muslim) men who entered the field of battle only a few escaped; some authors even state that their number did not reach a thousand.

[1328] J. Glubb: *A Short History;* op cit; p.190.
[1329] Ibid.
[1330] Ibid.
[1331] A. Thomson; M.A.Rahim: *Islam*; op cit; p. 102.
[1332] M.L. de Mas Latrie: *Traites de Paix*; op cit; p.73.
[1333] W. Durant: *The Age of Faith*, op cit; p.314.
[1334] Al-Marrakushi: *Kitab al-Mujib;* op cit; p. 236; A. Thomson-M.A. Rahim: *Islam in Andalus*; op cit; p. 106.
[1335] T.B. Irving: Dates, Names and Places: The end of Islamic Spain; in *Revue d'Histoire Maghrebine;* No 61-62; 1991; pp 77-93; at p. 81.

The battle was like a curse, not only to al-Andalus, but to the whole Maghrib, and the defeat is to be ascribed to the bad policy of An-Nasir, for although the Muslims in Al-Andalus were well trained to war and accustomed to fight with the Christians, that Sultan and his vizier entirely disregarded their advice, and even offended some of them; and the consequence was that the minds of the Andalusian officers were alienated and the Christians gained victory.

However this may be, certain it is that this defeat may be regarded as the real cause of the subsequent decline of Western Africa and Al-Andalus-of the former country, because the loss sustained in the battle was so great that her districts and towns were almost depopulated through it-of Al-Andalus, because the enemy of God was thereby enabled to extend his conquests; for after the death of An-Nasir, the empire of the Muwahhidun (Almohads) became convulsed, the princes of the royal family, who held the government of Andalus, each seized the opportunity of extending his own power and authority; and in the subsequent decline of their empire at Morocco, they came at length not only to hire the enemy's troops, but to surrender to the Christian kings the fortresses of the Muslims, that they might secure their aid against each other.'[1336]

The Almohad defeat at Las Navas de Tolosa in 1212, indeed, 'broke the back of Muslim power in the Peninsula.'[1337] It hastened the fall of Al-Nasir, and much worse, began the disorganisation of the kingdom.[1338] Almohad Spain broke into small and independent states. The ensuing intrigues, assassinations, petty state building, civil wars and general turmoil both demoralised the Muslims and invited Christian invasion.[1339] Thus, King James of Aragon marched into Valencia in 1238 to support one side of an Islamic civil war, itself a complex of factions enmeshed in a wider Muslim infighting.[1340] Before then, between 1229 and 1235, the Balearic Islands fell to this same James of Aragon.[1341] Cordova, the once mighty capital of Muslim Spain, ridden with intrigues, and local conflict fell easily in 1236. In 1246, Fernando III (1217-52), the King of Castile, occupied Murcia.

Two years later, in 1248, Seville, the Almohad capital, just like Cordova, fell victim to the jealousies of internal factions; thus, like Cordova, a sudden

---

[1336] Al-Maqqari: *Nafh al-Tib*; op cit; vol 2; p. 323.
[1337] B. Lewis: *Cultures in Conflict*; Oxford University Press; 1995; p. 19.
[1338] M.L. de Mas Latrie: *Traites de paix;* op cit; p.72.
[1339] R. I. Burns: Muslims in the Thirteenth Century Realms of Aragon: Interaction and Reaction, in *Muslims under Latin Rule*, (J.M. Powell; ed) op cit; pp 57-102; at p.73.
[1340] Ibid.
[1341] M.L. de Mas Latrie: *Traites de paix*; op cit; p.74.

opportunistic conquest for Fernando.[1342] Fernando was greatly assisted by the military help of Mohammed I of Grenada, for Seville's Muslim inhabitants put up a desperate resistance.[1343] Recounting the siege, Ibn al-Idhari says that it intensified during the year and the surrounding districts and regions became filled with Christian forces.[1344] They captured a large number of the inhabitants and seized some of their children in ships, with which they maintained a tight blockade, kept up bombardments from mangonels and destroyed all amenities, both small and great.[1345] The people, according to the chronicler, became dismayed and staggered around like drunkards even though they were not drunk; a great many died of starvation... they began to chew skins; the fighting men among the populace and the ranks of the army perished.[1346] It was in the end hunger and despair that had reason of the Muslims, more powerful weapons than all the military appliances by the Christian besiegers, more than the combined efforts of a thoroughly organized hierarchy, and more than the benedictions and indulgences of the Pope.[1347] The seventeen month siege and the fierce battle for the city had their impact. Ibn Al-Idhari writes that:

`All the population was immersed and floating in a sea of death because of the terrors and agonies that had befallen them, the description and explanation of which would be protracted and would exhaust both pen and paper.'[1348]

It was with greatest reluctance that the Muslims consented to give up the great mosque, which with its minaret was both sacred and the most conspicuous monument of the city.[1349]

The victorious Fernando III reunited Leon and Castile, pushed the Catholic frontier to Grenada, made Seville his capital, the Great Mosque his cathedral, and the Alacazar his residence.[1350] Subsequently, Muhammad II of Grenada allied himself to Christian forces to rid himself of his Merinid co-religionist Abu Yusuf; an alliance between Castile and Grenada re-conducted in the

---

[1342] Felipe Fernandez Armesto: *Before Columbus;* op cit; p.52.

[1343] Rodrigo de Zayas: *Les Morisques: et le racisme d'etat*; Ed Les Voies du Sud; Paris, 1992; p.173.

[1344] Ibn al-Idhari: *Al-Bayan al-Mughrib*; ed. A. Huici Miranda; Tetuan; 1963; pp. 381-5; in *Christians and Moors in Spain*; edited by C. Melville and A. Ubaydli; Aris and Phillips Ltd; Warminster; 1992; vol 3; p. 145.

[1345] Ibid.

[1346] Ibid.

[1347] S.P. Scott: *History*; op cit; vol 2; p. 413.

[1348] Ibn al-Idhari: *Al-Bayan;* op cit; p. 149.

[1349] S.P. Scott: *History*; op cit; vol 2; p. 413.

[1350] W. Durant: *The Age of Faith*, op cit; p.697.

capture of the last Muslim stronghold (other than Grenada): Tarifa (1275-76).[1351] Now the whole of Spain, except Grenada was in Christian hands.

The loss of Muslim Spain in the mid 13th century spelled the end for Muslims and their civilisation. The ultimate consequence, as to be seen below, was Muslim extermination.

[1351] Rodrigo de Zayas: Les Morisques; op cit; p.174.

The Critical Historical Role of the Almoravids and Almohads

History has been as unkind to the Almoravids as it has been to the Seljuks and the Mamluks. The film El-Cid exaggerates everything negative about them. Yet, Almoravid and Almohad intervention in Spain had a decisive impact on the fate of the Muslims. In place of disunited Muslim princelings, they offered a united Muslim front to fight invading northern Christians. At the time of the Almoravid and Almohad intervention, the crusades were proceeding in the East, nearly wiping out the Muslim presence there. What would have happened to the Muslim world if the Almoravids and Almohads had not intervened, and the Muslims had been conquered by the Christians in 1090 rather than two centuries later, and had the Spaniards and Portuguese advanced into North Africa then, to join with the other Crusaders, who were advancing and mass slaughtering Muslims in the East? This is not difficult to imagine. By delaying the Spanish take over by nearly two centuries, Almoravids and Almohads saved the Muslims of North Africa from extermination.

The Loss of Al-Andalus, and the Destruction of Islamic Civilisation

The last chapter has showed the devastation in the East caused by the crusades and the Mongols, and how Islamic scholarship and civilisation were shattered, and great centres of Islamic learning and scholarship such as Jerusalem, Merw, Baghdad, Aleppo, etc, were destroyed. The period of decline of Islamic civilisation happened in the 13th century, precisely the time when Al-Andalus and its great centres of learning: Cordova, Valencia, Murcia, Seville, etc, were devastated and lost by the Muslims. The following outline on some of the scholars who lived in Seville when it was in Muslim hands shows how the loss of such places had a disastrous impact on Islamic science and learning.

Abu Bakr Muhammad Al-Ishbili (b. 1108-1109) studied in Seville and Cordova, and died in Cordova in 1179.[1352] He compiled a bibliography (*Fihrist*) containing more than 1400 titles of books composed by Spanish Muslims on every subject.[1353] This Fihrist was edited by Francisco Codera and Julian Ribera y Tarrago late in the 19th century.[1354]

Abu'l Khair (fl early 12th century) was the author of a book *Kitab al-Filaha,* which deals with all matters pertaining to farming science.[1355]

Abu Zakariya Ibn al-'Awwam al-Ishbili was a Hispano-Muslim agriculturist who flourished at Seville about the end of the 12th century. He wrote a treatise on agriculture, *Kitab al-filaha,* which was the most important mediaeval work on the subject.[1356]

Abu Abbas Mufarraj, often called al-Nabati, or Ibn Rumiya (son of the Christian woman), also al-Hafiz (he who knows the Qur'an and Hadith (Tradition) by heart), was a Hispano-Muslim botanist born in Seville in 1165-6 or 1171-72, and died in Spain, very probably in ca. 1239-40.[1357]

Ibn Abdun Mohammed B. Ahmad flourished at the end of the 11th centuryand lived under the early almoravids, wrote one of the main books on Hisba (State inspection).[1358]

[1352] G. Sarton: *Introduction to the History of Science*; op cit; vol 2; p. 444.

[1353] Ibid.

[1354] Francisco Codera and Julian Ribera y Tarrago: *Index librorum de diversis scientiarum ordinibus quos a magistris didicit;* Biblioteca arabico-hispanica, vols. 9 and 10, Saragossa, 1894-1895.

[1355] Abu'l- Khair *Kitab al-Filaha*; in V. Lagardere: *Campagnes et paysans d'Al Andalus;* Maisonneuve; Larose; Paris; 1993; at p. 265.

[1356] Ibn Al-Awwam: *Kitab al-Filaha;* French tr: (Le Livre de l'Agriculture), by Clement-Mullet; 2 tomes in 3 vols, Paris 1864-1867.

[1357] G. Sarton: *Introduction;* op cit; vol 2; p. 650.

[1358] E. Levi Provencal: *Seville Musulmane au debut du XII siecle* (le Traite d'Ibn Abdun sur la vie urbaine et les corps de metiers); Maisonneuve; Paris; 1947.

Ibn Zuhr (Avenzoar) (b. 1091? 1094?) in Seville was the most illustrious member of the famous Ibn-Zuhr family that produced six generations of physicians in direct descent.[1359] He wrote six medical texts, of which three are still to be found in the British Museum and the Bibliothèque Nationale.[1360] His three extant works, in chronological order, are *Kitab al-iqtisad fi islah al-anfus wal-ajsad,* Book Concerning the Reformation of Souls and Bodies, completed in 1121-1122, for the Almoravid prince Ibrahim ibn Yusuf ibn Tashfin-to whom Ibn Zuhr had been the wazir. *Kitab al-taysir fi-l-mudawat wal-tadbir,* Book Concerning Therapeutics and Diet. *Kitab al-aghdhiya,* Book of Foodstuffs, composed for the first Almohad caliph, 'Abd al-Mu'min, who ruled from 1130 to 1163.[1361]

One of the mathematicians of Seville was Ibn al-Yasamin al-Ishbilli.[1362] Ibn al-Yasamin (fl second half of the 12th century; d. 1204) was originally of North African Berber descent. His mathematical works have been studied by many authors.[1363]

Jabir ibn Aflah was an astronomer who wrote *Kitab al-haiaa,* also called Correction of the Almagest, *Islah al-Majisti,* which was soon translated into Latin by Gherardo Cremonese under the title: *Gebri filii Affla Hispalensis.*[1364]

Al-Bitruji (known as Alpetragius) was born in Morocco, lived in Seville and died around 1204. Al-Bitruji's '*Kitab-al-Hay'aH*' was popular in 13th century Europe, and was translated by Michael Scot under the title `On the Sphere,' and was also translated into Hebrew by Moses Ibn Tibbon in 1259.[1365]

[1359] A. Whipple: *The Role of the Nestorians and Muslims in the History of Medicine.* Microfilm-xerography by University Microfilms International Ann Arbor, Michigan, U.S.A. 1977, p.52.

[1360] Ibid.

[1361] G. Sarton: *Introduction;* op cit; vol 2; p. 232.

[1362] A. Djebbar: Ibn al-Yasamin; in *Encyclopaedia of the history of Science, technology, and Medicine in Non Western Cultures;* ed by H. Selin; Kluwer Academic Publishers. Dordrecht/Boston/London, 1997; pp. 414-5.

[1363] See, for instance:

-S. Jalal: *Manzumat Ibn al-yasamin fi amal al-Jabr wal hisab*; Kuwait; Mu'assassat al-Kuyat li taquadhum al-ilmi; 1988.

-M Souissi: *Al-luma al-maradiniya fi sharh al-Yasminiyya;* Kuwait; 1989.

T. Zemouli: *Mu'allafat Ibn al-Yasamin ar-riyaddiya*; master thesis; E.N.S. Algiers; 1993.

[1364] H. Suter: *Die Mathematiker und Astronomen der Araber*; 1900; p.119; Nachtrage, 1902; p. 174.

[1365] J. Samso: Al-Bitruji; in *Dictionary of Scientific Biography;* volume 15; supplement 1; Ed C. C. Gillispie; Charles Scribner's Sons, New York, 1973 ff. Pp. 33-6; at p. 33.

These and many other scholars lived in Muslim Seville. After the city was taken by the Christians, in 1248, it did not produce one single Muslim scholar to this day. The same can be said of all other towns and cities that fell in Christian-Mongol hands: Jerusalem, Baghdad, Cordova, etc. All of them beacons of enlightenment under Islamic rule became places where Islamic learning was banished when the Muslims lost them.

3. The Elimination of the Muslims in Spain:

Once they lost power in the 13th century, the Muslims learnt the rules of the Christian victors. The defeated Muslims had to wear a distinctive garb, live in a separate section of each city, and bear especially heavy taxation.[1366] They were regularly moved en masse within Spain whenever the occasion arose. In 1247 James I ordered their expulsion from Aragon. Over 100,000 of them left.[1367] Newly Christian Majorca seems to have lost the larger part of its Muslims to flight and expulsion, whilst its smaller neighbour, Minorca had its Muslim population entirely enslaved.[1368] Any urban Muslims remaining after each early conquest were removed to a suburb outside the main walls.[1369] Floods of Catalan settlers appropriated the lands conquered from Muslims.[1370] In 1248, Pope Innocent IV ordered the king of Aragon 'to permit no Moors save as slaves.'[1371] Even the freedom of ordinary commercial dealings with the Muslims was discouraged, and in 1250 it was decreed that no one could buy from, or sell anything to a Muslim unless he had first obtained a licence to do so.[1372]

After their wealth, it was their faith. Muslims were summarily jailed and tortured for refusing to eat pork or drinking wine; neighbourhood gossip and surveillance were also introduced mainly to keep an eye on anyone whose clean and neat person betrays that of a Muslim who regularly performed his 'ablutions'.[1373] Later, the Inquisition was established to undertake the job of uprooting such a faith by the use of torture and burning at the stake, and watch over the final elimination of Islam and Muslims from Spain.[1374] This final woe of the Muslims followed the capture of Grenada, the last Muslim stronghold in Spain.

[1366] W. Durant: *The Age of Faith*, op cit; p.700.
[1367] Ibid.
[1368] R. I. Burns: Muslims in the Thirteenth Century Realms of Aragon; op cit; p.67.
[1369] Ibid; p.65.
[1370] Ibid; p.63.
[1371] A. Thomson-M.A. Rahim: *Islam in Andalus*; op cit; p. 115.
[1372] Ibid.
[1373] T.B. Irving: Dates; op cit. p. 81.
[1374] H.C. Lea: *A History of the Inquisition of Spain*, 4 vols; The Mac Millan Company, New York, 1907. See volume three.

a. The Fall of Grenada:

The fate of the Nasrid rulers of Grenada was sealed at the victory of Salado de Tarifa, won in 1340 by the Castilians and Portuguese, putting an end to Moroccan interventions to save Muslim Spain; although the Nasrid held for another century and half (until 1492, to be precise).[1375] Muslims always retired to Grenada, where the Sierra Nevada, or snowy ridges, provided some defence, and where a succession of prudent rulers sustained Grenada and its dependencies-Xeres, Jaen, Almeira, and Malaga against repeated Christian assaults.[1376] Commerce and industry revived, art flourished, and the little kingdom survived until 1492 as the last European foothold of `a culture that had made Andalusia for many centuries an honour to mankind.'[1377]

The conquest of Grenada was a combined outcome of the Spanish monarchs, Ferdinand's and Isabella's, decision to overthrow the emirate, the Pope's crusading zeal, and Jewish finance.[1378] Before the attack, the Christian monarchs launched a sustained campaign of devastation against the Nasrid realm that is its economy, before they engaged in a clinical conquest of one town and city after the other.[1379] A regular army was built to replaces feudal horsemen; artillery was reformed, peasants armed en masse under the name of St Hermandad (fraternity), and a special corps of thirty thousand *talladores* para military forces was charged with burning crops, expelling labourers, and cutting fruit trees in all Muslim lands; ready for the fight to the death Spain was delivering to the Muslims.[1380]

Just at the moment when the Muslims of Grenada needed all their forces to withstand the Christian attack, they were seriously weakened by dynastic quarrels: jealousies in the harem of the emir.[1381] `Such a suicidal mania invaded the minds of the rulers of Grenada,' Lane Poole says, `at a time when every man they could gather together was needed to repel the invasion of the Christians, they wasted their strength in ruinous struggles with each other, and one would even intercept the other's army when it was on the march against the common enemy. The people of Grenada, divided into various factions, aided and abetted the jealousy of their

---

[1375] G. Sarton: *Introduction*; Volume III; op cit; p.38.

[1376] W. Durant: *The Age of Faith*, op cit; p.314-5.

[1377] Ibid.

[1378] J. Read: *The Moors in Spain and Portugal*; Faber and Faber, London, 1974; p.211.

[1379] H. Terrasse: *Islam d'Espagne*; Librairie Plon; Paris; 1958; p. 243.

[1380] M.L. de Mas Latrie: *Traites de Paix*; op cit; p.323.

[1381] R. Merriman: The Conquest of Grenada; in *The Islamic World and the West;* Edited by A.R. Lewis; John Wiley and Sons, Inc; London; 1970; pp. 137-144; at p.138.

sovereigns always fickle.'[1382] The Catholic monarchs were happy at the divisions amongst Muslims, which they supported so as to neutralise their fighting spirit.[1383] The Muslims of Grenada could have held out for more than the ten years that it took to reduce the kingdom had it not been for such outbreak of a bitter family feud.[1384] This feud involved Abu'l Hassan 'Ali (Mulay Hassan), ruler of Grenada, and his son Mohammed XII, known as Boabdil.[1385] It was the latter's subjection to Ferdinand, which contributed as much as any other cause to the overthrow of Muslim power in Grenada.[1386] Boabdil, it was, who would eventually open the way to Christian forces to occupy all outer defences of Malaga in 1484, Ronda and its mountain bastion, and eventually Grenada itself.[1387]

Whilst revolt and sedition were rife in the Muslim camp, the Christian side presented enthusiastic unity and devotion such as Spain had seldom witnessed before.[1388] Further impetus to the Catholic rulers was given by the Pope's call for a crusade.[1389]

Facing the Christian onslaught was Abu'l Hassan and, above all, his brother, Al-Zeghal. Their forces fought the Spanish forces with such determination, that despite the shortcomings and betrayal of some emirs, it took ten years of implacable struggle to secure the triumph of Christianity.[1390] The seventeen strongholds and eighty boroughs of the Emirate (of Grenada) had to be conquered one by one.[1391] In Al-Zeghal, Lane Poole says, we see `the last great Moorish king of Andalusia. He was a gallant warrior, a firm ruler, and a resolute opponent of the Christians. Had he been untrammelled by his nephew (Boabdil), Grenada might have remained in the hands of the Muslims during his life.'[1392] It was, indeed, Boabdil's war in alliance with the Christians against his father and uncle (Al-Zeghal), which eventually led to the fall of Grenada.[1393] Boabdil, despised by the Christians, and hated by the majority of the Muslims, thanks to the money given to him by the Spaniards, and also their logistic support,

---

[1382] S. Lane-Poole: The Moors in Spain; op cit; p.248.
[1383] R. De Zayas: Les Morisques; op cit; p. 182.
[1384] J. Read: The Moors in Spain and Portugal; op cit; p.212.
[1385] Ibid; p.196.
[1386] S. Lane-Poole: The Moors in Spain; op cit; p. 246.
[1387] Ibid; p.247.
[1388] Roger B. Merriman: The Conquest of Grenada; op cit; p.139.
[1389] H. Terrasse: Islam d'Espagne; Librairie Plon; Paris; 1958; p. 243.
[1390] M.L. de Mas Latrie: Traites de paix; op cit; p.323.
[1391] Ibid.
[1392] S. Lane-Poole: The Moors in Spain; op cit; p.248.
[1393] J. Read: The Moors; op cit; p.215.

worked towards destroying the last combative powers of the kingdom.[1394] Boabdil offered a promise to the Muslims of Grenada that districts loyal to him would be spared the ravages of war.[1395] He also did his best to foil the efforts of his uncle Al-Zeghal, whilst the Christians were gradually narrowing the circle that they had drawn round the doomed kingdom.[1396] The Muslim civil war raged until 29 April 1487, when at last Boabdil had the upper hand in Grenada, and could install himself in the Alhambra after having all the supporters of al-Zeghal put to death.[1397] Profiting from the civil war between Muslims, Ferdinand occupied Loja, Illorca, and Moclin;[1398] more crucially, even, thanks to Boabdil the way to Malaga lay open.[1399]

The battle for Malaga in 1487 was particularly fierce, and Queen Isabella herself was present at the siege. The city defence was led by Ez-Zegry who inspired the citizens and his following of North African troops to resist to the last. When the Spanish King tried to bribe him, he dismissed the messenger with courteous disdain; and when the city was summoned to surrender Ez-Zegry said:

`I am here not to surrender but to defend.'[1400]

Ez-Zegry and his followers resisted the bombardments and renewed assault; the walls were mined by the Spaniards, yet the garrison held out.[1401] During the siege of Malaga, the vigilance of the Castilian fleet prevented any relief by sea coming from North Africa.[1402] Al-Zeghal tried to relieve the city after he had gathered what was left of his army, but again, Boabdil intervened, and cut to pieces the rescue party despatched by his uncle.[1403] This sealed the fate of the starved people of Malaga, who after a siege of three months forced Ez-Zegry to open the gates. The Spaniards took possession of the city in August 1487; Ez-Zegry was cast into a dungeon never to be heard of again.[1404] Ferdinand imposed the harshest conditions: the whole population was condemned to slavery.[1405]

[1394] R. De Zayas: *Les Morisques;* op cit; p. 184.

[1395] L.P. Harvey: *Islamic Spain: 1250-1500;* The University Of Chicago Press; Chicago; 1990; p. 288.

[1396] S. Lane-Poole: *The Moors in Spain*; op cit; p.251.

[1397] R. De Zayas: *Les Morisques;* op cit; p. 187.

[1398] J. Read: *The Moors;* op cit; p. 215.

[1399] Ibid.

[1400] S. Lane-Poole: *The Moors in Spain*; op cit; p.253-4.

[1401] Ibid.

[1402] R. Merriman: The Conquest of Grenada; op cit; p. 140.

[1403] Ibid.

[1404] S. Lane-Poole: *The Moors in Spain*; op cit; p. 254.

[1405] R. Merriman: The Conquest of Grenada; op cit; p. 141.

One third was transported to North Africa to be exchanged for Christian captives detained there; another third was appropriated by the state as payment for the expenses of the campaign; the rest were distributed among the nobles, the Pope, and the sovereigns of friendly lands.[1406] All Christians who had converted to Islam found there were tortured to death with sharp pointed reeds; all conversos (Jews who had converted to Islam) were burnt alive.[1407] Thousands more were massacred and young boys were picked up by priests to catechise them, then Malaga was burnt down.[1408]

In December 1489, after fierce resistance, and after the fall of his last bastion, Baza, Al-Zeghal's resistance ended. The castles that dominated the fastness of the Alpuxarras yielded one by one to Ferdinand's prestige and gold.[1409] Boabdil was pleased to see his uncle Al-Zeghal dethroned by their Catholic majesties.[1410] Now Grenada remained alone. Its turn had arrived.

Grenada had enjoyed a brief period of resumed peace and prosperity whilst the Spaniards dealt with other Muslim strongholds, although its inhabitants were apprehensive of Christian encroachments on its outskirts. Boabdil, evidently in the belief that he would be left in possession of the kingdom as promised by the Christians, despatched messages of congratulation to Ferdinand on his successive conquests (Malaga, Ronda, Baza...).[1411] Boabdil, though he heard his name cursed in the streets of his capital as a traitor in league with the infidels, indulged in blind confidence, believing he had nothing to fear.[1412] His turn to submit came next, though. After the fall of Almeria and the surrender of Al-Zeghal he was called upon to deliver the city.[1413]

Boabdil would eventually hand over the keys of the city to the Catholic monarchs. Not before another episode of stiff Muslim resistance, which Lane Poole recounts (here in an abridged form):
'The defence of Grenada was led by Musa, who rose against the desire of others who saw the utility of surrender. When the enemy came in sight, Musa had the gates open. 'Our bodies,' he said, 'will be the gates.' The

---

[1406] Ibid.
[1407] H.C. Lea: *The Moriscos of Spain*; Burt Franklin; New York; 1968 reprint; p.17.
[1408] T.B. Irving: Dates, Names and Places; op cit; p.80.
[1409] S. Lane-Poole: *The Moors in Spain*; op cit; p.259.
[1410] Ibid.
[1411] Ibid; p.258.
[1412] Ibid; p.259.
[1413] J. Read: *The Moors in Spain and Portugal*; op cit; p.216.

young men were kindled by such words, and when he told them: 'we have nothing to fight for but the ground we stand on; without that we are without home or country.' They made ready to die with him. With such a leader Muslims cavaliers performed prodigious feats of valour that divided the city from Christian camps. They challenged Christian knights and had them killed in duel one by one nearly extinguishing them so that Ferdinand forbade the knights from duelling with Muslims.[1414]

Famine, again, defeated the stiff resistance. When surrender was announced, Musa would not be party to surrender. He armed himself cap a pie, and mounting his charger rode forth from the city never to return. It is said that as he rode he encountered a party of Christian knights, and answering their challenge, slew many of them before he was unhorsed, and then disdaining their offers of mercy, fought stubbornly upon his knees, till he was too weak to continue the struggle; then with the last effort he cast himself into the River Xenil, and heavy with armour sank to the bottom.'[1415]

Boabdil handed over the keys of Grenada, and left the Alhambra by a little frequented route. After a brief but courteous exchange with Ferdinand and Isabella, he continued his journey into exile, while the Catholic Monarchs made their triumphant entry into the city; the singing of the Te Deum and the hoisting of the banner of Santiago over the citadel symbolising the end of Muslim Spain.[1416] A secret agreement had been concluded, guaranteeing the safety of Boabdil and his family and granting him the small principality of the Alpujarras on the coast south of Granada and the retention of 30,000 pieces of gold, together with certain other benefits.[1417]

So ended almost eight hundred years of Muslim rule in Spain. Boabdil had surrendered the last outpost without a fight, and the bitter reproach of his mother 'Aisha, who had herself played no little part in its downfall, rings down the centuries as his epitaph:

'Weep like a woman for what you could not defend like a man.'[1418]

For the first five years after the fall of Grenada the terms of the capitulation, that the Muslims were safe in their property and beliefs under the Christians, were scrupulously honoured.[1419] Then things changed.

[1414] S. Lane-Poole: *The Moors in Spain;* op cit; p.264.

[1415] Ibid; p.266.

[1416] J. Read: *The Moors in Spain and Portugal*, p.217.

[1417] Ibid; p.219.

[1418] Ibid.

[1419] Ibid; p.220.

b. The Suppression of Islam:[1420]

The suppression of Islam from any society is always gradual, relentless, and aims at its basics. The first symbol of Islam set for suppression was personal cleanliness. There were at some point nine hundred public baths in Muslim Cordova; an important feature in all Muslim towns, for among Muslims, cleanliness is not just 'next to godliness,' but also an essential preparation for any act of prayer or devotion.[1421] 'While the medieval Christians forbade washing as a heathen custom,' Lane Poole notes, 'and the monks and nuns boasted of their filthiness, insomuch that a lady saint recorded with pride the fact that up to the age of sixty she had never washed any part of her body, except the tips of her fingers when she was going to take the mass-while dirt was the characteristic of Christian sanctity, the Muslims were careful in the most minute particulars of cleanliness, and dared not approach their God until their bodies were purified.'[1422]

This contrast between Islam and Western Christendom was quite dramatic. De Zayas reminds us how in France, neither King Henry IV nor the Sun King, Louis XIV, nor his court, ever washed.[1423] (Incidentally, even the century of enlightenment, the 18th, was devoid of washrooms and baths, and until the 20th century, the best apartments of Paris were without baths, just as the palace of Versailles.)[1424]

Thus, in order to suppress Islam, was decided the suppression of baths, public and private.[1425] One of the first acts of Isabella after the conquest of Grenada was the foundation of innumerable monasteries on Islamic sites, and the demolition of baths on account 'of the scandal the sight of apartments devoted to ablution and luxury caused every good Christian, as well as for the reason that their use was always considered entirely superfluous in a monastic institution.'[1426] Philip II ordered the destruction of all public baths on the ground that they were relics of infidelity.[1427] Recurrently measures were passed not just that all baths, public and private were to be destroyed, but also that no one in future was to use them.[1428] As an earnest enforcement, all baths were forthwith destroyed, commencing with those of the king.[1429]

[1420] See S.M. Imamuddin: *A Political History of Muslim Spain;* Najmah and Sons Ltd; Dacca; 1961; chapter XVI, pp. 187 ff. for a good outline of the persecutions of Muslims.

[1421] S. Lane Poole: The Moors; op cit; pp. 135-6.

[1422] Ibid.

[1423] R. De Zayas: *Les Morisques*; op cit; note 260; p.682.

[1424] Ibid.

[1425] T.B. Irving: Dates, Names and Places; op cit; p.85.

[1426] S.P. Scott: *History*; Vol II, op cit; p.261.

[1427] S. Lane Poole: *The Moors;* op cit; pp. 135-6.

[1428] Marmol Carvajal: *Rebellion*; op cit; pp. 161-2, Pedraza: *Historia*; op cit; fol.239.

[1429] H.C. Lea: *A History of the Inquisition in Spain*; op cit; vol 3; p.336.

The Muslims still bathed whenever they could, but it had become increasingly hard because their public baths had been destroyed.[1430] They still washed their hands before eating, which was not the case amongst Christians; a difference, which also led to considerable religious conflicts.[1431] The hunt for a clean and neat person as they might be a Muslim who regularly performed their `ablutions' was continuous.[1432] One Bartolome Sanchez appeared in the Toledo Auto da fe of 1597 for bathing, and although overcoming torture, he was finally brought to confess and was punished with three years in the galleys, and perpetual prison and confiscation.[1433] Michael Canete, a gardener, for washing himself in the fields while at work, was tried in 1606; there was nothing else against him but he was tortured.[1434]

Putting clean linen on a corpse for burial was also a suspicious practice, which warranted prosecution. Abstinence from pork and wine was of course a highly suspicious circumstance, which frequently appears in the Inquisition trials of Muslims; and refusing to eat of animals that had died a natural death was also a very compromising practice.[1435] Thus were jailed Muslims for refusing to eat pork or drinking wine, and having always to live under neighbourhood gossip and surveillance.[1436]

New laws were passed to the effects just cited. Lane Poole says:
`The `infidels' were ordered to abandon their native and picturesque costumes, and assume those of Christians; to give up bathing, and adopt the dirt of their conquerors; to renounce their language, their customs and ceremonies, even their very names, and to speak Spanish, behave Spanishly, and re-name themselves Spaniards.'[1437]
One law introduced on 25 May 1566 stipulated that the `Moors had to abandon the use of Arabic, change their costumes, that their doors must remain open every Friday and other feast days, and (of course) that their baths, public and private, to be torn down.'[1438] The reasons doors and windows were to be left open on Friday and Islamic feast days was to watch in case they prayed.[1439] The possession of books or papers in Arabic was almost conclusive proof of disobedience with severe repercussions.[1440] A

[1430] R. De Zayas: Les Morisques; op cit; p. 198.
[1431] Ibid.
[1432] T.B. Irving: Dates, Names and Places; op cit; p.81.
[1433] H.C Lea: The Moriscos of Spain; op cit; p.129.
[1434] Ibid.
[1435] Ibid; pp.129-30.
[1436] T.B. Irving: Dates, Names and Places; op cit; p.81.
[1437] S. Lane Poole: The Moors; op cit; p. 273.
[1438] Rodrigo de Zayas: Les Morisques; op cit; p.230
[1439] T.B. Irving: Dates, Names and Places; op cit; p.85.
[1440] H.C Lea: The Moriscos of Spain; op cit; p.131.

commission of thirteen members, most of them high ecclesiastical dignitaries and presided over by Don Alonso Manrique, Grand Inquisitor of Spain, had been appointed, and its recommendations were published in a royal edict which banned the Muslims from using their family name, their dress and their language; compelling their women to show their faces, visits inside their homes, and not to lose sight of the Inquisitorial palace, whose officials were directed `to conduct and punish with customary rigor all infractions of religious discipline.'[1441]

On January 1, 1568, Christian priests were instructed to take all Muslim children, between the ages of three and fifteen, and place them in schools, where they should learn Castilian and Christian doctrine.[1442]

All these laws and measures needed force to be implemented, and from much earlier. In Aragon, at the close of the 15th century, fifty thousand Muslims were put to death and double that number compelled to renounce their religion.[1443] The Grand Inquisitor, Torquemada, revered in the annals of the Church as one of her most famous champions, and also the confessor of Queen Isabella, credited with the tortures of a hundred thousand `heretics' and the grief and misery of other unnumbered multitudes, inspired such policy.[1444]

In reaction to such measures the Muslims rose in rebellion. The last, and most formidable Muslim uprising was in the Alpujaras (the high peaks south of Spain) in 1568-1571. The numbers of those who rebelled did not exceed 4,000, before their numbers rose to 30,000, the bulk of the adult population of the region.[1445] Muslims, however, had been disarmed, had no military training, no munitions of war, no fortress and little money, whilst against them was the great Spanish monarchy, regarded as the most powerful in the world, with navies on every sea and armies in almost every land.[1446]

The uprising was to last until the Spring of 1571. It was a mixture of bravery, betrayal, and wholesale slaughter of Muslims. The Muslims were too few in number, and were fighting in atrocious conditions, while their women and children died of cold. Still, both women and children fought alongside the men, and women fought with bravery often superior to that

---

[1441] S.P. Scott: *History*; Vol II, op cit; p.259-60.
[1442] H.C. Lea: *A History of the Inquisition*; op cit; vol 3; p.336.
[1443] S.P. Scott: *History*; Vol II, op cit; p.167.
[1444] Ibid; p.171.
[1445] H. Kamen: *Spain: 1469-1714*; Longman; London; 1983; p. 173.
[1446] H.C. Lea: *The Moriscos of Spain;* op cit; p.232.

of the men, on foot and against Christian cavalry.[1447] The Muslims received aid from Algiers, the small coastal town of Sorbas, near Almeira, held by them, received weapons, munitions and Turkish volunteers.[1448] The Algiers government of Uluch Ali, one of the best Ottoman navy commanders, did not have sufficient means to carry out a large scale invasion, but his men could still reach the Spanish coast despite the Spanish coastal guard.[1449] More volunteers came from Morocco.[1450] It was not enough to win the war, but it explains why the uprising lasted until the Spring of 1571.[1451] The Christian Spaniards, for their part, brought armed men from Italy and Germany to join with the Spanish army in a war that was to cost them 60,000 soldier lives.[1452] The Spaniards also reinforced their ranks by releasing from prison all kinds of criminals and armed them.[1453] The war degenerated into a pandemonium of massacre of Muslims and pillage; nothing could restrain the ferocity of the troops as the armies were followed by merchants and adventurers ready to buy on the spot whatever was brought in: goods, cattle, slaves; in fact many of the so called military movements were merely slave hunts.[1454] In the end, the Muslim uprising was repressed in blood and fire. It was the last uprising before the Muslim presence in Spain was terminated some forty years later.

[1447] Luis del Marmol: *Historia del rebellion y castigo de los moriscos del reyno de Granada;* fol 113.r

[1448] R. De Zayas: *Les Morisques*; op cit; p. 235.

[1449] Ibid.

[1450] Ibid.

[1451] Ibid.

[1452] H.C. Lea: *The Moriscos of Spain;* op cit; p.308.

[1453] Luis del Marmol: *Historia del rebellion*; op cit; fol 129r and v.

[1454] H.C. Lea: *The Moriscos of Spain;* op cit; p.239.

The Inquisition

The Inquisition is a medieval Catholic invention. Its purpose was to remove `heretics' from the midst of Christians. In Spain, its main victims were the Muslims and Jews. Generally, they ended up tortured in dungeons, confessing whatever their accusers sought to make them confess, burnt at the stake, or disappeared for ever, their properties confiscated, their families thrown into perpetual want. The best work on the subject of Christian persecution of Muslims and the Jews by the Inquisition is by Henry Charles Lea. Today's works by Western `scholars' on the subject are not worth looking at. The best and most succinct work, which captures Lea's erudition, and outlines best the persecution of the Muslims and Jews is by Thomson and Rahim, and from it are derived the following brief extracts.

`The Inquisitors felt it their duty to investigate their (the Muslims' and Jews') minds, and to eliminate anyone whose words or deeds confirmed their suspicion. Their methods were even more callous and efficient than the ones which had been employed by the medieval Inquisition in France. According to Mariana:

`What caused the most surprise was that children paid for the crimes of their parents, and that accusers were not named or made known, nor confronted by the accused, nor was there publication of witnesses: all of which was contrary to the practice used of old in other tribunals.... And what was most serious was that because of these secret investigations, they were deprived of the liberty to hear and talk freely, since in all cities, towns and villages there were persons placed to give information of what went on. This was considered by some the most wretched slavery and equal to death.'[1455]

[1455] A. Thomson-M.A. Rahim: *Islam in Andalus;* op cit; p. 121.

c. The Elimination of the Muslims:

Because the Muslims were masters of skills, they were still needed for the well being of Spain. However, under papal pressure, the Spanish ruling classes were forced to terminate the Muslim presence. The removal of the Muslims was deemed necessary to purify Christian land. The Dominican Inquisitor Bleda, thus, held:

`The sins of these people are such that there are eyes to see them and hands to touch them, that even the plague which has devastated the kingdom in these latter years also come from their presence, and also resulting from their presence are all the woes and miseries which we suffer from, as well as the maritime disasters affecting us.

Oh Lord, give us a land that is purified and freed from heretics, and heavens will be given to you in exchange. If you expelled these heretics from our land, you will obtain the help of God to exterminate your enemies.' [1456]

In the eyes of devout Christians, according to Scott, Muslims were worse than pagans, even if they possessed all the requisites for good citizenship, and even if their intercourse with their neighbours was marked by evidence of honour and probity.[1457] They were suspected of practising Islam in secret, and the jealousy with which they guarded the privacy of their domestic life prevented the verification of this suspicion.[1458]

Archbishop of Grenada, Gurrero, returning from Trente in 1563, passed by Rome, and paid a visit to Pope Pie IV. The Pope listened and praised the zeal of this preacher who told him that `the flock was only Christian by name.'[1459] So the pope gave him a letter for King Philip II, remonstrating the king, that the scandal had lasted too long, and that it was time to rid the land of that `diabolical sect.'[1460] The Inquisitors themselves described `the Moriscos as Moors who would always be Moors and, if the Inquisition did not convert them, it at least compelled them to sin with less publicity and thus diminished their evil example.'[1461]

In exchange with the King in December 1601, Archbishop Ribera quoted the Old Testament texts ordering the enemies of God to be slain without mercy and setting forth the duties of kings to extirpate them.[1462] Don Juan de

---

[1456] In R. De Zayas: *Les Morisques*; op cit; pp. 468-9.
[1457] S.P. Scott: *History*; Vol II, op cit; p.259.
[1458] Ibid.
[1459] R de Zayas: *Les Morisques*; op cit; p.229.
[1460] Ibid.
[1461] Archivo hist.nacional, Inq.de Valencia, Leg.5, fol.185. 186 etc.
[1462] H.C. Lea: *The Moriscos of Spain*; op cit; p.308.

Ribera, Archbishop of Valencia incessantly worked for the ruin of these supposed heretics, either by exile or extermination.[1463] 'The Moriscos are obstinate, dogmatising heretics, and the only remedy is to drive them out of Spain: evils to be cured must be torn up by the roots, leaving no fragments to send up fresh shoots.'[1464] The Muslims were accused of every crime: treason, murder, kidnapping, blasphemy, sacrilege, and for Ribera, even the destruction of the Armada (the Spanish Fleet) was a divine judgment for the indulgence exhibited towards the enemies of the faith, and that the recent occurrences of earthquakes, tempests and comets was also attributed to the same cause.[1465] A letter from the king to Ribera confided 'in the divine favour, he had resolved on the expulsion of this evil race.'[1466]

The final removal of the Muslims throughout Spain was settled in the years 1609-1610. The operations were kept secret, and were conducted with military art, which combined both extreme trickery and ruthlessness. The policy was presented to the Muslims to concern only specific groups and regions. Thus, as the promulgation of the Valencia edict of expulsion alarmed both the Muslims in the neighbouring kingdoms, and in order to calm them, King Philip, on October 20, 1609, ordered the new viceroy, the Marquis of Aytona, to assure them that the matter did not concern them.[1467] Measures were also taken to carry the expulsion by successive steps. The expulsion of Muslims of Castile had been resolved upon by the council of State of September 15, 1609, but it was not to be attempted until the results in Valencia were known.[1468] And in order to avoid organised resistance, the removal was to be swift. A first order of the expulsion of the Andalusians and Murcians was signed by Philip III on 9 December 1609, and the modalities for expulsion were made public on 12 January in Seville, and on the 18th in Murcia. The edict required:
'The Moriscos to depart, under the pain of death and confiscation, without trial or sentence... to take with them no money, bullion, jewels or bills of exchange.... just what they could carry.'[1469]

So successful was the enterprise, in the space of months, Spain was emptied of its 'Moors'. Expelled were the Muslims of Aragon, Murcia, Catalonia, Castile, Mancha and Extremadura... Expelled were the people of Grenada

---

[1463] S.P. Scott: *History*; op cit; vol 3; p. 311.

[1464] H.C. Lea: *The Moriscos of Spain*; op cit; p.308

[1465] S.P. Scott: *History;* op cit; vol 3; p. 311.

[1466] H.C. Lea: *The Moriscos of Spain*; op cit; p.316,

[1467] Ibid; p.337

[1468] Ibid; p.348.

[1469] Ibid; p.345

who had throughout their lives, and who through various enquiries about them, had shown their good Christian credentials. A family, the Herrador, who for hundreds of years had been undoubted Christians, even holding positions in the Church and magistracy had yet to struggle against exile and confiscation.[1470] Most were herded like cattle onto ships, never certain of their destination. Many had to suffer the worst pain of having their children taken away from them to be baptised as Christians. Many atrocious deeds were committed on Muslims, which is needless to dwell upon here.[1471]

Many Muslims rose in rebellion, and fled to the Mountains. Unarmed, they were caught and butchered. In the Sierra del Aguar, 3000 died fighting. In the Muela de Cortes, 9,000 surrendered, were offered promise of safe conduct, before 6,000 of them were butchered on the spot.[1472] Most Muslims left without resistance. One of the Faquihs being asked why they obeyed a simple letter from the king, replied:

`Do you not know that many of us bought or stole boats in which to cross to Barbary with much danger? then why, when we are offered safe and free passage, should we not avail ourselves of it to go to the land of our ancestors, under our king the Turk, who will let us live as Moors and not as slaves, as we have been treated by our masters?'[1473]

[1470] Ibid; p.375.
[1471] This author is not going to go into the detail of the worst barbaric treatment the Muslims have been victim of. This is not the object of this work.
[1472] A. Thomson; M.A. Rahim: *Islam in Andalus;* op cit; p. 224.
[1473] H. C. Lea: *The Moriscos of Spain;* op cit; p.331.

How to Justify the Elimination of the Muslims

The Muslims had to be eliminated so as `to preserve the purity of the Christian land.' The mass elimination of Muslims from Spain, which was judged barbaric a century or so ago by most Western writers, increasingly today, is justified by modern Western historians and `scholars.' At the time the Muslims were eliminated, and in order to justify their elimination, they were depicted as barbaric criminals whose elimination was necessary for the safety of the country. Here is an excellent passage by De Zayas who shows how `Muslim crimes' were then exaggerated so as to justify their mass elimination:

`If I say: `yesterday a man killed another,' it would be assumed that this man, the murderer, could have acted differently, but this is a matter for justice to decide. However, if I say, `a Norman butchered a young, pregnant woman, and took great delight at such killing,' or `This morning, an Andalusian Muslim murdered an innocent French girl under the horrified eyes of her mother,' everyone would agree that all Normans, or Andalusians, are dreadful people, and that as a matter of emergency, it is necessary to take extreme measures against them. This is precisely what happened in Spain, as extracted from a note sent to the King of Spain, Philippe III, by a certain Martin Gonzales de Cellorigo Oquende, solicitor for the Inquisition of Valladolid. In seeking to demonstrate that the Muslims were murderers of the worst kind, he cited a horrific case:

`Andre Alonso, a good Christian, was taking five mules loaded with merchandise on the road of Valladolid to Burgos. He was attacked, robbed, decapitated, and his naked remains put in a bag. His head was never found, nor were ever recovered his mules, or merchandise. As at the time no corpse could be identified, that body could have been that of any person. The murderers were never found, but this hardly held our Inquisitor from using this incident and inflammatory rhetoric much reminiscent of today's media: this crime could only have been the work of the Moors, barbaric murderers infesting the highways; proof that it is necessary to put an end to their killings of the followers of Truth (i.e the Christians); these Moors giving free rein to their murderous deeds.'

This technique, (of using one horrific incident, committed (or not) by Muslims, and to generalise it to the whole community, to justify severe measures against them,) De Zayas concludes, is of course aged today, but `it still serves its purpose.'[1474]

[1474] R. De Zayas: *Les Morisques;* op cit; pp. 282-3.

EIGHT

THE OTTOMANS
(13th-18th Centuries)

A hundred and eighty years before the death of Barqooq, during Genghis Khan's invasion of Persia in 1220, a small Turkman tribe, of about four hundred families, fled the Mongol conqueror and settled at Surgut, on the Seljuk-Byzantine frontier, under the suzerainty of the Seljuk Sultan.[1475] Orthogrul became the soldier and subject of Aladin, and governed fifty-two years both in peace and war. He was the father of Thaman, or Athman, whose Turkish name has been melted into the appellation of the caliph Othman.[1476] Orthogrul was a heathen but his son, Othman, became a Muslim. Curiously enough, Othman was born in 1258, the year of the destruction of Baghdad by Hulagu. The descendants of Othman were to assume the name of the Othmanlis, a word corrupted in Europe to Ottoman.[1477] The Othmanlis' task, Glubb claims, was holy war, for the many centuries of existence of their empire, religion and war their guiding stars.[1478] Of course the Othmanlis also had a great system of administration and architecture, but these are not matters for this work to go into.[1479] It was the Ottomans, who, for centuries, kept the light of Islam fiercely alive, advancing and protecting the realm in hundreds of battles. It was the Ottomans who gave us Othman, himself, Bayazid I, Mohammed the Conqueror, and Suleyman the Magnificent, who became the heirs to other great Muslim heroes, whose careers and deeds have been seen in the previous chapters.

[1475] J. Glubb: *A Short History*; op cit; p.220.

[1476] E. Gibbon: *The Decline and Fall*; op cit; vol 7; p.23.

[1477] J. Glubb: *A Short History*; op cit; p.220

[1478] Ibid; p.230.

[1479] See for instance: O Aslanapa, *Turkish Art and Architecture* (1971); K. A. C. Creswell, *Early Muslim Architecture*, 2 vols. (1932-1940), Early Muslim Architecture, 2nd ed., I (1969); G Goodwin, *A History of Ottoman Architecture* (1971); E. Knobloch, *Beyond the Oxus: Archaeology, Art, and Architecture of Central Asia* (1972).

1. From Othman to Bayazid:

The 14th century witnessed a swift and lightening Turkish advance in Europe, Ottoman armies registering a succession of victories. From his stronghold at Yenishehr, Othman sent out expeditions against the nearest Greek towns, and captured many fortresses before the armies of the emperor moved out against him. When at length he met the Byzantine army at Baphoeum, in 1301, he crushed it and ravaged the whole of Bithynia, so that the Greeks dared not venture outside the walls of Nicaea.[1480] Encouraged by this success, Othman pushed his forces nearer the sea, then, gradually he advanced on the second city of the empire, Nicaea; and slowly he brought up his armies against Brusa, and erected two forts, whence for ten years he pressed the siege.[1481] Nicaea, the cradle of the Greek Church, for two generations the capital of the Greek Empire, was closely blockaded.[1482] Meanwhile Othman's flying cavalry ravaged the country as far as the Bosphorus and the Black Sea; the Turks' vessels harried the coast, the whole country trembling before Othman's unwearied onslaught.[1483] He had laid his plans well, and the great city of Brusa capitulated in 1326; Orkhan, his son, planted the Ottoman flag on its walls, and hastened to Sugut in time to tell the good news to his father.[1484] Othman lived to hear of the victory, and then died contented, at the age of seventy, after a reign of twenty-six years. His last wish was to be buried at Brusa, the new capital of the growing state; and this was soon done, and there did his sepulchre stand to the present century. His sword is still preserved at Constantinople, and each successive Sultan of his posterity was solemnly invested with the founder's blade by way of coronation.[1485]

Under Othman's son Orkhan, the Turks registered further advances. By the 1340s, the whole south coast of the Sea of Marmara and the Adriatic shore, but for a few cities, were in the hands of the Ottomans.[1486] The emperor Andronicus the Younger was vanquished and wounded by Orkhan, who subdued the whole province of Bithynia, as far as the shores of the Bosphorus and Hellespont. The Christians confessed the justice and

---

[1480] Finlay: History of Greece; iii; p. 387, in S. Lane Poole: *Turkey;* Khayats; Beirut; 1966 ed; originally published in 1908; p. 19.

[1481] S. Lane Poole: *Turkey;* op cit; p. 19.

[1482] Finlay: History pf Greece; iii; pp. 423-4; in S. Lane Poole: *Turkey*; op cit; p. 20.

[1483] S. Lane Poole: *Turkey*; op cit; p. 20.

[1484] Ibid.

[1485] Ibid; p. 23.

[1486] D. Vaughan: *Europe and the Turk*; Liverpool University Press; 1954; p. 10.

clemency of a reign which claimed the voluntary attachment of the Turks of Asia.[1487] In 1358 an earthquake hit the cities of Thrace; houses crumbled to the ground, and even the walls and fortifications fell to the trembling earth, while the terrified inhabitants fled from their shaking houses. Among the rest, the walls around Galipoli fell down, the people deserted the city, and over the ruins the Turks marched in. The Emperor in vain protested; Orkhan declared that providence had opened the city to his troops, and he could not disregard so clear an instance of divine interposition.[1488] The shore of the Hellespont was quickly garrisoned with Ottoman soldiers.

Orkhan died in 1359. He had lived to carry his arms to the confines of Asia Minor, and had even seen his horse-tails flying on the western shores of the Hellespont. His son, Murad, who was to succeed him, was to lead the Ottoman armies as far as the Danube.[1489] In 1371, the Turks crushed an alliance of Serbs, Hungarians, Wallachians and Napolese at the battle of Cernomen.[1490] In 1375, crossing the Balkans, the Turks took Nissa, one of the strongest fortresses of the Byzantine Empire. After a siege of twenty-five days the city capitulated, and the despot of Serbia, attacked in the heart of his kingdom, obtained peace on condition of his paying an annual tribute of a thousand pounds of silver, and furnishing a thousand horsemen to the Ottoman armies.[1491] The Kral of Bulgaria did not wait to be conquered, but humbly begged for mercy. Thus was the greater part of the two northern quarters made tributary to the Sultan.[1492] The Greek Emperor, who had not scrupled to become a convert to the Latin Church in order (as he vainly hoped) to secure the aid of the Pope and the Catholic powers, finding the Ottomans irresistible, declared himself a vassal of Murad.[1493] In 1380 the Turks captured Sofia and Nish, the northern Serb capital. Then, in 1389, the first Great battle of Kossovo took place, where the whole of Serbian nobility and power were finished. Serbia was now reduced to a small part of her former territory, and even this was brought under Turkish suzerainty.[1494] The Turkish armies were now fighting in Bosnia, Albania in the Peloponnesus and Wallachia.[1495] But the islands and fringes of the eastern

---

[1487] E. Gibbon: *The Decline and Fall*; vol 7; op cit; p.26.

[1488] S. Lane Poole: *Turkey*; op cit; p. 34.

[1489] Ibid; p. 35.

[1490] D. Vaughan: *Europe;* op cit; p. 21.

[1491] S. Lane Poole: *Turkey*; op cit; p. 40.

[1492] Ibid.

[1493] Ibid.

[1494] P. Wittek: The Ottoman Turks, from an Emirite of March warriors to an Empire; in *Royal Asiatic Society of Great Britain and Ireland*; 1965; pp. 33-51; reprinted in *The Islamic World and the West;* Edited by A.R. Lewis; op cit; pp. 106-18; at pp. 114 -5.

[1495] Ibid.

Mediterranean: Lesser Armenia, Cyprus, Rhodes, Crete, and the Aegean archipelago continued to be held by Christendom long after the Ottomans had broken into the Balkan Peninsula.[1496] For not too long, it seemed. The Turks had a mighty leader then: Bayazid (ruled 1389-1403).

Bayazid was known as the Thunderbolt, a title conferred to him on account of the rapidity of his movements in warfare.[1497] To stop Bayazid, Sigismund, King of Hungary and brother of the Emperor of the West, together with Pope Boniface IX (Pope1389-1404) preached a Crusade in 1394.[1498] Hungary has become the bulwark of Catholic Christendom, and her only chance of survival lay in arresting the advance of the Turks into the heart of Europe.[1499] In 1396 an army of Burgundians under John the Fearless, of Frenchmen under Marshal Boucicault, and of Hungarians under King Sigismund was formed.[1500] The Western armies reached Buda about the end of July. There, they found King Sigismund waiting with a force of some sixty thousand men.[1501] His vassal Mirceas, voyevod of Wallachia, had joined him with another ten thousand; and about thirteen thousand men came from Poland, Bohemia, Italy and Spain.[1502] English and German knights also came in large numbers, forming a total army of over 100,000 men, the elite of several nations.[1503] Amongst these were the Count de la Marche, three cousins of the French King, many of the flower of French chivalry, the Count of Hothenzollern, and the Grand master of the Knights of St John of Jerusalem, all accompanied by their followers.[1504] The aim of such a large Christian army was to defeat the Turks, cross the Hellespont, and rescue the Holy Land from `the Infidels.'[1505] Sigismund advised caution and prudence, but his allies envisaged a great offensive. The Turks would be overwhelmed and the Christian armies would advance triumphantly through Anatolia to Syria and the Holy Land itself.[1506] On hearing of the presence of the combined Christian armies, Bayazid made for the Danube,

---

[1496] J.J. Saunders: *Aspects of the Crusades*, op cit; p.48.
[1497] Sir Edwin Pears: The Ottoman Turks to the fall of Constantinople; in *The Cambridge Medieval History*, Vol IV; op cit; pp 653-705; p.674.
[1498] A.S. Atiya: *Crusade,* op cit; p. 148.
[1499] Ibid; p. 146.
[1500] D. J. Geanakoplos: *Medieval Western Civilisation, and the Byzantine and Islamic Worlds*, D.C. Heath and Company, Toronto, 1979; p.378.
[1501] S. Runciman: *A History of the Crusades*; op cit; vol 3; p. 457.
[1502] Ibid.
[1503] Sir Edwin Pears: The Ottoman Turks; op cit; p. 675.
[1504] S. Lane Poole: *Turkey;* op cit; p. 51.
[1505] Ibid.
[1506] S. Runciman: *A History of the Crusades*; op cit; vol 3; pp. 457-8.

and waited for the attack.[1507] In the battle which ensued, the Turks gave Europe its first lesson of their prowess.[1508] This battle is narrated by Lane Poole, and from his text are the following extracts:

`The allies marched through Serbia, whose king alone remained true to his treaty with Bayazid, and his lands were therefore plundered; they took Vidin and Orsova (where in both places, the Muslim population was slaughtered), and sat down before the strong city of Nicopolis, which, with Vidin, Sistova, and Silistria, formed the four great frontier fortresses on the Danube. Vidin had already surrendered; Nicopolis was the next to be attacked. Six days they pressed the siege by land and river, yet the Ottoman governor refused to surrender. The French knights, however, were not disturbed by this obstinacy, which was of the utmost value in detaining the invading army until the Sultan should come up with them; they ridiculed the mere thought of Bayazid's advance, declared that he would not dare to cross the Hellespont, and, betaking themselves to the wine and women that they had brought in shiploads down the Danube, they boasted in their cups that were the sky to fall, they would hold it up with their spears. When scouts brought word that the Sultan was within six hours' march of Nicopolis, the jovial boon-fellows laughed them to scorn, and Marshal Boucicault threatened to have the bearers' ears cut off for raising a false alarm. Bayazid heard of these "brave words," and in return swore that he would stable his horse at the high altar of St. Peter's at Rome. He was upon the allies before they could credit their eyes. When the Turkish troop were seen advancing in their usual perfect discipline, the young French nobles, full of wine and conceit, clamoured to begin the fight, and disregarding the counsel of Sigismund, who knew that the practice of the Turks was to put their worst troops in the van of battle, the hot-headed Frenchmen charged madly upon the foe, after first celebrating the occasion by a massacre of Turkish prisoners who had vainly trusted to their word of honour. Down they charged upon the Turkish front, and falling like a whirlwind upon the luckless skirmishers, whom Bayazid had thrown forward, cut them in pieces. Hacking right and left, the chivalry of France rode over their bodies, till they reached the Janissaries who were drawn up behind them; ten thousand of the flower of the Turkish army fell, before the Janissaries took refuge under cover of the cavalry. Still unchecked, the triumphant cavaliers rode pell-mell at the famous squadrons of the Sipähis, and five thousand horsemen went down before their stormy charge. Right through the third line of the enemy they rode, exulting in their victory; and ascending the high ground beyond, where

---

[1507] Edwin Pears: The Ottoman Turks; op cit; p.675.
[1508] Ibid.

they expected to see but the flying ruck of the Ottomans-they suddenly found themselves confronted by a forest of forty thousand lances, the main body of the Turkish army. Then they remembered, too late, the counsel of Sigismund; and seized with panic fear, the knighthood of France broke up and fled for its very life, pursued by the horsemen of Asia.....

The Christian infantry could not witness this fearful flight without dismay; the Hungarians and Vlachs on the right and the left wings of the main body took to their heels. The centre alone stood firm, where the king's own Magyar followers, the Systerians under Hermann Count of Cilli, and the Bavarians under the Elector, covered the retreat of the French cavaliers, and advanced in serried ranks, twelve thousand against the Turks.....

The battle was at an end; the remnants of the Christian army was cut down round the royal standard, and Sigismund was dragged away from the fatal field by the Count of Cilli, and harried into a boat by which he reached the Venetian fleet which was waiting to cooperate with the army at the mouth of the Danube. Instead of joining the attack, the task of the Venetians was narrowed to saving the few surviving leaders of a vanished host.'[1509]

The battle ended in a total disaster for Christian Europe; the elites of many nations had been slaughtered, a defeat, which spread great dismay amongst their countrymen and monarchs of Europe.[1510] Bayazid had won a great victory; in his rage, remembering the massacres of Muslims, he ordered his prisoners, to the number of three thousand, to be killed in cold blood, only sparing the few noblemen for whom a high ransom would be charged.[1511] The numbers of dead vary greatly, and many amongst the survivors died later in captivity; so considerable were the losses, the sad roll-call lengthened of those for whom the great French families mourned.[1512]

Four years later, by 1400 the Turks were masters of almost the whole of Anatolia, and had taken nearly all the European possessions of Byzantium, and there remained only Constantinople.[1513] The elites of the Christian armies had been decimated, and the road to Europe was open, except for the unexpected irruption of Timur the Lame (Timur Lang).[1514]

[1509] S. Lane Poole: *Turkey*; op cit; pp. 52-6.

[1510] E. Pears: The Ottoman Turks; op cit; p. 676.

[1511] S. Runciman: *A History of the Crusades*; op cit; vol 3; p. 461.

[1512] D. Vaughan: *Europe;* op cit; p. 39.

[1513] Paul Wittek: The Ottoman Turks-from an emirite; op cit; pp. 114 -5.

[1514] J.W. Draper: *A History*; op cit; Vol II; p.106.

From behind Bayazid erupted Timur the Lame, a `Muslim' of Mongol origins, but allied with Western Christendom. Prior to his war against Bayazid, Timur had already devastated the rest of the Muslim land in the late 1380s-1390s. In 1388 he invaded northern India and destroyed the Turkish armies; then in 1398, he sacked Delhi, massacred its inhabitants, and carried the treasure of the sultans home to Transoxeania.[1515] Conditions in northern India remained chaotic for a long time thereafter; and many cities in ruin.[1516] Everywhere his hordes went, farms, orchards, irrigation works, dams, schools… were razed to the ground.[1517] In Siwas, Timur had 120,000 people massacred, and in Aleppo, in Syria, and in Baghdad, it was another huge massacre, sparing none, regardless of age or sex.[1518] Timur even ordered his men to trample children reading the Qur'an.[1519]

After devastating the Muslim world, and supported by Western powers, Timur turned his attention to Bayazid. At the decisive battle of Angora, on 28 July 1402, Bayazid was betrayed by local contingents, who en masse deserted to Timur's side during the battle.[1520] At this battle, Timur had invited the Castilian embassies, that included Enrique Payo de Soto and Hernan Sanchez de Palazuelos, at their head, to watch the fierce fighting.[1521] The embassy returned to Castile with the news of the immense victory by Timur, which avenged previous Ottoman victories against the Christians.[1522] Bayazid was taken prisoner, put in a cage; his capital Brusa taken and burnt down.[1523] Worse for Bayazid, his Serbian wife, whose hand had been the price of Serbian autonomy thirteen years before, fell into the power of Timur, who compelled the Serbian Sultana to pour out his wine in the presence of her husband, no longer `the Thunderbolt' of Islam.[1524] Timur's victory had just stopped a Turkish advance that had begun to terrorize Christianity.[1525] Bayazid died eight months later, and Timur survived his humbled prisoner but two years. In that time, however, he had overrun the Turkish land in Asia, had occupied Nicaea, Brusa, and the other chief cities

---

[1515] E.R. Wolf: *Europe and the People without History*; University of California Press; Berkeley; 1982; p. 45.
[1516] Ibid.
[1517] N. Smith: *A History of Dams,* The Chaucer Press, London, 1971; p. 86.
[1518] Sir Edwin Pears: The Ottoman Turks; op cit; pp.679-80.
[1519] Ibid; p.684.
[1520] Paul Wittek: The Ottoman Turks-from an emirite; op cit; p.115.
[1521] R.De Zayas: *Les Morisques;* op cit; p. 136.
[1522] Ibid.
[1523] Sir Edwin Pears: The Ottoman Turks; op cit; p.682.
[1524] W. Miller: The Balkan States; *The Cambridge Medieval History,* Vol IV; op cit; pp 552-93; p.562.
[1525] A. Mieli: *La Science Arabe;* op cit; p.149.

of the coast.[1526] 'The Empire of the Turks, built up with so much skill and bravery, till it had become the terror of Europe, crumbled to dust before the Asiatic despot,' says Lane Poole.[1527] The history of the Ottomans seemed to have suddenly come to an end.

[1526] S. Lane Poole: *Turkey;* op cit; p. 73.
[1527] Ibid.

The Great Othman

Lane Poole describes Othman:
`Personally, like the first Caliphs of the Arabs, he was simple and primitive in his tastes and habits. He left neither silver nor gold behind him; but only a salt-bowl-symbol of hospitality,-a spoon, a braided coat and white linen turban, his standards, a fine stud of horses, a yoke of oxen, and some flocks of sheep, whose descendants still browse upon the pastures of Brusa. Simple as was his dress, his figure was imposing. His arms reached below his knees, his thighs were those of a horseman and his prominent nose, black hair and beard, and swarthy hue, procured him the name of 'Black Othman," for black is a colour of honour in the East, and indicates strength of character as well as bodily vigour and energy. Black Othmān transmitted his Physical characteristics to several generations of his successors, and for at least three hundred years there sat no Sultan on the Ottoman throne who was not distinguished for personal courage. Bravery is the heritage of the Turk.'[1528]

[1528] Ibid; pp. 23-4.

2. Turkish Revival and the Conquest of Constantinople:

Timur's irruption had given Europe a salutary respite, and weakened the Ottomans considerably, even allowing the Europeans to recover much of their territory. At the moment when Timur's armies were ravaging the southern shores of the Bosphorous and the Greek empire was almost rousing from its long sleep and retaking its lost provinces in Europe, the Turkish power might well be said to be annihilated; yet within a dozen years the lost provinces were reunited under the strong and able rule of Mohammed I, and the Ottoman Empire, far from being weakened by the apparent crushing blow it had received in 1402, rose stronger and more vigorous after its fall, and, 'like a giant refreshed prepared for new and bolder feats of conquest.'[1529]

In June 1444 a truce was concluded for ten years between the Ottoman Murad II (1421-51) and the king of Hungary John Hunyadi and his allies. Murad, a philosopher, who loved meditation, and who wished to live at peace accepted the truce, but his enemies would not allow him; the treaty solemnly accepted was almost immediately broken.[1530] The story, whether told by Turks or Christians, showed bad faith on the side of the Christians, the Pope Legate Cardinal Julian Cesarini declaring that an oath with the infidel might be set aside and broken.[1531] The Battle of Varna followed. At the battle, the Turks displayed the violated treaty upon a lance.[1532] The battle ended with a crushing Turkish victory, the Christian army totally destroyed.[1533]

Threatened by the Turks, the Byzantine Emperor rushed in 1452 to declare in St Sophia the Act of Union between the two churches, East and West, thereby acknowledging the primacy of Rome.[1534] Which was opposed by the population and also by the future Patriarch Gennadios and other dignitaries, one of whom, Lucas Notaras said: 'it would be better to have in Constantinople the rule of the Turkish turban than the Latin mitre.'[1535]
Still, an alliance of Catalans, Spaniards, Germans and Sicilians, Genoese and Venetian pirates,[1536] and mercenaries from other nations came to the aid of

---

[1529] Ibid; p. 75.
[1530] Sir E. Pears: The Ottoman Turks; op cit; p. 691.
[1531] Ibid.
[1532] Ibid.
[1533] A.S. Atiya: *Crusade;* op cit; p. 150.
[1534] Ibid; p. 151.
[1535] M. Ducas: Historia Byzantina; ed. By I. Bekker (*Corpus Scriptorum Historia Byzantinae*; Bonn 1834; p. 264; in A.S. Atiya: *Crusade*; op cit; p.151.
[1536] A.S. Atiya: *Crusade*; op cit; pp 151-2.

the empire to fight the Ottomans.[1537] Constantinople submitted to three successive Ottoman assaults in two days (May 28-9) 1453. Following the third assault, to the Church of St Sophia, said Draper rushed a crowd of women and children, priests and monks, religious virgins, and men, superstitious to the last, in this supreme moment, expecting the fulfilment of a prophecy that, 'when the Turks should have forced their way to the square before that church, their progress would be arrested, for an angel with a sword in his hand would descend from heaven and save the city of the Lord.' The Turks burst into the square, but the angel never came.[1538] The Turks took the city.

The Ottoman taking of Constantinople caused an explosion of emotions in Christian Europe. For Christian I, King of Denmark and Norway, 'the Grand Turk was the beast rising out of the sea described in the Apocalypse.'[1539] A Georgian chronicler wrote: 'on the day when the Turks took Constantinople the sun was darkened.'[1540] Contemporaries dwelt in their writing upon every morbid detail of the inhumanity of the Turks, and the stereotyped Turk, savage and bloodthirsty, swooping down upon innocent Christians, and massacring them indiscriminately, became firmly established in the tradition of the West.[1541]

In truth, there was hardly any ground for such tales of Turkish horrors. At the taking of Constantinople, the Turks caused less harm than the Latin crusaders when they looted the city in the wake of the fourth crusade of 1204.[1542] As soon as they entered Constantinople, the Ottomans recognised the collective existence of religious minorities, instituting them into nations, giving them the autonomy in religious matter, judicial, cultural, and health care.[1543] The Greek Orthodox Patriarch was established at the head of the first of the Christian *Millet* of the empire, this high personality weighing with all his spiritual and temporal authority on all Orthodox of the Empire, from the Adriatic Sea to the Arab/Persian Gulf.[1544]

[1537] Sir E. Pears: The Ottoman Turks; op cit; p.657

[1538] J.W. Draper: *A History*; op cit; Vol II; p.108.

[1539] *Loci e libro veritatum*; ed. J.E.T. Rogers (Oxford, 1881); p. 158; *Chronicles of London*, Ed. C.L. Kingsford (Oxford, 1905); p. 164.

[1540] Quoted in A.A. Vasiliev: *History of the Byzantine Empire*; vol I; Madison, 1952; p 655.

[1541] Note 47: Cf. M. Gilmore: *The World of Humanism*; 1453-1517 (New York, 1952); pp 20-1, who believes that such a view of the Turk was the product of the literature of the 16th century.

[1542] A.A. Vasiliev: *History*; vol 1; op cit; p 653.

[1543] Y. Courbage, P. Fargues: *Chretiens et Juifs*; op cit; p.9.

[1544] Ibid; p.205.

The Taking of Constantinople
(Abridged from the lengthy description by Gibbon)[1545]

`In the beginning of the spring of 1453, the Turkish vanguard swept the towns and villages as far as the gates of Constantinople.... (Mohammed II) first halted at the distance of five miles; and from thence advancing in battle array, planted before the gates of St. Romanus the Imperial standard; and on the sixth day of April formed the memorable siege of Constantinople...

The reduction of the city appeared to be hopeless, unless a double attack could be made from the harbour as well as from the land; but the harbour was inaccessible: an impenetrable chain was now defended by eight large ships, more than twenty of a smaller size, with several galleys and sloops; and, instead of forcing this barrier, the Turks might apprehend a naval sally, and a second encounter in the open sea. In this perplexity, the genius of Mahomet conceived and executed a plan of a bold and marvellous cast, of transporting by land his lighter vessels and military stores from the Bosphorus into the higher part of the harbour. (Although) the distance is about ten miles; the ground is uneven, and was overspread with thickets.... A level way was covered with a broad platform of strong and solid planks; and to render them more slippery and smooth, they were anointed with the fat of sheep and oxen. Fourscore light galleys and brigantines, of fifty and thirty oars, were disembarked on the Bosphorus shore; arranged successively on rollers; and drawn forwards by the power of men and pulleys. Two guides or pilots were stationed at the helm, and the prow, of each vessel: the sails were unfurled to the winds; and the labour was cheered by song and acclamation. In the course of a single night, this Turkish fleet painfully climbed the hill, steered over the plain, and was launched from the declivity into the shallow waters of the harbour, far above the molestation of the deeper vessels of the Greeks...

As soon as Mahomet had occupied the upper harbour with a fleet and army, he constructed, in the narrowest part, a bridge, or rather a mole, of fifty cubits in breadth, and one hundred in length: it was formed of casks and hogsheads; joined with rafters, linked with iron, and covered with a solid floor. On this floating battery he planted one of his largest cannon....

The fortifications, which had stood for ages against hostile violence, were dismantled on all sides by the Ottoman cannon: many breaches were opened; and near the gate of St. Romanus, four towers had been levelled with the ground.

[1545] E. Gibbon: *The Decline and Fall*; op cit; vol 7; pp. 159-93.

Mahomet, to the prince he offered a rich equivalent, to the people a free toleration, or a safe departure: but after some fruitless treaty, he declared his resolution of finding either a throne, or a grave, under the walls of Constantinople....

Several days were employed by the sultan in the preparations of the assault. On the evening of the twenty-seventh of May, he issued his final orders; assembled in his presence the military chiefs, and dispersed his heralds through the camp to proclaim the duty, and the motives, of the perilous enterprise.

In this holy warfare, the Muslims were exhorted to purify their minds with prayer, their bodies with seven ablutions; and to abstain from food till the close of the ensuing day.... The camp re-echoed with the Muslim shouts of "God is God: there is but one God, and Mohammed is the apostle of God."

Far different was the state of the Christians; who, with loud and impotent complaints, deplored the guilt, or the punishment, of their sins. The celestial image of the Virgin had been exposed in solemn procession; but their divine patroness was deaf to their entreaties: they accused the obstinacy of the emperor for refusing a timely surrender.

The Night preceding the 29 of May, the troops, the cannons, and the fascines, were advanced to the edge of the ditch, which in many parts presented a smooth and level passage to the breach; and his fourscore galleys almost touched, with the prows and their scaling-ladders, the less defensible walls of the harbour.... At daybreak, without the customary signal of the morning gun, the Turks assaulted the city by sea and land; and the similitude of a twined or twisted thread has been applied to the closeness and continuity of their line of attack.

In that fatal moment, the Janissaries arose, fresh, vigorous, and invincible. The sultan himself on horseback, with an iron mace in his hand, was the spectator and judge of their valour: he was surrounded by ten thousand of his domestic troops, whom he reserved for the decisive occasion; and the tide of battle was directed and impelled by his voice and eye. His numerous ministers of justice were posted behind the line, to urge, to restrain, and to punish; and if danger was in the front, shame and inevitable death were in the rear, of the fugitives. The cries of fear and of pain were drowned in the martial music of drums, trumpets, and attaballs (drums); and experience has proved, that the mechanical operation of sounds, by quickening the circulation of the blood and spirits, acts on the human machine more forcibly than the eloquence of reason and honour. From the lines, the galleys, and the bridge, the Ottoman artillery thundered on all sides; and the camp and city, the Greeks and the Turks, were involved in a cloud of smoke which could only be dispelled by the final deliverance or destruction of the Roman Empire.

The first who deserved the sultan's reward was Hassan the Janissary, of gigantic stature and strength. With his cimeter in one hand and his buckler in the other, he ascended the outward fortification: of the thirty Janissaries, who were emulous of his valour, eighteen perished in the bold adventure. Hassan and his twelve companions had reached the summit: the giant was precipitated from the rampart: he rose on one knee, and was again oppressed by a shower of darts and stones. But his success had proved that the achievement was possible: the walls and towers were instantly covered with a swarm of Turks; and the Greeks, now driven from the vantage ground, were overwhelmed by increasing multitudes. Amidst these multitudes, the emperor, who accomplished all the duties of a general and a soldier, was long seen and finally lost.

The victorious Turks rushed through the breaches of the inner wall; and as they advanced into the streets, they were soon joined by their brethren, who had forced the gate Phenar on the side of the harbour. In the first heat of the pursuit, about two thousand Christians were put to the sword; but soon the victors acknowledged, that they should immediately have given quarter if the valour of the emperor and his chosen bands had not prepared them for a similar opposition in every part of the capital. It was thus, after a siege of fifty-three days, that Constantinople, which had defied the power of Chosroes, the Chagan, and the caliphs, was irretrievably subdued by the arms of Mahomet The Second.'

3. From Constantinople to the Siege of Vienna:

After Constantinople, the Ottomans expanded in the Balkans and Greece. The Black Sea became Ottoman lake. In the heart of Anatolia, the emirate of Kraman was again absorbed into the empire.[1546] Between 1459 and 1467, Serbia and Bosnia submitted to Ottoman rule. Vlad of Valachia and Etinne of Moldavia were soon defeated. In 1475, Turkish warships took Caffa, the main Genoese outpost. Under Bayazid II (1481-1512), between 1499 and 1502, the Turks took from the Latin, the Morea and the Aegean islands.[1547]

Just as a century earlier, the Ottomans were once more threatening to overwhelm the whole of Europe, and once more, like a century before, the Turkish advance was held up by diversions arising on their Asian front, this time, the work of the Safavids of Persia.[1548] In 1505, the Safavid Shah Ismail sent a letter to the doge in Venice; he said:
`To the sultan of the Venetians, our great friend,... Words cannot explain, nor pen write, nor intellect comprehend the love that we have for you...'[1549]
In 1510, Ismail sent to the Ottoman Sultan Bayazid II in Istanbul a gift: the head of the defeated Ottoman ally, the Central Asian monarch: Shaiban Khan.[1550]
Shah Ismails' mortal enemies were the Ottoman Turks, whose eradication was vital to him, and he viewed the Christians as his brothers and partners in a struggle to the death against the Turks.[1551] Thus, he became not just a hero for the Christians, but also a saviour of Christendom.[1552]

Shah Ismail diverted Turkish efforts from Europe, but at the Battle of Chaldiran (1514), the Turks crushed the Safavids, as here recounted by a European contemporary:

[1546] P.M. Holt: *Egypt and the Fertile Crescent: 1522-1922;* Cornell Paperbacks; Ithaca; New York; 1966; p.27.
[1547] A.S. Atiya: *Crusades;* op cit; p. 154.
[1548] V.J. Parry: Renaissance Historical Literature; in *Historians of the Middle East*; Ed by B. Lewis and P.M. Holt; Oxford University Press; London; 1962; pp. 278-289; at p. 279.
[1549] Sanuto: I Diarii: 6: 269 in P. Brummett: The Myth of Shah Ismail Safavi: Political Rhetoric and `Divine' Kingship; in J. V. Tolan: *Medieval*; op cit; pp 331-59; p. 348.
[1550] P. Brummett: The Myth of Shah Ismail Safavi; op cit; p. 331.
[1551] Ibid; p. 332.
[1552] Ibid.

'The Turks slew many of his people, and he (Ismail) took flight. The Turk followed in pursuit, still slaying many, until he arrived in the land of Persia, whence he turned back to Turkey. This was the first time that Xeque Ismael had been overcome, by which he was greatly grieved, and determined to meet the Turk another time, but provided with artillery and in much greater strength than before.'[1553]

These conflicts between Safavids and Turks, as Saunders concludes, were fatal to Islam's chances of successfully meeting the European challenge on the seas.[1554]

The Turks also diverted great armies elsewhere to fight the Spaniards and Portuguese who were threatening Muslim North Africa. Ceuta in Morocco was taken by the Portuguese in 1415, and on 18 February 1416 Prince Henry was delegated his first powers to defend this newly conquered place.[1555] In 1458, the Portuguese subsequently took Ksar-el-Srir, an advanced outpost towards Tangiers, and made further advances into Anfa between Azemour and Rabat. A great expedition against Tangier in 1463 was unsuccessful, but the town eventually fell in 1471, followed soon by Arzila.[1556]

The treaty of Alcacovas of 4 September 1479 between Spain and Portugal delimited their respective zones of influence. And following the taking of Grenada in 1492, it became the turn for Spain to lead the offensive against North Africa, in pursuit of the Spanish-Papal policy of prolonged attack on Islam.[1557] The project of carrying the crusade against the Muslims to the other side of the Mediterranean was upheld from 1492. Archbishop Cisneros vociferously urged the permanent occupation of the central Maghrib and the foundation of a Spanish empire.[1558] The Spaniards took Melila (1497), Mers el-Kebir (1505), and in 1509, seized Wahran (Oran) and in 1510 Bejaia and Tripoli.[1559] Ferdinand's orders to his border commanders were to maintain these posts as defensive bastions where only Christians resided while allied Muslim tribes provided a shield against the hostile confederations of the

---

[1553] M.L. Dames trans of: The Book of Duarte Barbosa, vol 1; London; 1918; pp. 82-7 in J.J. Saunders ed: *The Muslim World on the Eve of Europe's Expansion*; Prentice Hall Inc; New Jersey; 1966; pp. 37-8.

[1554] J.J. Saunders: *The Muslim World;* op cit; p. 6.

[1555] P. Chaunu: *European Expansion in the Later Middle Ages*; tr by K. Bertram; North Holland Publishing Company; Amsterdam; 1979; p. 112.

[1556] M.L. de Mas Latrie: *Traites de paix*; op cit; p.324.

[1557] F. Fernandez Armesto: *Before Columbus;* Mc Millan; London; 1987; p.148.

[1558] J.M. Abun Nasr: *A History of the Maghrib*; op cit; p. 162.

[1559] A C. Hess: *The Forgotten Frontier*; The University of Chicago Press, Chicago and London, 1978; p.42.

outer frontier.[1560] The Spaniards built a massive fort, the Penon, on an island in Algiers harbour, from which the city could be bombarded at a range of only three hundred yards.[1561] Algeria was on the way of being overwhelmed by Spanish conquest. The Sheikhs of Algeria called for the Ottoman Turks to intervene, the Turks `being the most formidable nation of the period, and the most warlike people of that time.'[1562]

On behalf of the Ottoman sultan, the Barbarossa brothers, sons of a coasting trading of Mitylene on the Island of Lesbos, but possibly of Albanian origin,[1563] arrived and established their headquarters in the Algerian eastern town of Jijel, and on the Island of Djerba. In 1515, the elder brother, Arooj, recaptured Algiers from the Spaniards.[1564] Later in the same year, a Spanish fleet with ten thousand men was sent against Algiers under the command of Diego de Vera. Arooj was informed, and waited for it to land, before slaying the whole Spanish army on the shores of the city.[1565] In 1517, Khair Eddin, the other Barbarossa brother, defeated a new Spanish expedition under Ugo de Moncada in front of Algiers; considerable numbers of Spaniards were taken prisoners and sent to Selim I in Constantinople.[1566] The danger of a Christian conquest of North Africa was, thus, averted by the arrival of the so called Barbarossa brothers.[1567] Bejaia was retaken from the Spaniards in 1555 by Salah Reis, Beylerbey of Algiers; whilst Tripoli was recovered in 1551 by Sinan Pasha and Turgut. The Spaniards renewed attempts to retake these places were repulsed. To avert further Christian advance, Turks and Algerians constituted the fraternity, which fought Christendom for centuries, and which Western historians call corsairs.

Having just saved North Africa from Christian expansion, the Turks pursued their advance elsewhere despite the fact that the Christian West was now immensely stronger. The 16th century, it ought to be reminded, was the century when Europe expanded into America, and drew huge resources from that continent, just as it did from Africa.[1568] Huge Western Christian armies, equipped with artillery and powerful navies scoured the

---

[1560] Ibid.
[1561] J. Glubb: *A Short History*; op cit; p.262.
[1562] G. Fisher: *The Barbary Legend;* Oxford; 1957. p. 36.
[1563] J. Glubb: *A Short History*; op cit; p.262.
[1564] Ibid.
[1565] R. De Zayas: *Les Morisques*; op cit; p. 157.
[1566] Ibid; p. 159.
[1567] J. Glubb: *A Short History*; op cit; p.262.
[1568] See R. Garaudy: *Comment l'Homme;* op cit; on the exploitation of these continents and the wealth derived from them.

land and seas. And all of them were leagued against the Turks. The most remarkable feat, Lane Poole notes, 'that the Turks achieved during this glorious century (16th century) was that they survived it. With such forces as were arrayed against them, with a Europe roused from its long sleep, and ready to seize arms and avenge its long disgrace upon the infidels, it was to be expected that the fall of the Ottoman power must ensue. Instead, this power was not only able to meet the whole array of rejuvenated Europe on equal terms, but emerged from the conflict stronger and more triumphant than ever.'[1569]

Under Suleiman I, the Magnificent (1520-66), the Turks managed to take Rhodes in 1522. On August 29, 1526 was fought the Battle of Mohacs, in which the Franco-Hungarian armies were literally wiped out by a supposedly broken Turkish front; the Hungarian elite as well as the French, all perishing, and perished the Hungarian kingdom, too.[1570] Three years later, in 1529, Suleiman put Vienna under siege. At that time, from the Adriatic to the Gange, to the Gulf of Bengal, from the Steppes of Russia or Turkmenistan to the sands of Arabia and Sahara, Driault holds, the Ottomans had made of their diverse tribes an empire larger than that of the Arabs before them, greater than that of Alexander.[1571] As Sir Edward Greasy says:
'Sultan Suleyman left to his successors an empire to the extent of which few permanent additions were ever made, except the islands of Cyprus and Candia, and which under no subsequent Sultan maintained or recovered the wealth, power, and prosperity which it enjoyed under the great lawgiver of the house of Othman. The Turkish dominions in his time comprised all the most celebrated cities of biblical and classical history, except Rome, Syracuse, and Persepolis. The sites of Carthage, Memphis, Tyre, Nineveh, Babylon, and Palmyra were Ottoman ground; and the cities of Alexandria, Jerusalem, Smyrna, Damascus, Nice, Brusa, Athens, Philippi, and Adrianople... obeyed the Sultan. The Nile, the Jordan, the Orontos, the Euphrates, the Tigris, the Tanais, the Borysthenes, the Danube, the Hebrus, and the Ilyssus, rolled their waters 'within the shadows of the Horsetails.' The eastern recess of the Mediterranean, the Propntis, the Palus Maeotis, the Euxine, and the Red Sea, were Turkish lakes. The Ottoman crescent touched the Atlas and the Caucasus; it was supreme over Athos, Sinai, Olympus, Pelion, Haemus, the Carpathian and the Acroceraunian heights. An empire of more than forty million square

---

[1569] S. Lane Poole: *Turkey;* op cit; p. 166.

[1570] D. Vaughan: *Europe;* op cit; p. 114.

[1571] E. Driault: *La Question d'Orient*; Librairie Felix Alcan; Paris; 1921; p.26.

miles, embracing many of the richest and most beautiful regions of the world, had been acquired by the descendants of Ertoghrul, in three centuries from the time when their forefather wandered a homeless adventurer at the head of less than five hundred fighting men.'[1572] Never has Islam been so powerful. Christianity was shaking in fear.[1573]

The Turks were not just in control of a vast empire militarily, they also demonstrated able organisation, skilful administration, and excellent treatment of their subjects. More importantly, as Finlay insists:
`The respect with which Othman and his successors were regarded by the countless Muslims and Christian tribes, subjects who flocked to their standards and gladly submitted to their authority, is sure proof of real superiority. Other barbarous races have risen to power and conquered rich provinces, only to succumb to the vices to luxury and demoralisation. The Ottomans long retained their pristine vigour and morality.'[1574]
16th century travellers also commented upon the prosperity and happiness of Ottoman society. Christian peasants in the conquered lands were not dispossessed of their lands, and their rights and privileges were protected by Ottoman laws.[1575] All religions are to be found side by side in the vast pacific dominion of the Sultan, and Catholicism was deemed freer in Constantinople and at Smyrna than at Paris and at Lyons; no law restraining its outward practice.[1576] Equally in the 17th century, the Frenchman De la Croix, an interpreter at Constantinople, witnessed in his unpublished *Memoires*, how the Ottomans allowed the same freedom of worship for Christians just as they could find in France; and was impressed by the treatment of slaves, noting that their spiritual needs were not at all neglected, benefiting of chapels inside the prisons where they can pray in all freedom.[1577]

What is also remarkable is that no nation other than the Ottomans ever managed to put together a succession of remarkable rulers. As Lane Poole sums up:
`No other dynasty can boast such a succession of brilliant sovereigns as those who conducted the Ottomans to the height of renown in the 14th, 15th, and

---

[1572] Sir E. Greasy: *History of the Ottoman Turks*; 1877 ed; p. 197.

[1573] E. Driault: *La Question d'Orient*; op cit; p.26.

[1574] Finlay; History of Greece; iii; p. 475; in S. Lane Poole: *Turkey*; op cit; p. 76.

[1575] David. M. Traboulay: *Columbus and Las Casas;* University Press of America, New York, 1994; p.70.

[1576] J. Davenport: *An Apology;* op cit; pp.126-7.

[1577] In A. Gunny: *Images of Islam in Eighteenth Century Writing*; Grey Seal, London, 1996; p.18.

16th centuries. Orkhan, the taker of Nicaea and founder of the Janissaries; Murad I, the conqueror of Kosovo, Bayazid I, the victor at Nicopolis; Mohammed I, the restorer of the shattered empire; Murad II, the antagonist of Hunyady and of Skandeberg; Mohammed II, the conqueror of Constantinople; Selim I, who annexed Kurdistan, Syria and Egypt; and Sulayman the Magnificent, the victor on the field of Mohacs, and the besieger of Vienna. Never did eight such sovereigns succeed one another (save for the feeble Bayazid II) in unbroken succession in any other country; never was an empire founded and extended during two such splendid centuries by such a series of great rulers.'[1578]

[1578] S. Lane Poole: *Turkey;* op cit; p. 78.

Conquered People Under Turkish Rule

The following extracts from Turkish directive following the conquest of Cyprus in 1572 show how the Turkish state was extremely eager to protect its conquered subjects. The Firman of May 6, 1572 addressed to the Beylerbey, Kadi and Defterdar of Cyprus says:

`The island of Cyprus has been captured by force; therefore the situation of the reaya (conquered subjects) somewhat deteriorated. So, no violence should be done to them; they should be treated with justice. It is important both in the enforcement of the decision of the shari'a and in the levying of state taxes, to regard and protect them, so that the country may thus revert to its former prosperous state. Thus, I order that you must be careful in giving the reaya who are a trust from God to us, as much protection and mercy as you can, abstaining from such actions as may lead to their dispersion. It is my desire to ensure that everybody may attend to his daily work and concerns with a mind free from discomfort and anxiety, and that the island may be restored to its former flourishing condition. Those responsible for scattering the reaya through oppressing them and imposing too heavy taxes on them shall be chastised.'[1579]

[1579] A. Refik in *Edebiyat Fakultesi mec.* V (1926); p. 71; Document 47; in H. Inalcik: Ottoman Policy and Administration in Cyprus after the Conquest; reprinted in H. Inalcik: *The Ottoman Empire: Conquest, Organization and Economy;* Variorum; London; 1978; pp. 5-23; at p. 7.

4. The Decline of the Ottomans:

A number of factors leagued against the Ottomans, and caused their decline. One such factor was the weaker rulers who followed Suleiman the magnificent, which at once stimulated discontent among the subject people, and cupidity and ambition among the Western powers.[1580] 'As successive sultans increasingly abandoned the cares of government for the pleasures of the harem,' Vaughan observes, 'corruption and incompetence spread through the administration and weaknesses at the centre encouraged provincial governors to deal as they pleased with their districts.'[1581] Ottoman sultans such as Selim II and Murad III were endowed with negative virtues such as drunkenness and lechery that allowed authors to praise the Spanish ruling class by contrast.[1582] When an able ruler Murad IV had ascended the throne in 1623, it was after sixty years of confusion under seven weak sultans.[1583] By the time he had come to power, much had already worked against the Ottomans.

The Ottomans were severely weakened by their wars with the Safavids of Persia. The defeat of Ismail Shah in 1514 at Chaldiran was not the end of Safavid wars against the Turks. In 1533, just as the Ottomans were engaged in their wars in Europe, Shah Tahmasp launched an offensive from the rear against them, capturing Tabriz and overrunning the country to the north of the city.[1584] Western powers kept the momentum, sending missions, envoys, and armaments to the Safavids.[1585] From England Anthony Sherley travelled to Persia, and also to Morocco to stir them against the Turks.[1586] The Moroccans refused to ally themselves with the Christians against the Turks, but Sherley had great success with the Safavids.[1587] From the Portuguese they received artillery, and their needs in this respect were also met by Philip II of Spain so as to fight the Ottomans.[1588] Early in the 17th century, better armed, the Safavids launched their greatest onslaught on the Ottomans in a thirteen year war from 1603 to 1619. They managed to wrest from them Erivan, Shirvan and Kars. In a

---

[1580] D. Vaughan: *Europe and the Turk*; op cit; 212.
[1581] Ibid.
[1582] A.C. Hess: *The Forgotten Frontier*; op cit; p.194.
[1583] J. Glubb: *A Short History*; op cit; p.234.
[1584] S. Chew: *The Crescent and the Rose*; Oxford University Press; 1937; p. 252.
[1585] Ibid.
[1586] Ibid; pp. 239-97.
[1587] Ibid.
[1588] D. Vaughan: *Europe;* op cit; p. 209.

concerted push, the Spaniards launched in 1603 an assault on Turkish North Africa to coincide with Safavid's renewal of hostilities in the east.[1589] The wars against the Safavids stretched the Ottomans,[1590] then after a seven year break, the Safavid attacks resumed in the 1620s.[1591]

The Western alliances against the Turks grew stronger, too. In 1538 the Holy League against the Turks was formed. Even the king of France, although an ally of the Sultan, made his vow against Islam.[1592] On the Western front, the Turks fought Hungarians, Austrians, Spaniards, Venetians, Poles, Russians, armies of the Pope, and also the French and the English.[1593] In the East, the Ottomans fought the Safavids and Armenians on land, and the Portuguese in the Red Sea and the Arabian Sea for decades uninterrupted after the 1550s.[1594] In the West, in 1571 the Turks and their Algerian allies suffered a crushing defeat, their fleet decimated at the Battle of Lepanto off the Greek coast by the united Christian navies. The Venetian navy remained a constant threat throughout the 1640s, especially in the Dardanelles, culminating in 1656 in the destruction of the Ottoman navy, thus blocking the Mediterranean route to the Muslims.[1595] The Ottomans registered some victories in Wallachia, Crete, Novigrad during the 1660s,[1596] but, throughout the 1670s, until they lifted their second siege of Vienna, in 1683, they had to face alliances of Poles, Austrians, Russians, Ukrainians, and also the French, all leagued against them.[1597] In 1683, the Turks were forced to lift their second siege of Vienna pressed by an alliance of Austrians, Poles and Germans. The banner seized from the Grand Vizier was sent to Pope Innocent XI and proudly displayed on top of the main portal of St Peter's.[1598] It was the best symbol of Turkish reversal of fortunes.

1699, the last year of the 17th century was the last year of an era, too. Weakened by incessant wars, the Ottomans signed the treaty of Karlowitz, signalling the end of Ottoman might. At this juncture, England, in the person of Lord Paget, her ambassador at the Porte, offered her mediation, which was

---

[1589] Ibid.

[1590] Ibid.

[1591] H. Inalcik: An Overview of Ottoman History; in *The Great Ottoman, Turkish Civilisation*; ed by H. Inalcik; Ankarra; 2000; pp. 3-104; at p. 96.

[1592] B. Heyberger: Les Chretiens Arabes et l'ideologie de la croisade (XVII-XVIII siecles) in *De Toulouse a Tripoli*, op cit; pp: 221-36; p.222.

[1593] See for details E. Driault: *La Question d'Orient*; op cit.

[1594] P. Coles: *The Ottoman Impact on Europe*; Thames and Hudson; 1974; p. 78.

[1595] See for details E. Driault: *La Question*; op cit; and for brief accounts H. Inalcik; An Overview; p. 97.

[1596] Ibid.

[1597] Ibid; p. 98

[1598] Delumeau, p. 269; in A Gunny: *Images;* op cit; p. 2.

accepted. Here, for the first time, Russian and Turkish envoys met in a European congress, and Turkey admitted once and for all the principle of intervention by other powers. By this treaty, Austria kept Transylvania and Hungary north of the Marosch and west of the Theiss, with most of Slavonia; Poland recovered Podolia and Kaminiec; Venice retained Dalmatia and the Morea or Peloponnesus.[1599]

The 18th century witnessed further slides in Ottoman fortunes. The wars with Russia were a dominant aspect of Ottoman history during the century, one conflict ending, one peace treaty signed, before another war erupted, and generally, turning to the Russian advantage, and large territorial gains at the Ottoman expense. What helped Russia was mostly the fact that the Ottomans were engaged on many fronts. Hence, the 18th century opened with a peace treaty with Russia, before the Ottomans and the Russians went to war again in 1711, signed a peace treaty the following year, only for the Ottomans to find themselves at war with Venice two years subsequently, and at war with Austria two years after that, in 1716.[1600] In 1716, Prince Eugene took Belgrade, and by the peace of Passarowitz (1718), Austria obtained the rest of Hungary.[1601] Turkey found itself, throughout the 1720s, warring against the Safavids, and against the Russians who had invaded the Caucasus region and Georgia.[1602] During the 1730s, the Turkish armies fought the same foes (Russians and Safavids) besides being stretched on yet another front against Austria, in Serbia.[1603]

Russia remained a determined Turkish foe, especially under Catherine the Great (ruled 1762-1796), when Russia began her attempts to break through to the Mediterranean, and in pursuit of this objective, fighting no less than ten wars against the Ottomans, from Catherine's reign until the First World War.[1604] In 1774 after five years of war, the Turks were defeated, and signed the treaty of Kainardji.[1605] The treaty conformed to the conditions Russia had put down. She took Azov, Kinburn, Ienikale... and proclaimed the independence of Crimea. Russia made herself the protector of the Danubian principalities; and paved the way for her future supremacy of the Black Sea

---

[1599] S. Lane Poole: *Turkey;* op cit; p. 241.
[1600] H. Inalcik: Chronology of the Ottoman Empire; op cit; pp. 91-104; at p.99.
[1601] S. Lane Poole: *Turkey;* op cit; p. 211.
[1602] H. Inalcik: Chronology of the Ottoman Empire; op cit; p.99.
[1603] Ibid.
[1604] J. Glubb: *A Short History*; op cit; p.251
[1605] Details in E. Driault: *La Question*; op cit; at pp. 54-5; and A. Sorel: *The Eastern Question*; Howard Fertig; New York; 1969; pp. 247-8.

by obtaining free right to navigate it. Russia was now the guarantor of the Tartar independence, and Turkey promised to take into its view the representations made by Russia on behalf of the Greek Church of Constantinople and its ministers, and to accept measures taken by Russia on behalf of the principalities of Moldavia and Wallachia. This, Driault notes, meant that Russia now had the right to intervene in the internal affairs of Turkey.[1606] The Treaty of Kainardji was for Russia only a break, Sorel points out. The independence of the Tartars was but a step towards their annexation to the Russian Empire; the right of representation on behalf of the Christians was merely an instrument of propaganda and domination, and the very clauses of 1774 contained all the motives for the fresh war upon which the Tsarina was already preparing to embark.[1607] In 1788, occurred the siege of Ochakov, a strongly garrisoned place, which was expected to hold the northerners back from Moldavia and Wallachia. The Russians took the place, and gave free reign to their appetite for pillage and murder, and for three days the slaughter was merciless; only some three hundred people were left alive out of forty thousand.[1608] The following year, the Russian general, Suvorov, advanced on Ismail on the Delta of the Danube, some forty miles from the Black Sea. The place was taken by a night assault, and street fighting ensued. The Russians overwhelmed the Turkish defence, and then, for three days, the inhabitants were given up to the brutality of their conquerors, butchery raging without mercy, thousands being slain.[1609]

In January 1792 the Treaty of Jassy was signed, which amongst others gave Russia the role of protector of Christians living under Turkish sovereignty. Subsequent concessions the Ottomans were to make to the Balkan Christians and to the Armenians were rejected, and demands for independence were made at the instigation of Russia.[1610]

Had Russia, from amongst the bigger nations, been alone in fighting the Ottomans, the Turks would surely have escaped with their powers intact. The problem was that France and England were determined to destroy Turkey. The French, most particularly, played a crucial role in the Russian victory over the Turks in 1769.[1611] Voltaire, the influential French philosopher, relentlessly called the sovereigns of Europe to arms against the Turks for the

---

[1606] E. Driault: *La Question*, op cit; p 55.
[1607] A. Sorel: *The Eastern;* op cit; p. 259.
[1608] S. Lane Poole: *Turkey;* op cit; p. 256.
[1609] Ibid.
[1610] J. Glubb: *A Short History*; op cit; p. 251.
[1611] Beer; vol i., p.256; in A. Sorel: *The Eastern Question*; op cit; p. 55.

glory of their crowns and the profit of their states.[1612] To Catherine II of Russia, he suggested the partition of Turkey:

'Your majesty should be beating the Turks towards Jassy or elsewhere... and afterwards I would come and beg a dinner of you at Sophia, or at Phillipopolis in Romania; after which we would partition (Turkey) in a friendly manner.'[1613]

The only problem for Voltaire was that Frederick the Great, the Prussian emperor, was totally opposed to the idea of partitioning Turkey.[1614]

The project of partitioning Turkey remained high on the agenda, though. Count Massin, another Frenchman, who had been in the service of Russia as rear admiral, in 1771, made secret proposals to both Austria and Russia for the dismembering of Turkey under six different hypotheses, where the two countries would find mutual interest.[1615] The first two hypotheses supposed a European alliance to drive the Turks completely out of Europe, the Dardanelles, Constantinople and lands that were to be transferred to Russia. These proposals, Sorel holds, issued in a veil of secrecy, soon passed into that of official diplomacy, and were to receive solemn sanction from Catherine herself.[1616]

The dismemberment of Turkey was a powerful dream of another contemporary French ideologue, Volnay, who held:

'I swear that by the ruin of so many empires destroyed: the Empire of the Crescent shall suffer the fate of the states whose scheme of government it copied. A foreign people shall chase the sultans from their metropolis; the throne of Orkhan shall be overturned; the last relict of his race shall be cut off, and the hordes of Oguzians (the Turks by their pre-Ottoman designation), deprived of their head, shall be scattered.'[1617]

The French sought, and were, to profit greatly from the Turkish collapse. In 1686, already, Father Jean Coppin, published a book 'Le Bouclier de l'Europe ou la Guerre Sainte' (The shield of Europe, or the Holy War) in which the dismantlement of the Turkish realm was envisaged, and in which Egypt was attributed to France.[1618] The colonisation of Egypt and the Turkish realm in North Africa was to become a major French objective during the colonial era as to be seen in the final chapter of this work.

[1612] Voltaire in A. Sorel: *The Eastern*; op cit; p. 55.
[1613] Voltaire to Catherine II, May 27, 1769.
[1614] In A. Sorel: *The Eastern,* op cit; p. 89.
[1615] Details in A. Sorel: *The Eastern*, pp 159-60.
[1616] Ibid; p. 159.
[1617] Volnay: *Les Ruines*; Paris; 1798-9; chap ii; in N. Daniel: *Islam;* op cit; p.72.
[1618] G. Hanotaux: (vol 5 written by H. Deherain): *Histoire de la Nation Egyptienne*; Paris; Librarie Plon; 1931 (referred to from now on as Hanotaux/Deherain); p. 202.

Turkish Morality

`I confess,' says M. Ubbicini, `that this confidence in a man's word, this dignity and reserve please me. I know not why the seller with us should affect to place himself so much below the buyer. In Turkey there is no such distinction. In fact, the seller troubles himself little about his sale, and sees, without jealousy, the greater success of his neighbour. `My turn will come tomorrow', he says. When the voice of the muezzin is heard, he performs his prayers and prostrations in his shop, in the middle of all comers and goers, as little disturbed as if he were in the desert, or he goes to the nearest mosque leaving his merchandise under the guardianship of the public faith.'[1619]

An English traveller, in a letter addressed to the Daily News, says:
`Yesterday, I hired a Bulgarian peasant, with his wagon, to carry my luggage and that of my companions, consisting of trunks, portmanteaux, carpet bags, cloaks, furs, and shawls. Wishing to buy some hay to stretch ourselves on during the night, a Turk, polite, if ever a man was, offered to accompany us. The peasant unyoked his oxen and left them with all baggage in the street. When I saw that he was also going away, I said: `some of us must remain here.' Why? Asked the Turk with surprise? To watch over my goods.' Oh, replied the Muslim, `they may remain here all week, night and day, and no one will touch them.' I yielded, and when I returned, I found all safe. Observe that the Turkish soldiery were continually passing the spot. Let this be told to the Christians from the pulpits of London. Some will think that they dream. Let them awake.'[1620]

[1619] J. Davenport: *An Apology for Mohammed;* op cit; p. 124.
[1620] Ibid; p. 125.

nine

ISLAM IN AFRICA AND ASIA

As al-Faruqi note, `nothing is further from the truth than the claim that Islam was spread by the sword, or that Hollywood image of the Muslim rider or foot soldier charging the enemy with a view to kill, subdue, or convert. Unfortunately, in their resentment, the enemies of Islam did much to implant that image in the minds of generations of people. The Muslim faithful who is supposed to lay down his life in such process of forceful conversion of others knows only too well that God has commanded him never to coerce anyone into the faith (Qur'an 2: 256). He knows that God even warned his Prophet against any such practice (10: 99. 88: 22) and that the responsibility of the faithful cannot go beyond presentation of the claims of faith. Finally, he knows only too well that it is God Who guides, not he: and that God guides some and permits others to go astray (13: 27). If he did not, how could he be the "faithful" in question? And if he did, how could he indulge in such condemnable crimes? Logic, however, is not the forte of the falsifiers of history.'[1]

Thomas Arnold, likewise, says:

`These stupendous conquests which laid the foundations of the Arab Empire, were certainly not the outcome of a holy war, waged for the propagation of Islam, but they were followed by such vast defection from the Christian faith that this result has often been supposed to have been their aim. Thus the sword came to be looked upon by Christian historians as the instrument of Muslim propaganda, and in the light of the success attributed to it the evidences of the genuine missionary activity of Islam were obscured.'[2]

Indeed, as the following shows, it is the attraction of Islam, not the sword, which led most people in most continents to adopt Islam as their faith.

---

[1] I.R. and L.L. Al-Faruqi: *The Cultural Atlas*; op cit; p. 218.

[2] Thomas W. Arnold: *The Preaching of Islam*; Lahore: Sb. M. Ashraf, 1961, pp. 56-7.

1. Islam in Africa:

Islam spread in the African continent through a variety of means; coming from different directions, and at different times in the past centuries. Everywhere, Western Christian powers sought to halt its advance, and yet, many Westerners themselves admit the revolution Islam brought to the continent. These points are the object of this outline.

a. The Spread of Islam on the Continent:

The role of trade was very important in the spread of Islam. The relationship between Islam and trading has frequently been stressed, and trade has an important place in Islamic tradition, and there is a body of legislation governing contracts, exchange, loans, market conduct and the like.[3] Initially Berber merchants carried Islam across the Sahara into Sahilian states before the Murabit movement got moving, and all nomads in north East Africa where trade routes link the Red Sea with the Nile quickly became Muslim.[4] From the land of the Berbers, Islamisation extended to the pagan tribes of the Sudan. The Lamtuna and the Jadala, two clans of the Sanhaja, distinguished themselves in bringing Islam to the pagans, and through their efforts, the whole Fulbe tribe became Muslim before the end of the 11th century.[5] Most of the citizens of Jenne and Timbuktu, founded in 494H/1100, were Muslim. These cities became great centres of Islamic learning and they taught Islam to the Mandingos who conquered Ghana and became the greatest Muslim activists, bringing Islam to the Hausa people.[6] Islam was also brought into the Western Sudan by Egyptians and Nubians coming to dwell or to trade. Their presence and missionary activity brought Islam to the Lake Chad area.[7] Merchants and black pilgrims met in the streets of Cairo, and black embassies were set up in the

---

[3] See:
R, and D. El Mallakh: Trade and Commerce, in *The Genius of Arab civilisation*, J. R. Hayes Editor; Source of Renaissance, Phaidon, London, 1976; pp 193-205.
M. Rodinson: *Islam and Capitalism;* Paris, 1966.
[4] S.Trimingham: *The Influence of Islam upon Africa;* Longman, London and New York, Librairie du Liban, 2nd edition, 1980; p.38.
[5] I.R. and L.L. Al-Faruqi: *The Cultural Atlas*; op cit; p. 226.
[6] Ibid.
[7] Ibid.

cities of the Maghrib.[8] Neither the kings of the Sudan nor the Sultans of East Africa went to war with the purpose of converting their people.[9] Trade was the main consideration and Islam showed enough flexibility to ask no more of the conquered peoples than they pay taxes.[10]

The Islamic expansion progressed in various directions. Southward, by the 11th century, Arab penetration had reached Soba, twelve miles north of modern Khartum, where they built a large mosque.[11] In the 14th century the Juhaynah tribe in particular had already converted most of the Dongola, according to the Moroccan traveller Ibn Battuta. Establishment of the Funj Empire in the 16th century signified the near extinction of Christianity in the northern area of the present Sudan.[12]

On the East Coast, contacts were made with the Arabs before Islam and continued to grow vigorously thereafter. Maqdisu (Maqdishu, Magadoxo) was founded c. 339H/950 by Muslim immigrants who called themselves Ummah Zaydiyyah (Emozaydij) or the followers of Zayd ibn Ali. Other immigrants founded cities of their own further south.[13] 'Ali, son of Sultan Hassan of Shiraz, emigrated with his black mother and followers, and founded the city of Kiloah. The news of their prosperity encouraged many more to emigrate, thus reinforcing the Islamic presence and mission to the tribes inhabiting the hinterland. Their efforts were assisted by those Muslims descending from the north through the Nile valley. Notable among their achievements was the conversion of the Galla and Zayla' peoples reported by Ibn Hawqal in the 9th century to be Christians, and by Abul Fida in the 14th to be Muslims.[14]

In the 14th century, the most powerful state of the Western Sudan was that of Melle or Mali, which had risen to importance about a century before, after the conquest of Ghana by the Mandingos. The Mandingos are one of the finest races of Africa, whom Leo Africanus calls the most civilised, the most intellectual and most respected of all the black people,[15] whilst modern travellers praise them for their industry, cleverness and

---

[8] D.T. Niane: Editor: *General History of Africa;* Heinemann-California-UNESCO; 1984; Introduction; p . 7
[9] Ibid; p. 3
[10] Ibid.
[11] I.R. and L.L. Al-Faruqi: *The Cultural Atlas*; op cit; p. 222.
[12] Ibid.
[13] Ibid; p. 227.
[14] Ibid.
[15] Leo Africanus: *Della Descrittione dell'Africa; by Giovani Lioni Africano;* Ramusio; vol 1; p. 78.

trustworthiness.[16] These Mandingos have been among the most active missionaries of Islam, which has been spread by them among the neighbouring people.[17] According to the Kano Chronicle it was the Mandingos who brought the knowledge of Islam to the Hausa people; the date is uncertain, as are most dates connected with the history of the Hausa states.[18] But the importance of the adoption of Islam by the Hausas cannot be exaggerated; they are an energetic and intelligent people, and their remarkable aptitude for trade has won for them an immense influence among the various peoples with whom they have come in contact; their language has become the language of commerce for the Western Sudan, and wherever the Hausa traders go-and they are found from the coast of Guinea to Cairo-they carry the faith of Islam with them.[19]

Where intermarriages with Arabs and Berbers have been frequent, a steady process of infiltration has gone on, and this, added to the propagation activities by the Fulbe, Hausa and Mandingo, who contributed to the more rapid growth of a Muslim population.[20]

The Muslim expansion in the continent remained continuous for centuries until our modern times. Tunjar Arabs emigrating from Tunis to Darfur and other southern lands took the faith with them. One of them, Ahmad, was liked by the heathen king of Darfur, and he was taken into his employment and patronage. He later married his patron's daughter and established a dynasty which continued the task of proselytizing native Africans.[21] By 1017H/1608 most of the Wadai and Baghirmi peoples were converted to Islam, making possible the establishment by 'Abdul Karim in 1021/1612 of Wadai as the centre of Islamic influence throughout West Africa.[22]

From the late 18th century, the Fulbe people mobilized and dedicated themselves to the propagation of Islam under the leadership of Shaykh 'Uthman dan Fodio. They were eminently successful as they introduced Islam as far as Adamana in the south-east, founded the city of Ilorin in Yoruba land, and made the centres from which Islam radiated to the south and southwest. The Sufi orders of Mirghaniyyah (founded by Mohammed 'Uthman al Amir Ghani n 1251/1835, the Tijaniyyah stemming from

---

[16] W. Winwood Reade: *African Sketchbook;* vol 1; p. 303.
[17] T. Waitz: *Anthropologie der Naturvolker;* Leipzig; 1860; pp. 18-9.
[18] T. Arnold: *The Preaching of Islam*; op cit; p. 322.
[19] Ibid.
[20] Ibid; p. 324.
[21] I.R. and L.L. Al-Faruqi: *The Cultural Atlas*; op cit; p. 226.
[22] Ibid.

Algiers, and the Sanusiyyah from its bases in Kufrah and Jaghbub in southeast Libya consolidated and continued the gains made earlier.[23]

It is odd that in places, it was Western colonisation, which indirectly spread Islam. The Dutch encouraged Muslims from the Malay Basin to emmigrate to South Africa in order to work in the new plantations they were operating near the Cape of Good Hope. These intermarried with their Dutch masters as well as with the native Africans, and multiplied their numbers.[24] Together with Muslim immigrants from India who settled on the east coast of South Africa, they constitute a significant presence in the land.[25]

Having spread through the continent, Islam had a considerable impact on local African society.

b. The Islamic Impact on Africa:

The impact of Islam on African society is summed up by Trimingham. Islam for the ordinary adherent is not an intellectual exercise. It is absorbed and maintains its hold because it is a system of life.[26] Islam brings a fixed system of belief and action, not variable according to family or locality. Pilgrimage to Makkah has played an important role in giving African Muslims a conception of Islam as a world religion and the consciousness of possessing a common religious inheritance. Travelling the whole way through Muslim lands gave the impression that Islam was the religion of Africa.[27]

In practical Islam moral conduct is following what God allows and refraining from what He forbids. Theoretical and practical morality for the Muslim means the study and practice of the way of life (*sunna*) of the Prophet, the exemplar who followed the right path; but since all this has been codified it is simply a matter of following the law. The social ethics of Islam are directed to maintain the harmony and solidarity of the community, the consensus (*ijma'*) of the community being the criterion.[28] The duties incumbent upon the community are summarised in the maxim, `to command

---

[23] Ibid; p. 227.
[24] Ibid.
[25] Ibid.
[26] J. S. Trimingham: *The Influence of Islam;* op cit; p.53.
[27] Ibid; pp. 62-3
[28] Ibid; p.67.

right and forbid wrong'; right and wrong are defined by the law.[29] Social harmony involves the stressing of positive virtues such as benevolence, humility, truthfulness, condemnation of envy, and care of orphans.[30]

Although the communal aspect of moral conduct has been stressed, it should be mentioned that personal responsibility is a keynote of the Qur'an[31] and its outreach in institutions; the five pillars, for example, are duties incumbent upon the individual. Observance of Islam means avoiding the tabooed such as: intoxicants, eating pig and carrion; contact with dogs; whistling; mutilations, incising and tattooing.[32]

Observing such precepts of Islam brought considerable changes to African society, which have been observed at all times by travellers and writers on Africa.

Shortly after the adoption of Islam, Kanem rose to be a state of considerable importance and extended its sway over the tribes of the Eastern Sudan to the borders of Egypt and Nubia; the first Muslim king of Kanem is said to have reigned either towards the close of the 11th or the first half of the 12th century.[33]

Ibn Battuta gives a good description of the people of Mali under Islam:

'The Black people possess some admirable qualities. They are seldom unjust, and have great abhorrence of injustice than any other people. Their sultan shows no mercy to anyone who is guilty of the least act of it. There is complete security in their country. Neither traveller nor inhabitant in it has anything to fear from robbers or men of violence.

They are careful to observe the hours of prayer, and assiduous in attending them in congregations, and in bringing up their children to them. On Fridays, if a man does not go early to the mosque, he cannot find a corner to pray in, on account of the crowd. It is a custom of theirs to send each man his boy [to the mosque] with his prayer-mat; the boy spreads it out for his master in a place befitting him [and remains on it] until he

---

[29] Ibid; p.68.

[30] Ibid; pp.68-9.

[31] On the day of Judgement each person will be held responsible for his deeds, 'The fate of every man have we bound around his neck...., neither shall any laden soul be charged with the burden of another'; sura xvii.13, 15; vi.34.

[32] J. S. Trimingham: *The Influence of Islam*; op cit; p.57.

[33] C.H. Becker: Geschichte des ostlichen Sudan; *Der Islam;* vol 1; Strassburg; 1910; pp. 162-3.

comes to the mosque. Their prayer-mats are made of the leaves of a tree resembling a date-palm, but without fruit.[34]

Another of their good qualities is their habit of wearing clean white garments on Fridays. Even if a man has nothing but an old worn shirt, he washes it and cleans it, and wears it to the Friday service. Yet another is their zeal for learning the Qur'an by heart.'[35]

The positive impact Islam had on African society was observed by later Western writers and travellers. Smith notes, how:

'We hear of whole tribes laying aside their devil worship, or immemorial fetish, and springing at a bound, as it were, from the very lowest to one of the highest forms of religious belief. Christian travellers, with every wish to think otherwise, have remarked that the Black person who accepts Islam acquires at once a sense of the dignity of human nature not commonly found even among those who have been brought to accept Christianity.'[36]

Smith adds:

'Nor as to the effects of Islam when first embraced by a Black tribe, can there, when viewed as a whole, be any reasonable doubt. Polytheism disappears almost instantaneously; sorcery, with its attendant evils, gradually dies away; human sacrifice becomes a thing of the past. The general moral elevation is most marked; the natives begin for the first time in their history to dress, and that neatly. Squalid filth is replaced by some approach to personal cleanliness; hospitality becomes a religious duty; drunkenness, instead of the rule becomes a comparatively rare exception. Though polygamy is allowed by the Koran, it is not common in practice...; chastity is looked upon as one of the highest, and becomes, in fact, one of the commoner virtues. It is idleness henceforth that degrades, and industry that elevates, instead of the reverse. Offences are henceforth measured by a written code instead of the arbitrary caprice of a chieftain-a step, as every one will admit, of vast importance in the progress of a tribe.'[37]

The Islamic impact is also on the economic and cultural levels. Muslims proved to be excellent traders and came to dominate the commercial world, helping to foster progress in sciences, philosophy and technology wherever

---

[34] Ibn Battuta: *Voyages d'Ibn Battuta*, Arabic text accompanied by Fr tr by C. Defremery and B.R. Sanguinetti, preface and notes by Vincent Monteil, I-IV, Paris, 1968, reprint of the 1854 ed; vol 4; pp. 421-2.

[35] Ibn Battuta: *Travels in Asia and Africa;* tr and selected by H.A.R. Gibb; George Routledge and Sons Ltd; London, 1929; pp. 329-31.

[36] R.B. Smith: *Mohammed;* op cit; p. 38.

[37] Ibid; pp. 42-3.

they settled. Merchants from Arabia and the Gulf opened up the eastern coasts of Africa, from the Horn to Madagascar, to international trade.[38] The rich trading settlements of Sofala, Kilwa, and Mogaidishu became Africa's outlets to the Indian Ocean. Along the coast, from the Horn to Madagascar, an original Muslim civilisation developed around the Muslim trading settlements: the Swahili civilisation.[39]

Browne, an Englishman, who undertook extensive travels in Central Africa in the years 1799 and 1806,[40] remarks that, among the idolaters of Sheibon and of other places, the only persons who he saw wearing decent clothes, or indeed clothing at all, were Muslims; that it was to the introduction of Islam a century and a half before his time that Darfur owed its settled government and the cultivation of its soil; and that the people of Bergoo were remarkable for their zealous attachment to their religion, and read the Qur'an daily. In this summary we hear of the use of decent clothing, and the arts of reading and agriculture, attributed to Islam.[41]

Mungo Park, educated as he was for the Scotch Church, and cruelly persecuted as he was throughout his travels by 'Moorish banditi,' Smith notes, would not be likely to be a friend of Islam, and many of his remarks show a strong bias against it: his testimony, therefore, is all the more valuable. His travels lay almost exclusively among Muslims or semi Muslim tribes, and he found that the Black people were everywhere summoned to prayer by blasts blown through elephants' tusks. On reaching the Niger, the main object of his wanderings, he found, to his surprise, that Sego, the capital of Bamharra, was a walled town, containing some 30,000 inhabitants, that the houses were square and very often white washed, and that there were Muslim mosques in every quarter. 'The view of this extensive city,' he writes, 'the numerous canoes upon the river, the crowded population, and the cultivated state of the surrounding country, formed altogether a prospect of civilisation and magnificence which I little expected to find in the bosom of Africa.'[42]

His impression of the women was most favourable. 'I do not recollect, he says, 'a single instance of hard heartedness towards me among the women. In all my wanderings and wretchedness I found them uniformly kind and compassionate.' One of the first lessons in which the Mandigo women instructed their children was the practice of truth.[43]

---

[38] D.T. Niane: *General History of Africa;* op cit; p. 2
[39] Ibid; p.3
[40] See Pinkerton: *Voyages*; vol xv and xvi.
[41] In R. B. Smith: *Mohammed*; op cit; p. 44.
[42] Mungo Park's Travels; Cap I. Nd fin; in R.B. Smith: *Mohammed;* op cit; p. 45.
[43] In R. B. Smith: *Mohammed*; p. 46.

Mungo Park adds: 'the beverages of the pagan Negroes are beer and mead, of which they frequently drink to excess. The Muslims amongst them drink nothing but water.'[44]

As to education, Mungo Park found schools and active teachers everywhere.[45] In Africa, we are assured, at all hands, that the Muslim population has an almost passionate desire for education. Wherever Muslims are numerous, they establish schools themselves; and there are not a few who travel extraordinary distances to secure the best possible education.[46]

The Revd Edward Blyden, a native Black African and Christian missionary, counters those who attack Islam, and says:

'If those Christians who are so unmeasured in their denunciations of 'Mohammedanism' could travel, as I have travelled, through those countries in the interior of West Africa, and witness, as I have witnessed, the vast contrast between the pagan and 'Mohammedan' communities-the habitual listlessness and continued deterioration of the one, and the activity and growth, physical and mental, of the other; the capricious and unsettled administration of law, or rather absence of law, in the one, and the tendency to order and regularity in the other; the increasing prevalence of ardent spirits in the one, and the rigid sobriety and conservative abstemiousness of the other-they would cease to regard the 'Mussulman' system as an unmitigated evil in the interior of Africa.'[47]

Everywhere, Christian missionaries found the same effect, and also noticed the spread of Islam on the continent, and sought to put a halt to such a spread.

c. Western Efforts to Block the Progress of Islam in Africa:

Dr Barth, whose travels took him in Northern and Central Africa, in regard to the rapid spread of Islam, says, that:

'A great part of the Berbers of the desert were once Christians, and that they afterwards changed their religion and adopted Islam;' and he describes 'that continual struggle which, always extending further and

---

[44] Mungo Park; Cap Vii; in R.B. Smith: *Mohammed;* op cit; p. 46.
[45] In R. B. Smith: *Mohammed;* p. 47.
[46] Ibid; p. 41.
[47] Ibid; pp. 50-1.

further, seems destined to overpower the nations at the very Equator if Christianity does not presently step in to dispute the ground with it.'[48]

The effort to hamper the advance of Islam in Africa, as in other continents, is not new, though, and explains much of the hostile depictions and other measures against Islam. The hostile depictions of Islam and their anti Islamic propagandist nature have been seen in chapter two to warrant any more space here. But on top of such propaganda, Western Christendom always sought to remove Islam wherever it found it established. In Africa, the original Portuguese settlers found the Arabs established along the coasts of Mozambique and in the interior. They exterminated those established in the former; but they failed to dispossess the latter, and it has been proved to be the case, that some of the *Terra parum cognita* in the interior remained Muslim.[49] When the Portuguese arrived on the eastern coast, their aim was to cut out Swaheli middlemen and Muslim shippers. They established themselves at Sofala, the nearest port to Zimbabwe, in 1505, and later at Tete, a river port on the Zambezi.[50]

This European incursion, with the slave trade from the 16th to the early 19th century, and then with the rush to the interior and the colonial pillaging of the raw materials caused considerable decline to Africa.[51] According to Abbe Reynal:

'In the midst of so much glory, wealth, and conquest, the Portuguese had not neglected that part of Africa which lies between the Cape of Good Hope and the Red Sea, and in all ages has been famed for the richness of its productions. The Arabians had been settled there for several ages; they had formed along the coast of Zanguebar several small independent states, abounding in mines of silver and gold. To possess themselves of this treasure was deemed by the Portuguese an indispensable duty. Agreeable to this principle, these Arabian merchants were attacked and subdued about the year 1508. Upon their ruin was established an empire extending from Sofala as far as Melinda, of which the island of Mozambique was made the centre....'[52]

---

[48] Ibid; p. 49.

[49] Ibid; note 1; p. 56.

[50] A. Pacey: *Technology in World Civilization*, The MIT Press, Cambridge, Massachusetts, 1990; preface, p.71.

[51] R. Garaudy: *Comment l'Homme devient Humain*. Editions J.A, 1978; p.272.

[52] W. Howitt: *Colonisation and Christianity*: Longman; London; 1838. pp. 178-9.

Being absolute masters of the Eastern Seas, they (the Portuguese) extorted a tribute from the ships of every country; they ravaged the coasts, insulted the princes, and became the terror and scourge of all nations.[53]

The Western slave trade, which reached its peak in the 18th century, shattered not just Muslim communities, but the whole of African society and economy, and permanently. Garaudy and Howitt explain this disastrous impact in great detail.[54] It is not that African society, as generally held in Western writing, was initially backward, thus, clearing the conscience of the slave traders from their responsibility in its backwardness, but rather, as a whole, Black Africa, in the 15th century, before slave trading, Garaudy explains, was not inferior to Europe.[55] Coming from Goa or Egypt, Islam penetrated as far as Chad, and met in Nigeria an old black civilisation, which was remarkable for its art, possibly tributary to Mediterranean classical influences, which it soon adopted.[56] The African states of Ghana, Mali and Songhay shared in the great age of Islamic civilisation from the 9th to the 16th centuries.[57] On his return from his pilgrimage to Makkah in 1324, Mansa Musa brought back with him the Muslim poet and architect, Es Saheli, who built the famous mosques and learning academies of Timbuktu and Gao.[58] Timbuktu ranked with Alexandria, Fez, Seville, Cordova and Constantinople as a great centre of learning.[59] Blyden speaks of the story of the Hejazi jurist who sought employment in Timbuktu, but who, finding too many scholars there, went on to Fez where he found employment more easily. He quotes with relish many honourable appearances of a black skin in Islamic literature, as an encouragement to African learning.[60]

Economically, the textiles of Congo and Guinea were as high quality as those of Europe; Nigerian decorated hides and leather were appreciated in Europe, getting to it via North Africa; and metal works, of copper in particular, of Katanga and Zambia, and iron works of Sierra Leone, were much superior to those they were made to import by force later from Europe.[61] The Empire of Ghana was a thriving commercial centre, and its large capital city, Kumbi Saleh, was an important centre of trade and

---

[53] Ibid.

[54] R. Garaudy: *Comment l'Homme*; op cit. W. Howitt: *Colonisation and Christianity*. op cit.

[55] R. Garaudy: *Comment l'Homme*; op cit; p.271.

[56] E Perroy: *Le Moyen Age,* Presses Universitaires de France, 1956; p.525.

[57] D. M. Traboulay: *Columbus and Las Casas*; University Press of America, New York, London, 1994. p 69.

[58] Ibid; p.70.

[59] G.O. Cox: *African Empires and Civilisations;* New York; 1974; p. 161.

[60] Blyden in N. Daniel: *Islam, Europe, and Empire*; Edinburgh University Press; 1966; p. 314.

[61] R. Garaudy: *Comment l'Homme*; op cit; p.271.

scholarship, where Islamic theology and history were studied.[62] In Zimbabwe, Rhodes mercenaries and traffickers found huge constructions, and mines well exploited. Bronze metal in Benin was better quality than the Portuguese. European superiority was only in terms of gun fire.[63]

It was Western Christendom, and above all the slave trade it inflicted on Africa, which destroyed these progresses of the African continent, and made the prosperity of the slave trading nations.[64] In 1540, only 400 Africans were deported, a figure, which rose to nearly 300,000 every year in the 18th century.[65] Due to losses during capture, transportation, deaths at the plantations, etc, 100 million Africans perished as a result of the slave trade.[66]

---

[62] D.M. Traboulay: *Columbus and Las Casas*; op cit; p 69.

[63] R. Garaudy: *Comment l'Homme;* op cit; p.271.

[64] E. Williams: *Capitalism and Slavery*; North Carolina; 1944.
Catherine. C. Vidrovitch: Villes Africaines; op cit;at p.1390.
M. Craton: *Sinews of Empire: A Short history of British slavery;* Garden City; NY; Doubleday; 1974.

[65] R. Garaudy: *Comment l'Homme*; op cit; p.275.

[66] Ibid.

A Description of Muslims in the Gambia in 1731

Francis Moore, an eighteenth century traveller, writes:
"In every kingdom and country on each side of the river are people of a tawny colour, called Pholeys (i e. Fulbe), who resemble the Arabs, whose language most of them speak; for it is taught in their schools, and the Qur'an, which is also their law, is in that language. They are more generally learned in Arabic, than the people of Europe are in Latin; for they can most of them speak it; though they have a vulgar tongue called Pholey. They live in hordes or clans, built towns, and are not subject to any of the kings of the country, though they live in their territories; for if they are used ill in one nation they break up their towns and remove to another. They have chiefs of their own, who rule with such moderation, that every act of government seems rather an act of the people than of one man. This form of government is easily administered, because the people are of a good and quiet disposition, and so well instructed in what is just and right, that a man who does ill is the abomination of all... They are very industrious and frugal, and raise much more corn and cotton than they consume, which they sell at reasonable rates, and are so remarkable for their hospitality that the natives esteem it a blessing to have a Pholey town in their neighbourhood; besides, their behaviour has gained them such reputation that it is esteemed infamous for anyone to treat them in an inhospitable manner. Though their humanity extends to all, they are doubly kind to people of their own race; and if they know of any of their body being made a slave, all the Pholeys will unite to redeem him. As they have plenty of food they never suffer any of their own people to want; but support the old, the blind, and the lame, equally with the others. They are seldom angry, and I never heard them abuse one another; yet this mildness does not proceed from want of courage, for they are as brave as any people of Africa, and are very expert in the use of their arms, which are the assagay, short cutlasses, bows and arrows and even guns upon occasion. . . They are strict Muslims; and scarcely any of them will drink brandy, or anything stronger than water.'[67]

---

[67] Francis Moore: *Travels in the Inland Parts of Africa*; London; 1760; pp. 75-7.

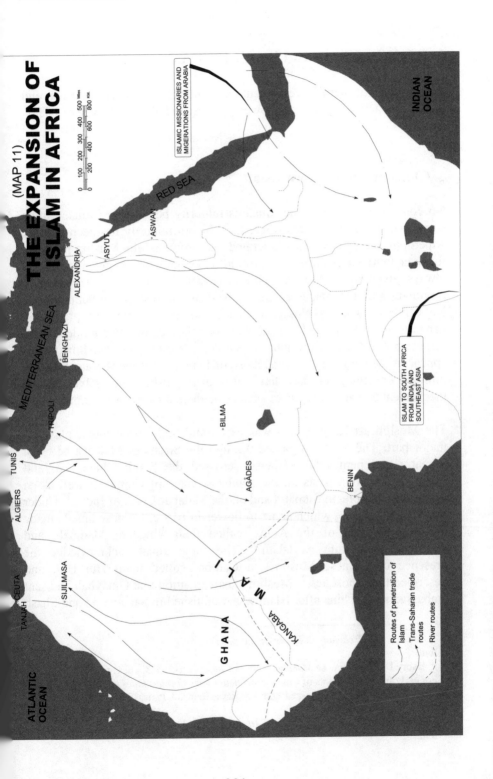

THE EXPANSION OF
ISLAM IN AFRICA
(MAP 11)

ISLAMIC MISSIONARIES AND
MIGRATIONS FROM ARABIA

ISLAM TO SOUTH AFRICA
FROM INDIA AND
SOUTHEAST ASIA

INDIAN
OCEAN

RED SEA

MEDITERRANEAN SEA

ATLANTIC
OCEAN

ALEXANDRIA
ASYUT
ASWAN
BENGHAZI
TRIPOLI
TUNIS
ALGIERS
CEUTA
TANJAH
SIJILMASA
GHANA
KANGABA
MALI
BENIN
AGADES
BILMA

Routes of penetration of
Islam
Trans-Saharan trade
routes
River routes

2. Islam in China and South East Asia:

We observe the same developments in South East Asia as in Africa, and the same reaction by Western powers seeking to halt the advance of Islam.

a. China and South East Asia:

No country ever treated the Muslims minority better than China. Unlike some places and continents where the Muslim minority has been entirely wiped out, the Chinese have tolerated and promoted the Muslim presence for over fourteen centuries. As Arnold notes the Chinese government has always given to its Muslim subjects (except when in revolt) the same privileges and advantages as are enjoyed by the rest of the population.[68] No office of state is closed to them; and as governors of provinces, generals, magistrates and ministers of state they enjoy the confidence and respect both of the rulers and the people.[69] Not only do Muslims names appear in the Chinese annals as those of famous officers of state, whether military or civil, but they have also distinguished themselves in the mechanical arts and in sciences such as mathematics and astronomy.[70]

The Muslim arrival in China was early, and trade, once more, played a major part. The Muslims passed through the Straits of Malacca between Sumatra and peninsular Malaysia, crossed the South China Sea, and established trading posts on the southeast coast of China, as well as en route, for example, in Sumatra and on the Malabar Coast of India.[71] Under the T'ang Dynasty, which came to power in 618 c, Chinese annals made the first mention of the Arabs, called their kingdom Madinah, and described their faith as Islam.[72] The same annals acknowledge the presence of Chinese Muslims in Canton, called them Hui Hui, and described their mosques.[73] Muslim annals mention that Qutaybah had sent ambassadors to China after Islam was established in Samarqand and Shash

---

[68] T. Arnold: *The Preaching of Islam;* op cit; p. 312.
[69] Ibid.
[70] P. Dabry De Thiersant: *Le Mahometisme en Chine*; Paris; 1878; vol 1; p. 247.
[71] For early Islamic accounts of China, see *Relations des Voyages faites par les Arabes et les Persans dans l'Inde et a la Chine*, ed. et tr. Langles et Reinaud, Paris, 1845, deux petits volumes, Imprimerie Royale.
[72] I.R. and L.L. Al-Faruqi: *The Cultural Atlas*; op cit; p. 224.
[73] Ibid.

(modern Tashkent), and Chinese annals mention an ambassador called Sulayman who was sent by the Umayyad Caliph, Hisham in 108H/726 to Emperor Hsuan Sung.[74] Under the Abbasids, Al Mansur sent a body of Muslim troops at the request of the Emperor's son, Su Tsung, in 139/756 to help him recover his throne from a usurper, and the Muslim force decided to stay in China rather than return home.[75] These Muslims who went to fight for the emperor in China and then were granted the right to stay there, proved the greatest ambassadors of Islam. Le Bon says:

'They are animated in general of a great spirit of rightness and honesty. Those who hold public functions are liked and respected by the populations, and those who deal in trade have an excellent reputation. They are charitable due to religious principles, and seem only to form one and large family all of whose members protect and support each other. What proves above any other thing their superiority is that despite their original task, thanks to subtle concessions they managed to make to the requirements of their country of adoption, also thanks to the brotherly fraternity that linked them all, they managed to grow and expand, whilst all other foreign religions which tried to implant in China have only passed by or vegetated.'[76]

In the middle of the 10th century, following the extensive trade links, an important Muslim colony grew in Canton.[77] Descriptions of China by Muslims, however, date from the early 9th century, through the work of a merchant: Suleyman, whose accounts were taken up by Abu Zeid Hassan.[78] He says that boats sailing for China departed from Basrah and Siraf. They brought cargos from Siraf and Oman on boats and loaded them on ships sailing for China because waters were shallow near the coasts. Fresh water was loaded at Siraf and Muscat. From there ships sailed to Oman, and from there to India; then the island of Sander Faulat (Singapore); Jinji (Chinji) and then anchored near the gate of China. Ships passed between hills of the Straits of China. They entered the Chinese Gulf, and lay anchor in Khanfua (Khanpua).[79]

Jitsizo Kuwabara gives a complete history of the Arabs in China during the T'ang and Sung dynasties.[80] We are informed that from the 8th to the

---

[74] Ibid; p. 225.

[75] Ibid.

[76] G. Le Bon: *La Civilisation des Arabes*, op cit; p.48.

[77] J.H. Kramers: Geography and Commerce, in *The Legacy of Islam* (edited by T. Arnold and A. Guillaume,) op cit; pp 79-97; at p. 95.

[78] *Relations des Voyages faites par les Arabes et les Persans;* op cit;.

[79] A.S.S.Nadvi: *Arab Navigation*; S. M.Ashraf publishers; Lahore; 1966; pp. 55-8.

[80] Jitsizo Kuwabara: *To so jidai ni okeru Arab-jin no Shina Tsuho no gaiko; kotomi So matsu no Teikyo-shihaku Saiiki-jin Ho Ju-ko no jiseki* (Piu Shou-Keng, a man of the Western regions, who was superintendent of the Trading Ships' office in Chiuan-chou

end of the 15th century the Arabs travelled to China from the Gulf, crossing the Indian Ocean, and passing through the Malay Peninsula, coming to Canton, where they carried trade.... They brought their wives with them, but a few traders married Chinese women. A record shows that an Arab marrying a Chinese lady of the imperial family was promoted to high official position.[81]

The widespread dislocation of people produced by the Mongol invasions of Central, South, and West Asia (in the 13th century) caused many Muslims to emmigrate to distant, safer places. Some emigrated to China, or to the lands leading to it. 'Abdul Rahman became head of the imperial finances and collected the taxes.[82]

In 1420, mosques were built in the capitals Singnanfu and Nankin, and the Muslim presence was conspicuous enough to have been earlier observed by Marco Polo (1275-1292) in Yunnan and its capital, Talifu.[83] A few decades later, that presence was evident throughout the south coastal region of China. Finally, under the Ming Dynasty (1369-1644), its founder Emperor Hungwu recognized his Muslim subjects and conferred upon them numerous privileges.[84]

Gradually, the number of Muslims increased. They were to be found particularly in the northern provinces and in Yunnan, most often engaged in cattle, horse, and sheep raising, caravan trading, inn keeping, and mercantile operations, although some were farmers and some served as Chinese officials.[85] They avoided pork, alcohol, and opium and the worship of idols and ancestors, and made the pilgrimage to Makkah. The Qur'an was not translated into Chinese, though, and only a few mosque officials knew Arabic.[86] Except for those in Sinkiang and adjacent regions in northwest China, the Muslims of China tended to become Sinicized: most of them retained or adopted Chinese names and dress.[87] Subject to the same government regulations and restrictions as Buddhists and Taoists,

---

towards the end of the Sung dynasty, together with a general sketch of trade of the Arabs in China during the T'Ang and Sung eras) Tokyo; Iwanami; 1935. Reviewed by Shio Sakanishi; *ISIS*; vol XXX; pp. 120-1.

[81] Ibid; p. 120.

[82] I.R. and L.L. Al-Faruqi: *The Cultural Atlas*; op cit; p. 225.

[83] Ibid.

[84] Ibid.

[85] L. Gottschalk et al: *History of Mankind*; vol 4; part one; UNESCO, 1969; p. 346.

[86] Ibid.

[87] Ibid.

in general, they lived in harmony with the other Chinese.[88] Migration into the northwest areas seems to have been considerable in the 18th century, and the total number of Muslims in China and Sinkiang possibly exceeded ten million in that century.[89]

b. The Malay Basin:

The history of the Malay Archipelago during the last 600 years furnishes us with one of the most interesting chapters in the story of the spread of Islam by peaceful efforts. In every instance, in the beginning, Muslim work had to be carried on without any patronage or assistance from the rulers of the country, but solely by the force of persuasion, and in many cases in the face of severe opposition, especially on the part of the Spaniards.[90] The Spaniards were among the Western powers (Portugal, Holland, England, and France) that had penetrated the region from the end of the 15th century onward, seeking to counter Islam and its influence. But in spite of difficulties, and with varying success, the Muslims prosecuted their efforts with untiring energy, perfecting their work wherever it has been partial or insufficient.[91]

It is impossible to fix the precise date of the first introduction of Islam into the Malay Archipelago, but trade played a central role in both its introduction and diffusion. Islam may have been carried by Arab traders in the early centuries of the Hijrah, and from the 10th to the 15th century, and until the arrival of the Portuguese (in the 15th century), they were undisputed masters of the trade with the East.[92] It is probable that they must have established their commercial settlements on some of the islands of the Malay Archipelago, as they did elsewhere, at a very early period. In the Chinese annals, under the date 674, an account is given of an Arab chief, who from later notices is conjectured to have been the head of an Arab settlement on the west coast of Sumatra.[93] Bases in Sumatra, at the Malacca straights, must have been founded to make the trade with Canton

---

[88] Ibid.
[89] Ibid.
[90] T. Arnold: *The Preaching of Islam*; op cit; p. 367.
[91] Ibid.
[92] Ibid.
[93] W.P. Groenweldt: Notes on the Malay Archipelago and Malacca, compiled from Chinese sources; *Verb. Bat. Gen. van K. en Deel*; xxxix; 1880; pp. 14-5.

(China) possible.[94] The period from the 7th to the 13th centuries witnessed a steady influx of Muslim traders and immigrants who settled in the region to conduct its prospering foreign trade.[95] These traders married native women, learned the native tongues, preached Islam to those with whom they came into contact, and gradually, developed a viable measure of security and popularity.[96]

The dislocations resulting from the Mongol invasions (13th century) caused many to emmigrate to Southeast Asia. Hence, from the 13th century, the area witnessed a great expansion of Muslim power. Scholars, disbanded soldiers, craftsmen, and people of all walks of life and races poured into the Malay Basin in search of peace and security, away from the Mongols and other wars.[97]

Although the annals mark 'Abdullah Arif as founder of the first Muslim state in Atcheh in Sumatra (modern Indonesia) in the mid-12th century, it is likely that pettier kingdoms of Muslims must have been formed earlier and that "Sri Paduka Sultan" 'Abdullah's monarchy was the high point of a long development. Marco Polo reported that Perlak (northeast corner of Sumatra) was already a Muslim kingdom in 692/1292.[98]
It was from Java (Indonesia) that Islam was first brought into the Lampong districts, which form the southern extremity of Sumatra, by a chieftain of these districts, named Minak Kamala Bumi.[99] Islam was introduced into Palembang (Indonesia) about 1440 by Raden Rahmat, but although the progress was slow, the Colonial Reports of the Dutch government drew attention to the continued spread of Islam amongst the so-called heathen populations of the various districts.[100]
It was mainly from Sumatra that Islam spread in Malaysia in the 13th and 14th centuries.[101] Smaller colonies of Muslims were also set up by seafarers on the east coast of Malaysia, and these developed into the modern states of Trengganu (which has the oldest Muslim inscription of the area, the Trengganu Stone bearing the date of 702/1303) and Kelantan,

---

[94] I.R. and L.L. Al-Faruqi: *The Cultural Atlas;* op cit; p. 228.
[95] Ibid.
[96] Ibid.
[97] Ibid.
[98] Ibid.
[99] H.D. Canne: Bijdrage tot de Geschiedenis der Lompongs; *Deel*; XI; 1862; p. 510.
[100] T. Arnold: *The Preaching of Islam;* op cit; p. 375.
[101] I.R. and L.L. Al-Faruqi: *The Cultural Atlas*; op cit; p. 228.

and planting other Muslim colonies in Thailand, Cambodia, and Vietnam.[102]

Sometime after their final conquest by the Annamites (about 1470) the Chams of Cochin-China became Muslim. Intermarriage with Indians introduced some Muslims into the Arakan area of western Burma, while others from Yunnan in China established themselves in northern Burma. But an effort to plant Islam in Cambodia about 1650 failed.[103]

In Bengal, Chittagong had for centuries been a centre of Arab maritime trade. Surrounding it was a strong Buddhist community whose religion had fallen into a primitive pattern and involved human sacrifices.[104] Islam did not progress with any great speed until after the death of King Kans (796H/1393). When he died, his son ascended to the throne as an enthusiastic and committed Muslim sovereign. Within the space of a century, the overwhelming majority of the people had converted to Islam.[105]

As in Africa, Western Christendom sought to stem the progress of Islam, succeeding in places and failing in others. When the Portuguese captured Malacca (1511), they thereby eliminated one of the most important Islamic centres in the East, but the Grisek-Tuban centre in Java remained, and others quickly developed.[106] Acheh, in western Sumatra, emerged as a Muslim rival to the Portuguese at Malacca and gradually extended its sway over western Sumatra. The displaced sultans of Malacca established themselves at Johore in south Malaya, threatening Malacca and influencing the nearby areas and western Borneo.[107] Despite Western efforts, Islam still made progress. Only in the northern Philippines, after the establishment of the Spanish at Manila (1571), did Christian influence conspicuously turn Islam back.[108] Elsewhere in the region, Islamic political control pushed onward from the coast into the interior, and although the actual conversion of the hinterland was a slow process, when

---

[102] Ibid.
[103] L. Gottschalk et al: History; op cit; p. 345.
[104] I.R. and L.L. Al-Faruqi: *The Cultural Atlas*; op cit; p. 226.
[105] Ibid.
[106] L. Gottschalk et al: History; op cit; p. 344.
[107] Ibid.
[108] Ibid.

the Dutch and the English arrived *(c.* 1600) most of that part of the world was at least nominally Muslim.[109]

The gradual extension of European political control over the Malaysian coasts in the 17th and 18th centuries did little to shake the hold of Islam. Demak declined, but Mataram rose and by 1601 dominated south and central Java, and under Sunan Agung (1613-45), a fervent Muslim, it conquered the Hindu kingdom of Balambang on the eastern tip of Java and gained control over all of that island but Bantam.[110] Agung established close relations with Makkah, brought new Islamic contacts to Java, exerted his influence in southern Borneo, and crossed swords with the Dutch at Batavia.[111] About 1604 a Muslim trader converted the Raja of Macassar, and thus began the conversion of the Bugis of Celebes, who, in turn extended Islam into Borneo and the islands east of Java.[112] From Brunei and the Suli area, Islam spread into Mandanao and the Manila Bay region, where it was stopped by the Spanish conquest. Ternate and Tidore remained Islamic centres for the area of the Moluccas and Banda Islands despite repeated counter-measures by the Portuguese, Spanish, and Dutch.[113] The Europeans succeeded in getting permanent Christian footholds only on Amboina and at some points in the Moluccas and northern Celebes.[114]

As elsewhere, wherever it became established, Islam transformed the primitive mentality completely. This is described by al-Faruqi:

`The most important element in this account is the encounter of Islam with the primitive mentality of the pre-Islamic Malay. That mentality fragmented human existence into countless separate tribes. It pictured the world as alien, frightful, and above all full of spirits which it had to appease and placate. These tribes relied on food gathering, or the least agriculture to survive, and related their miseries to fantastic myths in terms of which they understood themselves and the reality around them. They lived on cannibalism, instituted human sacrifice, tolerated infanticide, and never saw the nakedness of the body or the need to clean it. They never realized the need to read and write, to record human experience, and they existed without civilization, or even awareness of human culture. Where the West impinged upon it before Islam, as in Africa, Westerners bartered

---

[109] Ibid.
[110] Ibid; p. 345.
[111] Ibid.
[112] Ibid.
[113] Ibid; p. 344.
[114] Ibid; p. 345.

goods without ever developing native trade or industry and, besides bringing with them hitherto unknown diseases which debilitated the people, introduced gin and rum with all their attendant consequences.... Instead of developing native trade and industry or laying down foundations for the development of learning and civilization, Hinduism pushed primitive mythology to a higher degree of complexity and sophistication. As to the impact of Buddhism, it may have taught the Malay how to build temples and carve statues to the Buddha. But as in the other cases of contact, the primitive mentality remained primitive.'[115]

The Islamic impact, on the other hand, was powerful. Islam eliminated superstition and spirits and ascribed all causation to one supreme Creator Whose will is orderly and Whose patents in creation are eternal. It dissolved the tribe, repudiated its loyalties, and grouped the people into nations and empires, imbuing them with loyalty for causes greater than themselves.[116] It ended cannibalism, human sacrifice and infanticide once and for all; outlawed alcohol and nakedness, imposed cleanliness, and made necessary the wearing of shoes.[117] It banned raiding and plunder, and safeguarded life and property. It ordered the family and its internal relations on a footing of justice, and raised women to a status not reached by many of the civilized nations of modern times.[118] It established schools and imposed literacy on all its adherents, giving them a lingua franca with which to communicate internationally, and made possible the translation of books on religion and law to make their observance wider and deeper.[119] It ordered them to build houses that lent privacy to their families and mosques in which to congregate for worship and the conduct of public affairs. It encouraged travel, trade, and industry and brought to the converts the best and most advanced learning known to other Muslims in the world.[120] In short, conversion to Islam meant for the primitive a leap into civilization, from a miserable existence lacking in decency and dignity to one replete with both, and beautified with the products of Islamic poetry and art.[121]

As Gottschalk et al note, at the beginning, many local customs infringed on the understanding of Islam, however, in the 17th and 18th centuries took

---

[115] I.R. and L.L. Al-Faruqi: *The Cultural Atlas*; op cit; p. 227.
[116] Ibid.
[117] Ibid.
[118] Ibid.
[119] Ibid.
[120] Ibid; p. 228.
[121] Ibid.

place a purification of East Indian Islam.[122] Some of the more unacceptable native practices were eliminated, and some of the more basic tenets of Islam gained wider currency and deeper understanding or were associated with elements of the native tradition that were too precious to surrender.[123] In this process new teachers and missionaries from India and the Middle East or East Indians who had gone to these areas to study were important agents. Pilgrimages to Makkah also played a part; many local rulers sending their sons there, and merchants, nobles, and others who could afford it themselves made the pilgrimage.[124] The mosque schools were also effective media of education, as were the private schools, and in rural communities, villagers received elementary instruction in prayer halls from leaders who had received some training.[125]

---

[122] L. Gottschalk et al: History; op cit; p. 345.
[123] Ibid.
[124] Ibid.
[125] Ibid.

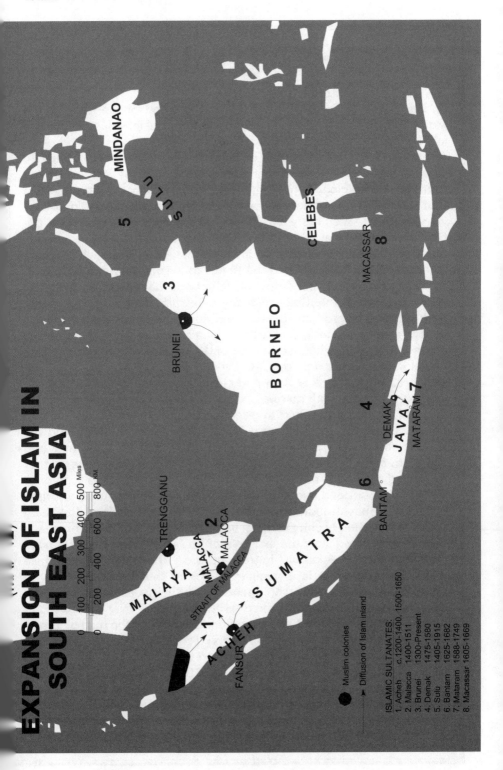

EXPANSION OF ISLAM IN SOUTH EAST ASIA

ISLAMIC SULTANATES:
1. Acheh   c.1200-1400, 1500-1650
2. Malacca   1400-1511
3. Brunei   1300-Present
4. Demak   1475-1580
5. Sulu   1405-1915
6. Bantam   1625-1682
7. Mataram   1588-1749
8. Macassar 1605-1669

● Muslim colonies

→ Diffusion of Islam inland

MALAYA

TRENGGANU

MALACCA

MALACCA

STRAIT OF MALACCA

SUMATRA

ACHEH

FANSUR

BRUNEI

BORNEO

SULU

MINDANAO

CELEBES

MACASSAR

DEMAK

JAVA

BANTAM

MATARAM

An Instance of how Islam Spread in South East Asia

This story is transmitted to us by Arnold:

`In the annals of Queda, one of the northernmost of the states of the Malay Peninsula, we have a curious account of the introduction of Islam into this kingdom, about 1501, as follows:

A learned Arab, by the name of Shaykh Abd Allah, having come to Queda, visited the Raja and inquired what was the religion of the country, "My religion," replied the Raja, "and that of all my subjects is that which has been handed down to us by the people of old. We all worship idols." "Then has your highness never heard of Islam, and of the Qur'an which descended from God to Muhammad, and has superseded all other religions, leaving them in the possession of the devil?" "I pray you then, if this be true," said the Raja, "to instruct and enlighten us in this new faith." In a transport of holy fervour at this request, Shaykh Abd Allah embraced the Raja and then instructed him in the creed. Persuaded by his teaching, the Raja sent for all his jars of spirits (to which he was much addicted), and with his own hands emptied them on the ground. After this he had all the idols of the palace brought out; the idols of gold, and silver, and clay, and wood were all heaped up in his presence, and were all broken and cut to pieces by Shaykh Abd Allah with his sword and with an axe, and the fragments consumed in the fire. The Shaykh asked the Raja to assemble all his women of the fort and palace. When they had all come to the presence of the Raja and the Shaykh, they were initiated into Islam. The Shaykh was mild and courteous in his demeanour, persuasive and soft in his language, so that he gained the hearts of the inmates of the palace. The Raja soon after sent for his four aged ministers, who on entering the hall, were surprised at seeing a Shaykh seated near the Raja. The Raja explained to them the object of the Shaykh's coming; whereupon the four chiefs expressed their readiness to follow the example of his highness, saying, "We hope that Shaykh Abd Allah will instruct us also." The latter hearing these words, embraced the four ministers and said that he hoped that, to prove their sincerity, they would send for all the people to come to the audience hall, bringing with them all the idols that they were wont to worship and the idols that had been handed down by the men of former days. The request was complied with and all the idols kept by the people were at that very time brought down and there destroyed and burnt to dust; no one was sorry at this demolition of their false gods, all were glad to enter Islam. Shaykh Abd Allah, after this said to the four ministers, "What is the name of your prince?" They replied, "His name is Pra Ong Mahawangsa." "Let us change it for one in the language of Islam," said the Shaykh. After some consultation, the name of the Raja was changed at his request to Sultan Muziaf al-Shah, because, the shaykh said, it is a celebrated name and is found in the Qur'an.

The Raja now built mosques wherever the population was considerable, and directed that to each there should be attached forty four of the inhabitants at least as a settled congregation, for a smaller number would have been few for the duties of religion. So mosques were erected and great drums were attached to them to be beaten to call the people to prayer on Fridays. Shaykh Abd Allah continued for some time to instruct the people in the religion of Islam; they flocked to him from all the coasts and districts of Queda and its vicinity, and were initiated by him into its forms and ceremonies.'[126]

---

[126] In T. Arnold: *The Preaching of Islam;* op cit; pp. 377-8.

3. Islam in India:

We left India in chapter four when Ghaznavid power was about to pass into the hands of the Ghurids.

a. Muslim India: From the Ghurids to the Mughals:

Mohammed Ghuri, a brilliant Turkish general, moved into northern India from his base in Ghazni. At the first battle of Tarain in 1191, however, he was successfully opposed by a coalition of Rajput chiefs under Prithvi Raj, at Tarain (modern Taraori), near Karmal. The Rajputs attacked with such vigour that both wings of the Muslim army were driven from the field.[127] The centre stood under Mohammed Ghuri, who was nearly killed, his life saved by a young soldier, and the battle ending in the first major Muslim defeat in northern India.[128] Mohammed Ghuri, on his return home, meted exemplary punishment to the army chiefs who had fled from the battlefield, and as a severe penance for himself, did not wear fine cloth or engage in any festivities for a year, but concentrated all his energies on preparation for a return to India.[129] He returned to the same battlefield in 1192, and on this occasion the Rajput chiefs were overcome by the mobile armoured cavalry of the Turks.[130] Prithvi Raj fled but was later killed; Delhi was captured and the surrounding territories of northern India were absorbed by the Muslims.[131]

Mohammed Ghuri died fourteen years after the victory at Tarain, leaving nearly all of Northern India under Muslim rule. In Aibak, Iltutmish, Nasir Eddin Qabacha, and Mohammed Bin Bakhtyar Khalji, he left a group of very able officers, who could complete his task.[132] Many of them, who later became rulers of India, were originally slaves, who later on became generals, governors, and more trustworthy than sons or other relatives of

---

[127] S.M. Ikram: *Muslim Civilisation in India;* op cit; 1964; p. 38.
[128] Ibid.
[129] Ibid.
[130] E. Wright ed: *The Medieval and Renaissance World;* Hamlyn Publishing; London; 1979; p. 332.
[131] Ibid.
[132] S.M. Ikram: *Muslim Civilisation in India;* op cit; p. 40.

rulers.[133] Bakhtyar Khalji, for instance, commanding a small force, conquered Bihar and Bengal.[134]

Ghiyath Eddin Tughluq, a provincial ruler, had come to Delhi to punish the Hindu slave who usurped power from the last Khalji Sultan.[135] That usurper, Khusraw Khan, had put to death the family of the sultan, whilst his Hindu companions destroyed mosques and many copies of the Qur'an.[136] Influential Muslim figures outside Delhi called upon the army general, Ghazi Malik, to intervene, and following his successful intervention, he was established as Sultan, under the name of Ghiat Eddin Tughluq Shah, the first ruler of the Tughluq, a dynasty, which lasted nearly a century.[137]

Ghiat Eddin Tughluk, who became sultan of Delhi in September 1320 was the son of a Turkish slave of Balban and a Jat woman.[138] Whilst his rule was marked with success, that of his son, Mohammed, was a disastrous experience due to his misrule, compounded by terrible natural disasters.[139]

The greatest Tughluq ruler was Firuz, who took over from Mohammed, in a rule which lasted from 1351 to 1388, a period marked by a return to purer values of Islam, and great achievements on the ground; during Firuz's rule no less than 200 towns were founded, together with 40 mosques, 30 colleges, 30 reservoirs, 50 dams, 100 hospitals, 100 public baths, and 150 bridges, besides a whole new capital near Delhi.[140]

The Sayyid and Lodi dynasties ruled the Muslim provinces of India after the Tughluq Sultanate, but did not add to Muslim territories.[141] Nonetheless the Islamic advance proceeded through the usual peaceful means. All along the western coast, the Hindu princes of the pepper ports welcomed the Arab and Persian merchants who linked them to the Gulf, the Red Sea and the trade of the Levant, and gave them freedom to build mosques and to worship. In the Vijayanagar armies Muslim troops were employed in the administration of the Bahmani Hindu clerks and revenue officials.[142] In time a considerable number of Hindus were converted to Islam; Muslims forming a brotherhood in which everyone was equal in the

---

[133] Ibid; pp. 40-1.
[134] I.R. and L.L. Al-Faruqi: *The Cultural Atlas;* op cit; p. 218.
[135] Ibid.
[136] S.M. Ikram: *Muslim Civilisation in India*; op cit; p. 69.
[137] Ibid.
[138] Ibid; p. 70.
[139] Ibid.
[140] Ibid; pp. 74-5.
[141] I.R. and L.L. Al-Faruqi: *The Cultural Atlas*; op cit; p. 218.
[142] E. Wright ed: *The Medieval and Renaissance World;* op cit; p. 336.

sight of God.[143] This concept of equality appealed to large numbers of the poorer classes of the people who were traditionally kept down by the rigid Indian caste system.[144] In this respect, Ikram counters, once more, the argument that Islam was spread by the sword.[145] He shows that the very distribution of the Muslim population does not support the idea that it was spread by the sword, for if that was the case, one would expect to find the Muslims as a majority in parts controlled by them. Instead, the percentage of Muslims is low around Delhi, Lucknow, Ahmadabad, Ahmadnagar, and Bijapur, the principal seats of Muslim political power.[146] Even in the case of Mysore, where Sultan Tipu is said to have forced conversion to Islam, Muslims only represent 5% of the total population, whilst in Malabar, where there has never been Islamic power, the percentage of Muslims rises to 30% of the total population today.[147]

Muslim rule in India was followed by great cultural developments. Throughout the 13th century, after the sack of Baghdad in 1258, there was a steady influx of artists and learned men who fled to India to escape from the Mongols.[148] At Delhi the various sultans patronized the arts and encouraged the emergence of schools where religious studies, literature and scientific subjects were taught. Even rulers such as Ala Eddin Khalji, who was almost illiterate, supported literary activity as much as any of the other sultans, and during his reign, Delhi became the centre of the Muslim cultural world.[149] Ikram provides an excellent outline of the accomplishments in learning, literature and the arts during this period (prior to the Mughals).[150] Other than the construction of schools and colleges in all provincial capitals, a flowering of literature and arts took place, and there also was a remarkable outburst in architecture, Muslim experience brought from Baghdad, Cairo, Damascus and Cordova, drawing on the skills of Indian stonemasons, the result a profusion of mosques, palaces, and mausoleums unmatched anywhere else.[151]

Beyond the immediate area of Muslim control, life for the Hindu peasant went on much as it had done before the Islamic conquest. In the rural areas

---

[143] Ibid; pp. 333-4.
[144] Ibid.
[145] S.M. Ikram: *Muslim Civilisation in India;* op cit; pp. 123 ff.
[146] Ibid
[147] Ibid; p. 124.
[148] E. Wright ed: *The Medieval*; op cit; p. 334.
[149] Ibid.
[150] S.M. Ikram: *Muslim Civilisation in India;* op cit; p. 112 ff.
[151] Ibid; pp. 113-20.

Hindu landowners retained much of their power, and Hindu merchants were largely in control of trade and commerce.[152] Agricultural products, textiles, herbs and scents were sent to nearby countries and to South East Asia.[153] The textile industry, in particular, developed during the Muslim period, and different and improved varieties of cloth were introduced by the Muslims from Persia and Arabia, and large factories, some of which employed several thousand weavers, were set up.[154]

b. From the Mughals to the Pre-colonial Period:

The Mughal Dynasty was founded by Babur following his victory over the Lodis at Panipat in 932H/1516. A period of consolidation followed. In 971/1564, Gondwana was annexed, and Akbar marched against Chitor and conquered it.[155] The only territorially significant addition after that was Jinji in 1698, and Koukan in 1700, which followed the successful termination of the Maratha's resistance to Muslim Mughal power. From then on, Muslim political and military power went on the decline.[156] The six great Mughals and their reigns were: Babur 1527-1530; Humayun 530-1556; Akbar 1556-1605; Jehangir 1605-1627; Shah Jahan 1627-1658; Aurangzeb 1658-1707

When Akbar died in 1605, his empire stretched from Kandahar to Calcutta, from the Himalayas to the Deccan Plateau. His administration, both strong and efficient, attracted and was made from the talents of Turks, Uzbek, Persian, Indian, and Rajput alike.[157] He forbade mutilation or other cruelty as the accompaniment of capital punishments. He re-formed and re-modelled his army, paying his troops in cash from the treasury instead by assignments on the revenue, and besides fortifications and other public works, he erected many magnificent buildings.[158] System and method were introduced into every part of the public service, and the whole of his establishments present an astonishing picture of magnificence and good order, where unwieldy numbers are managed without

---

[152] E. Wright ed: *The Medieval*; op cit; p. 334.
[153] Ibid.
[154] Ibid.
[155] I.R. and L.L. Al-Faruqi: *The Cultural Atlas;* op cit; p. 218.
[156] Ibid.
[157] E. Wright ed: *The Medieval*; op cit; p.344.
[158] J. Davenport: *An Apology;* op cit; p. 103.

disturbance, and economy is attended to in the midst of profusion.[159] He ignored or softened the religious differences between his subjects, and his court provided the unifying experience of common imperial services and fostered a common culture.[160]

Akbar's successor, Jahangir (1605-27), was rather weak, making no territorial advance, and worse, his state being marked by extravagant expenditure.[161] The lavish style of living introduced at the royal court was initiated by the nobility, and an era of extravagance, with its concomitants of corruption and demoralisation among officers of the state, was inaugurated.[162] This corroded the structure of the Mughal government. Ikram blames primarily for this condition the influence of Jahangir's wife, Nur Jahan, who encouraged extravagant expenditure, and the loss of the spiritual side of life in favour of materialistic values; gracious living becoming the goal of human existence.[163]

The reign of Shah Jehan (1627-1658), the grandson of Akbar, was the most prosperous ever known in India. His own dominions enjoyed almost uninterrupted tranquillity, and good government.[164] Shah Jehan ruled over his territory not as ruler but as father. His vigilance over his internal government was unremitting, and for the order and arrangement of his territory, and the good administration of every department of the state.[165] It was during the reign of this prince that the famous Delhi canal was constructed under the superintendence of his architect, Ali Murda Khan. After having ministered to the necessities of the husbandmen, during a course of several hundred miles, this magnificent aqueduct was made subservient to the luxury and taste of the imperial city.[166] A thousand streams flowed from its solid bed on either side, and spreading themselves through masonry channels, into every quarter of Delhi, `disported, in varied shapes, through marble jets, or cooled the fevered limbs in sculptured baths, or trickled over the gorgeous flowers in harems, lawns and terraces, or, anon, flowed to the humble houses of labourers, and slaked the poor man's thirst, and bathed the poor man's brow.'[167]

---

[159] Ibid.
[160] E. Wright ed: *The Medieval*; op cit; p.344.
[161] S.M. Ikram: *Muslim Civilisation in India;* op cit; pp. 177-80.
[162] Ibid; pp. 178-9.
[163] Ibid.
[164] J. Davenport: *An Apology for Mohammed;* op cit; p. 104.
[165] Ibid.
[166] Ibid.
[167] Ibid.

On the Muslim accomplishments in India, Davenport notes how:
'It may not be altogether un-instructive to compare the noble and enduring works of these Eastern princes with the progress made in a like direction in our own country, or indeed, in any Western kingdom, at that period. The two pictures, it is greatly to be feared, would not bear comparison. In this country (England), we know, at any rate, that at the epoch alluded to, we possessed not a single canal; that our roads were, with few exceptions, mere cattle tracks; that our large cities could not boast the supply of water, or of the police protection accorded to the humblest town within the empire of Delhi; nor had an English traveller, journeying from London to Highgate, in those early days, so great a certainty of reaching his destination in safety, as had any Shah Jehan's subjects in travelling from the Punjab frontier to Delhi, or from the latter city to Allahabad.'[168]

Aurangzib (1618-1707), the last Mughal, was a fearless soldier, industrious, and an able administrator.[169] He ruled more of India than any previous monarch, and in a court that had become a byword for luxury, he lived a life of austere piety.[170] About him, Lane Poole says:
'Nothing in life-neither throne, nor love, nor ease weighed for an instant in his mind against his fealty to the principles of Islam.'[171]
   The arrival of Western companies coincided precisely with the demise of Mughal power, itself subsequent to the passing of Aurangzib. After a long reign of fifty years, and just before his death, realising Western scheming, he begged his sons to remain united:
'I foresee,' he wrote, 'that there will be much bloodshed. May God the Ruler of hearts implant in yours the will to succour your subjects, and give you wisdom in the governance of the people.'[172]
His foresight presaged the fratricidal struggle, the sufferings of the people. But reality was worse:
'A veil concealed from his (Aurangzib) dying eyes the shame and ignominy of the long line of impotent successors that desecrated his throne, the swelling tide of barbarian invaders from the south, the ravages of Persian and Afghan armies from the north, and the final triumph of the infidel traders upon whose small beginnings in the east and west of his wide dominions he had hardly condescended to bestow a glance.'[173]

---

[168] Ibid.
[169] S.M. Ikram: *Muslim Civilisation in India*; op it; p. 189.
[170] Ibid.
[171] S. Lane Poole: *Arangzib*; Oxford at the Clarendon Press; p. 64.
[172] Ibid; p. 205.
[173] Ibid; pp. 205-6.

Infidels, who would soon fall on India, as on the rest of the Muslim realm, and plunge it into turmoil.

Conclusions

This chapter has shown that Islam was not spread by the sword as distorted history maintains. Islam, instead, was responsible for great accomplishments in these continents. It is these accomplishments that Western colonial powers would eventually destroy. Their invasion was aimed at stopping the progress of Islam and looting its lands. The final chapter of this work shows this abundantly.

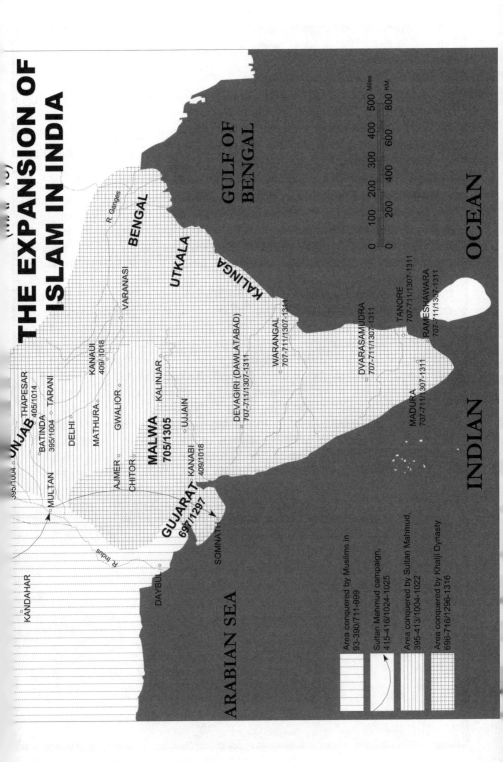

THE EXPANSION OF ISLAM IN INDIA

KANDAHAR

R. Indus

395/1004
MULTAN

PUNJAB THAPESAR
BATINDA 405/1014
395/1004 TARANI

DELHI
MATHURA GWALIOR

KANAUJ
409/1018

VARANASI

R. Ganges

BENGAL

UTKALA

AJMER
CHITOR

KALINJAR
MALWA UJJAIN
705/1305 KANABI
409/1018

KALINGA

DAYBUL

GUJARAT
697/1297

SOMNATH

DEVAGIRI (DAWLATABAD)
707-711/1307-1311

WARANGAL
707-711/1307-1311

ARABIAN SEA

DYARASAMUDRA
707-711/1307-1311

GULF OF
BENGAL

TANORE
707-711/1307-1311

MADURA
707-711/1307-1311

RAMESHAWARA
707-711/1307-1311

INDIAN

OCEAN

Miles
0 100 200 300 400 500
0 200 400 600 800 KM.

Area conquered by Muslims in
93-390/711-999

Sultan Mahmud campaign,
415-416/1024-1025

Area conquered by Sultan Mahmud,
395-413/1004-1022

Area conquered by Khalji Dynasty
696-716/1296-1316

A Tale from Muslim India

A British gentleman, Mr Holwell who had resided in Bengal in the early 17th century, says:

`In truth, it would be almost cruelty to molest this happy people, for in this district are the only vestiges of the beauty, purity, piety, regularity, equity and strictness of the ancient Hindostan government. Hence the property as well as the liberty of the people, are inviolable. Here, no robberies are heard of, either public or private. The traveller, either with or without merchandise, becomes the immediate care of the government, which allots him guards, without any expenses, to conduct him from stage to stage; and these are accountable for the safety and accommodation of his person and effects. At the end of the first stage he is delivered over, with certain benevolent formalities, to the guards of the next, who, after interrogating the traveller as to the usage he had received in his journey, dismiss the first guard with a written certificate of their behaviour, and a receipt for the traveller and his effects, which certificate and receipt are returnable to the commanding officer of the first stage who registers the same and regularly reports it to the Rajah.

In this form, the traveller is passed along through the country, and if he only passes, he is not suffered to be at any expense for food, accommodation or carriage for his merchandise or luggage; but it is otherwise if he is permitted to make any residence in one place above three days, unless occasioned by sickness or any unavoidable accident. If anything is lost in this district, for instance, a bag of money or other valuable, the person who finds it hangs it on the next tree, and gives notice to the nearest choutry or place of guard, the officer of which orders immediate publication of the same by beat of tom-tom, or drum.'[174]

---

[174] J. Davenport: *An Apology for Mohammed;* op cit; pp. 105-6.

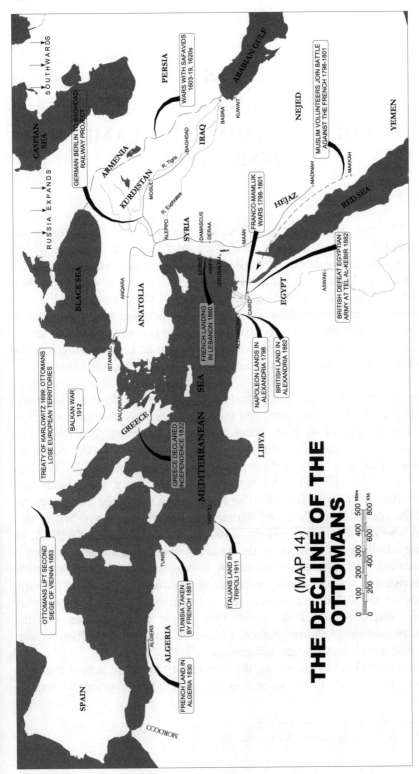

(MAP 14)

THE DECLINE OF THE OTTOMANS

TEN

COLONISATION AND ISLAMIC RESISTANCE

The 18th and 19th centuries witnessed the systematic colonisation of Islamic lands. Those that were not, were later occupied in the early 20th century. The colonisation of the Islamic world was aimed at stemming the advance of Islam and undermining its influence wherever it was established, and also exploiting the resources of the Islamic world. These objectives were suppressed from colonial rhetoric, and colonisation, instead, was presented as a civilising mission of barbaric Islamic societies. Under the banner of Islam, Muslims rose in armed resistance against the colonial powers. These are the points covered in this chapter.

A crucial remark needs to be made at this juncture, though. Generally, modern works by Westerners, and even by some Muslims, have cleansed Western history of its dark deeds. We even hear and read today that Western colonisation brought civilisation and progress to the colonised people. This is a great fallacy. This chapter, relying on old Western sources, above all, will show that the colonial history was bloody and destructive, and that it left a terrible legacy from which the Muslim world and the continents of Asia and Africa have not recovered yet. Whilst this work shows the colonial history in its real image, it avoids dwelling, or going into its worst aspects, i.e the widespread massacres and genocides it committed. The destructive impact of colonisation can indeed be amply demonstrated without having recourse to unravelling the most barbaric deeds of the colonisers, which serves no purpose other than opening graves that should be kept sealed. This author, indeed, agrees with the modern British journalist, Robert Fisk, who, in a recent editorial said: `Some buried bones are best left un-dug.'[1795]

Which should not be, however, the opportunity for those behind the mass graves to say that there never was any as modern Western historians,

---

[1795] R. Fisk: *The Independent;* 10 December 05; p. 39.

generally, hold, and as, generally, inept, corrupt, Westernised modern 'Muslim' 'intellectuals' acquiesce.

1. The Aims of Colonial Powers:

There were primarily two major aims for Western military conquest of the Islamic land:
-To stem the advance of Islam, and remove it wherever it was established.
-To exploit, or some would say, to loot Islamic lands.

These two aims follow an established tradition. Hence, the early (in the late 15th century) intruders into the Islamic world, the Portuguese, followed the twin objectives of destroying the Islamic presence, and to loot Islamic wealth. The 19th century historian, Howitt, notes how the Portuguese were nothing loath. They were, in the expressive language of a great historian, 'all on fire for plunder and the propagation of their religion!'[1796] These aims were very clear to the Portuguese commander, Albuquerque, who, whilst devastating the Muslim Eastern trade and land, to his men insisted on:
'The great service which we shall perform to our Lord in casting the Moors out of this country and of quenching the fire of the sect of Mahomet so that it may never burst out again hereafter.'[1797]
After service to God, he alluded to the service to his king 'for,' he said 'I hold it certain that if we take this trade of Malacca away from them, Cairo and Mecca will entirely be ruined.'[1798]

 Holland's aims, following its intrusion in Muslim South East Asia, were the same as those of Portugal, but the atrocities committed by its people, perhaps, worse. The Dutch literally wiped out whole Muslim populations in places. Howitt says of them, that at home the people of Holland were moderate, kindly and liberal; abroad their rapacity, perfidy, and infamous cruelty made them resemble devils rather than men.[1799] When they took over Malacca in 1641, and the Dutch commander then tauntingly asked the

---

[1796] W. Howitt: *Colonisation and Christianity*: Longman; London; 1838; pp. 173.4.
[1797] In K.M. Panikkar: *Asia and Western Domination*; George Allen and Unwin Ltd; London; 1953; p. 49.
[1798] Ibid.
[1799] W. Howitt: *Colonisation*; op cit; p. 192.

commander of the Portuguese garrison, as he marched out, when he would come back again to the place, the Portuguese gravely replied: `when your crimes are greater than ours!'[1800]

In the East, Holland's most lucrative posts were at Java, Bantam and the Moluccas. No sooner had they gained ascendancy that they surpassed the Portuguese in perfidy and cruelty.[1801] The Moluccas were the source of cloves, nutmeg, and the nutmeg fleece called mace, particularly on the Island of Banda.[1802] In 1621, in order to ensure their control of these places and trade, the Dutch exterminated or deported the local people to Batavia, to be replaced by colonists from Holland who were granted land tracks planted with nutmeg trees, together with the services of Company slaves for cultivation.[1803] Such was the scale of their massacres, one province, Banywawngi, which in 1750 had upwards of 80,000 souls, in 1811, was reduced to 8,000.[1804]

The British intrusion also had the same aims of seeking to stem the Islamic advance, and to exploit the resources of the Islamic land. In Africa, for instance, as recognised by a War Department witness, Captain Clarke, the British military presence was to support the weaker (and pagan) coastal tribes against the stronger (and Muslim) ones inland. He saw no evidence of the success of Christianity, whilst `the Koran enforces on the Pagan a purer morality, which raises him above cannibalism, man-stealing, and degrading fetish, and leads him to a new civilisation which, creating in him new wants, teaches him, and to some extent, at least, to value the lives and industry of others'. The Muslims, he maintains, would have reached the coast if `Britain had not lent the Ashantis the support of its name.'[1805]

In India, likewise, from the initial moment of their arrival, the British broke Islamic held power, and used subsequent developments, and even incidents such as the revolt of 1857, to implement measures aimed at shifting power which once belonged to the Muslims in favour of the Hindus.[1806]

[1800] Ibid; p. 198.
[1801] Ibid; p. 192.
[1802] E.R. Wolf: *Europe and the People Without History*; University of California Press; Berkeley; 1982; p. 238.
[1803] Ibid.
[1804] W. Howitt: *Colonisation*; op cit; p. 200.
[1805] Select Committee, Report on Africa (Western Coast) in N. Daniel: *Islam; Europe and Empire;* University Press, Edinburgh, 1966; p. 297-8.
[1806] R.C. Majumdar: *History and Culture of the Indian people*; 11 vols; Bombay; 1951-1969. vol IX: p. 661.

Islam was seen as a powerful obstacle in front of colonial aims, and vanquishing it remained a central preoccupation of Western colonial ideology. Buchanan, thus, held: the Muslims would never 'bend humbly to Christian dominion while they remained Muslim.'[1807] A view adhered to by both Western officials and Christian missionaries.[1808] Sir William Muir (1818-1905), Lt Governor of the vast territory known as the North West provinces of India, acknowledged that Islam was 'the only undisguised and formidable antagonist of Christianity.[1809] A view shared by the leading missionary figures such as E.A. Freeman, who, in his *History,* stated, that Islam was 'an object of abhorrence... essentially an obstructive, intolerant system.' Mohammed might not have been 'the Antichrist of scripture,' but Islam was 'emphatically anti-Christian,' the 'Bitterest foe to Christian faith and Western law.'[1810] In Algeria, Thomson notes: 'the identification of the Arabs as fanatical Moslems marked them out as the implacable enemies of the French.'[1811]

Pan Islamism, that is the solidarity of Muslims fighting colonial powers, remained the focal point of attack due to its opposition to Western domination. As such, Rodinson notes, pan Islamism was deemed 'a sinister conspiracy.'[1812] So strong was Western obsession that Western Christendom was progress and civilisation, and Islam backwardness, that any opposition to the former was 'a sign of resistance against progress,' and 'whenever there was any show of anti-imperialism, even if it was purely local reaction, pan-Islam was blamed.'[1813] In this respect, as Rodinson points out, whilst European armies were colonising continents (adding to those they had already subjugated in the Americas and Oceania), they still held that it was Pan-Islamism that was attempting at domination, that bore an aggressive ideology, and that was the fruit of international conspiracy.[1814] In Pan Islam, Westerners were apt to see 'an illusory unity of purpose and meticulous attention to the execution of evil designs that relied on the most treacherous methods to oppose the

---

[1807] Buchanan: *Memoir of the Expediency of an Ecclesiastical Establishment for India;* London; 1805.

[1808] N. Daniel: *Islam; Europe; and Empire;* op cit; p.252.

[1809] Sir William Muir: The Mohammedan Controversy, in N. Daniel: *Islam, Europe;* op cit, p. 32.

[1810] E.A.Freeman: *The History and Conquests of the Saracens*; Oxford: John Henry and James Parker; 1856; London; Mc Millan 1876; 3rd ed; p. 72.

[1811] A. Thomson: *Barbary and Enlightenment:* Brill; Leiden; 1987; p. 111.

[1812] M. Rodinson: *Europe and the Mystique of Islam*; tr R. Veinus; I.B. Tauris and Co Ltd; London; 1988; p.127.

[1813] Examples can be found in Daniel: *Islam, Europe;* op cit; pp. 385-6.

[1814] M. Rodinson: Europe; op cit; p.127.

Europeans'.[1815] Through the popular press, popular literature, and even children's books, this view had a lasting effect on the thinking of many Europeans, and it also influenced scholars (for some of whom, Pan-Islamism became an obsession), particularly when they gave their supposedly competent advice to overseers of colonial policies.[1816]

 The crusade spirit and the subjugation of the Islamic lands were closely associated, amongst the French, most particularly. This was obvious from the very early stages of the French entry in Algeria in 1830:
'You have renewed with the crusades' declared the French leading General de Bourmont to his soldiers.[1817]
'Our war in Africa is a continuation of the Crusades,' said Minister Poujoulat to General Bugeaud in 1844.[1818]
'According to me,' said another French general, E. Pelissier: 'This is the second act (the independence of Greece being the first); this is the second act, I say, in the Mediterranean, of the inexorable absorption of the Muslim world by the Christians, a task being undertaken with great success by both the English and Russians in India and Central Asia.'[1819]

The war on Islam was never isolated from the other ultimate objective: the loot of Islamic wealth. James Grey Jackson, for instance, tells us that the conquest of Algeria would result in the 'civilisation of the Berbers' and their conversion to Christianity.[1820] He then remarks that conquest should lead to the occupation of her neighbours, and he enumerates the advantages that would follow:
'1. An incalculable demand for spices and East Indian manufactures of silk and cotton.
2. A similar demand for coffee and sugar manufactured and un-manufactured; as well as for other articles of West Indian produce.
3. An incalculable demand for all our various articles of manufacture. In addition, Britain would obtain from this fine country:
a. An immense supply of the finest wheat and other grain that the world produces.

[1815] Ibid.
[1816] Ibid.
[1817]A. Surre-Garcia: l'Image du sarrasin dans les mentalites de la litterature Occitanes: *De Toulouse a Tripoli*, op cit; pp 181-9; at p.186.
[1818] Ibid.
[1819] E.D. Pelissier: *Quelques mots sur la colonisation Militaire en Algerie;* Paris; 1847; in N. Daniel: *Islam; Europe*; op cit; p. 330.
[1820] J.G. Jackson: *An Account of Timbuctu and Hausa;* London; 1820; p.463.

b. Direct commerce with the interior of Africa.'[1821]
 He pursues:
'The fertile and populous districts which lie contiguous to the Nile of Sudan, throughout the whole of the interior of Africa would become, in a few years, as closely connected to us, by mutual exchange of benefits as our own colonies; and such a stimulus would be imparted to British enterprises and industry, as would secure to us such a store of gold as would equal the riches of Solomon....'[1822]

Whilst these aims were central for the colonial powers, they were, however, hidden behind the veneer of `Civilising Mission,' ie, that Western colonisation only aimed at civilising barbaric Islamic societies.

2. The `Civilising Mission':

Just prior, and throughout the colonial period, Islamic lands, most of which were under Turkish guardianship, were depicted by Westerners as nothing other than dens of barbarism, despotism, murder and mayhem. The French Count St Priest, in 1777, thus held:
'There is no administration, no finance, only unruly populations, rebellious pachas, a riotous army, the pride of the barbarian, the hunger of the savage, rulers made into beasts by the culture of the harem, taught through tyranny, ministers and generals-mere animals-picked out of an ignorant mass, swarming with intrigues, adventurers and favourites put in power by chance of circumstances, this is Turkey.'[1823]
    Algeria, under Turkish rule, was deemed the hot bed of despotism and barbarism, a country about which Chevaliers D'Avrieux says:
'This is more or less what I would say about this unpleasant country, inhabited by the dregs of the provinces of the Ottoman Empire, and which we can consider without fear of errors as the most unworthy rabble in Africa and as a lair of thieves, which I shall never regret having left.'[1824]
Pananti, who had resided in Algeria early in the 19th century, says:

[1821] In A. Thomson: *Barbary*; op cit; p. 136; 50; etc.
[1822] J.G. Jackson: *An Account;* op cit*;* p 463.
[1823] G. Hanotaux/H. Deherain): *Histoire de la Nation Egyptienne*; op cit; pp. 203-4.
[1824] Chevallier d'Arvieux: *Memoires;* R. P. Labat; 6 Vols; Paris; 1735; Vol V; pp. 288-9.

'These degraded people... monsters who vie with each other in the deepest hatred and bitterest hostility towards Christianity and civilisation'.[1825]

In 1788, the Frenchman Volnay, in his *Considerations sur la Guerre des Turcs,* goes as far as blaming the Turks for 'spreading the plague':

'It is through these barbarians that this scourge got to us; it is they, who, by their stupid fanaticism, spread contagion by breeding its germs. If just for this reason their rule could perish. May other people establish themselves in their place, and the sea and the land be freed from their enslavement (of others).'[1826]

Mark Twain, the 19th century writer/traveller, on his visit of Tangiers, writing to his mother, said:

'We are glad we came here among the Africans, Moors, Arabs, and Bedouins of the desert. I would not give this experiment for all the balance of the trip combined. This is the infernalist hive of infernally barbarians I have come across yet.'[1827]

Of a Syrian village he says:

'It is a hive of huts one storey high... and as square as a drygoods box.... A Syrian village is the sorriest sight in the world.'[1828]

When he reaches the village of Endor:

'They were the wildest hordes of half naked savages we have found thus far.... It was Magdala over again, only here the glare from the infidel eyes was fierce and full of hate... Dirt, degradation, and savagery are Endor's speciality.'[1829]

Islam was deemed the main cause behind this state of degradation and barbaric nature of these societies. Abbot Raynal describes the degradation and the misery caused by 'Islamic despotism,' noting that the Muslim 'invaders' destroyed Christian civilisation of North Africa 'thanks to their genius for destruction and their fanaticism, and replaced it with slavery and tyranny,' and so he calls for Christian conquest to free Barbary from 'a handful of barbarians.'[1830]

[1825] F. Pananti: *Narrative of a Residence in Algiers*; Tr. E. Blaquiere: London; 1818 F.; p 416.

[1826] Volnay: *Oeuvres Completes*; Paris; 1864; p. 765.

[1827] A.B. Paine ed: *Mark Twain's Letters;* London; Chatto and Windus; 1920; I; p. 130.

[1828] M. Twain: *Travelling with the Innocents abroad*; ed. D.M. Mc.Keithan; Oklahama Press; 1958; p. 215 f.

[1829] Ibid; p. 305 f.

[1830] Abbe Raynal: *Histoire philosophique et politique des etablissements et du commerce des Europeanens dans l'Afrique*; Paris; 1826; Vol I; pp 106 fwd and 137.

According to the governor General of the North Western Province of India, Sir Muir:

'We fail of finding anywhere the germ of popular government or approach to free and liberal institutions.' Islam kept Muslim nations 'in a backward and in some respects barbarian state.'[1831]

The leading missionary: J.D. Bate (1836-1923), notes:

'Islam reduces to a state of degradation every civilised state over which it obtains ascendancy and renders impossible the social and moral elevation, beyond a certain point, of even the most degraded people. Wherever Islam has obtained the sole ascendancy, the vast induction of twelve centuries tells one uniform tale-that the ascendancy has been the death knell of all progress and the signal for general stagnation.'[1832]

And Lord Baring, (Lord Cromer,) the true ruler of Egypt (behind the Egyptian khedive), says:

'Islam is progress for the Black man who adopts it,' but was also as a social system, 'a complete failure,'' because of its 'subjugation of women, the union of religion and law, toleration of slavery and sectarianism.'[1833]

The worst legacy of Islam upon society, according to Western views, is the enslavement of women. Women are enslaved by ghoulish, repulsive looking, Muslim men, and the pictures of naked, or half naked, women exhibited in slave markets, always take central place in contemporary Western paintings.[1834] In these paintings, the Oriental man is always predatory, lecherous, gross, loathsome, and the woman, frail, and beautiful, and also helpless. The behaviour of the Oriental only mirrors his repulsive physical features.[1835] These depictions are well summed up by Kabbani:

'Their (oriental men's) villainy is compounded by the fact that they are portrayed as traders in female bodies. They are the cruel captors who hold women in their avaricious grasp, who use them as chattels, as trading-goods, with little reverence for them as human beings. This idea was highly important in distinguishing between the barbarity of the Eastern male and the civilised behaviour of the Western male. One tied women up and sold them at slave auctions; the other revered them and placed them on pedestals. The European (and the Englishman in particular) cherished

---

[1831] W. Muir: *The Caliphate;* Smith and Elder and Co; London; 1883; p. 599.
[1832] J.D. Bate: *The Claims of Ishmael;* London; W. Allen; 1884; p. 301.
[1833] In N. Daniel: *Islam, Europe;* op cit; p. 470.
[1834] R. Kabbani: *Europe's Myths of Orient;* Mc Millan; 1986; pp. 78-9.
[1835] Ibid.

the notion of his gentlemanliness among savages. It was one added way of convincing himself that he was born to rule over them.'[1836]

This Islamic barbarism, in Western view became a syndrome, a stain on humanity, which the Christian West felt dutiful to remove. `Let us,' thus says Lord Cromer, `Let us in Christian charity, make every possible allowance for the moral and intellectual shortcomings of the Egyptians, and do whatever can be done to rectify them.'[1837]

Bayard Taylor, the American litterateur, in his work *Lands of the Saracens*,[1838] held:

`What a paradise might be made of this country, were it in better hands!' or more directly: `Give Palestine into Christian hands, and it will again flow with milk and honey.'[1839]

Shaler, an apologist for the colonisation of Algeria, insists:

`True civilisation could only come about by a transfer of responsibility into the hands of Christian nations who would favour agriculture, industry and commerce and thus civilise the region. The `primitive' was incapable of progressing by its own unaided efforts.'[1840]

For Abbe Raynal, the North Africans, cannot civilise themselves, and so must be taken in hand by the Europeans.[1841] The reason: the `Algerines were committed by religion, custom and heredity to see life from a particular viewpoint,'' and they would never become civilised unless forced to do so; thus `total conquest and permanent occupation were the only solutions.[1842]

For J.Grey Jackson:

`The only solution is conquest, and the conquerors should then set up a firm government to quell the inhabitants' religious prejudices, until they are reconciled to a rational government, mild compared to the present despotism. The only reason for hostility on the part of the inhabitants is to be their religious fanaticism.'[1843]

As Jackson elaborates, this conquest may not be welcome by those who are to be liberated, but once their fanaticism and bigotry are overcome,

---

[1836] Ibid; pp. 76-7.

[1837] Lord Cromer: *Modern Egypt;* London; 1908; 2 Vols; Vol 2; p. 538.

[1838] Bayard Taylor: *Lands of the Saracens*; New York; Putnam; 1855.

[1839] Ibid; p. 129.

[1840] W. Shaller: *Sketches of Algiers*; Boston; 1826; p.56.

[1841] Abbe Raynal: *Histoire philosophique et politique des etablissements;* op cit.

[1842] Perkins and Douglas Morris: *Gunfire in Barbary*; Havant; 1982; p. 175.

[1843] James. Grey Jackson: *An Account of Timbuctu and Hausa;* London; 1820; p 463.

they will realise how much their situation has improved. They are to be saved despite themselves.[1844]

Pananti, for his part, explains that once the civilised Christians are:

`Masters of North Africa, the harem walls must fall and suffer the miserable inmates to regain their natural rights in society, rendering the most beautiful part of creation what it should be, the happiness and consolation of mankind.'[1845]

Christians would convert `those who are now scarcely superior to the brute creation into good men and industrious citizens.'[1846]

The conquest `of Algiers' would `lead to the civilisation of Africa.'[1847]

And if the French respected Kabyle freedom they would be welcomed as liberators from their Turkish and Arab oppressors.[1848]

From the Western communist perspective, Rodinson wrote, `the Muslims remained culturally backward because of the powerful fanaticism intrinsic to Islam.'[1849] And to ascertain their enlightenment, which might take some time, though, `the revolutionary role, in Muslim countries,' had to belong to the European elite.[1850]

The Western coloniser, according to Fontana, thus, saw himself as a missionary of new times who proposed `to teach primitive peoples the true path of intellectual and material progress.'[1851] Regardless of their ideology, Westerners saw themselves as educators and guides, condemning Muslims for their lack of capacity to insert themselves in the march for progress.[1852]

`Political domination and economic exploitation needed the cosmetic cant of *mission civilisatrice* (Civilising Mission) to seem fully commendary,' Kabbani explains. `The image of the European coloniser had to remain an honourable one: he did not come as exploiter, but as enlightener. He was not seeking mere profit, but was fulfilling his duty to his maker and his sovereign, whilst aiding those less fortunate to rise toward his lofty level.

[1844] James. Grey Jackson: *An Account;* pp 457-63 in A. Thomson: Barbary; op cit; p. 131.

[1845] F. Pananti: *Narrative*; op cit; p.415.

[1846] Ibid; p 416.

[1847] Ibid; p. 412.

[1848] A. Thomson: *Barbary and Enlightenment:* Brill; Leiden; 1987; p. 109.

[1849] M. Rodinson: *Europe and the Mystique of Islam*; op cit; p.74.

[1850] Especially typical is Sidi Bel Abbes's famous letter written to the secretariat of the French Communist Party by the Communist militants of Algeria, which was published for the first time in H.Carrere d'Encausse, and S. Schram's: *le Marxisme et l'Asie 1853-1964*; Paris, 1965; pp. 268-71.

[1851] J. Fontana: *The Distorted Past,* Blackwell, 1995; p.130.

[1852] C.Grossir: *L'Islam des Romantiques*; Maisonneuve; Larose; Paris, 1984; p. 160.

This was the white man's burden, that reputable colonial *malaise* that sanctioned the subjugating of entire continents.'[1853]

3. A Brief Outline of the `Civilising Mission' at Work:

The `Civilising Mission' resulted in countless millions Muslim deaths; in Algeria alone, more than ten millions were killed or starved to death by the French.[1854] The following seeks to show how this `civilising mission' worked, but it will avoid dwelling on the worst instances of mass extermination of Muslims. The aim of this author is to deal with history and its dark episodes, but also to avoid the morbid and cruel, for, whilst it is important to depict correctly the past so as to make arguments against colonisation and genocide, it is wrong to dwell on its worst. Thus, only brief references to colonial atrocities will be made to show both the brutal nature of colonisation and, more importantly, to destroy the myth, which is cultivated and prevalent today, that colonisation was a civilising mission.[1855]

India:

In the preceding chapter, we left India with the Mughals. It was during their rule that the Western intrusion in the region began. The English, like other Westerners, came initially to India to `trade.' In 1600, the English East India Company was granted by Queen Elizabeth the monopoly on trade and navigation in the area between the Cape of Good Hope and the Straights of Magellan not occupied by a friendly power.[1856] In 1612, the first English establishment was made at Gujarat, followed by others at

---

[1853] R. Kabbani: *Europe's Myths*; op cit; p.6.

[1854] M. Lacheraf, in Louis Blin: *l'Algerie du Sahara au Sahel*, l'Harmattan, Paris, 1990; note 3, p 112.

[1855] In February 2005, the French Assembly voted to declare that the French colonization of Algeria brought progress and civilization to the Algerians.

[1856] E.J. Hamilton: The Role of Monopoly in the Overseas expansion and colonial Trade of Europe before 1800; in *The Making of Modern Europe*; Ed by H. Ausubel; The Dryden Press; New York; 1951; pp. 170-90; at p. 185.

Madras, Bombay, and Calcutta.[1857] Subsequently, the English acted as tax collectors and general administrators, first, and then, from this technically subordinate and transitory authority, began to gain complete control.[1858] The English faced initial competition from the French, the French, who, just like them (and the Dutch,) had entered the region as traders, via the French East India Company (Compagnie Francaise des Indes Orientales), which was established in 1604 by King Henry IV, also with exclusive rights to trade and navigate, and eventually to colonise in India and the East Indies.[1859]

Anglo-French expansionism was at first held in check by Aurengzib, the last Mughal ruler. He foresaw the Western schemes in the region, and in his final words before his death, he begged his sons not to fight each other.[1860] No sooner had he departed, however, that local feuds erupted.[1861] Stirred into rebellion and armed by incoming Western 'traders,' Rajputs, Sikhs and Jats rose against Mughal power, which resulted in a myriad of warring statelets controlled by the Europeans established along the coastlines.[1862] As Lane Poole puts it: 'the infidel traders upon whose small beginnings in the east and west of his (Aurengzib) wide dominions he had hardly condescended to bestow a glance,'[1863] now decided matters of the country.

The English colonial hero in India was William Clive, who, back home, was famed for stealing, blackmail, and terrorizing shop owners with his gang, before he was dispatched to India.[1864] There, his criminal skills were put to great use. Clive played the various local parties against each other in the phase that led to the so-called 'decisive Battle of Plassey' (1757) for the conquest of Bengal. This battle, in modern history books, is supposed to have been a great British victory; in truth, the British bought the support of the Zamindars (local tax collectors) against their Mughal ruler, Siraj al-Dawla.[1865] Clive used the intermediary of a Hindu merchant to buy off the

---

[1857] A. Zahoor: Muslims in the Indian Sub-continent; at: http://www.minhaj-audio.net/Astro/A%20Chronology%20of%20Muslims%20in%20the%20Indian%20Subcontinent%20-%20IV%20(1700-1800%20CE).htm
[1858] M.G.S. Hodgson: *The Venture of Islam;* Vol 3; The University of Chicago Press; 1961; p. 149.
[1859] E.J. Hamilton: The Role of Monopoly; op cit; p.183.
[1860] In. S. Lane Poole: *Aurengzib*; op cit; p. 205.
[1861] Ibid; pp 205-6.
[1862] E. Driault: *La Question;* op cit; p. 63.
[1863] S. Lane Poole: *Aurengzib*, op cit; pp 205-6.
[1864] S. Sharma: History of Britain; BBC2; 9 Nov 02.
[1865] E.R. Wolf: *Europe and the People Without History*; op cit; p. 244.

support of Meer Jafar, the commander-in-chief of the Bengal army.[1866] At the ensuing battle, the English took the field against Siraj al-Dawla, but Meer Jafar, in the midst of the engagement, went over to the English side with his troops, thus determining the fate of a great kingdom, and of thirty millions of people, with the loss of twenty Europeans killed and wounded, of sixteen Sepoys killed, and only thirty six wounded.[1867] Soon after, Siraj al-Dawla was seized and assassinated by the son of Meer Jafar; who was soon pulled down from the position he was placed by the English, to be replaced by his son in law, Meer Causim.[1868] The latter, Howitt notes, served for a time the purposes for which he was placed in power, resorting to every piece of cruelty to raise money from his subjects.[1869] As he was not good tool enough, the English removed him, and put back in power Meer Jafar, who 'although a criminal and imbecile, was preferable to Meer Causim, as he was an easier tool to deal with,' adds Howitt.[1870] Meer Jafar ruled as Nawab of Bengal [1757-60] to watch over British interests.[1871]

From their foothold in Bengal, the British expanded their territory rapidly, still relying on the cover of the East India Company, which, by 1765, had changed its character from that of a chartered trading organisation to that of a military and bureaucratic arm of the British government.[1872] The company took charge of some areas, and left others in charge of local rulers under its sponsorship.[1873] To conquer the rest of India, the technique remained as before: interference in the civil affairs of rulers.[1874] Benares had been a tributary of Oude; but in 1764, when the British commenced war against the Nawab of Oude, the Rajah of Benares joined them and rendered them the most essential services in exchange of protection and consideration.[1875] Soon, though, he was made to pay his tribute; and was summoned to keep maintenance of three battalions of Sepoys. He proved incapable of paying, and sought to corrupt Hastings, the British governor.[1876] Hasting took the money, and still pressed the Rajah for the payment of the rears, besides fining him 10 thousand pounds for delay; and soon troops were ordered to march in the Rajah territory to

---

[1866] S. Sharma: History of Britain; op cit.
[1867] W. Howitt: *Colonisation;* op cit; p. 220.
[1868] Ibid; p. 221.
[1869] Ibid.
[1870] Ibid.
[1871] A.Zahoor: *Muslims in the Indian sub-continent;* op cit.
[1872] E. Wolf: *Europe;* op cit; p. 245.
[1873] Ibid.
[1874] M.G.S. Hodgson: *The Venture of Islam;* op cit; p. 149.
[1875] W. Howitt: *Colonisation;* op cit; p. 230-1.
[1876] Ibid; p. 231.

enforce the decision.[1877] The Rajah lost his territory and possessions, and when the princesses, with their relatives and attendants to the number of three hundred women, besides children, withdrew from the castle, the capitulation was violated as they were plundered of their effects, and their persons rudely treated.[1878]

At best, Hodgson notes, the British were by no means uniformly successful in particular wars, the brilliant Muslim general turned ruler of Mysore (in the south western Deccan), Haydar Ali (d.1782) defeated them in the field and maintained his position against them in two wars.[1879] But British power outlasted all reverses and, when Indian powers were weak for a time, the British could always take advantage of this to expand their local base.[1880] This happened in the late 18th century, when India disintegrated into feuding states.[1881] As it divided into diverse confederations, the Maratha, Hyderabad, and Mysore, the British made the best of such divisions, defeating and conquering them separately; Hyderabad in 1789; Mysore in 1799; and the Maratha federation in the early 19th century.[1882] Only one state offered stiff resistance: Mysore, which fought four wars against the British. Tipu Sultan participated in all four Mysore wars, his rule beginning in the midst of one in 1760, and ending in the midst of another in 1799. Mysore became "the terror of Leadenhall Street;" the headquarters of the East India Company,[1883] but the British were supported during all four Mysore wars by the Marathas and the Nizam, thus a powerful confederacy against Tipu.[1884] During the brief fourth Mysore war, Tipu was killed in combat on 4 May 1799.

In their wars against Tipu, Howitt says, `the British heaped on his name all the odious crimes that make us hate the worst tyrants. Cruelty, perfidy, cunning, and all kinds of baseness, make up the idea of Tipu which we have derived from those who profited by his destruction.'[1885]
Yet, in the view of neutral historians, adds Howitt, quoting Mills:
`That the accounts which we have received from our countrymen, who dreaded and feared him (Tipu), are marked with exaggeration, is proved by this circumstance, that his servants adhered to him with a fidelity which

---

[1877] Ibid.

[1878] Ibid; p. 233.

[1879] M.G.S. Hodgson: *The Venture of Islam;* Vol 3; op cit; p. 149.

[1880] Ibid.

[1881] B. Sheikh Ali: *Wars and Agreements of Tipu Sultan* at http://www.islamicvoice.com/april.99/tippu.htm#

[1882] E. Wolf: *Europe*; op cit; p. 246.

[1883] B. Sheikh Ali: *Wars and Agreements of Tipu Sultan*; op cit.

[1884] Ibid.

[1885] W. Howitt: *Colonisation*; op cit; p. 247.

those of few princes in any age or country have displayed. Of his cruelty we have heard the most... yet, in his words: `I demand that male and female prisoners, as well English as Portuguese, who shall be taken by the republican troops, or by mine, shall be treated with humanity; and, with regard to their persons, that they shall (their property becoming the right of the allies) be transported, at our joint expense, out of India, to places far distant from the territories of the allies.

Another feature in the character of Tippoo was his religion, with a sense of which his mind was most deeply impressed. He spent a considerable part of every day in prayer, and had the conviction of Divine providence....

His country was accordingly, at least during the first and better part of his reign, the best cultivated, and his population the most flourishing, in India: while under the English and their pageants, the population of Carnatic and Oude, hastening to the state of deserts, was the most wretched upon the face of the earth.' [1886]

Indeed, as Howitt notes, once under firm control, India was looted of its wealth. Under a system of expropriation, the East India Company forced down the social scale of poverty ever larger numbers of people.[1887] Then, through taxation, millions were forced into ruin. Under the previous Islamic tax system, Le Bon explains, Muslim and Hindu farmers, who formed the majority, only paid one sixth of the final product from the land, now, they paid half of it.[1888] So much taxed, farmers were forced into economic ruin and starvation, whilst the market was open to English imports.[1889] The outcome was great famines in 1770 and 1783.[1890] In the Bengal famine, altogether a quarter of the population died.[1891] A contemporary, Abbe Reynal, had first witness accounts of these events:

`The unhappy Hindus were perishing every day by thousands under this want of sustenance, without any means of help and without any revenue. They were to be seen in their villages; along the public ways; in the midst of our European colonies, pale, meagre, emaciated, fainting, consumed by famine, some stretched on the ground in expectation of dying; others scarcely able to drag themselves on to seek any nourishment, and throwing themselves at the feet of the Europeans, entreating them to take them in as their slaves....

[1886] Ibid; p. 248-9.

[1887] In G. Le Bon: *La Civilisation;* op cit; 465.

[1888] Ibid.

[1889] Hyndman in G. Le Bon: *La Civilisation;* op cit; p. 465.

[1890] E. Wolf: *Europe;* op cit; pp. 244-5.

[1891] S. Sharma: The History of Britain; op cit.

Let us represent to ourselves, infants deserted, some expiring on the breasts of their mothers; everywhere the dying and the dead mingling together; and on all sides the groans of sorrow and the tears of despair.... During this whole time, six weeks, the Ganges was covered with carcasses; the fields and highways were chocked with them; infectious vapours filled the air, and diseases multiplied... It appears by calculation that pretty generally acknowledged, that the famine carried off a fourth part, that is to say about three millions. What is still more remarkable, is, that such a multitude of human creatures, amidst this terrible distress, remained in absolute inactivity. All the Europeans, especially the English, were possessed of magazines. These were not touched. Private houses were so too. No revolt, no massacre, not the least violence prevailed. The unhappy Hindus, resigned to despair, confined themselves to the request of succours they did not obtain; and peacefully awaited the relief of death.'[1892]

Mass starvation proceeded throughout the 19th century in parallel with systematic loot of the country. Writing later in the century, W.S. Blunt concluded:
'If we go on developing the country at the present rate the inhabitants will have, sooner or later, to resort to cannibalism, for there will be nothing but each other left to eat.'[1893] Hyndman notes that in the North-Western provinces, exports of grains were imposed, whilst 300,000 people died of hunger in a few months.[1894] In 1877, in the province of Madras, alone, 935,000 people died of hunger according to official reports.[1895] Millions were to die altogether.[1896]

Egypt:

The colonisation of Egypt, just as that of other Islamic countries, was the outcome of the declining fortunes of the Ottomans, who had put such lands under their protection. No sooner Ottoman power was undermined by Western nations leagued against it that the rush for the spoils began.
Three decades before the French taking of Egypt, the Duc de Choiseul, the French Minister for Foreign Affairs, in a dispatch to Count de Vergennes

---

[1892] Abbe Raynal: I; 460-4; in W. Howitt: *Colonisation;* op cit; pp. 270-1.
[1893] W.S. Blunt: *Ideas about India*; London; 1885; p.47.
[1894] G. Le Bon: *La Civilisation*; op cit; p. 466.
[1895] Ibid; p. 465.
[1896] A. Zahoor: *Muslims in the Indian sub-continent;* op cit.

in 1766, alluded to the decay of the Ottoman realm.[1897] Then opened the Question of the Orient, of an eventual sharing out of the Ottoman Empire; for the Duc of Choiseul the occupation of Egypt was the ideal form of compensation for the French losses in America and in India.[1898] It remained a fixation decades later, and in 1787, Lauzun, Duke of Biron reminded Count Montmorin how for Choiseul `the acquisition of this superb, fertile country, was his favourite project, the political romance which filled his dreams.' [1899]

To put the plan in action, Count St Priest, travelled to Turkey, saw a realm in decline, and on returning to France, in 1778, he presented the minister, count Vergennes a report where he favours the conquest of Egypt. He provides two arguments in favour of this project, arguments which kept re-occurring in all documents of the time: the fertility of the soil `on which every crop can be grown,' and the easy conquest in view of the political anarchy in Egypt.[1900]

At about the same time, in 1777, Baron Tott sent on a secret mission by the French government to study the situation in military and political terms in the southern Turkish shores, arrived in Alexandria, and then sojourned in Cairo.[1901] When he returned to France, Tott gave a secret Memoire to the minister of defence where he explained the condition of Egypt and the ways to conquer it.[1902] The French hoped to occupy Egypt permanently and to profit from its agriculture and trade under the guise of `liberating' the Egyptians from Mamluk rule.[1903] Subsequent complaints and calls for intervention by French merchants based in Egypt were only to serve as pretext for Bonaparte's (the future Napoleon) expedition.[1904]

On 12 April 1798, a decision by the French Directory charged Bonaparte, chief of the Army of the Orient, to take Egypt; he was also ordered to cut the Suez Isthmus, and `to secure the free and exclusive possession of the Red Sea for the Republic of France.'[1905] The apparent reason for this invasion was the bad treatment of French merchants based in Egypt by the Mamluk

---

[1897] G. Hanotaux/H. Deherain: *Histoire de la Nation Egyptienne;* op cit; p. 202.
[1898] Ibid.
[1899] Ibid; p. 203.
[1900] Ibid; p. 204.
[1901] Ibid; pp. 204-5.
[1902] Ibid.
[1903] P.M. Holt: *Egypt and the Fertile Crescent: 1522-1922;* Cornelll Paperbacks; Ithaca; New York; 1966; p.156.
[1904] Ibid; p.155.
[1905] In E. Driault: *La Question;* op cit; p. 74.

government.[1906] The merchants' appeal for French intervention was dramatic, indeed:

'We need urgent help, because our woes have reached the worst state.... French people suffer cruelly at the hands of the despot, and call on their country to rescue them.'[1907]

This was taken up by Bonaparte's proclamation to the people of Egypt on 2 July 1798, which included the following:

'For very long the Beys who rule Egypt have insulted the French nation, and have inflicted injuries on its tradesmen. Now has arrived the hour of retribution.... People of Egypt! I have come to restore your rights, punish the usurpers, and more than the Mamluks, I respect God, his Prophet and the Qur'an...'[1908]

After landing at Alexandria, the French advanced on Cairo, defeating a Mamluk force under Murad Bey at Shubrakhit. The French then won the decisive battle of Inbaba, opposite the capital (the so called battle of the Pyramids) on 21 July 1798. The French conquest proceeded against stiff resistance but also the collaboration of some. Most of the Egyptian population behaved in a dignified way, and in the conquered cities, including Cairo, Egyptians made a point of looking after Mamluk families and their womenfolk who had been left behind.[1909] However, as Morsy points out, we find in every circle of society people who went out of their way to collaborate with the French.[1910] Amongst these were some merchants, some poets, such as Hassan al-Attar's poems warming with praise for the French; members of al-Sadat family collaborated, and so did local Christians such as Barthelemy, who at the head of the police, did much of the dirty work for the French.[1911] The French also relied on Christian Egyptians, raising them to the highest positions, especially as tax collectors, and went to extremes to encourage a firmer Copt stand.[1912] To further establish their control over a hostile population, a strong police force was set up, and local auxiliaries were recruited.[1913]

[1906] P.M. Holt: *Egypt and the Fertile Crescent;* op cit; p.155.

[1907] G. Hanotaux/H. Deherain: *Histoire de la Nation,* op cit; at p.209.

[1908] For lengthy details of this proclamation see Al-Jabarti: *Al-Jabarti's Chronicle of the First Seven Months of the French Occupation of Egypt;* Ed and tr by S. Moreh; Leiden, 1975; pp 39-47.

[1909] M. Morsy: *North Africa 1800-1900;* Longman; London; 1984; p. 79.

[1910] Ibid; p. 90.

[1911] Ibid.

[1912] Ibid.

[1913] Ibid; p. 79.

Mamluk resistance, on the other hand, was assisted by volunteers from the rest of the Arab world. 20,000 Maghribi came to fight in Egypt, via Makkah, the Moroccan Sheikh al-Kilani calling on the pilgrims to go to the Holy war.[1914] Volunteers from Makkah, Tunisia and Algeria, early in 1799, crossed from Jeddah and Yambo on boats, landed at Kosseir, crossed the desert to join Murad Bey on the Nile for embittered fighting against the French.[1915] Fierce fighting went on in the first half of 1799 at Dedecieh (11 February); Keneh (12-3 February); Abu Manah (17 February); Benout (3 March); Tahta (5 March); Coptos and Benout (8-10 March); Bir al-Bar (2 April); Bardis and Gige (5 April); Nexlet al-Hamah (9 April); Beni Adin (18 April); Mimieh (25 April); Abou Girge (28 April 17); Assouan (16 May 1799).[1916]

In their military encounter with the Muslims, the French view was that facing them were people burning with `religious fanaticism.'[1917] In reality, though, it was the French invasion which led to widespread mass slaughter of Egyptians, and the burning of whole populations in their towns and hamlets such as at Benout, in March 1799, at Beni Adin;[1918] Tahta, and at Abou Girge, where on 28 April 1799, the French commander Davout burnt the whole population of the town alive inside their homes.[1919] The French also carried public executions of prominent Egyptian figures on repeated instances such as in November 1798 and July 1799 so as to install a climate of terror.[1920] The French also destroyed much of Cairo.[1921]

Advancing on the Holy land, which was also another objective, the French captured Jaffa on 15 March 1799. To the garrison made of Albanians and Turks, they promised clemency if they surrendered. However, as Officer Peyrusse wrote:
`As it was recommended to save on powder for guns, the whole garrison was butchered with bayonets. That three days after an assault, when all passions had calmed down, and in such cold barbarity we butchered with knives 3000 men who had trusted our word. Posterity will give justice to this atrocity, and those who had given the orders will have their place amongst the butchers of humanity... This instance is going to show our

---

[1914] Ibid; p. 94.
[1915] G. Hanotaux/H. Deherain: *Histoire de la Nation*; op cit; p. 61 and p.379.
[1916] Ibid; p. 384-5.
[1917] Ibid; p. 385.
[1918] Ibid; p. 387.
[1919] Ibid.
[1920] M. Morsy: *North Africa*; op cit; p. 80.
[1921] P.M. Holt: *Egypt*; op cit; p.156 fwd.

enemies that they can never trust French loyalty; and sooner or later the blood of these 3000 men will fall back on us.'[1922]

In the same city, the French soldiers first looted everything before massacring the whole Muslim population. Commandant Malus narrates:

`The soldiers were everywhere slitting throats of men, women, children, old people, Christians, Turks, all that had a human figure. Doors were broken, houses crushed; women were wailing; father thrown upon the corpse of the son; the daughter raped on the corpse of her mother; smoke from bodies burnt alive; the smell of blood; the cries of the wounded; the shouts of the soldiers fighting over the loot of a dying victim; furious shouts of soldiers responding to the cries of despair by shouts of anger and re-doubled blows; at last men, gorged with blood (from their victims) and gold, falling, exhausted on the masses of corpses; this was the sight that that unhappy city gave.'[1923]

After taking Jaffa, the French besieged the seaport of Acre in order to establish communications with France (just as during the Third Crusade centuries before).[1924] The French relied on support from local Arab tribesmen; support which failed to arrive, though.[1925] Muslim volunteers also contributed to the failure of the French siege, which forced a French retreat back to Egypt on 13 June 1799.[1926] In the retreat, the French army was decimated by attacks of mounted Turks, Mamluk, and Arabs.[1927] In August 1799, Bonaparte left Egypt, leaving command in the hands of General Kleber. Kleber was assassinated by a Syrian Muslim, Sulayman al-Halabi; a man, Western historians, as Morsy points out, fail to tell, that he was not guillotined or shot, but was, instead, impaled; his slow, long drawn out death intended to strike terror into the hearts of Muslims.[1928] Sulayman was condemned to have his right fist cut off and burned, and to be impaled alive. At the moment of his execution, and while it lasted, four hours, he showed courage and calmness which only the knowledge of having committed the most praiseworthy and glorious act, and the assurance of having earned the palm promised to martyrs could give him.[1929] Sulayman showed no change of expression as his wrist was cut off, though he did cry

---

[1922] G. Hanotaux/H. Deherain: *Histoire;* op cit; p. 407-8.

[1923] Ibid; pp 406-7.

[1924] O.J. Thatcher; F.Schwill: *A General History of Europe;* John Murray publisher; London; 1919; p. 471.

[1925] G. Hanotaux/ H Deherain: *Histoire;* op cit.

[1926] M Morsy: *North Africa;* op cit; p. 93.

[1927] G. Hanotaux/H. Deherain: *Histoire;* op cit; pp 60 fwd.

[1928] M Morsy: *North Africa*; op cit; p. 94-5.

[1929] J. Miot: Memoires pour servir a l'Histoire des expeditions en Egypte et en Syrie; Paris; 1814; in N. Daniel: *Islam, Europe and Empire;* op cit; p. 106.

when a burning fragment struck his neck.[1930] Sulayman uttered no cry as the stake was driven in, and when it was raised and set in its hole he called out the shahadah and verses from the Qur'an.[1931]

Following the death of Kleber, general command of the French army went to Abdallah Jacques Menou, a French convert to Islam, to make the occupation more acceptable to Muslims. The French army had, however, lost much more considerable numbers of men, officers and equipment than first planned; and when the English came about, the whole of the French army was unable to mount effective resistance.[1932] The French capitulated on 2 September 1801, and left Egypt.[1933]

Although unsuccessful in its final aims, the French invasion had, however, dented Mamluk power considerably. It also, as Daniel claims, had planted the seeds of nationalism which the Arabs soon made their own;[1934] and which was to have considerable impact in stirring anti Ottoman feelings. Moreover, after the French departed, the Ottoman sultan, too weak, was made to appoint Muhammad Ali as Viceroy of Egypt in 1805. Divisions amongst factious Mamluks soon helped him acquire greater hold over the country.[1935] Muhammad Ali's scheme to control the country resided in his eliminating the Mamluks. On 1 March 1811, he invited their leadership to the Citadel to attend the investment of Ahmad Tusun Pasha, his son. No sooner had they entered, they were locked in, and were all shot down as they passed in procession down a rocky passage. Simultaneously Mamluk houses were sacked, and any Mamluks survivors were hunted down as far as Upper Egypt.[1936] Thus was wiped and permanently Mamluk power that had begun in 1250.

Muhammad Ali ruled Egypt from 1805 until 1848, and whilst severing his links with the Sultan, he built stronger ones with European powers. After the French left, those who collaborated with them were raised to higher positions by him, men such as Hassan al-Athar now promoted to the rectorship of al-Azhar; George Jawhari, a Copt appointed by Bonaparte as Collector in Chief of Taxation, now acted in the same capacity for Muhammad Ali, and with him those of his co-religionists who served in

---

[1930] N. Daniel: *Islam, Europe and Empire;* p. 107.
[1931] Ibid.
[1932] G. Hanotaux/Deherain): *Histoire*; op cit; p. 430.
[1933] G. Hanotaux/ Deherain: *Histoire*; op cit.
[1934] N. Daniel: *The Arabs;* op cit. p.2.
[1935] P.M. Holt: *Egypt;* op cit; p. 162.
[1936] Ibid; p. 178.

the Finance Department.[1937] Another collaborator with the French, Ahmed al-Mahruqi, head of the guild of merchants, was later put in charge of municipal affairs in Cairo.[1938] Muhammad Ali also de-established the Ulama and confiscated their waqfs (pious endowments), and fought both the Sudanese and the Wahhabi movement in Saudi Arabia.[1939] In 1832, profiting of Ottoman disarray in Europe, he rose against them. And whilst the Russian fleet took to the Bosphorus, Muhammad Ali's army engaged the Ottomans in Turkey proper.[1940] Fearing his power to grow beyond bounds, England and France intervened in 1840; the London agreement giving them powers to 'solve' the Egyptian question.[1941] This, eventually, opened the road for them to control Egypt proper; via economic and financial intrusion, and through the contract for the construction of the Suez Canal in 1865.

Gradually, the Egyptian economy passed under Western control. Already, in the 1830s, just as in Syria, European trade was killing off the traditional industries and changing the traditional trading patterns in Ottoman land.[1942] The Anglo-Turkish Convention of 1838, which outlawed monopolies, was applied increasingly in Egypt after 1841 and further reduced the prospects of his successors being able to emulate Muhammad Ali in retaining the profits of Egypt's trade in Egyptian hands.[1943]

The rising Western influence soon turned into open looting. Playing a central role in this was Ismail Pasha, the Khedive, who was put in control of the country in 1863 by Western powers. He was luxurious, voluptuous, ambitious, fond of display, and devoid of principles.[1944] Over and above the millions wasted in entertainments, in largess, in sensuality, in the erection of numerous palaces, he threw away millions on diverse failed schemes.[1945] To finance these, he borrowed heavily. A long series of loans amounting nominally to £68.5 millions were negotiated by major banking firms: Oppenheim, Fruhling and Goshen, the Anglo-Egyptian, and Bischoffsheim, and were raised successively between 1862 and 1873.[1946] A brief scrutiny at some such loans shows how the ruling elites borrowed in the name of the state, at extravagant rates, under conditions which

---

[1937] M. Morsy: *North Africa;* op cit; p. 91.
[1938] Ibid.
[1939] P. Lunde: *Islam;* Dorling Kindersley; London; 2002; p. 77.
[1940] H. Inalcik: Chronology; op cit; p. 101.
[1941] Ibid; p. 102.
[1942] J.C.B. Richmond: *Egypt 1798-1952*; Methuen & Co Ltd; London; 1977; p. 98.
[1943] Ibid.
[1944] Viscount Milner: *England in Egypt*; Edward Arnold; London; 1907; p.176.
[1945] Ibid; p.177.
[1946] M Morsy: *North Africa*; op cit; p. 173.

ended in bankrupting their country.[1947] Much of the borrowing was to finance events such as the ceremony on the occasion of the opening of the Canal of Suez in May 1869. The Khedive invited not just emperors of Europe, but also hundreds of other guests from Europe, all the invitations carried a free passage from Europe to Alexandria and back, board and lodging in Egypt and free travel within its borders,[1948] an opening, which must have added a sizeable sum to the cost of the Canal and thus to the Egyptian taxpayer.[1949] The debt of Egypt rose from under 3 millions to 89 million by 1876, whilst taxation of Egyptians increased by 50%.[1950] To bring the country to such bankruptcy, Milner notes, it required a cowardly and corrupt bureaucracy and, above all, an army of swindlers, mostly Westerners, who surrounded Ismail.[1951] Men like the Frenchman Bavray (an agent of the Rothschilds); private Paris bankers such as Marcuard and Dervieu, Herman Oppenheim, all advisers to the Pasha, procuring ready cash at great expense.[1952]

Financial bankruptcy paralleled loss of sovereignty. Indeed, to face with his mounting debts, the Khedive sold his shares over the Canal of Suez to Great Britain in 1875.[1953] News of the Khedive's willingness to sell had been communicated to Disraeli, then Prime Minister, by a journalist, possibly acting on Oppenheim's suggestion.[1954] The Prime Minister made a quick decision, and, without waiting for parliament consent, asked Lionel Rotschild to put up the necessary £4 millions.[1955] In 1875, thus, Disraeli was able to make Britain the largest single shareholder by acquiring the Khedive's 176,000 shares; a very sound investment it was going to prove, indeed.[1956] The British government paid a little less than £4 million for the khedive's shares in 1875, but by 1932 their estimate value was some 53 millions; and in the interval the government had received some 43 millions in interest; hence shares now in British hands were worth 24 times their initial value.[1957] The problem was not so much an economic as a political one, since Egypt no longer had any say in the canal which

---

[1947] J.C.B. Richmond: *Egypt 1798-1952*; op cit; pp. 100-1.
[1948] Ibid; p. 97.
[1949] Ibid.
[1950] Viscount Milner: *England in Egypt*; op cit; p.177.
[1951] Ibid; pp.177-8.
[1952] M Morsy: *North Africa;* op cit; p. 172.
[1953] Ibid; p. 173.
[1954] Ibid.
[1955] Ibid.
[1956] Ibid; pp. 175-6.
[1957] J.C.B. Richmond: *Egypt 1798-1952*; op cit; p. 97.

became an international enclave.[1958] The Khedive, and therefore Egypt, thus, deprived themselves of their share in the major international concern on national soil, and consolidating the power of a foreign company as a state within the state, and foreign nations as shareholders.[1959]

In 1882, a rebellion by Egyptian officers, led by Arabi, sought to alter the order, and save their country from bankruptcy. In retaliation, the British bombarded Alexandria on July 11, 1882, and British forces landed on August 1882; Cairo was occupied on 14 September 1882.[1960] Arabi was forcefully removed and things 'brought back to order.'[1961] The British now ruled, but via the Khedive. Lord Cromer, otherwise known as Sir Evelyn Baring, was between 1878-9 the British Commissioner to the Egyptian debt fund, and also general controller of Egyptian finance.[1962] He spent twenty four years in the country until his retirement in 1907, during which he exerted all important influence on the country's policies.[1963] His title, although modest, still gave him like every other European representative in Egypt the role of mentor of the Egyptian government, running the khedive's policies.[1964] As Lord Cromer, himself, wrote in 1893:

'My programme was to put a leading Muhammedan at the head of the government,' with a mission, as Daniel notes 'to save Egyptian society,' and 'make sure, the Khedive and the Egyptian ministers conformed to his (Cromer's) views.'[1965]

Recently, a prominent Egyptian journalist and political figure went through the 20th century period, and professed his amazement at how Egypt was ruined by British occupation, its wealth literally siphoned out. He was bewildered at the amount looted from Egypt shown in British official documents.[1966]

[1958] M. Morsy: *North Africa*; op cit; pp. 175-6.
[1959] Ibid.
[1960] J.C.B. Richmond: *Egypt 1798-1952*; op cit; pp. 129-31.
[1961] Ibid.
[1962] G. Hanotaux/H. Deherain: *Histoire*; op cit; pp. 60-1.
[1963] Ibid.
[1964] Ibid; p. 61.
[1965] In N. Daniel: *Islam, Europe;* op cit; pp. 469-72.
[1966] M. Haykal: Haykal; *Al-Jazeera*-25 August 05; 21-22 pm; seen by this author.

The French `Liberation' of Egypt

The contemporary Egyptian historian, Al-Djabarti, chronicles events of the French occupation of Egypt in the final years of the 18th century. He describes a particular incident:

`The French trod into the Mosque of al-Azhar with their shoes, carrying swords and rifles. Then they scattered in its courtyard and its main praying area and tied their horse to the Qibla. They devastated the students' quarter and ponds, smashing the lamps and chandeliers and breaking up the bookcases of the students, the mujawirun, and the scribes. They plundered whatever they found in the mosque, such as furnishings, vessels, bowls, deposits, and hidden things from closets and cupboards. They treated the books and Quranic volumes as trash, throwing them on the ground, stamping on them with their feet and shoes. Furthermore they soiled the mosque, blowing their spit in it, pissing and defecating in it. They guzzled wine and smashed the bottles in the central court and other parts. And whoever they happened to meet in the mosque they stripped. They chanced upon someone in one of the ruwaqs and slaughtered him. Thus they committed deeds in al-Azhar which are but little of what they are capable of, for they are enemies of the faith, the malicious victors who gloat in the misfortune of the vanquished, rabid hyenas, mongrels obdurate in their nature.'[1967]

One should remember that when the French army entered Egypt in 1798, its commanding officer, General Bonaparte (the future Napoleon), outlined the noble purposes of the French invasion. In his declaration to the Egyptian people on 2 July 1798, Bonaparte insisted that his only aim was to free Egypt from the Mamluk tyrants and despots.[1968] His declaration went:

` People of Egypt I have come to restore your rights, punish the usurpers, and more than the Mamluks I respect God, his Prophet and the Qur'an...'

`All Egyptians will be called to manage everything; the wisest, the best instructed; the most virtuous will govern; and the people will be happy.'

`Three times happier will be those who will side by us: they will prosper in their fortune and ranks. Happy will be those who remain neutral: they will have time to know us and will join us.'[1969]

[1967] Al-Jabarti in M Morsy: *North Africa 1800-1900*; Longman; London; 1984; p. 79.
[1968] For lengthy details of this proclamation see al-Jabarti: *Al-Jabarti's chronicle*; op cit; pp 39-47.
[1969] G. Hanotaux: *Histoire*; op cit; p. 254.

Algeria:

In April 1827 the Dey of Algiers (the ruler of Algeria on behalf of the Turkish sultan) angrily struck the French Consul, Deval, with a fly whisk; the reason: the French envoy's insolence over a disputed unpaid debt incurred by France.[1970] It was the excuse used by France to invade the country.[1971]

Three years after the fly whisk incident, in 1830, the conquest of Algeria began. The Turkish Dey proved no match for the French army that landed on July 5, 1830 at the bay of Sidi Ferruch, on the western outskirts of Algiers. A proclamation written in Arabic and diffused at the arrival of the troops asserted that the French had not come to take possession of the city;[1972] which anticipated 'with some genius, but not without duplicity, the promises of Louis Bonaparte to Abd el-Kader (1855) and those of Lawrence of Arabia to the Cherif of Makkah in 1916,' say Courbage and Fargues.[1973] To the Algerian population, the operation was presented as a temporary occupation, simply aiming at expelling the despotic Turks, and then to return the country to the Arabs, its legitimate masters.[1974]

No sooner, however, was the country under firm control, and in violation of agreements that had been made, the French seized private and religious buildings, and looted possessions, mainly in Algiers and its surroundings; besides sequestrating 650,000 ha of farming land.[1975] The French also looted the Algerian treasure-chest.[1976]

The French invasion 'to free Algeria from Turkish yoke,' soon turned into a bloody colonial enterprise. Duc de Rovigo, governor from 1831 to 1833, went on a campaign of devastation and had tribal leaders, who were lured to

---

[1970] C. A. Julien: *Histoire de l'Algerie Contemporaine, 1827-1871*; Presses Universitaires de France, 1964; pp. 21; 33.

[1971] R. Ageron: *Histoire de l'Algerie Contemporaine;* Presses Universitaires de France, Paris, 1964. For details on causes that led to the French invasion, see H Alleg; J. de Bonis, H.J. Douzon, J. Freire, P. Haudiquet: *La Guerre d'Algerie*: 3 volumes, Temps Actuels, Paris, 1981; Vol 1.

[1972] Y. Courbage, P. Fargues: *Chretiens et Juifs*; op cit; pp.108-9.

[1973] Ibid.

[1974] Ibid.

[1975] H. Alleg et al: *La Guerre d'Algerie*, op cit; Vol 1.

[1976] J. Fontana: *The Distorted Past*, Blackwell, 1995.p.137

Algiers by promises of safe conducts, slain.[1977] The French army had the Mitidja capital, Blida, razed to the ground; the devastated streets filled with corpses of old people, women, children and Jews.[1978]

Duke of Rovigo recommended to his subordinates: `heads! Bring heads, heads, block burst water mains with the head of the first Bedouin you meet.[1979] Colonel Montagnac admitted that `to chase away dark thoughts that besiege me, sometimes I have heads cut off.'[1980] In Letters from a soldier, he relates:

`Of the Algerian women we capture, some we keep as hostages and the rest are auctioned to the troops like animals. In the operations we have carried out during the last four months I have witnessed scenes that would melt the hardest heart, if one let oneself to be moved. I witnessed it all with a frightening indifference... Women and children caught on thick bush wood which they had to cross as they surrendered to us. We kill, we slaughter, the screaming of the terror stricken and the dying blends with the sounds of the beasts.'[1981]

The same ferocity was shown by the French in the eastern parts of the country. The fiercest onslaught was against the capital, Constantine, in 1836, which was defended by Hadj Ahmed Bey. Unlike what Yusuf, a `Muslim' who fought on the French side, and with great enthusiasm, had convinced the French, that the people would welcome them, the first campaign against the city ended in disaster.[1982] The French army retreated in painful conditions, before, in 1837, General Damremont with 20,400 men, and strong artillery moved, again, against the city, but not before last efforts were made to get Hadj Ahmed to negotiate, which he refused to do.[1983] The attack was launched, and on 13 October 1837, the city was taken. Muslim defeat was followed by the general massacre of its population.[1984] Hadj Ahmed, with a group of faithful followers retired to the southern marshes of Algeria where he fought on for another eleven years, but in 1848, old and sick, no longer able to ride on horseback; most of his men and private papers fallen in French hands, he surrendered,

---

[1977] C. Ageron: *Modern Algeria,* op cit; p.11.

[1978] C. A. Julien: Histoire de l'Algerie; op cit; p.67.

[1979] P. Christian: *L'Afrique Francaise;* Paris 1845-1846; Cited by H Alleg et al: La Guerre; op cit; vol 1; p. 64.

[1980] Y. Lacoste, A. Noushi, and A. Prennant: *L'Algerie: Passe, Present*; Editions Sociales; Paris; 1960; p. 306.

[1981] Ibid; pp. 306-7.

[1982] M. Morsy: *North Africa*; op cit; p. 136.

[1983] Ibid; p. 137.

[1984] Ibid.

too.[1985] Hadj Ahmed's pro Ottoman feelings, Morsy notes, were not such as to please either the French colonial historians or later Algerian (secular-Westernised) nationalists,[1986]and so was his role in resistance to Western Christendom obscured by modern history, just as was that of the Seljuk, the Mamluks, and the Ottomans.

In the west, although the French took Mers El-Kebir in 1830, and entered the Casbah of Oran in 1831, they had to face the more organised opposition of Emir Abd al-Kader, who had gathered around him substantial forces. Truces were agreed with the Emir, just to be broken by the French once they felt better prepared.[1987] General (later Marshal) Thomas-Robert Bugeaud, carried a total war on the Emir, devastating towns, cities, crops, and livestock; ravaging tribes, decimating settlements, even tribes friendly to the French were systematically exterminated.[1988] Marshall Bugeaud made it a rule of war to starve, destroy and confiscate crops and livestock, and burning all settlements, and to kill the largest numbers until Algerians submit or disappear.[1989] French generals, Cavaignac and Pelissier, smoked and walled in caves whole tribes that had sought refuge in them.[1990] It was common for men to be gratified with honours in infamous war deeds. One officer presented 500 pairs of 'Arab ears' to be rewarded by the government of the King with 50,000 francs and the legion d'Honneur for services rendered.[1991]

The French presented their enterprise as a civilising deed, and their killings as efforts towards pacifying the country, and removing fanatical, barbaric Muslims. The following incident expresses their sentiments:

'When Emir Abd al-Kader freeing his French prisoners said to them: 'I have nothing to feed you; I cannot kill you, thus I send you back home....' The prisoners full of admiration for the Emir, according to General St Arnaud: 'had their minds diseased,' and had been 'brainwashed.'[1992]

Eventually, Emir Abd al-Kader sought refuge and recruits in Morocco, and was joined by Sultan Abd Errahman to take a stand against French incursions, which resulted in the disastrous defeat of Moroccan forces at

---

[1985] Ibid.

[1986] Ibid; p. 138.

[1987] See R. Ageron: *Histoire de l'Algerie;* op cit. p. 13. C. A. Julien: *Histoire de l'Algerie*; p.104.

[1988] H. Alleg et al: *La Guerre d'Algerie*, op cit; p.77.

[1989] Ibid; p.70.

[1990] Ibid; pp. 66 and 69.

[1991] Ibid; p.68

[1992] General St Arnaud in a letter of 16 May 1842.

the Battle of Isly in 1844. Three years later, Abd al-Kader gave up the fight, and was forced into exile to Syria.

The French went on to submit other parts of the country: the Saharan oases (Zaatcha in 1849, Nara in 1850, and Ouargla in 1852), and Kabylia in 1857. Southern towns and cities were razed to the ground by gun and canon fire; corpses made mounts and filled wells.[1993] In Kabylia, a French officer recounts:

`Order was given to deliver a war of devastation... So our soldiers acted with ferocity... women, children were slaughtered, homes burnt down, trees razed to the ground, nothing was spared... Kabyle women wore silver bracelets to the arms and around their ankles. Soldiers cut all their limbs, and they did not always do it to the dead only.'[1994]

A mass uprising against the French took place in 1870; one of its apparent causes was the mutiny of Spahi regiments refusing to take part in the French war against Germany.[1995] The uprising against the French was mainly focused in the eastern and Kabyle regions, involving more than 200,000 fighting men.[1996] The superior French army won the day, but after a long, costly campaign. French reprisals included war indemnity of 36.5 million francs imposed on 298 peasant communities; a fine that ruined them.[1997] Great numbers of people, chosen at random, were taken to court and condemned to deportation abroad.[1998] There was mass execution of `rebels' and suspects, and now, the physical mass extermination of Algerians envisaged.[1999] It was suggested that Algerians be `driven into the desert', and that their elimination was part of a natural law which led to the `disappearance of backward peoples.'[2000]

The disappearance of the `barbaric, backward Muslims' was to leave room for the better people, i.e the white Europeans. Hence, as Algerian Muslims were being wiped out, Western European settlers were pouring in greater numbers to settle the country. They took over the lands expropriated from

---

[1993] Paul Gaffarel: l'Algerie: Histoire, conquete et colonisation, Ed. Firmin Didot, 1883; in H. Alleg et al: *La Guerre d'Algerie*, op cit; p.77.
[1994] Ibid.
[1995] M. Morsy: *North Africa*; op cit; p. 157.
[1996] Ibid; p. 158.
[1997] Ibid; p. 159.
[1998] Ibid.
[1999] M. Morsy: *North Africa*; op cit; pp. 287-8.
[2000] Ibid.

native Algerians, who in turn, were pushed onto arid and semi arid lands to eke a living.[2001] Homes were built, roads and infrastructure were erected, and many businesses and services were set up, and they all went to the settlers and to a tiny minority of subservient indigenous classes who assisted colonial rule. According to Etienne, the powerful and influential deputy of Oran (1881-1921), the Muslims had to stand aside to make way for the inevitable march of progress and technology in Algeria.[2002] For Marmier, Algeria was a land for a New France, to grow what the old France lacked, house the surplus population, expand industry and shipping, with no room for inferior natives.[2003] V.A. Hain of the Societie Coloniale de l'Etat d'Alger considered the whole population of Algeria beyond all redemption and only fit to be removed from the land.[2004] To justify the extermination of the Algerians, just as the extermination of the Indians in North America, and like the frontier settlers in the western United States, as Cook observes, 'the colon held that there was a constant threat from an uprising, but in this case it was not Sioux or Cheyenne Indians, but Algerian Muslims.'[2005]

To exterminate Algerians, other than by mass killing in the field of combat, forced mass starvation was implemented. After taking native lands, the French decimated the other source of Algerian livelihood: their livestock. A total of 18 million sheep, 3.5 million cattle, and one million camels were killed between 1830 and 1845.[2006] Greater numbers were killed in the following decades. Hundreds of thousands of Algerians were consequently starved to death.[2007] According to Dr Bodichon, one of the French theorists of colonisation:

'It matters little that France in her political conduct goes beyond the limits of common morality at times; the essential thing is that she establishes a lasting colony and that, later, she brings European civilisation to these barbaric countries. When a project which is to the advantage of all humanity is to be carried out, the shortest path is the best. Now, it is certain that the shortest path is terror. Without violating the laws of morality, or international jurisprudence, we can fight our African enemies

---

[2001] D. Sari: *La Depossession des Fellahs 1830-1962;* SNED, Algiers; 1978.

[2002] J.J. Cook: The Maghrib through French Eyes; 1880-1929; in A.A. Heggoy Editor: *Through Foreign Eyes;* University Press of America; 1982; pp. 57-92; at p. 77.

[2003] X.Marmier: *Lettres sur l'Algerie*; Paris; 1847.

[2004] V.A.Hain: *A La Nation. Sur Alger;* Paris; 1832; pp 31; 58 fwd.

[2005] J.J. Cook: The Maghrib through French Eyes; op cit; p. 63.

[2006] N. Abdi quoted in Louis Blin: *l'Algerie du Sahara au Sahel,* l'Harmattan, Paris, 1990; p. 68.

[2007] See Jo Melia: *The Triste sort des Indigenes d'Algerie;* D.Sari: *La Depossession;* op cit

by powder and fire, joined by famine, internal division, war between Arabs and Kabyles, between the tribes of the Tell and those of the Sahara, by brandy, corruption and disorganisation. That is the easiest thing in the world to do.'[2008]

French extermination policies caused the Algerian population to fall from 10 millions in 1830 to 2.1 millions in 1872 according to some sources.[2009] Others put at between 8 and 10 millions those who died following military uprisings, hunger and disease between 1830 and 1962.[2010] Comparative figures with Egypt show the scale of French devastation. In 1800, that is thirty years before the French entry, the population of Algeria was around 4 millions; that of Egypt between 3-4 millions; by 1890, Algeria had 4.1 millions; Egypt 10 millions; in 1920: Algeria's population had risen to 4.9 millions; whilst Egypt in 1927 had 14 millions.[2011] Statistical evidence of Algerian demographic trend up to the late 1880s seemed to show that the Algerians might become extinct.[2012]

The Algerians did not go extinct despite French endeavours. Once the shock of mass extermination passed, the Algerians organised and mobilised for the ultimate fight. Great men such as Sheikh Ibn Badis and his followers re-ignited the spirit of Islam and Arabism in Algerian hearts. In 1945, in the towns of Setif, Guelma, and Kherrata, Algerians went to the streets to call on the French to abide by their promise to grant Algeria its independence. The French response was to mass slaughter 45,000 of these demonstrators. Nine years later, in 1954, the Algerians rose in armed resistance. The shots that triggered the Algerian rising were in the Aures, in the Batna region. Soon, they were echoed from all parts of the country, the whole nation rising in arms to wrest its independence. The French reaction was massive and overwhelming. France poured in hundreds of thousands of military and the most sophisticated of its hardware to fight the Algerians. Algerian resistance was, however, one of the most glorious acts of recent centuries, a war of independence, whose real history, and greatness has not been written yet; certainly, with the Viet-Nam wars being one of the greatest ever wars of independence. After nearly eight years of fighting, and French ferocious mass killings, Algeria became

---

[2008] Cited in C.H. Favrod: *Le FLN et l'Algerie;* Paris; Plon; 1962; p. 31.
[2009] Louis Blin: *l'Algerie du Sahara;* op cit, p. 68.
[2010] M. Lacheraf, in L. Blin: *l'Algerie*; op cit; note 3; p. 112.
[2011] M. Morsy: *North Africa*; op cit; p. 9.
[2012] Ibid; pp. 287-8.

independent in 1962. 1.5 millions Algerians paid with their lives so as Algeria could live free, Arab and Muslim.

CONCLUSION

The Italian historian, Gabrieli, tells us:
'I am going to make a confession, a confession of somebody who had studied since his youth Muslim society, its faith and culture, without ever reaching any sympathy for it, sympathy which alone allows a good understanding of history. Well, this sympathy, I must say, I did feel, though, when listening to the voices of these Arabs, these Muslims, who, at a time of great peril during the crusades, still clung fiercely by their faith, their civilisation, and fought back, and died defending it, like this old sheikh from the Maghrib: Al-Findalawi, who, Ibn Al-Athir says, walked amongst the volunteers for the defence of Damascus (in 1148), and who was told to withdraw from the fight because of his old age, but who answered:
'I have given my life to God; He had accepted it; this engagement is still valid.' And, resolutely, and solemnly, he moved forwards towards death.'[2013]

It is the story and the heroism of countless millions of Findalawi like Muslim figures, which distorted history has ignored. It is the greatness of Muslim history, above all, which distorted history has belittled. Let this book be the first to begin the rewriting of Muslim history by Muslims, as it really happened, and not as it is presented by those who feel no sympathy for it, as Gabrieli himself admits, and Gabrieli, it must be said, is one of the best modern historians of Islam.

[2013] F. Gabrieli: Introduction aux historiens arabes des croisades; in *Cahiers de Civilisation Medievale;* vol 13; 1970; pp. 221-8; at p. 228.

SELECT BIBLIOGRAPHY

-Abu al-Fadail: *Tarikh al-Mansuri* in *Bibliotheca Arabo-Sicula*; Second Appendix; Leipzig; 1887.

-Abu'l Fida Ismail Ibn Khatir: *The Life of the Prophet Mohammed; A Translation of al-Sira al-Nabawiyya;* Translated by T. Le Gassick; Centre for Muslim Contribution to Civilisation; Garnet Publishing; 1998.

-J.M. Abun Nasr: *A History of the Maghrib;* Cambridge University Press; 1971.

-Abu Shama: *Kitab al-rawdatayn;* ed. M.H. M. Ahmad; 2 vols; Cairo; 1954; II.

-J L. Abu-Lughod: *Before European Hegemony,* Oxford University Press, 1989.

-C.R. Ageron: *Modern Algeria*, tr by M. Brett, Hurst and Company, London, 1990.

-A.I. Akram: *Khalid Ibn Al-Waleed;* Maktabah; Publishers and Distributors; Birmingham; England; 2004;

-Al-Baladhuri: *Kitab Futuh al-Buldan;* Ed de Goeje, Brill, 1866.

-H. Alleg; J. de Bonis, H.J. Douzon, J. Freire, P. Haudiquet: *La Guerre d'Algerie;* 3 vols, Temps Actuels; Paris, 1981.

-*The Alexiad of Anna Comnena,* tr. E.R. A. Sewter; Harmondsworth; 1969.

-A. Amari: *La Storia dei Musulmani di Sicilia,* 3 vols, (1933-9) Revised 2nd edition by C.A. Nallino, Rome.

-Syed Ameer Ali: *The Spirit of Islam;* London; Chatto and Windus; 1922.

-F F Armesto: *Before Columbus*: MaCMillan Education; London, 1987.

-Anonymous: *Akhbar Majmu'a,* ed. Lafuente y Alcantara, Madrid, 1867.

-T. W. Arnold: *The Preaching of Islam*; Lahore: Sb. M. Ashraf, 1961.

-T. W. Arnold and A Guillaume ed: *The Legacy of Islam;* 1st ed, Oxford; 1931.

-A.S. Atiya: *Crusade, Commerce and Culture*; Oxford University Press; London; 1962.

-Ibn al-Athir: *Al-Kamil fi'l Tarikh;* 12 Vols; ed C.J. Tornberg; Leiden and Uppsala; 1851-76.

-Ibn Al-Awwam: *Le Livre de l'Agriculture* d'In al-Awwam, tr. from Arabic by J.J. Clement-Mullet, Vol. I, Paris 1864.

Bibliography

-Al-Bakri: Descriptions de l'Afrique Septentrionale; in *Journal Asiatique*; 5th series; XII.

-Ibn Battuta: *Travels in Asia and Africa;* tr and selected by H.A.R. Gibb; George Routledge and Sons Ltd; London, 1929.

-Ibn Battuta: *Voyages d'Ibn Battuta*, Arabic text accompanied by French translation by C. Defremery and B.R. Sanguinetti, preface and notes by Vincent Monteil, I-IV, Paris, 1968, reprint of the 1854 ed.

-Beha Eddin: *The Life of Saladin*; London, Palestine Pilgrim's text Society, 1897.

-Al-Biruni: *Chronology of Ancient Nations*, tr. E. Sachau; London, 1879.

-D.R. Blanks; and M. Frassetto ed: *Western Views of Islam in Medieval and Early Modern Europe;* St Martin's Press; New York; 1999.

-C. Bouamrane-L. Gardet: *Panorama de la pensee Islamique,* Sindbad; Paris, 1984.

-Denise Brahimi: *Opinions et regards des Europeens sur le Maghreb aux 17em et 18em siecles*; SNED; Algiers; 1978.

-H.Bresc: *Un Monde Mediterraneen: Economies et Societe en Sicile*, 1300-1450: 2 vols, Rome-Palermo, 1986.

-H. Bresc: *Politique et Societe en Sicile; XII-Xv em siecle*; Variorum; Aldershot; 1990.

-J.A.Brundage: *The Crusades*; The Marquette University Press; 1962.

-T. Burckhardt: *Moorish Culture in Spain*, George Allen & Unwin, London; 1972.

-*The Cambridge Medieval History*, Vol IV: Edited by J. R. Tanner, C. W. Previte; Z.N. Brooke, 1923.

-*The Cambridge History of Islam*, vol 2, ed P.M. Holt, A.K.S. Lambton, and B. Lewis, Cambridge University Press, 1970.

-A. Castro: *The Structure of Spanish History*, English tr. with revisions and modifications by Edmund A.King. Princeton: Princeton University Press, 1954.

-S. Chew: *The Crescent and the Rose;* New York; 1974.

-C.R. Conder: *The Latin Kingdom of Jerusalem;* The Committee of the Palestine Exploration Fund; London; 1897.

-J.J. Cook: The Maghrib through French Eyes; 1880-1929; in *Through Foreign Eyes;* edited by A.A. Heggoy; University Press of America; 1982; pp. 57-92;

-Youssef Courbage, Paul Fargues: *Chretiens et Juifs dans l'Islam Arabe et Turc*, Payot, Paris, 1997;

-G.W.Cox: *The Crusades*; Longmans; London; 1874.

-Al-Dabbi: *Bughyayt al-Multamis fi Tarikh Rijal al-Andalus;* ed Francisco Codera and J. Ribera; Madrid; 1884-5.

-N. Daniel: *The Arabs and Medieval Europe*; Longman Librarie du Liban; 1975.

-N. Daniel: *Islam, Europe and Empire*, University Press, Edinburgh, 1966.

-N. Daniel: *Islam and the West*; Oneworld; Oxford; 1993.

-J. Davenport: *An Apology for Mohammed and the Koran*; J. Davy and Sons; London; 1869.

-*De Toulouse a Tripoli*, Colloque held between 6 and 8 December, 1995, University of Toulouse; AMAM, Toulouse, 1997.

-M. Defourneaux: *Les Francais en Espagne aux 11 et 12em siecles*; PUF; 1949.

-*Dictionary of the Middle Ages*; J.R. Strayer Editor in Chief; Charles Scribner's Sons; New York; 1982 ff.

-R. Dozy: *Spanish Islam: a History of the Muslims in Spain*; tr F.G. Stokes; London; 1913.

-J.W. Draper: *A History of the Intellectual Development of Europe*; George Bell and Sons, London, 1875.

-J.W. Draper: *History of the Conflict Between Religion and Science;* Henry S.King & Co; London; 1875.

-E. Driault: *La Question d'Orient*; Librairie Felix Alcan; Paris; 1921.

-W. Durant: *The Age of Faith*, Simon and Shuster, New York; 6th printing; 1950.

-Al-Duri: *Tarikh al-Iraq*; Baghdad; 1948.

-P. W. Edbury: *The Conquest of Jerusalem and the Third Crusade*, Scolar Press, 1996.

-N.Elisseeff: Nur al-Din: *Un Grand prince Musulman de Syrie au temps des croisades*; Damascus; 1967.

-*Encyclopaedia of Islam*, Leyden; Brill.

-M. Erbstosser: *The Crusades;* David and Charles; New ton Abbot; First published in Leipzig; 1978.

-J. L. Esposito: *Islam, the Straight Path;* Oxford University Press; 1998.

-F. Fanon: *Les Damnés de la terre,* Editions ENAG, Alger, 1987.

-I.R. al-Faruqi and L. L al-Faruqi: *The Cultural Atlas of Islam;* Mc Millan Publishing Company New York, 1986.

-Abu al-Fida: *Geographie d'Aboulfeda*, ed. and tr. M. Reinaud. 3 vols; Paris, 1840-83.

-R. Finucane: *Soldiers of the Faith*; J.M. Dent and Sons Ltd; London, 1983.

-G. Fisher: *The Barbary Legend;* Oxford; 1957.

-D.H. Fischer: *Historians' Fallacies,* London: Routledge & Kegan Paul, 1971.

-J. Fontana: *The Distorted Past, Blackwell,* 1995.

-C. Forster: *Mohametanism Unveiled;* London; James Duncan and John Cochran; 1829.

-F. Gabrieli: *Arab Historians of the Crusades;* London; Routledge; 1957.

-R. Garaudy: *Comment l'Homme devint Humain,* Editions J.A, 1978.

-M. Garcia-Arenal: Historiens de l'Espagne, Historiens du Maghreb au 19em siecle. Comparaison des stereotypes, *ANNALES: Economies, Societes, Civilisations*: Vol 54 (1999): pp; 687-703.

-D. J. Geanakoplos: *Medieval Western Civilisation, and the Byzantine and Islamic Worlds,* D.C. Heath and Company, Toronto, 1979.

-P. Geyl: *Use and Abuse of History,* Yale University Press, 1955.

-Al-Ghazali: *Manaqib al-Turk;* tr. Harley-Walker.

-E. Gibbon: *The Decline and Fall of the Roman Empire;* vol 5; ed.W. Smith; London, 1858.

-T. Glick: *Islamic and Christian Spain in the Early Middle Ages,* Princeton University Press, New Jersey, 1979.

-J. Glubb: *A Short History of the Arab Peoples;* Hodder and Stoughton, 1969.

-A. Gunny: *Images of Islam in Eighteenth Century Writing;* Grey Seal, London, 1996.

-M.A.S. Abdel Haleem: *The Qur'an;* Oxford University Press; 2004-5.

-G.Hanotaux: (vol 5 written by H. Deherain): *Histoire de la Nation Egyptienne;* Paris; Librarie Plon; 1931.

-A C. Hess: *The Forgotten Frontier;* The University of Chicago Press, 1978.

-W.Heyd: *Histoire du Commerce du Levant au Moyen Age;* Leipzig; 1885-6; reedit; Amsterdam 1967.

-C.Hillenbrand: *The Crusades, Islamic Perspectives,* Edinburgh University Press; 1999.

-P.K. Hitti: *History of the Arabs;* MacMillan and Co. Ltd; London; 1937.

-P.M. Holt: *Egypt and the Fertile Crescent: 1522-1922;* Cornelll Paperbacks; Ithaca; New York; 1966.

-W. Howitt: *Colonisation and Christianity:* Longman; London; 1838.

-R.G. Hoyland: *Seeing Islam as Others Saw it;* The Darwin Press, Inc; Princeton; New Jersey; 1997.

-R.S. Humphreys: *From Saladin to the Mongols;* State University of New York Press Albany; 1977.

-Ibn al-Athir: *Usd al-Ghabah fi Ma'arifat al-Sahabah* (Cairo; 1286 (H); vol iii.

-Ibn al-Athir: *Kitab al-Kamil*; ed K.J. Tornberg; 12 vols; Leiden; 1851-72.

-Ibn al-Athir: *Tarikh al-Dawla Al-Atabakiyya*; ed. Ab Al-Qadir Ahmad Tulaymat; Cairo; 1963.

-Ibn al-Idhari: *Al-Bayan al-Maghrib fi Akhbar al-Maghrib;* ed R. Dozy; Leyden; 1848.

-Ibn abd al-Hakam: *Futuh Misr of Ibn Abd al-Hakam;* Edited from the manuscripts in London, Paris, and Leyden by C. C. Torrey; New Haven; Yale University Press; London; Milford.

-Ibn Abbi Ussaybi'ah: `Uyun al-anba fi tabaqat al-attiba'*, edited by A. Mueller, Cairo/Konigsberg; 1884, reprint, 1965, vol 3.

-Ibn Al-Furat tr by U. and M.C. Lyons: *Ayyubids, Mamluks and Crusaders, selection from the Tarikh al-Duwal wal Muluk of Ibn al-Furat*; 2 vols, W. Heffer and Sons Ltd, Cambridge, 1971.

-Ibn al-Qutiyya: *Tarikh Iftitah al-Andalus,* ed. Madrid, 1868, tr. J. Ribera, Madrid, 1926.

-Ibn Bassam: *Kitab al-Dhakhira fi Mahasin ahl-Jazira*; ed. Fuad University, Cairo, 1939-44; more up to date edition by I. Abbas; Beirut; 1978-9 (8 volumes).

-Ibn al-Idhari: *Al-Bayan al-Mughrib*; ed. A. Huici Miranda; Tetuan; 1963.

-Mohammed Ibn Ishaq (151/769) and Mohammed Ibn Hisham (218/834): *Sirat al-Nabiy Salat Allahu Alayhi wa Sallam;* ed. M.M. Abd Al-Hamid; Cairo; 1963;

-Ibn al-Khatib: *Al-Hulal al-Mawshiyah fi Dhikr al-Akhbar al-Marrakushiyah*; Tunis (1329 H).

-Ibn Khaldun: *Kitab al-Ibar*; Cairo: Dar al-Tab'a al-Amira; 1867-8.

-Ibn Khaldun: *The Muqaddimah*, tr: F. Rosenthal, Bollingen series, XLIII; New York, Princeton University Press, 1958.

-Ibn Khallikan: W*afayat al-Ayan wa-Anba Abna al-Zaman*, Maymunyah Press, Cairo, 1888.

-Ibn Khalikan's *Biographical Dictionary*, tr., M. De Slane Duprat, Paris and Allen & Co., London, 1843.

-Ibn Hayyan: *Mukttabis* published by M. M. Antuna, under the title: *Chronique du regne du calife umayyade Abd Allah a Cordoue*, Paris 1937; tr into Spanish by Kh. Ghorayyib, in *Cuadernos de historia de Espana,* Buenos Aires 1952.

-Ibn Hisham: *Sirat Ibn Hisham: Biography of the Prophet* as abridged by Abdus Salam M. Harun; Al-Falah Foundation; Cairo; 2000;

-Ibn Qutaiba, *Uyun al-ahbar*, ed. C. Brocklemann; Berlin and Strasburg, 1900-8.

Bibliography

-Ibn al-Qalanisi: *The Damascus Chronicle of the Crusades*, tr of Ibn al-Qalanisi, H.A. R. Gibb; London, Luzac and Co, Ltd, 1932.

-Ibn al-Qalanisi: *Dayl tarikh Dimashk;* ed. H.F. Amedroz; Leiden; 1908.

-Ibn Shaddad: *Al-Nawadir al-sultaniyya,* ed J. El-Shayyal; Cairo; 1964.

-Ibn Sa'd: *Kitab al-tabaqat al-Kabir;* ed Sachau; Leiden, Brill, 9 vols, 1904-28.

-Ibn Taghri Birdi: *Al-Nujum al-Zahirah fi Muluk Misr wa'l Qahira;* ed. T.G.J. Juynboll; vol 2; Leyden; 1855.

-Ibn Taymiyya: *Lettre a un roi croise*; Trans. J.R. Michot; Louvain; 1995.

-Ibn Wasil: *Mufarrij al-Kurub fi Akhbar bani Ayyub;* Ed. G. Shayyal, S.Ashur, and H. Rabi'; 4 vols; Cairo.

-Al-Idrisi: *Min Kitab Nuzhat al-Mushtaq fi Ikhtiraq al-Afaq;* ed. M. Amari and C. Schiaparelli; Roma; 1878.

-S.M. Ikram: *Muslim Civilisation in India;* ed by by A.T. Embree; Columbia University Press; New York; 1964.

-Imad Eddin al-Isfahani: *Sana al-Barq al-Shami*; summarised by al-Bundari; ed. F. al-Nabarawi; Cairo; 1979.

-Imad Eddin al-Isfahani: *Al Fath al-Qusi fi 'l fath al-Qudusi*; Landberg Ed; Leiden; 1888.

-T.B. Irving: Dates, Names and Places: The end of Islamic Spain; in *Revue d'Histoire Maghrebine;* No 61-62; 1991; pp 77-93.

-Al-Jabarti: *Al-Jabarti's Chronicle of the First Seven Months of the French Occupation of Egypt.* Ed and tr by S. Moreh; Leiden, 1975.

-Al-Jahiz: *Opuscula*, tr. Walker, *JRAS*, 1915.

-M.Jameelah: *Islam and Orientalism*; M.Y Khan and Sons; Lahore; 1990.

-Ibn Jubayr: *The Travels of Ibn Jubayr*; Tr. R.J.C. Broadhurst; London; 1952.

-R. Kabbani: *Europe's Myths of Orient*; Mc Millan; 1986.

-Kamal Eddin: *Zubdat al-Halab fi ta'arikh Halab;* S. Dahan ed; Damascus; 1954.

-J.H. Lamonte: crusade and Jihad: in N.A. Faris ed: *The Arab Heritage*, Princeton University Press, 1944; pp 159-198.

-S.Lane Poole: *Saladin and the Fall of the Kingdom of Jerusalem*; Beirut; Khayats; 1964.

-S. Lane-Poole: *The Moors in Spain;* Fisher Unwin; London; 1888.

-S. Lane Poole: *Turkey;* Khayats; Beirut; 1966 ed; originally published in 1908.

-H.C. Lea: *The Moriscos of Spain*; Burt Franklin; New York; 1968 reprint.

363

-H. C. Lea: *A History of the Inquisition of Spain*, 4 vols; The Mac Millan Company, New York, 1907.

-G. Le Bon: *La Civilisation des Arabes*; IMAG; Syracuse; Italy; 1884.

-E. Levi Provencal: *Histoire de l'Espagne Musulmane*; Vol III; Paris, Maisonneuve, 1953.

-H. M. J. Loewe: The Seljuqs: in *The Cambridge Medieval History*, Vol IV: Edited by J. R. Tanner et al; 1923; pp 299-317.

-Al-Makrizi (Al-Maqrizi), Ahmad Ibn Ali. *Al-Mawaiz wa Alitibar fi dhikr al-Khitat wa-Alathar;* ed by A. A. al-Mulaiji. 3 Vols. Beirut: Dar al-Urfan. 1959.

-Al Makrizi: *Histoire des sultans Mamlouks de l'Egypte*, Etienne M. Quatremere, tr., 2 vols; 1837-1845.

-Al-Makrizi: *Kitab al-suluk;* ed. S.F. Ashour; Cairo; 1972.

-Al-Marrakushi: *Kitab al-Mujib fi talkhis akhbar ahl al-Maghrib;*2nd ed; R. Dozy; Leyden; 1881.

-Al-Maqqari: *Nafh Al-Tib;* tr. by P.De Gayangos: *The History of the Mohammedan Dynasties in Spain*; 2 vols; The Oriental Translation Fund; London, 1840-3.

-Al-Muqaddasi: *The Best Divisions for Knowledge of the Regions*, a tr. of his *Ahsan at-taqasim fi Ma'rifat al-Aqalim* by B.A. Collins, Centre for Muslim Contribution to Civilization, Garnet Publishing Limited, Reading, 1994

-M.L. de Mas Latrie: *Traites de Paix et de Commerce, et Documents Divers, Concernant les Realations des Chretiens avec les Arabes de l'Afrique Septentrionale au Moyen Age,* Burt Franklin, New York, Originally Published in Paris, 1866.

-Maria Rosa Menocal: *The Arabic Role in Medieval Literary History,* University of Pennsylvania Press, Philadelphia, 1987.

-D. Metlitzki: *The Matter of Araby in Medieval England,* Yale University Press, 1977.

-Viscount Milner: *England in Egypt*; Edward Arnold; London; 1907.

-M. Morsy: *North Africa 1800-1900;* Longman; London; 1984.

-Mudjir Eddin: *Al-Euns al-jalil bi Tarikh el-Qods wa'l Khalil*, tr. into French as Histoire de Jerusalem et Hebron, by H. Sauvaire; Paris; Ernest Leroux; 1875; and 1926.

-Awad (Munis: *al-Rahhala al-awrubiyyun fi al-bayt al-maqdis*, Cairo, 1992.

-D. C. Munro, "Urban and the Crusaders", Translations and Reprints from the *Original Sources of European History*, Vol 1:2, 1895, pp. 5-8

-D.C. Munro: The Western attitude toward Islam during the period of the Crusades; *Speculum* Vol 6 No 4, pp. 329-43.

Bibliography

-Mustawfi-Qazwini: *Ta'rikh-i-Guzida;* ed. E.G. Browne; Leyden; 1910-1913.

-Baron G. d'Ohsson: *Histoire des Mongols*: La Haye et Amsterdam; 1834.

-Z. Oldenbourg: *The Crusades*; tr from the French by A. Carter; Weinfeld and Nicolson; London; 1965.

-E. Pears: The Ottoman Turks to the fall of Constantinople. In *The Cambridge Medieval History*, Cambridge University Press, 1923; Vol IV: Edited by J. R. Tanner et al. pp 653-705.

-P. Pelliot: *Mongols and Popes; 13th and 14th centuries;* Paris; 1922.

-P. Pelliot: Les Mongols et la Papaute; In *Revue d'Orient Chretien*; 1923-1924; and 1931-2.

-M.M.Pickthall: *The Meaning of the Glorious Quran;* Ta ha Publishers; London; first printing 1930.

-J.M. Powell, Editor: *Muslims under Latin Rule, 1100-1300,* Princeton University Press, 1990.

-H. Prutz: *Kulturgeschichte der kreuzzuge*; Berlin, 1883.

-H.U. Rahman: *A Chronology of Islamic History: 570-1000 CE*; Mansell Publishing Limited; London; 1989.

-J. Read: *The Moors in Spain and Portugal*; Faber and Faber, London, 1974.

-J.C.B. Richmond: *Egypt 1798-1952*; Methuen & Co Ltd; London; 1977.

-S. Runciman: *A History of the Crusades*, Cambridge University Press, 1962.

-E.W. Said: *Orientalism;* London, 1978.

-Z. Sardar; M.W. Davies: *Distorted Imagination*; Grey Seal Books; London, 1990.

-D.Sari: *La Depossession des Fellahs 1830-1962;* Algiers; SNED; 1978.

-J.J. Saunders: *Aspects of the Crusades*; University of Canterbury publishing; Canterbury; 1962.

-J.J. Saunders: *The History of the Mongol Conquests;* Routlege & Kegan Paul; London; 1971.

-S.P. Scott: *History of the Moorish Empire*; in 3 vols; The John Lippincott Company; Philadelphia; 1904

-R. Schwoebel: *The Shadow of the Crescent: The Renaissance Image of the Turk*; Nieuwkoop; 1967.

-K. I. Semaan ed: *Islam and the Medieval West;* State University of New York Press/Albany.1980.

-E.Siberry: *The New Crusaders*; Ashgate: Aldershot; 2000.

-Sibt al-Jawzi: *Al-muntazam fi tarikh al-muluk wa'l umam*; X; Hyderabad; 1940; VIII/ 2.

-A.G. Slama: *La Guerre d'Algerie*, Decouvertes, Paris, 1996.

-R.B.Smith: *Mohammed and Mohammedanism*; London; Smith Elder; 1876.

-A.Sorel: *The Eastern Question*; Howard Fertig; New York; 1969

-B. Spuler: *History of the Mongols*; London, Routledge& kegan Paul, 1972.

-W.B. Stevenson: *The Crusades in the East*; Cambridge University Press; 1907.

-R.W. Southern: *Western Views of Islam in the Middle Ages*, Harvard University Press, 1978.

-D. E. Stannard: "Genocide in the Americas" *The Nation*, (October 19, 1992 pp. 430-34).

-B. Stora: *Histoire de la Guerre d'Algerie*, La Decouverte, Paris, 1993.

-Al-Sulami: Un Traite Damasquin du debut du XIIem siecle, ed Siwan, *Journal Asiatique*, 1966.

-J.W. Sweetman: *Islam and Christian Theology*; Lutterworth Press; London; 1955; Vol I; Part II.

-Al-Tabari: *Tarikh al-Umum wal Muluk*; Cairo; 1939.

-Al-Tabari: *The History of al-Tabari (Tarikh al-rusul wa'l muluk;)* tr. by M. Fishbein; State University of New York Press; 1997; vol 3; and subsequent ones.

-A.D. Taha: *The Muslim Conquest and Settlement of North Africa and Spain*; Routledge; London; 1989.

-Tanukhi: *Jami' al-Tawarikh;* ed. D.S. Margoliouth; vol 1; London; 1921.

-The first and second Crusades from an Anonymous Syriac Chronicle; tr by A.S. Tritton; with notes by H.A.R. Gibb; *Journal of The Royal Asiatic Society (JRAS)* 1933; pp 69-101.

-A. Thomson: *Barbary and Enlightenment:* Brill; Leiden; 1987.

-A. Thomson and M.A.Rahim: *Islam in al-Andalus*; Taha Publishers; London; 1996.

-P. Thorau: *The Lion of Egypt;* tr by P.M. Holt; Longman; London; 1992

-J.V. Tolan ed: *Medieval Christian Perceptions of Islam*; Routledge; London; 1996.

-D. M. Traboulay: *Columbus and Las Casas*; University Press of America, New York, London, 1994.

-J. S. Trimingham: *The Influence of Islam Upon Africa*; Longman, Librairie du Liban; second edition 1980.

Bibliography

-William of Tyre: *A History of Deeds Done Beyond the Sea*; 2 Vols; tr and ed by E. Babcock and A.C. Krey; Columbia University Press; 1943; repr 1976.

-Al-'Umari: *Al-Ta'arif bi al-Mustalah al-Sharif;* Cairo; 1312.
-Usama Ibn Munqidh: *Kitab al'Itibar;* tr P.K. Hitti; Beirut; 1964.

-L.Valensi: *Le Maghreb avant la Prise d'Alger;* Paris; 1969.
-D. Vaughan: *Europe and the Turk*; Liverpool University Press; 1954.

-C. Waern: *Medieval Sicily;* Duckworth and Co; London; 1910.
-E.Williams: *Capitalism and Slavery*; North Carolina; 1944.
-P. Wittek: The Ottoman Turks, from an Emirite of March Warriors to an Empire; in *Royal Asiatic Society of Great Britain and Ireland*; 1965; pp. 33-51
-E.R. Wolf: *Europe and the People Without History*; University of California Press; Berkeley; 1982.

-Yaqut, ibn-' Abd Allah al-Hamawi, *Irshad al-Arib ila Ma'rifat al-Adib*, also referred to as *Mu'jam al-Udaba*, (Dictionary of Learned Men,) ed., D.S. Margoliouth (Luzac, 1907 ff);

-R de Zayas: *Les Morisques et le racisme d'etat;* Ed Les Voies du Sud; Paris, 1992.

INDEX

Index